THE AMERICAN
RADICAL PRESS

1880-1960

THE AMERICAN
RADICAL PRESS

1880-1960

Edited with an Introduction by
Joseph R. Conlin

Volume I

GREENWOOD PRESS

WESTPORT, CONNECTICUT • LONDON, ENGLAND

Library of Congress Cataloging in Publication Data
Main entry under title:

The American radical press, 1880-1960.

    Essays on various periodicals, many having been
written as introductions for Greenwood Press' Radical
reprint series.
    Includes bibliographical references.
    1. Socialism—Periodicals—History. 2. Communism—
Periodicals—History. 3. Radicalism—Periodicals—
History. 4. Labor and laboring classes—United States
—Periodicals—History. I. Conlin, Joseph Robert, ed.
HX1.A49   335'.00973   72-9825
ISBN 0-8371-6625-X

Library of Congress Catalog Card Number: 72-9825

ISBN: 0-8371-6625-X   Set
ISBN: 0-8371-7282-9   Vol. I
First published in 1974

Greenwood Press, a division of Williamhouse-Regency Inc.
51 Riverside Avenue, Westport, Connecticut 06880

Manufactured in the United States of America

To Anastasia Lenore

CONTENTS

VOLUME II

PART EIGHT

PART NINE

PREFACE

THIS project very directly originated with the publication in 1964 by the Yale University Library of Walter Goldwater, *Radical Periodicals in America 1890-1950*. This bibliography was well known to historians of American radicalism and was well exploited by them. But, as with all catalogues and librarians, it was taken for granted and seemed well on its way to obscurity. Then, while planning a reprint edition of Dwight MacDonald's *Politics*, Harold Schwartz and Harold Mason of Greenwood Press took note of Goldwater's list, and, in a fortuitously immodest decision, expanded their plans 109 times. When Greenwood concluded its reprint project, *Radical Periodicals in the United States 1890-1960*, several years later, the house had retrieved and reprinted 109 of the most important radical publications of the past seventy-five years in 410 physical volumes.

Just as important as the new accessibility of these important sources was Greenwood's commissioning of introductory essays to each of the reprinted titles by scholars expert in the field of radical history, and, in some cases, by the actual editors of the journals. It was soon obvious that this mass of work collectively represented a significant contribution to the growing literature in American radical history, itself a field which offers important perspectives on general American studies. The tasks of editing the essays, devising a plan of organization, and consulting the contributors for revision began early in 1972. Because some important radical periodicals were already quite accessible before the reprint program, and therefore were not included in it, Greenwood Press and the editor commissioned several additional essays, which are published here for the first time.

The manner in which the essays are organized is probably not superior to any of several alternate arrangements, but in view of the complexity of American radical development, a combination of chronological, organizational and tendential, and *genre* characterization seemed the most useful. Problems were unavoidable. For example, *Catholic Worker* is listed as an "independent" journal in Part Nine; it could just as well have been listed in Part Eight as an anarchist publication or even in Part Eleven, "Personal Journalism." Likewise, *Radical Review* appears with other De Leonist publications in Part Seven but, as a theoretical journal, would also have fitted comfortably in Part Ten. In the end, the editor's apology must be that to choose any of the other alternatives would have left a comparable criticism intact. A comprehensive index should resolve any of the user's initial inconvenience.

Another potential criticism is the omission of articles on many radical periodicals, some of which have indisputable importance and others of which have special importance to specific scholars. Again, there is no completely defensible explanation, only an apology. Goldwater listed 321 periodicals in his bibliography and he defined "radical periodical" in such a way as to exclude many that other bibliographers would quickly commend. This book has been proscribed by the limits of expertise, time, space, and expense. It includes 100 essays with five elaborative notes on 119 different periodicals and some consideration of numerous other periodicals. While it is not exhaustive, this book does provide a comprehensive view of the radical press in America between 1880 and 1960 and, in effect, a history of American radicalism itself.

No editor of a book with contributions from 58 different writers ever had such easy and willing cooperation as did the editor of this volume; to them must go my first and most grateful acknowledgments. As ever, I turned to my friend, colleague, and comrade, Thomas Wagstaff, with my knottiest problems and, as always, received unfailingly good advice. To Herbert Cohen, a scholar-publisher of a sort quickly vanishing, who was liaison with me and the other writers of the original introductions during the reprint project, my renewed appreciation. And, finally, to Robert Hagelstein, Jeannette Lindsay, and Betty Pessagno of Greenwood Press, with whom I amassed an appallingly large correspondence during the preparation of this book, and who invaluably aided its completion, my many thanks.

THE AMERICAN
RADICAL PRESS

1880-1960

INTRODUCTION

THE social and political tumult of the 1960s inspired, among other things, a great revival of interest in the history of American radicalism. A number of historians, themselves generally "political," examined, minutely dissected, and reassessed the anarchist, socialist, and quasiradical movements of the late nineteenth and twentieth centuries. The result is an ample and insightful literature, produced despite the unique resource problem of the new historians of radicalism. For these historians conventional and valuable sources such as the personal correspondence of the radical movement leaders (and certainly that of their subordinates), minute books, and organizational logs are almost nonexistent. Generally, the American Left simply did not compile businesslike records, and personal letters were either lost or destroyed in an urgent moment.

In some cases, this lack of records was due to the semibohemian scorn for all things "bourgeois," an attitude that frequently accompanies radical politics in America: radicals rejected anything "businesslike" or orderly along with the social system. At other times, the lack of files was the result of mere carelessness: Big Bill Haywood of the Wobblies, for example, kept the day's impedimenta in his hatband. On the other hand, such inconsideration for future historians might have derived from conspiratorial whimsy or even plain paranoia. One student Communist leader of perhaps four comrades at a midwestern university incinerated his "papers" upon hearing the news of John F. Kennedy's assassination in 1963. It is safe to conjecture that comparably unsettling incidents in other years consigned far more interesting documents to oblivion.

There were also some very sound reasons for not preserving records. During the 1918 Chicago trial of some one hundred Wobblies for sedition, the prosecution glibly distorted the documents they had seized in order to depict the Industrial Workers of the World (IWW) as a subverter of the war effort. The government snatched sentences from their context

3

and suppressed the exonerating mass of material. In reality, the IWW's central office had trimmed and temporized on the war issue, striving circumspectly to avoid the harassment that eventually destroyed it anyway. The files were apparently so blameless that, although forewarned of the government's raid and seizure, the Wobblies kept their papers intact and ready for confiscation. But the prosecutors released the documents neither to the defense nor to the public nor, for that matter, to posterity. In this instance, it was the federal government which destroyed a warehouse filled with ''historical sources,'' presumably to avoid any further historian's reversal of their conviction. Numerous such instances of willful government distortion of evidence in political trials provided even the most level-headed radical activist with a reason for abjuring a personal archive.

Until recently, not even personal interviews have proved a fruitful source for historians of the Left. By the late 1960s, when a brief vogue for things ''radical'' promoted some loquacity among then obscure Old Left veterans, oral history techniques were producing some nice results. But, as late as 1964, recollection of the McCarthy days and bitterness over betrayals and faded loyalties made ''old radicals'' a taciturn bunch —when they could be found at all. Walter Goldwater observes as ''an interesting fact'' that he was handicapped in his bibliographic work with radical periodicals because

> many individuals and groups which have been chiefly involved, and from whom much of the information must be sought, not only fail to assist in supplying this information, but to a large extent refuse it and hinder its being obtained. Some individuals have denied having been involved in the publication of the very periodicals which list them as editors; some organizations have denied the existence of their organs, and on being confronted with copies have denied any knowledge of them.[1]

As a result historians engaged in direct research have had to rely most heavily on just these orphaned periodicals. In no other area of historical inquiry has reliance on the press been greater.

Fortuitously, as if in compensation for the other research problems, the radical historians have had access to a great many periodicals. Goldwater lists 321 "radical periodicals" in his bibliography, but, he quickly adds, his list is highly selective. He does not, for instance, include the journals of the scores of labor unions which, for at least some period of their history, adopted a Socialist program and devoted their publications to its promulgation. Nor did Goldwater's bibliography seek to encompass the many pacifist newsletters and magazines which were also radical, or the bulletins of the countless ad hoc committees which have germinated and flourished for a season in twentieth-century America, heralding the struggles for everything from the extrication of Tom Mooney to the repeal of antihomosexuality laws. Finally, no bibliographer could fantasize uncovering the titles and dates of every mimeographed alarum sheet that bone-weary malcontents have sold or given away on streetcorners and at supermarkets for the past half-century.[2]

Alas for the perfectionist cataloguer in individualistic America—it is not even merely a matter of the identifiable organizations. When factionalism accelerated to its orgiastic frenzy of the 1930s, especially among the Trotskyists, groups took shape which, like the "Marlenites," were "literally a family party, the majority faction of which was alleged to consist of Mr. and Mrs. George Marlen and their parents, children and collateral relations." Then there were the "Weisbordites" of whom Dwight MacDonald has written. Also a Trotskyist splinter, the group had so many defectors that, finally, only Mr. and Mrs. Weisbord remained.

Then there was a divorce, and the advance-guard of the revolution was concentrated, like a bouillon cube, in the small person of Albert Weisbord, who sat for years at his secondhand desk behind the dusty glass door proudly emblazoned REVOLUTIONARY LEAGUE OF AMERICA—HEADQUARTERS writing his party organ and cranking it out on the mimeograph machine. This contrivance played the same part in the American revolutionary movement that machine guns did in the Russian. The mimeographs were the instruments of production, which, as any Marxist schoolboy knows are the base of power of every ruling class, and many a faction fight was decided by who seized control of them first.[3]

Indeed, it was a rare leftist fragment which did not have "an organ."

Even individuals who could stomach no semblance of organizational affiliation proved perfectly willing to issue a "review" or a "newsletter," a willingness which added to the enormous and uncountable total.

The condition of the Socialist press alone at the turn of the century indicates the extent of the literature. At least 600 distinct periodicals were published during the Socialist party's happiest days. In 1912 alone there were 323 avowedly Socialist periodical publications issued in the United States, including 5 English-language dailies and 8 dailies in foreign languages; 262 English weeklies and 36 in other languages; and 10 English and 2 foreign-language monthly magazines.[4]

Again, during the late 1960s, which are sometimes thought to mark another radical apogee, the number of "Movement" and "Underground" newspapers reached extraordinary proportions. The "underground press" movement began in 1965. By early 1969 (the peak, after which the phenomenon rapidly deflated), there were perhaps 500 such periodicals. The *Wall Street Journal* estimated in April 1968 that underground newspapers had a combined circulation of 333,000; a few months later, Liberation News Service, a clipping agency for radical and counterculture journals, claimed 4.6 million readers.[5]

These sheets were not all "socialist" by any means. But while they were often juvenile, they were "radical" in a vaguely anarchist or bohemian manner. In September 1968, Liberation News Service put its subscribers into two categories: "Movement" or politically radical (44 papers) and "Underground" or "counterculture" (111 papers). But even the latter bandied about talk of "revolution" with glorious aplomb. And popular consensus, sympathetic and otherwise, placed all of them beyond the pale of political convention.

This vast literature comprises a rich cultural record. American radical periodicals approached genuine artistry in the *Masses* and the highest refinement of the journalist's craft in half a dozen others. At the other extreme, there is the reliable thickheadedness of the *Daily Worker*'s editorials. And, in more recent years, quality ranged from the frequently seminal economic analysis of *Monthly Review* and the venturesome curiosity of *Studies on the Left* to the obscenity-mongering of much of the "underground press."

Moreover, the radical press *is* the chief source for understanding the radical experience in America. The thought, dreams, and activities of the radicals are recorded there and, to a great extent, only there. The value to those who are curious about that subject is obvious. Beyond them, whatever insights "radical man" can give to illuminate us on the human condition cannot be known and understood without these sources. The scholar and the nonprofessional student committed to historical method will regard the cant, obfuscation, and tomfoolery with which the wisdom is mixed as minor impediments indeed.

It would be difficult to overestimate the importance of the radical press to those researching in it and quite impossible in the case of those involved in the original publications. As Max Shachtman quipped to a symposium at the University of Illinois in 1968, "a radical group without a paper is a contradiction in terms."[6] The old Trotskyist campaigner had spent his career among overreachers. (When he left the tiny Socialist Workers party in 1940, James P. Cannon pointed his finger at him from the rostrum and stated, "Very well, Comrade Shachtman, we will seize power without you!").[7] But this remark was pure understatement. Indeed, American radicals deemed the publication of some sort of periodical to be so vital that it is by no means frivolous to suggest that the movements, parties, factions, and tendencies that make up American radical history were actually subsidiary to their organs.[8]

There are good reasons why this should be so. The chronic political condition of organized anticapitalism in the United States has been its feebleness. With a few exceptions—like the Socialist Labor party in the 1890s, the IWW, and the Socialist party early in the twentieth century, and then the Communists of the Great Depression—radical movements were not really "movements" at all. They were followerless cadres; there never really was a rank-and-file. These cadres, moreover, were generally comprised of educated and articulate middle-class radicals who naturally found "publications work" highly appealing. So, the "movements" were frequently identical in personnel to their "publications staffs."

This fact has had an ironic consequence in some of the writing about radical history. There is a hackneyed *caveat* in the training of historians, that one writes from the sources and not about them. As regards the radicals and their periodicals, some historians have written fastidiously from the newsprint without recognizing that in large part they were writing about little else but a desk, a typewriter, a printing press, and a busy mind. There are in some of the histories more than a few "mass demonstrations" footnoted to a radical newspaper that represent only the reveries or the ill-advised propaganda devices of a revolutionary journalist.

Certainly the radicals themselves took their publications to heart. Dwight MacDonald, one of the most scathing mockers of the American Left, could wax testy as late as 1958 because the Socialist Workers party "monotonously rejected" his contributions twenty years before.[9] In recalling his own career as a Trotskyist Communist during the 1930s (however much he repudiated it in later years), Max Shachtman still remembered fondly and emphasized most boastfully the hapless party's "achievements . . . in the field of publications."

> It succeeded in getting out a weekly newspaper, even though every once in a while poverty dictated the skipping of an issue; and a presentable monthly theoretical revue. Its small but compact youth organization managed with some irregularity to put out a monthly paper of its own. In addition it published at certain periods of time little newspapers in the Yiddish language, in Greek, and even a few issues in the Polish language.[10]

The fact is that even in organizations of considerable substance, the "party press" seemed the most significant revolutionary endeavor. From Daniel De Leon, who devoted most of his time to the Socialist Labor party's *People*, through Big Bill Haywood who gruffly complained of the deskwork but nevertheless put in a stint editing the *Miners Magazine*, there have been few active radicals who have not directed a large share of their labor on behalf of the new society to journalism. No other facet of radical political activity in the United States—not strikes, not subversion, not demonstration, not terrorism, not oratory—has claimed more attention or time. When he was attempting to organize a Socialist daily newspaper in Oklahoma, Oscar Ameringer remembered the enthusiastic response of Socialists as, "Sure the Comrades wanted the Daily. How could we hope to capture the state without a daily paper?"[11]

Historians of other than radical subjects might do well to pay attention to the pre-1919 radical press as sources for their own work. The successful Socialist dailies such as the *Milwaukee Leader*, the *New York Call*, and the *Cleveland Citizen* might especially serve as indispensable correctives for distortions in the capitalist press. The definitive histories of American journalism give them scant attention.[12] Yet these were excellent newspapers of record, employing competent and even peerless reporters and editors and possessing what seem in retrospect to have been the highest ethics in the business.

Before 1919 there was a relatively innocuous sectarianism on the American Left; the Socialist party and the IWW and even the anarchists looked out and forward rather than inward upon themselves. Even those differences among comrades which did exist received scant journalistic attention beyond the editorial columns, except during a few rare crises. These were radicals confident in their future rather than inherently pessimistic. As a result, they looked about them, seeking to learn from the stuff of ''the news'' instead of tooling and recasting it to fit the hour's requirement.

The quality of pre-1919 radical journalism can also be ascribed to the fact that the foremost Socialist dailies were controlled by the moderate wing of the Socialist party. This is not to say that the moderates were any less sectarian or any more perspicacious than their revolutionist fellows. On the contrary, the Socialist ''Right'' contributed more than its share to the myopic factionalism that transformed the American Left; and their errors of analysis were at least equally consequential to those of the revolutionists.

While it did not necessarily blaze the best trail to socialism, the moderate line was conducive to excellent journalism. The moderate Socialists (like Victor Berger of the Milwaukee papers) regarded their papers as agencies which served a public need and which, they hoped, through the highest journalistic standards, would demonstrate their ''legitimacy'' to a non-Socialist readership. In practice, moderate Socialist government was ''honest government,'' ''clean government,'' ''good government.'' Socialists were hardly able to construct ''socialism in one city''—in Milwaukee or Berkeley or Schenectady or in other cities which they captured. The idea was to govern honestly and efficiently, thus presenting to the citizenry a stark contrast to the corruption then endemic in American municipal governance. In their newspapers, they sought to work the equivalent: to contrast the honest reportage of the Socialists to the seedy flamboyance of the "yellow press" and tabloids and the dignified omissions of the genteel press. The result, for journalism, was salutory.

Upton Sinclair recounts several illustrations of how the Socialist press was superior, as journalism, to the capitalist publications of the age in *The Brass Check*, his diffuse but valuable polemic on the American press. He describes muckraking articles he wrote which were suppressed after the warmest assurances that they would be published, and mass meetings, of up to 5,000 persons, which would be unknown to posterity if historians relied solely on standard newspaper sources.

In 1907, a year after he published *The Jungle*, Sinclair addressed a Packingtown, Chicago overflow audience, haranguing that virtually nothing had been done to remedy the conditions in the meatpacking industry which he had so dramatically publicized. He discussed a *New York Herald* investigation that had exonerated the packers and had been widely circulated. "You are the people who know about these matters," he told his slaughterhouse worker audience, "are they true?" "There was a roar of assent that rocked the building," Sinclair continued, and he asked, "Now tell me this, ought they be made known to the American people? Would you like them to be made known to the American people?"

Then I looked over the edge of the platform to a row of tables, where sat the reporters looking up, and I talked to them for a while. I said: "You are newspaper men; you know a story when you see it. Tell me now—tell me straight—is not this a story?" The newspaper men nodded and grinned. They knew it was a "story" all right. "The public would like to read this—the public of Chicago and the public of all the rest of America—would they not?" And again the newspaper men nodded and grinned. "Now," said I, "play fair with me; give me a square deal, so far as you are concerned. Write this story just as I have told it tonight. Write it and turn it in and see what happens. Will you do that?" And they pledged themselves, the audience saw them pledge themselves. And so the test was made, as perfect a test as anyone could conceive. And next morning there was just one newspaper in Chicago which mentioned my speech in the Stockyards district—the "Chicago Socialist." Not one line in any other newspaper, morning or evening, in Chicago![13]

Socialist newspapers could sometimes force the establishment press to respond. It was in *The Appeal to Reason* (which Sinclair called "the refuge of suppressed muckrakers") that *The Jungle* was first published. Sinclair and others could always place suppressed researches there, but they preferred not to use the radical journals. Publishing with them, Sinclair wrote, "has always been my last recourse." Although the audience of journals like the *Appeal* was by no means small, it was an audience of the already converted. To make the proper impact, dissenting journalists sought to sell their work to the established press. When *The American* discontinued Kenneth Turner's articles on the barbarities of the Diaz regime in Mexico and the writer had to turn to *The Appeal to Reason*, Sinclair lamented characteristically, "poor Turner."[14] But historians ought to think differently; to them, the old Socialist party press can provide the very correctives for posterity that Sinclair despaired of in his own time.

After 1919, on the other hand, American radical newspapers are generally worthless as accurate sources of data on the world at large, and as a rule, are far less reliable than the better establishment journals. The principal cause is that the post-1919 Socialist and Communist newspapers reflect the same sectarianism which has accounted for the decline of socialism in America as a mass movement (and which has provided the occasion for the richly deserved merriment at the expense of the "Old Left").[15] Robert Bendiner recalled that his cronies in journalistic studies at City College read the *Daily Worker* "solely for laughs." He cites a memorable headline above the account of an atheistic speech by party member Anthony Bimba which announced, "THERE IS NO GOD —BIMBA" and quotes this jewel as "a news lead never dreamed of in your schools of journalism":

That the Socialist Party is the third capitalist party and is allied with the gangsters and bosses and is the most ruthless tool in the hands of the capitalists against the workers, was apparent at the Socialists' open-air meeting on Mathon Street, Brighton Beach on June 26.[16]

It is perhaps too easy to make sport of portentous theoretical journals that issued three numbers in 1926, or of intercollegiate reviews that dripped blood and sounded the tumult of the *proletaire* through their mailing wrappers. The radicals themselves seem rarely to have missed an opportunity to jibe at the publications of their heretical fellows. Max Shachtman, who so warmly recalled his own Socialist Workers party's "few issues in the Polish language," could ridicule the journals of opposing radicals as being "filled with inconceivable resolutions which scorned the dimensions of breadth and depth and concentrated exclusively on length."[17] And Dwight MacDonald, while editor of *Politics*, gleefully devastated "rival" radical journalists and formulated the principle that "the smaller the sect, the more grandiosely optimistic it usually is in its editorial pronouncements." MacDonald cited a mimeographed journal which crossed his desk in 1944. It was entitled *International Review*, with the heading: "*Issued by the Revolutionary Workers League for the International Contact Commission. Affiliates: Central Committee of the Red Front of Greater Germany; Revolutionary Workers League of the U.S.; Leninist League of Great Britain.*"[18]

But there is a serious aspect to the decline in radical journalism after 1919. The nature of periodicals literally changed. They no longer looked outward and forward but came to be consumed in the petty infighting which characterized American radicalism after the Bolshevik Revolution: spieling the Comintern line in the case of the Communist journals; reflexively opposing the same, regardless of merits in the case of the Socialists; and—for lack of a better explanation—displaying sheer crankiness in the case of the Trotskyists. In speaking of battles within the International Ladies Garment Workers Union between Socialists and Communists, Norman Thomas observed the thankless nature of editing a labor newspaper. "The last thing anybody wanted," he said, was an objective statement of the news.[19]

Corollary to this sectarianism, radical news reporting came to be characterized by plain pigheadedness and by what Mary McCarthy, referring to the Communists, called their "lack of humor, their fanaticism, and the slow drip of cant that thickened their utterance, like a nasal catarrh.'' A journalist who served briefly on the staff of the *New Masses* described a not untypical instance of how party line stultified good Socialist newswriting:

> The solemnity with which the affairs of the Left were conducted were enough in itself to separate it from the mainstream of American politics, which, whatever its weaknesses, has always had the redeeming attribute of self-ridicule. It was a jolt to me to discover that, coming to the *New Masses*, I had come to a synod of Calvinists, for whom joking about any aspect of the party line seemed as wicked as joking about original sin would have seemed to Cotton Mather.[20]

The result of this pious abhorrence of the traditional cynicism of journalism is illustrated by a report from Washington in the *Daily Worker* during the early 1930s. The headline was ''HOOVER SMIRKS AT ALL THE MASS SUFFERING.'' The article began: ''Let the workers die! What does he care, so long as they die quietly, without demonstrating, making a noise about it, threatening to storm the gates of power!''[21]

If anything, the Trotskyist journals were worse. Dwight MacDonald made the point in his comment on an article by Joseph Hansen in *Fourth International*. Hansen had written:

> When the history of our country is written by future historians, they will not look for material at Hyde Park where Roosevelt employs a staff to file away minutiae about himself. They will dig painfully into . . . the files of Trotskyist publications, to find out what the real figures of American history were like.

MacDonald observed that ''evidently Roosevelt will be lucky to get a footnote in future histories of the period 1930-1950.''

> The chapters compiled from the files of Trotskyist publications promise to be epic: CHAPTER IX: 1929 DEPRESSION BEGINS, JAMES P. CANNON AND MAX SCHACHTMAN LEAVE COMMUNIST PARTY. CHAPTER XII: CIO LAUNCHED, LITTLE STEEL STRIKE, JAMES P. CANNON AND MAX SCHACHTMAN LEAVE SOCIALIST PARTY. CHAPTER XV:

NAZI-SOVIET PACT, WORLD WAR II BEGINS, JAMES P. CANNON AND MAX SCHACHTMAN LEAVE EACH OTHER.[22]

If the relative merits of the radical and capitalist presses in the United States have any correlation with the stability of the capitalist order, it must be argued that the Socialist opportunity was indeed best before 1919 (as several historians have argued from other perspectives). Then, the Socialist press was better journalism, unafraid of honest transmission of fact whereas the establishment papers distended, selected, and suppressed. After 1919, it was a different story. Except for the fringe, the conventional American press began to improve and, in its best parts, became far more reliable in at least its reportage in comparison to the grim and obtuse propaganda of the radicals.

There are plenty of exceptions to these generalizations on the respective merits of the capitalist-radical press before and after 1919. There was rank silliness in many radical publications before 1919. And more recent fact sheets like George Seldes' *In Fact* and *I. F. Stone's Weekly* regularly shamed well-financed news agencies with their shoestring "scoops" and exposés. Even the Communist and Trotskyist papers—even the underground journals of the New Left—now and then revealed that important stories were ignored or buried in the dailies. *Ramparts*, a radical monthly of the 1960s, scored many such sensations. But, on the whole, the capitalist press has improved and radical journalism has declined.

This change has much to do, no doubt, with the changing vagaries of newspaper economics. The competition of television and the soaring real costs of production have in recent years produced a well-known decrease in the number of conventional newspapers and magazines. Fewer and fewer large cities in the United States have more than two newspapers, and many have only one; among middle-sized cities, the two-newspaper town is practically unknown. Whether such monopoly has led to a sobering sense of responsibility among newspaper publishers is debatable. But the competitive sensationalism that had so much to do with news distortion has apparently declined.

While rising costs have buffeted the capitalist press, they have practically killed off the radicals. There is no stridently self-styled "radical" daily newspaper in the United States today; the last one to fold was the

Communists' *Daily Worker*, which went on a weekly schedule in 1958.

Decline of income has as much to do with this trend as rising costs. The "underground press" craze proved briefly practicable (and in a few cases highly profitable) through a liberal admixturing of sexual titillation with revolutionary slogans. But financing a newspaper through subscriptions has in recent years been even less reliable than through subvention. Organizations with patrons and a treasury like those of the Communist party and the Socialist Workers party manage, through subsidy, to publish regularly. But the New Left, based largely on political fads, suffered from the protean essence of faddism. Even a once solvent publication like *New Left Notes* (of the Students for a Democratic Society) has gone the way of *Dr. Robinson's, Mother Earth Bulletin*, and the *Road to Communism*.

The American radical press flourished best when discontent provided subscribers and patrons. Some publications were remarkably successful. Charles S. Kerr's *International Socialist Review*, for example, with a circulation of only 3,000-6,000 until 1908, switched to a popular (and brilliantly managed) format in that year, just in time to coincide with the rapid growth of the Socialist party and IWW. It was selling 50,000 copies of each issue in 1912. Kerr's company was organized as a cooperative, and in addition to the *ISR* profitably published Marxist classics in book form. In 1910, the company was so successful that it was charged with "monopoly" and had to be endorsed for purity by the Socialist party's National Executive Committee.[23]

Most of the other nonsubsidized radical publications of the Socialist party's heyday were strictly private enterprises. One of the most successful was *Wilshire's Magazine*, the scion of the wealthy eccentric Gaylord Wilshire. Curiously, instead of costing him money, the magazine actually bankrolled numerous of Wilshire's harebrained projects. Eventually, Wilshire's other interests dragged his magazine into oblivion. But *The Appeal to Reason* of Girard, Kansas, owned the championship list of subscribers. At its peak, the weekly mailed out 750,000 copies, and on the occasion of the trial of Big Bill Haywood for the murder of Frank Steunenberg, it sold, or distributed free, one million copies of a special issue.

In more recent times, small journals with modest production costs have maintained themselves successfully. *Science and Society* and *Monthly Review* are perhaps the most signal examples. *I. F. Stone's Weekly*, which became more radical in the 1960s, had a profitable circulation until its sole contributor decided he was unable to shoulder the workload necessary to continue. MacDonald's *Politics* is another example of a magazine suspended not so much for financial as for personal reasons. *Studies on the Left*, partly subsidized, partly dependent on subscription, was discontinued at the end of the 1960s as much because of an editorial split as an empty purse.

Radical periodicals have discontinued for quite a variety of reasons, but in most instances it has been for lack of money. Oscar Ameringer, one of the finest radical journalists, describes the experience of hundreds of radical publication journals:

By the time I started promoting the Oklahoma daily I had learned that it takes lots of money to launch a newspaper and still more to keep it going. Formerly I had undertaken the job rather lightly: I used to proclaim the glad tidings that I was about to fill a long-felt need and asked for subscriptions. When enough subscriptions at one dollar per year had been gathered to pay for the first issue I brought out the first issue. When enough money had accumulated to pay for the second issue I brought out that, and so on until about the fourth issue when the flow of money began to dwindle and I owed my subscribers forty-eight issues which I could not publish. About that time I started to stand off the printer and defer the salary of ye editor, publisher and general manager. When the printer refused to be stood off any longer and the editor-publisher had exhausted his credit with butcher, baker, and grocer, he would make a swing around the faithful to raise money, and keep it up until there were no more faithful to corral. Soon thereafter appeared a boxed notice in the paper to the effect that, due to the insidious opposition of plutocracy and certain financial difficulties, the paper would suspend until further notice.[24]

The plutocracy's "insidious opposition," of course, could operate with great effect. Not so curiously, it had its greatest effect in the earlier period, during World War I and the Great Red Scare, when the radical opposition was something to be reckoned with. The Post Office Department withdrew second-class mailing privileges from some 75 newspapers during the war, many of which were radical. The most famous case was that of the *Milwaukee Leader* and its chief personages, especially Ameringer and Victor Berger, who made heroic efforts to keep the journal going. For a time, they sent the 18,000 mail subscriptions first class, at two cents a mailing. But the Post Office revoked their letter privilege, confiscating as much outgoing mail as possible and returning incoming mail to the sender stamped "Undeliverable under the Espionage Act." Eventually, even the sturdy *Leader* collapsed.

Since that time, however, coinciding with the era of radical desuetude, the government has taken no systematic action against revolutionary periodicals. Not even during the time of Joseph McCarthy's ascendancy was a journal effectively suppressed. I. F. Stone recounts that, at the time he launched his personal newsletter, he had been active for several years in left-wing causes and had authored, among other dissenting pieces, the first magazine article against the Smith Act. "There was nothing to the left of me but the *Daily Worker*," he wrote.

Yet, I was able to get second-class mail privilege without a single political question. As George Seldes had before me, I encountered old-fashioned civil service courtesy and political impartiality in the post office, and the second-class mail privilege when I started was my bread and butter. The difference between the second-class rate and the cheapest third-class rate was the equivalent of my salary.[25]

By the 1960s, when it could be argued that the "radical" underground press was scarcely more than pornography, a nonpolitical if not necessarily legitimate ground for suppression, legal interpretation and social attitude were such as to tolerate anything. A godsend to the radical press apparently, but such "tolerance" from a society in disarray—if not decay—seems a gratuitous italicization of the radicals' eclipse.

J.R.C.
Davis, California
April 1973

NOTES

1. Walter Goldwater, *Radical Periodicals in America 1890-1950: A Bibliography with Brief Notes* (New Haven: 1964), p. vii.

2. Goldwater explicitly excludes from his list: daily newspapers, "purely trade union publications," local and sectional publications, literary magazines, "periodicals appealing to special groups (no matter how large), such as women, Protestants, or members of the staff of the New York Public Library." However, he then selects three daily newspapers "since it was felt they were too important to leave out altogether"; a few journals published abroad are included; "local or sectional publications" are listed "where a national audience is written or hoped for"; literary magazines are listed if "the political aspect is dominant"; and there were "many borderline cases." These inconsistencies are noted, not to denigrate Goldwater's invaluable achievement, but to illustrate the enormity and complexity of the periodical literature. Goldwater, *Radical Periodicals*, pp. vii-viii.

3. Dwight MacDonald, *Memoirs of a Revolutionist* (New York: 1958), pp. 16-17. Also see Robert Bendiner, *Just Around the Corner* (New York: 1968), pp. 102-103.

4. Goldwater, *Radical Periodicals*, p. vii.

5. Massimo Teodori, *The New Left: A Documentary History* (New York: 1969), pp. 78, 495; Ethel G. Romm, *The Open Conspiracy: What America's Angry Generation is Saying* (Harrisburg, Pa.: 1970), pp. 16-17.

6. Quoted in Rita J. Simon, *As We Saw the Thirties* (Urbana, Ill.: 1967), p. 19.

7. Bendiner, *Just Around the Corner*, p. 113.

8. Trotskyists within the Socialist party of America (SPA) in 1936 took their factional title from their pre-existing organ, but the clearest case of the periodical tail wagging the organizational dog was the relationship at the end of the 1920s between the *Forward* of New York (the world's largest Yiddish language newspaper), and the SPA. The journal gave the party's national office $500 per month for operating expenses. David A. Shannon suggests, "without this help it is doubtful that the office could have remained open."

9. MacDonald, *Memoirs*, p. 18.

10. Quoted in Simon, *As We Saw the Thirties*, p. 22.

11. Oscar Ameringer, *If You Don't Weaken* (New York: 1940), p. 310.

12. Lucy M. Salmon's *The Newspaper and the Historian* (New York: 1923), for example, does not even mention them. Frank L. Mott, *American Journalism 1690-1960* (New York: 1962), James M. Lee, *History of American Journalism* (Boston: 1923), and George L. Bird and Frederic E. Merwin, eds., *The Newspaper and Society* (New York: 1946) consider the Socialist daily press almost solely in connection with the withdrawal of second-class mailing privileges during World War I—in other words, in a purely passive role.

13. Upton Sinclair, *The Brass Check: A Study of American Journalism* (Long Beach: Privately published by the author, 9th edition, 1928), p. 53.

14. Sinclair, *Brass Check*, pp. 52, 82.

15. Irving Howe and Lewis Coser, *The American Communist Party: A Critical History* (Boston: 1957), for instance, is laced with a gloss that jibes at Communist party foibles.

16. Bendiner, *Just Around the Corner*, p. 78.

17. Simon, *As We Saw the Thirties*, p. 32.

18. MacDonald, *Memoirs*, p. 284.

19. "The Reminiscences of Norman Thomas," Part I, p. 27, Oral History Project, Columbia University Library.

20. Mary McCarthy, "My Confession," *The Reporter* 9 (December 22, 1953): 32; Bendiner, *Just Around the Corner*, p. 100.

21. Bendiner, *Just Around the Corner*, p. 78.

22. MacDonald, *Memoirs*, p. 273.

23. Walter Rideout, *The Radical Novel in the United States* (New York: 1956), pp. 96-97.

24. Ameringer, *If You Don't Weaken*, p. 308.

25. I. F. Stone, *The Haunted Fifties* (New York: 1963), p. viii.

Part One

EARLY RADICAL PERIODICALS

THE social dislocations of industrialization in the United States during the last quarter of the nineteenth century produced ripple after ripple of social criticism and a few significant waves. There was little cohesiveness to the whole; rather, the ferment was characterized by the wide variety of panaceas that it elicited and by the diversity of the individuals and groups which it attracted. But all of the discontent was to devolve, after the turn of the century, into the two wings of the reform movement: the Progressives and the Socialist party of America.

In a sense, the Socialist movement in the United States ought to be traced back to the communitarians of the early and middle nineteenth century who planted dozens, perhaps hundreds, of utopias from New England to the Middle Border and California. But despite the durability of the communitarian tradition (Eugene V. Debs was among others committed to that ideal in the latter 1890s), twentieth-century American socialism is more clearly descended from those Gilded Age radicals who believed that social transformation involved the whole of society.

Somewhat ironically, one of the most important progenitors of organized socialism was himself a lifelong believer in competition and a critic of the Socialists. Henry George, a Jeffersonian and disciple of Herbert Spencer, published, in 1879, *Progress and Poverty* which explored the seeming paradox that, as the United States progressed, impoverishment seemed likewise to increase. George concluded that the chief cause of want amidst plenty was rent, the "unearned increment" on landownership which bled the many for the sake of a few. As a solution, he proposed, simply, a "single tax" which would expropriate all such rents. In effect, this was socialization of the land but George and his disciples took great pains to "conservatize" their program by pointing out that the industrial entrepreneur would equally benefit wage-workers through the more profitable use to which he could put his capital. George had a great many disciples. His book and his subsequent propagandizing aroused enthusiastic support in "Single Tax Clubs" throughout the country and, in 1886, he ran a very strong second in the contest for mayor of New York City, losing to the Democratic candidate but outpolling the Republican, Theodore Roosevelt. This was certainly the apogee of the Single Tax movement but, while it declined thereafter, many of those whom it stimulated to contemplation of society went on to more comprehensive programs.

Among these disciples was Daniel De Leon, a figure of unclear personal origins. In 1886 he was a lecturer at Columbia University who became an active supporter of George's candidacy. This action probably cost him promotion to a professorship. De Leon, who by then had begun reading Marxist writings, left Columbia and from there moved quickly to the leadership of the Socialist Labor party (SLP), the oldest Socialist organization in the United States. Before De Leon, the SLP was a small, introspective, largely German-language society, not much more than a *Turnverein* whose members haggled over old world politics. During the 1890s, stimulated by depression conditions in American industry and guided by De Leon, the party grew and scored several local electoral victories.

De Leon realized that the SLP's political weakness lay primarily in its foreign immigrant constituency. Himself apparently of foreign birth, he strived consistently to win native Americans to his party. But De Leon's own major weakness was also political. He was a man of firm conviction who, once settled on solutions to a problem, could tolerate no deviation from his thought within the party. Repeatedly, he expelled talented men and groups from the SLP—later, he would eject his own son for expressing reservations on a favorite point. Ex-SLP members were to be prominent in the Socialist party of America when it was founded in 1900-1901.

On his hegira from the Single Tax to Marxism, De Leon was a "Nationalist," a supporter of the ideals expressed in Edward Bellamy's *Looking Backward*. Published in 1888, *Looking Backward* caused an even greater sensation than George's *Progress and Poverty*. The novel told of an America in the year 2000 where the competitive principle had been abandoned peacefully in favor of a cooperative society in which, in effect, the great corporations of the nation had been merged into one great socially owned trust.

"Nationalism" did not face the problem of "foreignness" that plagued De Leon's SLP. Quite the contrary, it was frequently criticized by Marxian Socialists because of its seemingly sole concern with the United States and its concurrent disinterest in socialism's internationalist ideals. Indeed, many prominent Nationalists were to out-jingo the most reactionary chauvinists during the Spanish-American War. But Bellamy's influence was unparalleled by that of any other individual. "It is doubtful," wrote William D. P. Bliss, himself an important Socialist, "if any man, in his own lifetime, ever exerted so great an influence upon the social beliefs of his fellow beings as did Edward Bellamy." So pervasive was Bellamy's effect, albeit briefly, that scarcely a Socialist after the turn of the century failed to pay personal homage to *Looking Backward* and the Nationalist Movement.

Another important source of American radicalism was the Knights of Labor. Although its early leaders were, as often as not, cautious, conservative men, the Knights pioneered in the industrial unionism which was later to be regarded as practically synonymous with social revolution; the ideals of the Order posited a social organization beyond the wage system. Displaced by the class-collaborationist American Federation of Labor by the 1890s and quite near its demise by that time, the Knights nevertheless left a legacy of working-class radicalism which somewhat nurtured but more often proved to be a frustrating failure for later radicals.

Eugene V. Debs and his American Railway Union played a similar role. While simply a wage-conscious trade union leader at the time he led a strike against the Pullman Company in 1894, Debs attracted national attention as a result of his militancy, the moral simplicity of his ethics, and his attractive personality and platform manner. Jailed for a year after the unsuccessful strike, Debs was courted by a number of Socialists. After supporting William Jennings Bryan in 1896, he helped to launch the Social Democracy, at first a communitarian venture but later the core of the SPA.

The Socialist who most assiduously pursued Debs was Victor Berger of Milwaukee. An Austrian immigrant, Berger had taught school in Milwaukee and then turned to journalism, first in the German language and then in English. This shrewd politician realized that, to be successful, his Social Democratic Federation needed to extend its support beyond the German bloc in Milwaukee. Berger was eventually successful in establishing political hegemony in Milwaukee through a combination of working-class support and good, honest government, but before 1900 he was still a minor figure in the city's politics. As the leader of the most vital local organization, he was a key figure in putting together the national Socialist party.

Fabianism was never strong in the United States but it claimed several prominent middle-class figures, who, eventually, like their British exemplars, supported political organization. Many of the Christian Socialists did likewise, although others never did join the SPA. These "Christian Socialists" were represented chiefly by several decidedly un-Marxist ministers such as Washington Gladden, W. D. P. Bliss, and George D. Herron who used pulpit and press to preach the moral iniquity of capitalist society.

Finally, another element in the history of nineteenth-century American radicalism was the great Populist rebellion. Regardless of its essentially non-Socialist nature and ultimate fiasco, it left behind a considerable reservoir of discontent which in part drifted to the Left. This was true among populistic farmers (the SPA's support in agricultural Oklahoma was proportionately greater than in any other state) as well as among hard-rock miners in the Rocky Mountain states who forged the most important anticapitalist labor union of its time, the Western Federation of Miners.

All of these movements published journals. Many of the leaders of radicalism in the 1890s were primarily propagandists and while they worked through universities, churches, lecture platforms, and books, periodical publications remained, as they would thereafter, the most important single means of spreading the word.

Journal of United Labor
CHICAGO, 1880-1889

Journal of the Knights of Labor
CHICAGO, 1889-1917

DAVID BRODY

"THE Knights of Labor are the first national organization created by the American working class as a whole; whatever be their origin and history, whatever their platform and constitution, here they are, the work of practically the whole class of wage-earners, the only bond that holds them together, that makes their strength felt to themselves not less than to their enemies, and that fills them with the proud hope of future victories. . . . To an outsider it appears evident that here is the raw material out of which the future of the American working-class movement, and along with it, the future of American society at large has to be shaped."

In these acute observations published in 1887, Friedrich Engels identified the features that have made the Knights of Labor a continuing subject of fascination—and frustration—for American labor historians. After a slow growth to roughly 100,000 members in 1885, the Order surged to over 700,000 the next year, and seemed poised for still greater success. The Knights of Labor became a mass labor movement whose dimensions exceeded anything that had happened before and, in some ways, in intent and structural possibilities, exceeded anything that has happened since. Engels was right, too, to express puzzlement over the ideology of the Knights, and to leave open the relationship between its vitality and its origins and program. For the Knights of Labor was perhaps unique in the extent to which it was a labor organization whose aims were left vague and whose actual impact seemed divorced from its official platform. Engels miscalculated only in his optimism over the future of the Knights of Labor, although he was shrewd enough to recognize that it constituted only "the raw material" of a working-class movement. The Knights declined swiftly after 1886. By 1890 the membership was 100,000 or less, and was no longer primarily wage-earning in character. After a brief alliance with the Populists, the Order ceased to have any significance.

One of the crucial sources for future study will have to be the journal of the Order, *The Journal of United Labor* (retitled *The Journal of the Knights of Labor* in 1889). First appearing on May 15, 1880, the *Journal* was a direct result of the creation two years earlier of a national organization from the hitherto autonomous district assemblies. Published originally as a monthly, then as a semimonthly, and finally, beginning in 1889, as a weekly, the *Journal* continued to appear until 1917 (save for a hiatus in 1904-1905), but its interest is limited to the period when the Knights was a significant movement, i.e., only until the early 1890s. The prime fact about the *Journal* was that it was an *official* organ, the instrument of the national officers (the secretary served as editor). So the *Journal* tells very little about the decision-making process, and virtually nothing about the factionalism within the Order or the developing conflict with the trade unions. On these points the convention proceedings and the Powderly Papers are far more useful. Nor is the *Journal* informative about the Order's reversals: the disastrous strikes of 1886, the Haymarket affair, the creation of the AFL are passed over in silence or given only brief and oblique mention. Here the independent press—most notably, *John Swinton's Paper*—far overshadow the *Journal* in value. During the years of expansion, the *Journal* does provide a crucial organizational record of finances, official rulings and directives, reports of organizers and district leaders, and, perhaps most important of all, a complete listing of local assemblies chartered and lapsed (including number, type, and location) since the previous issue. These data, too, dry up after 1886: the *Journal* records success, not failure (except by its silences). But the cardinal value of the *Journal* is as a mirror of the mind of the Order's leadership. For no other organization in American labor history are the questions of proper means and ends so salient; no other was the victim of such uncertainty, or in the end so clearly defeated by an inability to resolve ideological issues. For this central problem, the *Journal* provides an essential record.

The first editor, Charles Litchman, remarked on the significance of the journal's title: *United Labor*. "The name contemplates a time in the future when, with no uncertain sound, it can give voice to that grand undercurrent of mighty thought, which is today crystallizing in the hearts of men, and urging them on to perfect organization, through which to gain the power to make labor emancipation possible." (May 15, 1880) Here were incorporated the two undeviating points of doctrine. Foremost, of course, was the grand objective: the emancipation of the worker. Except in the most all-embracing of idealistic terms, the new order never received clear definition, but what was certain was that it would be fundamentally different from the existing system and that the Knights of Labor would be the instrument of the transformation.

The other certitude was that of labor solidarity. This had been a central notion from the very first, and, according to Norman Ware, was the one point that genuinely distinguished the Order from the trade unions of the 1870s. The trouble with unions, said T. V. Powderly, was that "they never recognised the fight of any other labor body of craftsmen to organize or strike to elevate themselves; they never dreamt that they were dependent on the other; they were not aware that when one class or branch . . . of labor was oppressed the others suffered." (June 15, 1880) The Knights of Labor seemed to offer a genuine alternative to the narrow unionism that was maturing in the 1880s. "Its principles," a district master workman wrote in the *Journal* (July 10, 1886), were "broad enough to embrace all branches of honorable toil into one common fold, without regard to nationality, sex, creed or color." Working among the miners of Shenandoah, Pennsylvania, he admitted that organizing Poles, Hungarians, and Italians—"these miserable foreigners"—was a hard job, but he had succeeded "in educating this servile class up to a higher standard of civilization." That the Knights did not transcend conventional American sentiment reveals how strong was the hold of the idea of labor solidarity. Only in the case of the Chinese (as frequent articles in the *Journal* make clear) was principle overborne by prejudice. "The great work of the Knights of Labor has been to organize labor which was previously unorganized," the *Journal* rightly boasted. (May 25, 1886)

But how was labor solidarity to lead to labor emancipation? The Order was silent on this point. Powderly and his circle did have some notion of the organization's function: namely, as a vast labor lyceum (in which, indeed, the *Journal* would be a major instrument). Unfortunately, this was a poor prescription for organizational success; the early issues of the *Journal* are filled with indications of discouragement among the members grown puzzled about the purposes of the Noble and Holy Order. For their part, the national officers were singularly reluctant to commit themselves to a specific course of action. The Order aimed at "a platform so broad and comprehensive that upon it can be conceived and matured every plan having for its ultimate object the emancipation of labor." (August 15, 1880) Pressed to act, the Order took up cooperation, one of the planks in the program borrowed from the defunct Industrial Brotherhood when the General Assembly was formed in 1878. After much discussion, the constitution was revised to provide "for immediate practical co-operation," which might prove to be "the crowning act." (September 1882) But little headway was actually made, quite clearly because the leadership did not want to commit the Order's energies in this direction.

And politics? Yes, said Powderly, legislation was crucial for achieving labor reform. But not by any direct involvement of the Order: partisan activity was corrupting in any form, whether independent or in support of the existing parties. The *Journal* predicted that, by means of education, "we will soon come out of the ruts of party thinking where we can as freemen see our rights and have the courage and independence to seize them." (September 1882) For the present, the order proposed an elevated kind of nonpartisan politics: the assemblies should discuss issues and candidates (but not parties!), so that the members "will see that their only safety lies in supporting only those men in whose hearts beat purely and warmly the pulsations of hearty sympathy for the oppressed of the land." (November 15, 1880) This was heady advice, but hardly calculated to cost the Order anything. The promising labor politics of 1886-1887, which he briefly encouraged, Powderly rejected with the injunction: "Let political parties alone as an Order." (March 1887)

Powderly's own pet plan—the only one, aside from temperance, about which he seemed to hold fixed convictions—was land reform, not Henry George's Single Tax, but the more primitive agrarian hostility to "private property in land . . . I believe God made the earth for all his children, and that only the fruits of the earth belong to man.'' (June 15, 1882) But Powderly did not impose land-for-use on the Knights, and it was taken up only briefly when the Order made common cause with the Farmers' Alliance at the end of the 1880s.

In reality, the Order's reform impulse never did get much beyond "education." Seeking to distinguish the Knights from the anarchists after Haymarket, the *Journal* stressed its belief that social evils would not end in a day. "These must await the gradual development of education enlightenment as well as beneficial legislative enactment." (November 25, 1886) Had this been all, the Knights probably would have passed into oblivion in the dark days of 1880-1881. That it did not was due to the other side to the movement.

The Order had originally taken the essential character of a labor union, i.e., men had organized within it on the basis of occupational interest and for the purpose of improving the terms of their employment. The founding local assembly was formed in 1869 by garment cutters, and succeeding assemblies likewise organized on occupational lines. There were very few "mixed" assemblies until national organization began in 1878, nor until then were any members not wage-earners. It was true that the Knights of Labor was a secret organization with an elaborate ritual, but, as Norman Ware pointed out, neither of these was uncommon to the unions of the 1870s, nor even a vague commitment to the cooperative commonwealth. The union impulse remained potent at the local and district levels after 1880, and was accepted in practice by the national leaders. In unguarded moments, they acknowledged that the Order was open to anyone "who desires to better his conditions." (February 1883) This led them to adjust the rules to admit national unions (such as the window glass workers, Local Assembly 300) and railroad workers on a systemwide basis, to make provision for strike funds and boycott (for which the Order's structure was admirably suited), and even to abandon the secrecy and the religious aspects of the ritual that had been the core of the Order's fraternal appeal.

But the acceptance of the union tendency was never wholehearted, nor, what was perhaps more important, never with a firm grasp of what was essential in that tendency. "The right to strike is undoubted," remarked Charles Litchman, "the policy and wisdom of exercizing the right are doubtful." (May 15, 1880) Powderly and his circle abhorred the resort to force, and feared the consequences for labor. "A strike brings in its train a series of evils which no man can see the end of," said Powderly. "If the men gain their point or lose it, it is all the same." The employer might "lay low" for a while, but he was sure to revive the fight and eventually crush the men. (August 15, 1880) Nor could Powderly see any functional relationship between day-to-day labor struggles and the larger ends of the movement. At the height of the militant phase of 1885-1886, Powderly was complaining that "the petty strikes and boycotts into which our Assemblies rush are deplorable in the extreme. Our Order can do a great deal of good if time is given to the general officers to think out a plan of action"—by which he certainly did not mean strike action. (January 10, 1886) Much earlier, a *Journal* editorial gave succinct definition to the Order's fundamental dilemma: "The trouble is that each man is so impatient to claim his own individual dividend, that he is unwilling to aid in that complete organization, without which *any* return is impossible." (August 15, 1880)

So here was a labor movement that, beyond any other, had captured the loyalty of American workers, but that lacked sympathy for their concrete concerns, a movement that presided over the greatest strike wave of its time, yet whose leaders abhorred the methods of industrial warfare. It is not any wonder that the Order broke apart on the union issue, and that the strike wave ended in disaster. Nor is it any wonder that the Order beat a hasty retreat from the very things that had given it its brief success.

These are pieces of the puzzle provided by a reading of the *Journal*, not all the pieces by any means, given the official character of the *Journal* and given the remarkable divergence between the elected leaders and some of the tendencies within the Order. But even the puzzle fully assembled would not yield up a ready key to the curious history of the Knights of Labor. The heart of the matter probably was timing. At a point of major social transition, the Order was too modern not to be skeptical of utopian solutions, but not yet capable of the unflinching analysis that might have produced a radical alternative (certainly not one that required acceptance of the class struggle). It was prescient in recognizing the weaknesses of a trade unionism that divided workers and benefited only a labor aristocracy, but was not itself prepared to settle for limited ends nor to accept the uses of economic power. The Knights of

Labor, in effect, stood at the crossroads, fatally incapable of moving in any direction. Joseph R. Buchanan, the toughest minded of the Order's leaders, gave a pungent postmortem: "The prohibitions of strikes, of political action, of mutual aid and the like, had raised the query, 'What are we organized for?' and no satisfactory answer being forthcoming, the unanswered left the Order."

Coventry, Warwickshire, 1973

Nationalist

BOSTON, 1889-1891

FREDERIC C. JAHER

BY the mid-1880s America had awakened to the transformations wrought by industrialism. Awareness of the impact of industrialization had been delayed because even in communities attuned to technological change, important innovations may significantly modify the social structure long before the people awake to their far-reaching consequences. Belated comprehension of these new forces was also a result of the secession crisis. For over thirty years, issues of slavery, expansion, disunion, civil war, emancipation, and reconstruction preempted the attention that might otherwise have been focused on industrial capitalism.

As the passions aroused by these issues subsided, the nation began to shift primary emphasis to other considerations. As the problems of slavery, the war, and its aftermath lost salience or were deemed solved, dramatic events of the 1870s and 1880s impelled America to confront the industrial system. The Credit Mobilier scandal which broke in 1872, the Panic of 1873, the Railroad Strikes of 1885-1886 and 1887, and the Haymarket Riot in 1886 revealed the venal connections between public officials and a new business type—the industrial magnate. These events also highlighted the deep rift between labor and capital and made Americans confront the fact that industrialism could bring poverty as well as progress.

One symptom of the widespread malaise of these troubled times was the plethora of fictional accounts of late nineteenth-century social problems. Beginning in the 1870s and multiplying in number through the 1880s and early 1890s hundreds of economic novels appeared. By 1888, the year in which Edward Bellamy's utopian novel, *Looking Backward*, was first published, fourteen other utopias, eleven fictional, had already been written in the United States since the Civil War. The projection of hopes or nightmares about the community, the literature of cataclysm or utopia, is a sure measure, both in degree and nature, of societal dislocation. Such writing, offering panacea or perdition (sometimes in the same volume), usually focuses as much upon contemporary agitation as upon a vision of the future.

By any standard—sales, literary influence, spur to subsequent action and organization—*Looking Backward* was the most important utopian novel ever conceived in this country. Along with the other outstanding works of this genre, William Dean Howells' *A Traveller From Altruria* (1894) and Ignatius Donnelly's cataclysmic *Caesar's Column* (1890), Bellamy's *Looking Backward* was more radical in indictment and solution than most social protest novels. The majority of works in this vein confined themselves to moderate suggestions for rehabilitating the character of selfish and corrupt captains of industry.

Looking ahead to 2000 A.D., Bellamy unfolded a vision of a harmonious commonwealth. Public ownership and equal distribution of the wealth created by an industrial army of citizens has ended the social strife, commercial waste, and political corruption and oppression that Bellamy felt had prevailed in his own time. Bellamy's version of the perfect society held particular appeal for Americans. The Nationalist state would be brought into existence by orderly democratic process. An enlightened electorate would perceive that the corporate concentrations of wealth and power and the abundance created by industrialism offered a basis for a cooperative commonwealth that could ensure plenty, and security, for all its citizens. As envisioned by Bellamy, only one short, evolutionary step would bring society from monopolistic capitalism to public ownership. Technology had already given men the tools, and the business trust provided the idea of organization with which to perfect society. Once public ownership and an equal distribution of wealth occurred, security and prosperity would belong to all men.

Although Bellamy shared the ideals and many of the principles of socialism, his emphasis on classlessness, peaceful transition, conventional morality, and patriotism (Nationalism, not socialism, was the label Bellamy gave his ideology) made his message palatable to Americans.

Indeed, traditional American values of morality, individualism, freedom, opportunity, and democracy would at last be realized. No longer would they be duplicitous slogans used to disguise ruthlessness, regimentation, and repression.

Looking Backward not only inspired subsequent utopian writing but also fathered a movement. In 1888 ex-army officers attracted by the notion of an industrial army, and Theosophists enthusiastic about the book's expression of humane sentiments of community brotherhood, founded the first organization dedicated to implementing Bellamy's ideals. In deference to the modesty of its namesake, this group, the Boston Bellamy Club, rechristened itself the First Nationalist Club of Boston. Seeing themselves as a model to encourage subsequent organizations, the Boston Nationalists were highly selective in their membership. The club's most famous members were the Brahmin reformers and literary luminaries Edward Everett Hale and Thomas Wentworth Higginson, the Christian Socialists William D. P. Bliss, Frances E. Willard, the Prohibitionist leader, Socialist Laurence Gronlund, urban reformer Solomon Schindler, and novelist and editor of *The Atlantic Monthly*, William Dean Howells. Of one hundred and seven members in 1889, twenty-six were women, thirteen clergymen, six physicians, three journalists, and several lawyers.

A composite portrait of the club reveals a membership similar in social class and outlook to Bellamy. The First Nationalist Club was a loosely knit aggregation of genteel, middle-class New England reformers. A glance at the diverse reform commitments of those who belonged indicates little ideological discipline. The interests and purposes of the organization, as manifested by its members and by the Theosophical leadership of its early years, focused on tolerant, abstract, theoretical, and humane statements of Nationalist principles and upon attempts to educate America in this creed.

The primary vehicle for propagating Nationalism was *The Nationalist*, a monthly magazine which served as both the club bulletin and as the chief organ for the entire movement. This journal, first issued in May 1889, was financed by the Nationalist Educational Association, a corporation formed by the First Nationalist Club. The original editor was Henry Willard Austin, a cousin of Frances E. Willard. Austin, son of a collector of the Port of Boston, was a Harvard graduate, a poet, lawyer,

Theosophist, and one of the founders of the initial Nationalist Club.

True to the aims of its parent, *The Nationalist* contained articles usually hortatory in tone and educational in aim. Contributors like Bellamy, Hale, Daniel De Leon, and Gronlund wrote long inspirational or declaratory essays on Nationalism or socialism, or upon problems like child labor and civil service reform. The treatment of these subjects tended to be abstract rather than concrete. The magazine was embellished by occasional literary flourishes, such as poetry from Thomas Wentworth Higginson. Reflecting the tolerance of the movement, *The Nationalist* opened its columns to reformers who advocated panaceas that differed from Nationalism.

Never a huge seller (it peaked at 9,000 subscribers), *The Nationalist* by 1890 faced bankruptcy. Willard, an alcoholic, proved to be an inefficient editor and was replaced by John Storer Cobb, a wealthy Englishman, and like Willard, a Theosophist and a lawyer. Change in leadership, however, did not improve the financial situation. Moreover, Bellamy, never a leader in the club, and having refused to edit the magazine because of ill-health, saw no point in continuing publication. He was becoming more interested in accomplishing concrete reform through political action than in declarative statements of ideology. The last issues of *The Nationalist* appeared in March-April 1891, but even before its demise Bellamy brought out its successor, *The New Nation*. The new journal, in which Bellamy played the chief role, more accurately reflected his current emphasis upon political activism.

Chicago, 1968

New Nation

BOSTON, 1891-1894

FREDERIC C. JAHER

THE early phase of the Nationalist movement was dominated by the First Nationalist Club of Boston, the second phase by the Second Nationalist Club of Boston. The Second Club, organized by Henry R. Legate in October 1889, was, in part, a reaction against the exclusiveness and deliberative orientation of the First Club. Under the leadership of Legate and Bellamy (who had been only one of several vice-presidents in the original organization), Nationalism became an activist, politically committed movement. The contemplative Theosophist influence declined as local Nationalist parties were formed, as adherents of the movement became candidates for office, and as clubs began to pressure state legislatures to pass enabling acts to permit communities to own and operate public utilities.

Henry Legate, president of the Second Nationalist Club, became the legislative agent for the Boston Nationalists and served on the State Committee of Massachusetts Populists. Bellamy, who approved of the support given by Nationalism to the Peoples' party, went with Legate to the Omaha convention in 1892 to advise the agrarians on a campaign platform. The shift to political engagement led to a break with Theosophy in 1891, an event which cost Nationalism many followers.

On January 31, 1891, the political wing of the Nationalist movement published the first issue of their organ, *The New Nation*. The prospectus for the magazine reflected its founders' disagreement with the theoretically directed *Nationalist* by proposing to pay more attention to concrete Nationalist reform programs. The editor, publisher, and financer of this journal was Edward Bellamy. Mason Green, an Amherst graduate who had worked for Samuel Bowles on *The Springfield Republican*, and who went to Omaha with Bellamy and Legate, was the managing editor. Legate became the assistant editor.

The fact that *The Nationalist* and *The New Nation* did not share personnel, format, and subject matter reflects the gap between the earlier and later phases of Nationalism. None of the editorial staff of *The Nationalist* was carried over to *The New Nation*, nor was anyone who ran the latter publication influential on the former. In fact, *The Nationalist* staff did not even turn over its subscription list to the founders of the new journal. A makeshift list had to be put together from Bellamy's private correspondence.

The two journals differed almost as much in format as in personnel. *The Nationalist* was published in the conventional style of the late nineteenth-century magazine. This monthly was composed mainly of lengthy, signed, topical essays with small departments for book reviews, poems, and letters to the editor. *The New Nation* came out weekly in a form that more closely resembled a newspaper, with triple-, later double-, columned pages, multiple headlines and subheadlines, few signed articles, most of the space devoted to news items, no book reviews, and several special features.

Differences in format lent themselves to differences in orientation and subject matter between the two publications. Signed articles and book reviews encouraged the abstract, declaratory discussions of Nationalist principles that dominated the older magazine. Similarly, headlines, multi-columned pages, and special features enabled the editors of *The New Nation* to emphasize news about practical reforms, concrete situations, and political activities. Special features underscored the specific content and programmatic orientation of Bellamy, Green, and Legate. One column, "Nationalistic Drift," devoted itself to events pointing toward Nationalism, e.g., increasing public ownership of utilities; "Read, Reflect and Inwardly Digest" recounted incidents of crime, suicide, swindling, etc., which would not happen in a Nationalist society; and "News From the Front" presented information on strikes and other social conflicts.

According to one estimate, 70 percent of the space in *The New Nation* was devoted to specific reforms. The most frequently mentioned cause or program was municipal ownership of gas and electric utilities, considered by Bellamy and his followers to be the crucial first step toward nationalization. Much space was also given to the Populists. News of their conventions and victories, and frequent reprinting of the 1892 Omaha platform, kept the agrarian crusade constantly before the eyes of *The New Nation* reader. The extensive and generous attention extended to the Populists and Socialists was characteristic of the tolerant attitude that marked Nationalism throughout its existence.

Although Bellamy felt that *The New Nation* had counteracted the dangerous tendency in Nationalism, accentuated by *The Nationalist*, of "being dissipated into a vague and foggy philanthropy," by 1894 he was no longer prepared to continue to balance the journal's deficit with his own royalties. Bellamy felt that *The New Nation* had made its contribution, and he now became preoccupied with another project, *Equality*, a sequel to *Looking Backward* that was published in 1897.

The weekly needed a patron because, like *The Nationalist*, it never had many subscribers. In its best year only 8,000 paid to read *The New Nation*. But after 1891 the movement began to lose members. The Panic of 1893 diminished the subscription list even further. With its sources of support gone, *The New Nation* suspended publication after the issue of February 3, 1894. The journal, and shortly thereafter the movement from which it sprang, passed into the oblivion that awaited all attempts to radically alter American society to fit some dream of the world as it should be.

Chicago, 1968

American Fabian
BOSTON, 1895-1900

JAMES B. GILBERT

FABIANISM, as an organized impulse in the history of American radicalism, had only a short and unimportant existence. While it was alive, from about 1896 to 1902, it was confined to a small group of intellectuals in Boston, New York, California, and a few other places. At best it was a stopgap movement, coming at a time when middle-class reformers were beginning to move beyond municipal reforms to choose either socialism or a national reform program such as Theodore Roosevelt proposed.

Like many other imported reform theories, Fabianism was quickly adapted to its American surroundings, and, if anything, it became a foreign description of a group of American attitudes. The Altrurian Club of New York (named after William Dean Howells' novel) argued that the word Fabian ought to be dropped by the fledgling movement because it sounded too foreign. Instead, they proposed to call the new group the Collectivist League. American Fabians acknowledged their debt to the British, but in the long run they owed as much or more to utopian Edward Bellamy, Laurence Gronlund, and the Christian socialism of William D. P. Bliss.

The American Fabian League and its publication, the *American Fabian*, were both established in 1895 by William Bliss. A reformer of inexhaustible energy and innumerable projects, Bliss had traveled to England in 1894 and had been deeply impressed by the work being done by the English Fabians. When he returned to Boston, he founded the *American Fabian*, a magazine that he hoped would unite divergent American reform groups and create a new reform movement. As the

39

major organ of American Fabianism, the magazine played an interesting but interim role for reformers in the unstable period prior to the organization of the American Socialist party and the appearance of national progressivism.

When it first appeared, the *American Fabian* was an outgrowth of *The Dawn*, the Christian Socialist magazine published in Boston by Bliss. The new magazine immediately suggested that its primary function should be the founding of an ecumenical reform movement: "The aim of the 'American Fabian,' " the first editorial announced, "is to unite social reforms and lead the way to a conception of Socialism, broad enough, free enough, practical enough to include all that is of value, no matter whence it comes, and replace jealousy between reformers by co-operation for the general good." The magazine and the movement it inaugurated were frankly eclectic, searching every philosophy and organization for usable ideas. It necessarily followed that the *American Fabian* was an educational organ, only secondarily devoted to politics. The magazine sought a middle position, hoping to bring together middle-class reformers and trade unionists. It felt compelled to move beyond the fixation of single-cause reforms, such as Prohibition and the Single Tax, but was also careful to dissociate itself from the rough Marxism of the Socialist Labor party.

In 1895, some limited attempts were made to organize Fabian clubs throughout the United States, but these met with little success. Small groups were founded in California; Madison, Wisconsin; New York; and Boston, but the Fabian League, for all practical purposes, never amounted to more than a paper organization. The magazine's ambitious correspondence school, which promised courses in economics, sociology, and political science based on the writings of the English Fabians, Bliss, Bellamy, and others, never amounted to much. By the beginning of 1896, Bliss proposed to move the magazine to New York, where a group of Fabians was willing to continue editing it. In its first year, the magazine was far from becoming the important journal Bliss intended. It did little more than print citations out of Bliss' *Encyclopedia of Social Reform* and suggest, in the broadest way, the meaning of Fabianism.

Perhaps one factor that impeded the magazine's success was vagueness about socialism, conceived as a mild sort of municipal ownership that Bliss called "voluntary socialism." The magazine believed that the

Socialist commonwealth could be introduced with little struggle: socialism, it explained, "simply needs a knowledge to be accepted." Although Bliss spoke to an accepted set of beliefs in American reform thought—to the positivist sense of the inevitable triumph of the good society—he did not succeed in organizing the reformers who accepted this idea. After about a year, Bliss was ready to undertake new tasks and left the magazine to his New York friends.

During the next two years, the *American Fabian* was edited by Prestonia Mann, who ran a part-time utopian community in the Adirondacks called "Summer Brook," and then by reformer William James Ghent. Once in New York, the magazine took on new energy and attracted new writers. The most important of these was Charlotte Perkins Stetson (Gilman), whom the American Fabians nominated to be the American George Bernard Shaw. During this time, the magazine clarified its political position and gradually began to focus its attention on such reform organizations as the New York Social Reform Club, of which Ghent was a member.

In the spring of 1897, the magazine still had high hopes for organizing a universal reform group. "The Fabian movement," the magazine editorialized, "—at present the most rational and moderate of all reform movements—is thus destined, perhaps to assume more and more a position of commanding importance in our social evolution." The political position remained much the same, if more elaborated. Fabian socialism would occupy a middle position, proposing a just society in which individualism and collectivism would reinforce and protect each other. A short statement of principles was adopted promising what amounted to state socialism, focusing on the need to equalize workers' wages and criticizing the role of competition in society. In line with its support for evolutionary change, the magazine identified elements of collective life that were already present in American society; for example, in urban patterns of life (Bliss had once written of the Brooklyn Bridge as a symbol of municipal socialism).

In New York, the magazine also altered its format, printing more original material and occasional poems, and reporting news of reform activities in New York City and elsewhere. It devoted more time to discussing European reformers such as Mazzini, Ruskin, and Tolstoi. By the end of 1898, the magazine reached a high point. It enthusiastically greeted as an ally of Fabianism, the Social Reform Club of New York, which included among its members a number of important urban reformers. However, it quickly became apparent that neither the Reform Club nor the magazine itself would fulfill a central role in American reform.

During the last year of its existence, the *American Fabian* came under the editorship of John Preston, until it stopped publishing in January 1900. All of the other Fabian publications disappeared by 1902. Preston blamed two things for the demise of his publication: the return of economic prosperity, and the general apathy of the masses. But Preston was right only in the short run. American radicalism was not entering a low period. Its most exciting and productive years were just ahead. Fabianism had never been a really serious contender for the attention of American reformers, nor had many intellectuals, Bliss and Ghent among them, given it their full attention. Many American intellectuals, however, held ideas similar to Fabianism, and for this reason the magazine has an importance beyond its limited life and influence. But most intellectuals were not seriously interested in the weak movement that was organized in its name.

College Park, Maryland, 1969

Social Crusader
CHICAGO, 1898-1901

Socialist Spirit
CHICAGO, 1901-1903

HOWARD H. QUINT

THE aftermath of the presidential election of 1896 was a time for stocktaking by Christian and Fabian Socialists in the United States. Almost all of them had supported William Jennings Bryan, the Democratic candidate, in preference to Charles H. Matchett, who headed the Socialist Labor party ticket, and William McKinley, the Republican standard bearer.

To the Christian and Fabian Socialists, McKinley's crushing victory was clear proof that the country was nowhere near ready to listen to, let alone support, a socialist political party. To have cast one's ballot for Matchett was, in effect, to have thrown away his vote, since the Socialist Labor candidate had no chance of winning or even making a respectable showing. Other decisions, too, weighed in their voting for Bryan rather than Matchett. The Socialist Labor party was rent by factional strife and not a few of the non-Marxist Christian and Fabian Socialists had been the victims of Daniel De Leon's editorial invective. Moreover, the Fabian and Christian Socialists, most of whom were former members of Edward Bellamy's Nationalist clubs, vehemently repudiated the class struggle thesis, the very cornerstone of the Socialist Labor program. It deeply offended their middle-class sensibilities.

But what to do? Clearly, political activity along Socialist lines was out of the question. Rather, as the Christian and Fabian Socialists read the situation, the task confronting those who desired social reconstruction was to concentrate on education, agitation, and organization in the manner of the British Fabians. Such a strategy demanded establishment of national, state, and local societies dedicated to propagandizing the ideals of the cooperative commonwealth. Where possible, such societies might be associated with church groups which would afford them a certain degree of respectability. Schools, colleges, and institutes would have to be founded to teach Socialist doctrines, not of the Marxist variety, to be sure, but such collectivist concepts as government ownership of railroads, telegraphs and telephones, and public utilities. And there was need, too, for new and better socialist publications to discuss political and economic issues without rancor or ideological rigidity.

During the period between the election of 1896 and the founding of the Socialist party of America in 1901, the Christian and Fabian Socialists went about their self-assigned task with enthusiasm. Their leading agitator, organizer, and spokesman was the Reverend William Dwight Porter Bliss, Episcopal clergyman and editor of the Christian Socialist paper, *The Dawn*. The indefatigable Bliss crisscrossed the nation on lecture tours and invariably left in his wake local social reform clubs dedicated to propagandizing non-Marxian socialism. He was also responsible for founding several Socialist journals, all of which, like the clubs, had an ephemeral existence. Significantly, both the clubs and the journals paid little attention to the wranglings currently going on among politically oriented Socialists. These controversies were to lead to a split in the Socialist Labor party and to the establishment of the Social Democratic party in 1898 and eventually of the Socialist party of America in 1901.

If Bliss was the plodding workhorse of the Christian Socialists, their charismatic leader was the Reverend George D. Herron. It was Herron, more than any other man, who diverted Christian Socialists from political inactivism and brought them into the fold of the Social Democratic party. He himself had joined the party in 1899 and for the next few years took a prominent role in its affairs.

Herron had rocketed to national fame through his passionate and widely publicized sermons on social redemption and his brief and stormy career as professor of applied theology at Grinnell College. Christian radicals who found the Fabian tactics of Bliss unrewarding had no difficulty in identifying with the dynamic Herron who did not try to obfuscate the existence of class conflict in America. While eschewing "class hatred" as such, Herron asserted that nothing could "obviate the hideous fact" that one class of human beings was living off another class. Only through a Socialist society would such exploitation end, and the time had come, he declared, for men of good will to band together behind a Socialist political party dedicated to this purpose—the Social Democratic party, to be precise.

Herron's greatest following was in the Chicago area, although he had disciples scattered throughout the country. Among them was the Reverend J. Stitt Wilson, who was later to become a reform mayor of Berkeley, California. Wilson organized the Social Crusade, a religious fraternity dedicated to "righteousness, justice and brotherhood." Its immediate concern was to arouse the conscience of men and women everywhere to the iniquities of the capitalistic system and to foster social and economic change along Socialist lines. To this end, members of the fraternity spoke wherever they could find an audience and organized local Social Crusade Circles. In 1898 they began publication of *The Social Crusader, a messenger of brotherhood and social justice*. Initially, *The Social Crusader* was almost indistinguishable from other Christian Socialist-Fabian magazines such as the *Social Economist*, the *Bellamy Review* and *Social Forum*. But as Herron moved toward open endorsement of the Social Democratic party so did *The Social Crusader*. In the 1900 presidential election it warmly endorsed Social Democratic party candidates, Eugene V. Debs and Job Harriman. The Social Democratic party, wrote Wilson, was not created out of a melange of demagogues, cranks, and eccentrics. It represented the coming together of the various forces in America that were making for a new cooperative society. It was the beginning of an effort to free the working people of the country from social injustice. And it was destined not only to remain but eventually to prevail. "As the new order appears on the horizon," Wilson predicted, "those who see it live in a new day already. And they form the advance guard of a new civilization."

In point of fact, Herron, while encouraging the work of the Social Crusade, did not become a member until January 1901. In September of the same year, the name of the *Social Crusader* was changed to *The*

Socialist Spirit. The Reverend Franklin H. Wentworth, a Christian Socialist clergyman from Chicago, continued on in the editorship inherited from Wilson, and the format of the little magazine did not differ essentially from what it had previously been. Two prominent Socialist writers, John Spargo and William Mailly, were recruited to write feature articles on developments in the world of socialism and labor. Like the editors of *Comrade, Wilshire's Magazine, The Coming Nation*, and *The International Socialist Review*, Wentworth sought to incorporate in *The Socialist Spirit* both good socialist propaganda and literary excellence. He wanted a magazine that Socialists could show with pride to their non-Socialist friends. And at the same time, he wished a temperately written journal that members of the Social Crusade, rechristened the Fellowship of the Socialist Spirit, could disseminate in the churches. Quite characteristic of Socialist magazines of the time, *The Socialist Spirit* had a section devoted to women and, equally characteristic, it was edited by Wentworth's wife, Marion Craig Wentworth.

The last issue of *The Socialist Spirit* appeared in February 1903. In all, eighteen issues had been published. Wentworth's editorial swan song was a familiar one. "A year and a half of the sincerest kind of effort" had demonstrated that the value of the magazine was not "commensurate with the life that has been poured into it." *The Socialist Spirit* had always been "a labor of love." But Wentworth was in no way discouraged. "I feel that I am eminently the gainer by the few poor things I have written . . . some of them forged in the white heat of mental and moral feeling; some of them produced under stress of great weariness of body and mind. I am the gainer because some of these things have brought me closer to my fellows; those who feel passionately as I do the unspeakable wrongs that flourish in the world—and that there is a remedy for them."

Amherst, Massachusetts, 1969

Part Two

THE SOCIALIST PARTY PRESS, 1900-1919

THE Socialist party of America was founded in 1900-1901. In 1919, as a consequence of divisions induced by the Bolshevik Revolution, the party split into three parties, and even more splinters. One of the three retained the name and much of the leadership of the pre-Bolshevik party but there the resemblance ended. The post-1919 Socialist party was quite as petty in its vendettas and quite as politically insignificant as the various Communist groups to its left. Before 1919, the Socialist party had been a large, open-membership organization with considerable electoral support. The party included hostile factions but, with few exceptions, it was a broadly based association, able to accommodate any who shared the goal of establishing a postcapitalist commonwealth. The party very nearly became a significant force in American politics and many American radicals since have developed the habit of looking back nostalgically on the period as ''a golden age.''

Initially, the party was put together piecemeal by a variety of local organizations, the remnants of 1890s reform groups, and visionary individuals. The largest components were a group of Socialist Labor party secessionists led by New York attorney Morris Hillquit; and Victor Berger's Social Democratic Federation, a significant political force in Milwaukee which also claimed loosely affiliated groups elsewhere in the country. Other elements included diehard Populists, former members of Nationalist clubs, Christian Socialists, some immigrant societies, and numerous individuals, some of them well-known figures but none of them more important than Eugene V. Debs.

Debs was no ideologue nor was he even very intellectual. His was a moral socialism, rooted in a Christian and a Jeffersonian hatred for injustice. In his lack of patience and of aptitude for the abstract, Debs finely personified the early Socialist party. Confronted with concrete and obvious injustices, the party was collectively not so much concerned with a unanimous agreement on the exact nature, cause, and remedy of those injustices as it was with working to correct them. In the meantime, the Socialists tolerated broad differences within, tacitly assuming that those differences would be adjusted as the party moved toward its socialist goal.

With this latitudinarian approach, the SPA scored increasing electoral successes. In 1900, Debs, the candidate of a still incompleted party, received 94,768 votes for president. In 1904, this total quadrupled to 402,460. Dishearteningly, the Socialist presidential vote in 1908 scarcely exceeded this but, in 1912, despite the fact that two of the three major party candidates stood for election as "Progressives," Debs won almost a million votes. In the meantime, especially in 1910, the Socialists scored dozens of local successes, even sending Victor Berger to Congress. Moreover, while some formerly Socialist trade unions lapsed from their commitment, socialism made appreciable gains in other parts of the AFL, and, in the Industrial Workers of the World, at least the left wing of the SPA had a seemingly vital working-class ally. The writings and speeches of capitalist politicians were flecked with apprehensions of the Socialists' growth and the SPA leaders themselves looked forward confidently to eventual victory.

Then, at this apex, the right wing of the party moved to recall William D. Haywood, the titular leader of the left wing, from his post on the National Executive Committee. The charges placed against him were largely trumped up. Basically, this move represented the belief of the respectability-conscious right wing that future success depended upon the party's dissociation from the ill-regarded IWW (with which Haywood was closely identified). Only then, the right wing reasoned, could progressive-minded middle-class people and anti-dual unionist AFL men be aligned behind the SPA.

This was the only significant instance of factional *action* in the early history of the SPA and its effects were destructive. Within months of Haywood's recall, the membership of the party declined drastically with no compensating influx of "moderate" reformists. In 1913 and 1914, many of the party's local electoral gains were wiped out. And, in 1916, when the right wing, under Berger's direction, managed to prevent the "revolutionist" Debs from taking the nomination, the party's poll in the presidential election dropped almost 50 percent.

With America's entrance into World War I, the SPA seemed to be recovering. No doubt this was largely because, after the American declaration of war, the Socialist party was the only significant political organization through which antiwar sentiment could express itself. Nevertheless, Victor Berger was again elected to Congress; Socialists scored successes in several state legislatures and came very close to capturing the municipal administrations of several large cities. In 1920, Eugene V. Debs, again the presidential candidate, but now in Atlanta Penitentiary where he was imprisoned for his opposition to the war, received nearly a million votes. But this was largely a sympathy vote. Just as the SPA had dismantled its own success in 1912 through a factional fight, its second apogee during the war was to be dissipated, this time conclusively, by the bitter internecine struggles engendered by the Bolsheviks' success in Russia. No other American radical movement ever rose to its heights, perhaps in part because the SPA's errors were never fully appreciated.

When well-funded and subscribed, the SPA published a large number and variety of periodicals: newspapers, journals, popular magazines, internal bulletins. Reflecting the character of the movement, these were not the highly disciplined issue of the central office but the autonomous ventures of local groups and individuals in voluntary support of the Socialist party. In 1912, at the peak, over three hundred Socialist periodicals were published in the United States. Almost every one of these disappeared during the next decade.

The Appeal to Reason

GIRARD, KANSAS, 1895-1917, 1919-1922

New Appeal

GIRARD, 1917-1919

PAUL M. BUHLE

THE *Appeal to Reason* is perhaps the only American radical periodical which belongs equally to the history of American radicalism and modern journalism. *The Appeal* was the most important evangelistic propaganda organ of the Left and the clearest expression of indigenous American socialism, but more than that, the only national political newspaper of its time to capture a half-million subscribers and maintain its financial integrity without massive infusions of funds and, for considerable periods, without advertising. The secret of the "Little Ole Appeal," as editors and readers alike called the paper, was the decisive link it created between the working class's heritage of despair in nineteenth-century America and the alternate indignation and hopefulness of the dispossessed in the twentieth century. *The Appeal* discovered in tens of thousands of its readers an "Army" for socialism and molded itself around this group's literary tastes and desire for self-education; in turn, the "Army" conquered new territories for socialism until the calamity of World War I and the dissipation of indigenous radicalism.

The father of *The Appeal* was J. A. Wayland—financier, Socialist, journalist wrapped up into a single remarkable individual. Born in poverty in Indiana in 1854, he became a partner in a printing and newspaper business at nineteen, then publisher of a Republican paper in staunchly

Democratic Missouri, and finally successful job printer in Pueblo, Colorado. In Pueblo, he made a small fortune by shrewd investment in real estate, and was converted to socialism through reading pamphlets and Edward Bellamy's *Looking Backward*. He returned for a time to Indiana to publish his own radical paper, *The Coming Nation*, and then moved his journal and hopes to the Ruskin, Tennessee, utopian colony. In 1895 he left Ruskin, cynical toward communitarian living; the same year he began *The Appeal to Reason* in Kansas City, and moved it to its final home in Girard, Kansas.

These were the first of the boom years for American magazines generally. Prior to 1890, the only periodicals available were the expensive, erudite journals like *Harper's*, or the trashy pulp press. Breakthroughs in the printing process in the 1880s and 1890s helped clear the way for a new and more popular journalism, as they did for the burgeoning "yellow press" of the great daily newspapers. S. S. McClure, Cyrus Curtis, William Randolph Hearst, and J. A. Wayland all recognized that millions of Americans thirsted for a real understanding of current events and interesting reading. All shared, too, the understanding that price was central: the worker could not afford to pay more than a few cents for a single issue, or a dollar or two per year at most for a subscription. But Wayland was unique among these giants in his fundamental devotion to a cause. If Curtis' *Post* sought to portray the virtue and glamor of business, Wayland was determined to tell the real story of what he considered "this so-called Christian nation," and to reinvest his profits to that end alone. He was also determined to remain very far from New York City and the new face of American capitalism: his was the America that was dying by degrees.

The Appeal to Reason, named in the heritage of Thomas Paine, was in its first years substantially the same as the earlier *Coming Nation*. The most notable feature of *The Appeal* was the twang of Wayland's own cadence in his columns of opinion, short and to the point:

People don't have titles in America! 'Gin the law, you know. Titled people make people work to keep 'em in luxury, you know, and Americans would never stand for that. No Sirree! Not while the Declaration is read every fourth, and the names of Lexington, Bunker Hill, Homestead and Coueur d'Alene are remembered! No

oppression in America, if you please. We are free. We are the great
people. The American eagle soars—wonder if it isn't sore?

The "One Hoss" editor, as he liked to call himself, earned the
admiration of his readers by his stubborn independence. As he wrote in
The Coming Nation, "Why should I write these lines and say 'we'? There
is no 'we' about it. There may not be another man in the nation who
coincides with all I write." Moreover, he did not patronize his readers:
far from it, he lambasted the ignorance of the "Voting Kings," the
workers who perpetuated their own misery by voting Republican or
Democratic: "Work, you slaves, so your master will make enough
money out of you to buy a titled husband for his daughter, so she can live
in Yurrup among decent people. . . . Will they learn better? O! maybe."

As Howard Quint puts it, *The Appeal* was full of "analogies, fables
and parables," the imagery of post-frontier humor that echoed the sly
folksiness of Uncle Jonathan and the frontiersman of the popular stage a
half-century earlier. Characteristic columns by individual writers had
titles like "Your Uncle," "Musings of a Mossback," "From My Snuff
Box," and "Warbling Wilbur," with their own terse paragraphs or more
extended commentaries, sometimes written in a stylized midwestern
dialect. Radical classics from the previous period of upsurge, the 1840s
to 1860s, were serialized; one of these classics was "A Voice to Mankind," written by the universal reformer and spiritualist Andrew Jackson
Davis. Antiforeign stereotypes as well as ethnic humor were not dis-
dained. In one front-page cartoon, "Sambo" says to a Civil War veteran:
"Guess you made a mistake massa. You'se a worse slave than I was fo'
de war," while a money-mad Count Rothschild whispers to Grover
Cleveland during a threat of war: "Vell Grover, my frient, if we can get
the beoples to think dere's going to be a vite we'll vin de game. Great
chances for us, I dell you. Some littl money for me and for you a crown, a
real golden crown, Grover, mit diamonts. More bonts, Grover, more
bonts."

The optimistic side of *The Appeal* was no less important than its
vitriolic attacks on capitalism, domestic and foreign. Wayland, along
with the Socialist faithful, believed, in a way hard to comprehend today,
that the process of revolution was essentially one of working-class

self-education: as the blows continued to fall upon them, workers would grow wiser and in time, they would become Socialists. As early as 1895, Wayland made the basis of his faith perfectly clear:

"Do you think it is possible to educate all the people to understand your theory?" is asked of me often. No. Nor is it necessary. If we can educate 10 per cent of the voters, we shall have it all our way. Do you think the voters in the old parties understand the "theories" they vote for? Not a bit. Less than 100 cunning men now control the whole machinery of government of the United States. The rest are puppets. Given a million posted men, and the balance is easy. And there are more than that studying our principles. The future is ours.

And that future rested upon agitation such as *The Appeal* could carry out. Wayland withheld fidelity to any one socialist party through the bulk of the 1890s, advising readers to subscribe to the Socialist Labor party's *The People* but disdaining to accept the SLP's discipline. Only with the rise of Eugene Debs' Social Democracy did Wayland commit himself, and only with the formation of the Socialist party in 1901 did *The Appeal* consider itself the unofficial organ of a movement.

The most dramatic event for *The Appeal* in these years was the formation of a group of "Patriots," later renamed simply the "Appeal Army," to distribute and solicit subscriptions for the periodical in an organized fashion. By 1899, the "Army" had its own column in *The Appeal*, with its own peculiar variant of *Appeal* humor. Such is the sincerity and pathos of the volunteer work:

Comrade Jensen, of Travers, Minn, does not say a word but ships us in 25 patients for one year's treatment. They will be properly cared for during that period.

Comrade Taylor, of Denison, Tex, captured a squad of 42 of the enemy and sent them to the APPEAL headquarters for judgment. They will be treated as prisoners of war and brothers.

The Falun, Kansas Trust, which is generaled by Comrade Neff, Jr., exploded one of its shells loaded with 50 slugs, on the office desk and scattered the Editor's copy all over the room. John ought to give us a little notice before he fires next time.

On a day's hunt at Poplar Bluff, Mo, Bro. Knecht captured 36 stray voters and put tickets in their hands for a year's excursion into the jungles of socialism. If they escape they will be out of luck.

Comrade Frank Fianke, of Redlands, Calafornia, shipped us 90 subs. When the thing exploded in the office, the gas engine took on a higher speed, the press ground its teeth a little harder and the rolls of paper groaned under an additional pressure.

Would naturally expect such treatment from W. H. Attlesea of Little Rock, Iowa. He hits us with a club weighing 33 subscriptions for a year. He is given to mistreating the "One Hoss" that way. Hope his character will improve with age.

These "salesmen-soldiers" rapidly came to be the heart of *The Appeal*, not only in matters of circulation and finance, but politically and spiritually as well. By 1913, the newspaper had reached a peak circulation of 750,000, with some 50,000 subscribers in Oklahoma alone. The "Army" then became a kind of party-within-a-party, its organizational efforts the primary thrust of Socialist agitation between elections, especially in the southwestern states but also in all localities where *The Appeal*'s circulation was concentrated. Such mass selling efforts were common to Socialist propaganda. In that sense *The Appeal*'s "salesmen-soldiers" were different from the Milwaukee *Social-Democratic Herald*'s "bundle brigade" (which distributed copies and sold subscriptions on weekends) only in its larger size. But the "Army" was also an immediate presence in *The Appeal*. When in 1904, the newspaper was forced to take advertising in order to maintain its low subscription rates, Wayland solicited the "Army" in his columns, as he was to do on other occasions. According to *The Appeal*'s own claims, the "Army" could have a decisive impact by combining its sales and political efforts. This impact could most notably be felt by the "Army's" role in freeing the leaders of the Western Federation of Miners, who had been "kidnapped" by the state of Colorado for being accessories to the murder of ex-Governor Steunenberg (a charge that was later disproved). *The Appeal* had published an edition of a million copies, with Debs' call (titled "Arouse Ye Slaves") to free the leaders of the miners by armed force if necessary. As a staff member remembered:

> Perhaps it was the need developed by the Colorado fight which made of the Appeal Army the efficient literature organization it has become. But it was the Army that made the Appeal, was the Army that saved Haywood, it was the Army which repeatedly snatched the paper from destruction, it was the Army that made the plutes tremble and that, alone of all agencies. The Appeal has grown and it has a circulation greater than any Socialist paper on earth, greater than any political paper on earth; but it is the ARMY THAT DID IT. Thirty thousand men and women working for nothing and doing things men never did before, is a spectacle that astonished the world.

Wayland's personal assessment of the "Army" confirmed this vision. When he was on the verge of quitting the operation in 1903, exhausted by the daily labors and uncertain of the progress made, he remembered himself asking, "Shall I sink self, even life if need be, for those who need it? And my wife said, 'The Army has been faithful to you,' and I decided."

A study by James R. Green of the top-ranking Army salesmen (honored in an *Appeal's Who's Who*, with biographical materials on the five hundred best soldiers) shows that they were primarily from the Midwest, Southwest or West, native-born, tending toward middle age, and mostly artisans, unskilled workers, or small and tenant farmers. These were the men who had been converted largely by reading *The Appeal* or its predecessor, *The Coming Nation*, and whose gospel, at least initially, had been the ethical texts such as Bellamy's *Looking Backward* rather than the Marxist classics. In an attack on prize-fighting, Debs perhaps best sketched out the ideal Army type: in counterposition to the city-slick "plug-hatted and patent-leather shoed" men who found entertainment in brutal beatings, Socialists were "at their humble cottages with their families, reading sound literature, studying the science of society." Like all stereotypes, this was an oversimplification; yet it captures the ethos of self-betterment which penetrated *The Appeal*'s essentially lower class supporters and audience. Wayland himself, a shy and retiring man known only by reputation to *The Appeal* audience, was properly depicted by a co-worker as only an agent of the Army, similar to the thousands he had influenced, who spent his leisure time "talking Socialism" to individuals he met, seeking to convince them one-by-one to the evangel.

The power of *The Appeal* was not without its drawbacks to the Socialist movement. The newspaper quickly became an end in itself, while the actual organization of Socialists in many places trailed along behind. *The Appeal*, moreover, reinforced a certain kind of naive expectation in the uses of the political process then common to indigenous socialism: while the economic and political frauds of capitalism were endlessly exposed, the very power of the sensationalistic revelations was a measure of the belief remaining in the "true" (if latent) possibilities for the democratic process. Socialists, then, were little prepared for the wave of legal and semilegal repression that swept across the country during World War I and most deeply damaged the Socialist movement in the Midwest and Southwest. *The Appeal* also tended to create "personalities" overnight with some dubious results. Charles Edward Russell, who did not join the Socialist movement until 1908, wrote a series of muckraking articles on government that helped him gain the nomination for governor of New York in 1910; Allen L. Benson was virtually unknown until his series of antiwar articles in 1914 catapulted him to the presidential nomination two years later. The later capitulation of both of these men from the Socialist ranks over the war issue was at least a painful reminder of the unreliability of the intellectuals whom *The Appeal* had raised to prominence based solely on their journalistic skills. Most of all, *The Appeal*'s very strengths ultimately proved to be their greatest weaknesses. Unlike the other Socialist newspapers and magazines, the very size of *The Appeal* audience demanded that it operate as a barometer of public interest on various issues and that it maintain itself in some ways like a bourgeois journal; unlike the *Saturday Evening Post* or *Munsey's*, however, *The Appeal* remained responsible above all to the propagation of socialism. Sometimes, as in the serialization of Upton Sinclair's *The Jungle, The Appeal* managed to do both. But the task required a unique interpretation and anticipation of the audience by the editor. Such a task could not be institutionalized politically, but depended upon personality.

Early in the life of *The Appeal*, Wayland had able help from Fred A. Warren, a Kansas newspaperman who had converted to socialism and became a staffer in 1900. Warren increasingly took over the newspaper from the aging Wayland, and may be credited with balancing the format between the intensely personal style of Wayland and the columns of Debs, serialization of popular Socialist literature, news reports and other random materials. The tremendous scale of labor and the repeated persecution of *The Appeal* by Post Office officials seeking to deny it second-class mailing privileges ultimately took their toll, however. A week after the tragic death of Wayland's wife in an automobile accident, Wayland announced that Warren was overtired and would be on a leave of absence, that "it will be of great help if the Army will continue its wonderful work . . . for that has been the thing that he has ever had in mind." When, in the following year, Wayland was accused of abducting a female employee of *The Appeal* for immoral purposes (the charge was later found to be an utter fabrication), Wayland could no longer fight. He committed suicide, leaving a note which read, "The struggle under the capitalist system isn't worth the effort. Let it pass." The columns of *The Appeal* were immediately filled with the Army's promises not to disgrace Wayland's memory by failing, demanding, "Stick to the Appeal, the Army will stick to you." Two years later, Warren resigned for medical reasons, his health broken at forty-two from years of overwork. Walter H. Wayland, who had worked at his father's paper since the age of twelve, took over the editorship, and a former business manager of the *New York Call*, Louis Kopelin, became managing editor. Under this new team, business sagged: the Socialist party had entered a period of stagnation generally, and the new, less exciting *Appeal* lost major circulation for the first time in 1913-1917, from around 760,000 to around 530,000. But the worst was ahead.

The entry of the United States into World War I divided Socialists across geographical and factional lines. Although there was a strong tendency for reform-minded Socialists to join the war effort, many (including some well-known pacifists) remained to carry on the agitational effort; conversely, while most revolutionary Socialists continued to oppose the war, a considerable number—especially from native-born stock—renounced the Socialist party. Under Louis Kopelin's editorship, *The Appeal* (renamed *The New Appeal* in 1917) supported Wilson's

Fourteen Points: Kopelin went so far as to claim: "Whatever may be our opinions of the capitalist system, the capitalists in no respect control the present administration of the U.S. government." This was a significant defection from the Socialist party's St. Louis Resolution against the War, and along with the entry of thousands of foreign-born workers through the language federation, it marked the eclipse of indigenous, rural-dominated socialism in favor of a more "European," metropolitan variety of proletarian struggle. *The Appeal* had not defected from socialism, however. After merging with *Upton Sinclair's* (a similarly pro-war journal), in 1919 it took back its old title and resumed its crusade against the trusts and government.

The days of glory had passed, however. *The Appeal* might demand the release of Debs from prison and even call for the support of the Russian Revolution, but it found a diminishing response from its old readership. The loss of second-class privileges for a time, the severe damage wrought to the rural Socialist movement during the war (capped by the disastrous and ludicrous "Green Corn Rebellion" in Oklahoma in 1918), and the prevailing disillusion at the failure of the Socialist mission proved insuperable barriers. The remarkable new owner and editor, Emanuel Haldemann-Julius, sought through fundraising efforts and new promotion to revive "the evangel." As he pointed out in 1921, the Socialist movement had been first built by the street-corner speaker and the Socialist periodical. In the decade after the onset of the native Socialist decline, street-corner speaking had lost its novelty and in many places had become illegal. More important, the capitalist press had expanded enormously, and especially since the war, had become propagandistically anti-Socialist. In short, "They have the ears of the workers . . . We expose the inside control of the public press. The masses, not seeing our exposure, continue to read the capitalist-controlled public press with unshaken confidence." Or alternatively, as Haldemann-Julius did not say, the urban masses read the public press with cynicism toward any political alternatives for the direction of society. Haldemann-Julius was shrewd enough to respond; but not with *The Appeal*.

The legacy of *The Appeal*, which finally folded in 1922, was a continuation of that great project for self-education among lower class Americans. The "Little Blue Books," which began to appear under the ownership of Haldemann-Julius during wartime, were 3-1/2 by 5 inches in size, priced from a nickel to twenty-five cents. For a dime, one could buy the classics of literature and politics from Paine to Ibsen, Dumas, Molière, Wilde, and George Washington. His "Campaign for Shakespere," banned from the mails on a Post Office technicality, offered an entire set for $2.35. As the reader purchased more, the price fell: for $1.95 each, some twenty-five books could be purchased. Haldemann-Julius prided himself for thus "Fordizing Literature"; well he might, for over the next forty years an estimated five hundred million bluebooks appeared under two thousand different titles. As Haldemann-Julius wrote in the 1920s:

What the crowd thinks and does has been and is very vital to thinkers, and to liberal-minded citizens, especially when they have felt the enormous fist of the ignorant, intolerant mob in their faces. What the crowd does and correspondingly what the crowd thinks, checks or advances, as culture is isolated or made popular, the degree of freedom and civilization that we can enjoy. To make knowledge popular is to make life as a whole freer and more intelligent.

Socialism had failed, at least for several generations, and with it *The Appeal* had fallen victim with the movement, marking out the limitations of the most accessible alternative to the bourgeois media that Socialists were ever to produce. Yet one cannot help believing that, had Wayland lived to see the Haldemann-Julius mission, he would have perceived that the continuous task of education of the masses was simply being performed under another name. This was the golden ideal of socialism at its political peak in Europe and America. In the reality that this education would be performed (although in the most limited and alienated fashion) by the bourgeois media systems and by the compulsory educational training of the working class, the ideal died and the task of socialism —whatever it was to become—was forever transformed.

Somerville, Massachusetts, 1973

Social-Democratic Herald

CHICAGO AND MILWAUKEE,

1898-1912

PAUL M. BUHLE

PERHAPS more than any other single publication, the *Social-Democratic Herald* embodied the development of American socialism from its nineteenth-century origins to its distinctive development in the urban United States of the Progressive period. The *Herald* was unquestionably mundane by the standards of other leading leftist journals of the time, such as *The Appeal to Reason* or *The International Socialist Review*. It scorned theoretical precision, sensationalism, and stylishness alike for the simple, straightforward propagation of socialism to the ordinary worker. Through such steady effort, the *Herald* succeeded in spreading and intensifying the loyalties of a particular working-class constituency to socialism. When it finally folded, the *Herald* still believed that the achievement of the Cooperative Commonwealth was not an idea, but a practical inevitability.

The *Herald* began as the organ of the Social Democracy of America, which had shortly before eliminated its utopian contingent and undertaken a practical political program. Socialism in 1898 was still a rough amalgam, and the paper reflected its disparate elements. Among its contributing staff were figures ranging from Jesse Cox, a blood descendant of James Fenimore Cooper and a prominent Chicago reformer; Eugene Dietzgen, son of the autodidact tanner Joseph Dietzgen whose theories of cognition paralleled Marx's elucidation of historical materialism; Joseph Barodness, semi-anarchist leader of the Jewish garment trade in Manhattan; James Carey, representative of the largely Irish, recession-ridden sector of shoe workers in Massachusetts who was the first Socialist to gain public office in the United States; to Gustave

Hoehn, leader of a German-American constituency of skilled workers in St. Louis.

The role of the *Herald*, then, was to help forge a distinctively American movement out of diverse groups and individuals. Thus the paper adopted a mixture of homespun commentary on values, local reports, and national political discussions. The first element in the explicit adaptation of socialism to historic Protestant values was perhaps the most unique. Debs' epigrams in the *Herald*, for instance, expressed his own attitude toward self-sacrifice: "I would rather be a slave than a master upon the principle that I would rather be a victim than the beneficiary of crime." Or, again, toward the work-ethic: "If you meet a man who does not want to work, the chances are that his father never had a chance to work." For Debs' election campaign of 1900, the paper published a remarkable poem in the same vein, written by the former trainman's friend, James Whitcomb Riley:

> And there's 'Gene Debs, a man 'at stands
> And just holds out in his two hands
> As warm a heart as ever beat
> Betwixt here and the Jedgement Seat

Yet, clearly, the difficulties of organization were not to be wholly overcome by moral principles, even insofar as German-American or Jewish Socialists, for instance, would fully accept Debsian sentiments at face value. Apart from its optimistic messages of electoral and agitational activities around the country, the *Herald* also contained fumbling but significant attempts to resolve the dominant ideological questions confronting Socialists. Primarily, these discussions took the form of debate over the proposed unification of the Social Democracy with a dissident faction of the Socialist Labor party. The latter group, more orthodox in its Marxism, tended to reflect the "European" orientation of Socialist workers in eastern cities. By contrast, the very heterogeneity of the Social Democracy led the organization to stress a more "American" model of state autonomy within any national agitation. After two years of negotiation and discussions, and a common presidential campaign in 1900, amalgamation was completed substantially along the lines that the *Herald* and the Social Democracy had sought.

The Unity Convention at Indianapolis in 1901 marked a new period for the *Herald* and for American socialism generally. In Chicago, where it had been founded, the paper had never been able to make ends meet, and in 1898-1899 had moved to the suburb of Belleville in order to lower printing costs. The leaders of the new, unified party voted to continue the *Herald* as the official national organ, but without the kind of long-term financial support that such a project would demand. Perhaps, in fact, the paper was being killed covertly: for more than a decade afterward, the party refrained from publishing any official journal, purportedly because of the general fear of potential national office tyranny. In any case, the financial collapse of the *Herald* neatly coincided with the desire of the Milwaukee Socialists for an established paper. Earlier, they had launched their own English-language sheet which, however, had barely survived the election of 1900; now, increasingly powerful, and with a strong local organization they sought to acquire national appeal by bringing the *Herald* to Milwaukee.

In later years, the *Herald* gave credit for the paper's transfer to Milwaukee to Victor Berger and to Elizabeth H. Thomas, a wealthy New England radical of Quaker descent who devoted her life and fortune to the *Herald*'s development. The first Milwaukee edition appeared in August 1901, with Victor Berger's stamp already affixed to its content. While *Herald* editor A. S. Edwards was temporarily retained as co-editor, his colleague became Fred Heath, one of Berger's most loyal converts to socialism. Berger himself wrote the editorials, the key political documents of each issue. As Milwaukee Socialists increased their power and influence, the paper's identity with Berger, "the architect of victory in Milwaukee," was tightened. Indeed, after Berger went to Congress in 1910 his lieutenants retouched a Walter Crane illustration designating the greatest living Socialists: alongside Bebel, Kautsky, and Jaures there was a single American—not Debs but Berger.

The first years in Milwaukee reflected the transition of the *Herald* from a nationally to a locally oriented paper. On the one hand, its issues retained columns by nationally known Socialists, such as Eugene Debs and Margaret Haile. "Bundle Brigades," groups of Socialists who would cover a certain neighborhood (often on Sunday) selling individual copies and subscriptions, operated for the *Herald* in a number of cities. On the other hand, the paper moved rapidly to create the local support and influence which would make it a financial and political success. In 1902, a joint-stock company was formed to take over its ownership and workers with spare cash were incessantly approached to buy shares toward the paper's expansion and improvement. Also, the *Herald* gained the endorsement of the Milwaukee Federated Trades Council as its official organ, thus securing the indirect support of all the city's considerable number of unionized workers. Controversy was generally banished from the paper, and the unfinished quality of the earlier format was replaced by a clean, highly readable propaganda sheet. Circulation never rose over 6,000 for regular issues, and the *Herald* lost money every year but 1910. Yet the national readership was gradually supplanted by a local base, and with party support the *Herald* repeatedly moved to larger headquarters and greater local and national influence.

The early period was also marked by the first steps in the establishment of "Milwaukee socialism" as a distinct political movement, promulgated above all in the *Herald*. Wisconsin Socialists had demonstrated their independence vis-à-vis the American movement by retaining the name of the "Social Democracy" within the state. Like the successful German municipal Socialists, they were labeled by the Left as "opportunist" for their electoral orientation and for their expectation of a peaceful victory over capitalism. But by their own lights, the *Herald*'s writers and followers were wholly principled. Once established, the Milwaukee brand of socialism was constantly reinforced by its success in reaching workers and convincing them to vote Socialist. Such practical results offered more proof to them of the viability of socialism than a thousand theoretical texts and left-wing complaints could rebut.

The Milwaukee Socialists regarded themselves and their counterparts all over the world (but particularly in Germany) as the historic pathfinders of a new society, ready to prevent the degeneration of the class struggle into barbarism and to offer in its stead a vision of a cooperative order that the vast majority of society would happily accept. For the Social Democrats, the masses in precapitalist society really had been inferior to the ruling classes which had directed progress. But in the capitalist period the leveling of social relationships due to common nationalities, speech, and education had led to the creation of a great class, the proletariat, which was now the equal of the property-owning class.

Within the modern working class, the Milwaukeeans saw four definite groups: the helpless, ignorant toilers whose capacity to think had been stolen, who were "stunned and toiled as the ox"; a complacent, inactive group of organized workers who still had the power to resist but were without a clear policy; the union leaders, who had some vision of the class struggle but had not yet become fully aware of the issues at stake; and the Socialists, who had both understanding of the issues and a program, and who sought to hasten the process of class struggle to a successful and peaceful conclusion. The possibility remained, as Berger pointed out, that increasing imbalance of wealth would lead to a "volcanic eruption . . . against the fat and satiated," with the effect of throwing mankind back to semibarbarism. But through socialism, the workers would be directed away from violence and toward a more positive expression: the political class struggle.

The mediation of the political class struggle was, of course, the task of the Social Democratic party. By its involvement in the day-to-day, ameliorative attempts of the proletariat, it would teach the workers their class interests, provide them with an indispensable world-view, and shunt aside their irrational and emotional tendencies. As Berger defined the party's role, "We educate, we enlighten, we reason, we discipline. And therefore, besides order, we bring also law, reason, discipline, and progress." For the purposes of education, the Milwaukeeans looked foremost to the electoral arena, especially in the municipality. By focusing on local issues of immediate concern, the Socialists took a stand on all the problems besetting the workingman, and gave concrete shape to otherwise abstract theories. The Socialists were, therefore, in Berger's words, "the greatest advocates of reforms of all kinds and every description the world has ever seen."

The Milwaukee Social Democrats saw the creation of socialism as eminently *constructive* in method, issuing from a struggle that, in Berger's calculations, might take a thousand years to bring to full completion. The reforms carried out in local and regional areas were seen as stepping stones to the new system, not socialism in a microcosm but concrete evidence of the Socialists' abilities to build a new society. The social basis for a postcapitalist order had, they believed, already been laid by the formation of the national corporations and trusts—which the Milwaukeeans, unlike the Populists and their political descendants, the rural Socialists, welcomed as a step toward capitalism's ultimate stage. What remained to be done was primarily the *nationalization* of production, with the factory system apparently directed in much the same manner but with profits turned over to human needs.

Politically, such positions pitted the *Herald* against other Socialist papers, and the Milwaukee Social Democrats against many other Socialist tendencies, helping to define further the peculiarly Milwaukeean brand of socialism. When the *Herald* denied the validity of the utopian and antitrust attitudes of rural radicals, and fought against the attachment of the Socialist party nationally to a revolutionary policy toward trades unions, the paper ruled against the past and future hopes of American radicals for a *community*, for a transformation in the *quality of life* which would develop from the transformation of the economic levers of production. Berger and his followers saw as anathema the very idea of a primitive communism with shared food, family space, and responsibilities. Berger repeatedly asserted, in the *Herald*'s pages, that socialism was solely an *economic* system which did not imply sweeping changes in social habits. Thus, the normative qualities of a kind of Calvinism were made the permanent qualities of socialism: work would lose its compulsion because labor would be universalized; work in the next society would become the standard of worth that money was under capitalism. There was no discussion in the paper of alienated labor, or the factory system as inherently oppressive to human aspiration.

The tactical concomitant to this defense of private life-styles and goals was a single-dimensional rationalism in the *Herald*'s appeal. The main obstacle to socialism, the *Herald* constantly reaffirmed, was the ignorance and superstition bred by the Roman Catholic Church particularly, and by the residues of the precapitalist era generally. Once workers learned to grasp the historical logic of their situation, they would necessarily come to a Socialist conclusion, convinced not so much by the Socialists themselves as by the flow of objective events. Thus followed the logic of Milwaukee Socialist agitation: a unidirectional stream of logical arguments which incited no more action than the casting of a ballot, or a Socialist agitational career for the most advanced members of the masses. In fact, the logic of this position led to a discouragement of any direct action in factories or elsewhere, for fear that such action would destroy the respect Socialists had built up in the community.

Quite naturally, the *Herald*'s political stance appealed not only to wage-earners but to all in the community who appreciated the humanitarian side of socialism and the relative administrative honesty and efficiency of its politicians. Perhaps because the *Herald*'s position was so antithethical to the workers' direct control of factories, the Socialists enjoyed some popularity with Milwaukee's middle classes while languishing (especially in view of their claim to being a proletarian party) among the new immigrant groups who populated the factories. To seek state power, the Socialists even appealed, somewhat hypocritically, to Wisconsin farmers: they sought to pick up the old Greenbackers' and Populists' traditions by promising to better the farmer's condition, with the added pledge that private ownership of farms would continue under socialism. Rural agitation met with scant success, and probably for this reason the *Herald* remained almost wholly a metropolitan Milwaukee paper. However, its strengthened position within the city and its growing appeal across class lines were evidenced in its columns' increasing attacks on political scandals among Milwaukee's major party politicians, and on advertisements by corporations such as Edison's.

In its formative years, then, Milwaukee socialism reflected in the *Herald* the wants and needs of its constituency; these supporters included an economically and socially ascending group of skilled workers, and a growing portion of public-spirited middle-class citizens. Such a development put the Milwaukee movement at the forefront of American progress, in the twentieth-century liberal sense, but not progress toward the creation of a revolutionary workers' movement.

In the long run the Milwaukee policies were bound to evoke embarrassment and hatred in those Socialists and labor agitators like Eugene Debs and "Big Bill" Haywood who sought to lift the lowest ranks of workers into control over the basic institutions of American society. Relations between Debs and Berger began to chill as early as 1903: the trainman's old mentor, who had come to teach him socialism in the Woodstock jail in 1894, now found new alliances within the united Socialist party. Berger turned to those leaders whose constituencies most resembled his own in size and stability: Morris Hillquit's Lower East Side Jewish Socialists, J. Mahlon Barnes' largely German Pennsylvania followers, and Max Hayes' *Cleveland Citizen* readers and supporters. As he fought in the Socialist party nationally for local autonomy of strategy,

Berger formulated in the *Herald* a basic policy toward the trades union movement which became known as the "two armed strategy."

Berger's experience with the American Federation of Labor had been a series of bitter exchanges with AFL president Samuel Gompers dating back to the late 1890s. As the futility of Socialist hopes for a takeover of the federation grew more apparent, and Gompers' attacks upon Berger increasingly vicious, Socialists inside and outside the federation called for a new and radical union movement. Ultimately, in 1905, this ferment resulted in the creation of the Industrial Workers of the World. As much as two years before, Berger had sought to prevent or discredit such a development by espousing a *neutrality* toward the internal politics of trades unions. Socialists, in his view, should support unions in every possible way, organize in their shops, or be loyal members if unions already existed. But any further action was strictly meddling. Thus, the *Herald*'s columns described the union and Socialist movements as two arms on a body, neither one of which should interfere with the other.

Similarly, the Milwaukee Socialists' political and labor policies, which blamed the "venality of the illiterate elements among the Poles, Italians and Slovenians" for the Republican machine's control of the Milwaukee mayoralty, made the Socialists willing victims of the racism that permeated the skilled workers. Berger spoke against unrestricted immigration of Orientals and eastern and southern Europeans into the United States, but was more obviously racist toward Negroes. As he wrote in 1902:

> There can be no doubt that negroes and mullatoes constitute a lower race. . . . The many cases of rape which occur wherever negroes are settled in large numbers prove, moreover, that the free contact with the whites has led to the further degeneration of the negroes, as of all other inferior races.

Thus, although Berger firmly believed in the proletariat as the fundamental messenger of socialism, he limited the "real American proletariat," basically, to the Old Immigration. Such an attitude was firmly in the tradition of American skilled labor, but against the future hopes for class solidarity.

The implications of the racist policy within the Social Democratic party were not, however, always simple or obvious. Because the Milwaukee Socialist vote depended in some measure upon the popularity of the national candidate, Debs was given enthusiastic support in every race between 1904 and 1912, despite Berger's personal opposition to his candidacy. Similarly, while Berger stood in the forefront of Socialist party resistance to the IWW's dual unionist policies, the repression of the Western Federation of Miners in 1907 led IWW leader William Haywood to become guest speaker at the *Herald*'s annual picnic, where he praised the Milwaukee Socialists for their financial and spiritual support.

The efficiency of Milwaukee socialism evoked great respect nationally, not only from Berger's cofactionalists but even from envious leftwingers. This national reputation followed from the Social Democracy's remarkable strength in Milwaukee and its energetic evangelicism among the masses of voters. Local official Walter T. Mills, in defending the Milwaukee movement against its detractors, noted that the Socialists' success was based upon the ultimate in efficient civil service: an uncorruptible meritocracy within the party, with all appointments remaining at all times strictly responsible to the party (party officials, for example, were given a signed but undated resignation from office at the time of office-taking). The paid staff and volunteers were extraordinarily efficient so that "over and over again throughout the year, to every house in Milwaukee are distributed—to each reader in his own language—the arguments of Socialism." Frequent public meetings were held, especially in the factories at noon, with logical, unemotional arguments for socialism directed at the workers. The Social Democracy's annual picnic was "the greatest propaganda meeting of the year," drawing up to 20,000 people and clearing considerable amounts of money. And above all, at the shops, through the unions, and at public events, workers were constantly contacted, recruited, and reinforced in their beliefs in the Milwaukee Social Democracy and in the vital connection between local politics and the social revolution of the future.

Such persistence paid off in Milwaukee from the turn of the century to World War I. By 1908, the Socialists had four members on the state legislature, ten members on the Milwaukee city council, four members on the school board, and five members on the county board. Berger warned that the election of Social Democrats could only bring greater efficiency and honesty, not socialism itself. Nevertheless, enthusiasm, as reflected in the *Herald*, continued unabated. By 1910, the Socialists had begun to plan for a daily paper and to raise bonds for a new office. The week after the mayoral election in 1910 the *Herald* trumpeted in a banner headline, "Socialists Sweep Milwaukee," reporting that Emil Seidel had been elected mayor with the greatest plurality for that office in Milwaukee's history. Seven months later another banner headline recorded, "Berger Goes to Congress," hailing the first Socialist candidate ever to be elected to national office in the United States. The sweep of city offices was augmented in the November elections with the ascension of thirteen Socialists to the state legislature. "These Are the Good Old Times," the *Herald* optimistically reported. The *Herald* became the newspaper of the party in office—with all the additional advertising revenue and influence which that position brought.

But political prosperity killed the *Herald*, for it made possible the launching of the *Milwaukee Leader* in 1911. This new Socialist daily soon relegated the *Herald* to roughly the same position as the *Vanguard*, a political journal kept up by the Social Democracy to augment the regular press and to spread the word of Milwaukee socialism across the country. When the *Herald* lost its local news function, it lost the vitality of its local connections, its advertising slid down to pre-1908 levels, and, although "bundle brigades" outside Milwaukee were refurbished for national distribution, it could not put itself through a second transformation.

The *Herald* closed out its last years on an optimistic note. Emil Seidel's mayoralty defeat in 1912 to a Republican-Democratic fusion candidate was seen as "victory in defeat," for it consolidated the Socialist ranks. Most Socialists were holding onto local office, despite all the pressure which priests and ward-bosses were exerting on the population. Ironically, the post-1911 paper was more important nationally, for it carried signed columns by such figures as Walter Lippmann and W. J. Ghent. Moreover, it was more attractive, with the addition of photographs and more Walter Crane sketches to fill out its pages. Whatever its own fate, it looked joyfully at the growth of "constructive socialism" nationally. By 1912, when Debs won nearly a million votes at the polls, 1,200 Socialists held public office, including 79 mayors in 24 states and some officials in 340 municipalities across the nation, the trend seemed unmistakably clear, as if Milwaukee had shown the way to the whole of the American Left.

Historical retrospect makes it easy to view the Milwaukee Socialists as superficial reformers, racists, or at best as opportunistic radicals who helped destroy the idealism of the Debsian Socialist movement. Such an analysis, however, misses both the simple sincerity of the *Herald* staffers and readers, and the significance they held for American socialism.

Unlike the Left of the 1930s, whose energizing visions were tied to the Soviet Union and the accomplishments of the Congress of Industrial Organizations, the Milwaukee Socialists saw the electoral victories, like the existence of the *Herald* itself, as mere *signs* of socialism's growth. The Social Democrats' faith was based not on the expectations of great mobilizations (such as the defense campaigns, unionization drives, and foreign-policy rallies of the "Red Decade") but rather on the promulgation of a rational doctrine through agitational speeches and literature. Consequently, unlike the latterday Communists and Socialists, the Milwaukee faithful never concealed their aims within a larger movement. Even Victor Berger's wartime campaign billboards, when repression was growing across the country, read boldly, "WAR IS HELL CAUSED BY CAPITALISM. SOCIALISTS DEMAND PEACE. READ THE PEOPLE'S SIDE. MILWAUKEE LEADER. VICTOR BERGER, EDITOR." The revolution they sought did not, for them, necessitate violence, a sudden overturn in the control of fundamental institutions; but they insistently, and sincerely, regarded the change as revolutionary.

The source of their strength was consequently also the source of their weakness. The movement was born in a time when modern liberalism had not yet siphoned from the radical movement the idealistic and/or efficiency-minded segments of the emerging new middle class. The Milwaukee Socialists could share the racism of the nation as a whole —against southern and eastern Europeans but particularly against non-Europeans—without immediately undermining their opposition to American capitalism. Because Milwaukee was so largely German-American, they could even oppose the war without becoming known in their own community as seditious or dangerously subversive. But like the Socialists of the Southwest, whose constituency was a dying class, being driven off the farms, and like the foreign-born Socialists whose children were being socialized and "Americanized" in the public schools, Milwaukee socialism was founded and built upon a declining sector of society. Given the failure of the Socialist party in the 1920s to spearhead a farmer-labor alliance or "Progressive" force (analogous to the British Labor party, as Berger himself wished), even the attachment of local liberals and progressives to the Milwaukee government meant less and less. And while German-Americans continued to move out of the factories, their places were taken by eastern and southern Europeans and finally by the blacks—the very groups whose temperament seemed antithetical to the advancement of Milwaukee socialism. By the late 1930s when the daily *Milwaukee Leader* failed, the Socialists controlled city hall as Socialists in name only: the grand experiment had dwindled to nothing more than its efficient bureaucratic infrastructure.

The *Herald* represented Milwaukee socialism in its prime, its growth years when its ideals were most certain, and in the first moment of its success in national politics. The paper also continued to reflect its heritage from the older *Herald* of the American Social Democracy, before the paper's transfer to Milwaukee. For despite the contradictions inherent in Debsian socialism from its ties to past *and* future, the Socialist movement as a whole shared generally in the pre-World War I dreams of an easy Socialist success. Most Socialists, even the most revolutionary-minded, had faith in the efficacy of propaganda to carry the message of capitalism's irrationalism and socialism's rationalism, as a fundamental force to bring the revolutionary period closer. Nearly all seemed to feel that the turmoil generated by America's transformation into an industrial nation was a sign of impending change in social systems. More articulately than any other single newspaper, the *Herald*, throughout its fifteen-year history, bore the hopes and hidden fears of this great optimism.

Somerville, Massachusetts, 1973

The Challenge

LOS ANGELES AND NEW YORK,

1900-1901

Wilshire's Magazine

TORONTO, NEW YORK, AND

BISHOP, CALIFORNIA, 1900-1915

HOWARD H. QUINT

DURING the period of its greatest influence and promise the American Socialist movement produced three particularly talented publisher-editors in A. J. Wayland and Fred Warren of the Girard, Kansas, weekly newspaper, *The Appeal to Reason*, and H. Gaylord Wilshire, who not immodestly named his magazine after himself. *The Appeal to Reason* and *Wilshire's Magazine* had the largest circulations, respectively, of all Socialist newspapers and magazines in the world. Since neither was a party organ or rigidly adhered to the doctrines of "scientific socialism," they were sometimes denigrated by those who insisted on Marxist orthodoxy. Nevertheless, *The Appeal* and *Wilshire's* were exceedingly effective in propagandizing socialism.

Gaylord Wilshire is today almost completely forgotten, though his name graces one of the principal districts and boulevards in Los Angeles as well as hotels, funeral parlors, stores, churches, golf courses, etc. What an "irony of fate," Wilshire wrote George Bernard Shaw in 1922, that so many of the churches of Los Angeles should be named after a man who preached socialism "and, incidentally, of course, atheism." Those who have studied the history of American radicalism will probably remember Wilshire as the "millionaire Socialist," if they recall him at all. But in fact, Wilshire, though comfortably wealthy when he began his publishing career, was not a millionaire nor anywhere close to being one. And he was never to become a millionaire. Whatever money he had, he put into the magazine, which never prospered. Furthermore, whatever money he subsequently was to make from selling stock in his gold mines in California and British Guiana was poured back into the magazine, with the exception of what was used for his own personal expenses. Since Wilshire lived well, traveled extensively, and spent freely with the ease of those who have had money all of their lives, such expenses were not inconsiderable.

Son of a wealthy Cincinnati industrialist, Gaylord Wilshire went to California in the mid-1880s to establish himself after a year's study as an unmatriculated student at Harvard. According to his own account, he attended classes of William James and J. Lawrence Loughlin, but this unofficial and abbreviated academic career hardly entitled him to be presented as a Harvard alumnus, which was sometimes done. He cynically permitted the public to consider him as such in order to create the impression, as he put it, that a wealthy and intelligent man could be a Socialist. But in addition, Wilshire was something of a poseur, which was unfortunate because he possessed a keen mind, personal warmth, and generosity of spirit.

During the spectacular land boom that engulfed California during the late 1880s, Wilshire was an active, though hardly major, speculator. But he had what many other speculators lacked, namely imagination in developing his properties, especially those in Los Angeles. While he hardly can be credited with planning the whole Wilshire district as it exists today, he was instrumental in designing Westlake (now MacArthur) Park and the beginnings of the famous boulevard that today bears his name. He and his associates, among them the future general, Leonard Wood, did well during the land boom. When the boom collapsed, he turned to such ventures as bill posting, an ostrich farm, a citrus fruit ranch, and an amusement park. Billboard advertising proved highly profitable, though Wilshire found himself in constant controversy with Los Angeles city officials over the sites and heights of his ungainly billboards.

Had Wilshire concentrated on business, he might well have become a leading Los Angeles capitalist, but in 1887 he read Edward Bellamy's

Looking Backward, which gave him a never-to-be-forgotten vision of the cooperative commonwealth. Moreover, he had made the acquaintance of William C. Owen, an English-born labor editor and philosophical anarchist who introduced him to more sophisticated forms of radical literature. Wilshire helped organize the Los Angeles Nationalist Club to propagate Bellamy's collectivist ideas, and in 1890 was the Nationalist party's candidate for the House of Representatives—the first Socialist actually to seek a seat in the United States Congress. Despite endorsement by the Farmers' Alliance and an active campaign, which featured an informal debate with Henry George, Wilshire did poorly but not sufficiently so to discourage him from running again for public office under Socialist auspices.

In 1891 Wilshire came into an inheritance and left Los Angeles for New York, which he believed offered a greater opportunity for Socialist agitation. He joined the Socialist Labor party and, though lacking any legal training, ran as its candidate for attorney general of New York. During this same year he founded a coaching school for Socialist orators and, more important, wrote a preface to the first American edition of the *Fabian Essays*.

The latter undertaking was also preparatory to a four-year visit to England where Wilshire again involved himself in Socialist politics and became acquainted with just about every notable figure of the British Left, including George Bernard Shaw and Henry M. Hyndman, with whom he maintained a lifelong correspondence. He was a frequent speaker at Socialist rallies and, just before returning to the United States in 1895, was proposed as a Social Democratic Federation candidate for Parliament from Salford.

Back in Los Angeles, Wilshire resumed his various business enterprises, read papers before the Southern California Scientific Society, bombarded the local papers with letters to the editor, helped found the Los Angeles Country Club, and was elected a member of a commission to help a new municipal charter. It was also at this time that he developed a close friendship with Dr. John R. Haynes, a wealthy physician, civic reformer, and advocate of direct legislation. On December 26, 1900, Wilshire began publication of a Socialist propaganda magazine, *The Challenge*, forerunner of *Wilshire's Magazine*.

Wilshire intended the name of his magazine to serve as a reminder of the standing challenge he had made to William Jennings Bryan to debate him on the trust problem. At various times since 1896, Wilshire had offered Bryan from $2,000 to $10,000 to debate the merits of socialism and capitalism, but the Nebraskan ignored him. Wilshire, of course, claimed that Bryan feared to confront him in an open forum.

The Challenge was very much a vehicle for Wilshire's own particular brand of socialism, though it published articles by all varieties of Socialists, as well as by non-Socialists. Wilshire constantly printed letters from his British friends praising *The Challenge* and, more to the point, its publisher. But if he annoyed some of the comrades by his "personal journalism," he was not nettled by their criticisms. He had both literary and editorial talent and, contrary to most Socialist magazines of the time, *The Challenge* was a well-edited and handsomely produced periodical, comparing favorably with many of the better non-Socialist journals of opinion.

The motto of *The Challenge*, "Let the Nation Own the Trusts," summarized Wilshire's theory as to how socialism would evolve in the United States. As early as 1887, he had reached the conclusion that the development of trusts in the United States was not only an inevitable consequence of capitalistic competition but also an open door to socialism. Acknowledging that the nation was in the throes of a fantastic industrial expansion, he insisted that such activity was ephemeral and temporary. The waxing industrial growth in the United States, according to his analysis, came less from the demands of workers for the necessities of life than from the need for new capital goods. But the day was quickly approaching when the nation's trustified industries would overexpand. And since their dramatic increase in production would not be accompanied by a comparable increase in distribution and consumption, a crisis would set in, bringing large-scale unemployment and general discontent. Confronted with this situation, the American people would insist that their monopolistic and trustified economy be placed under government ownership and a socialistic society established. Wilshire's cooperative commonwealth would eventuate, then, not through a class struggle and revolution but out of the very workings of capitalism.

Wilshire elaborated on this theme, a simplistic version of Marx's theory of capitalistic accumulation, in editorial after editorial and speech after speech. But Los Angeles was a relatively small city at the turn of the century and offered a poor forum for a man with such an apocalyptic message. In September 1901, Wilshire moved the office of *The Challenge* to New York City.

Publication of *The Challenge* in New York did not last long. President William McKinley's assassination brought in its wake a concerted drive by United States postal authorities to ban radical newspapers and magazines from the mails. The technique employed by Edwin G. Madden, third assistant postmaster general, was to deny them second-class mailing privileges. *The Challenge* was brought under this ruling. But Wilshire, ever resourceful, moved the magazine's offices to Toronto, Canada. Rechristened *Wilshire's Magazine*, it made its way back across the border unimpeded under Canadian second-class postal privileges. The cover of the January 1902, issue carried the caption: "Suppressed by the United States 'I' Be [*sic*] Now Under Protection British Crown." For four years Wilshire unsuccessfully fought the United States Post Office Department ruling in the federal courts while maintaining offices of the magazine in both New York and Toronto. Resumption of publication in New York in October 1904 resulted not from any judicial ruling but rather from the intervention of New York's "Easy Boss," Senator Tom Platt, who convinced postal authorities that the ban was depriving one of his constituents of Wilshire's printing business.

The cost of publishing *Wilshire's Magazine* ran high—$70,000 during its first year. Piece by piece, Wilshire mortgaged his properties to Dr. Haynes in order to obtain money to cover his mounting expenses. In July 1902, Haynes warned that if the existing state of affairs continued, Wilshire would be bankrupt by the following January. The collapse of the magazine was postponed when Wilshire's mother advanced him a sizable loan. He also borrowed money from Stanley McCormick of Chicago and other wealthy and sympathetic parlor radicals. To obtain thousands of new subscribers—and of course to attract advertisers on the basis of a large circulation—Wilshire offered subscription prizes including a ten-acre fruit ranch in Ontario, California, player pianos, collie dogs, oil painted tapestries, gramophones, billiard tables, bicycles, gold-filled watches, cameras, fountain pens, silk shirts, boxes of cigars, violins, shotguns, tonneau automobiles, symphony organs, typewriters, dinner dishes, etc. Subscriptions rolled in, but not fast enough for Wilshire, who at one point cut the price of subscription to ten cents a year. Despite this

feverish effort to increase circulation—Wilshire claimed 280,000 subscribers for the December 1905 issue—advertising came slowly. Worse
yet, the magazine increasingly had to depend on patent-medicine advertisements. In 1904 Wilshire began to sell stock in the Wilshire Publishing
Company, with the explanation that although he had personally put
$100,000 of his own money into the magazine, he had to have help from
his Socialist supporters. "There is an erroneous impression," he
quipped, "that Wilshire is a capitalist of somewhat greater magnitude
than Vanderbilt and Astor, and in fact only a little less bright in the
financial heavens than Rockefeller himself. . . ."

Wilshire's Magazine came under criticism from some Socialists for its
literary and intellectual rather than political orientation and also for its
lack of Marxian rigor. In reply the editor declared: *"Wilshire's* has never
pursued the narrow, petty policy of ignoring good merely because the
good does not emanate from an accredited Socialist source." To be sure,
Wilshire's was the most interesting and certainly the most readable
radical magazine of the Progressive period. Among its contributors were
George D. Herron, Charlotte Perkins, Gilman Stetson, George Bernard
Shaw, Walker Crane, William Thurston Brown, G. G. Hobson, Jack
London, William English Walling, Charles E. Russell, H. W. Macrosty,
Hall Crane, Richard LaGallienne, Julian Hawthorne, Odon Por, Leo
Tolstoi, Leonard D. Abbott, Eugene V. Debs, Gustavus Myers, Henry
M. Hyndman, Robert Rives LaMonte, and other radical intellectuals of
the era. The magazine carried a running commentary on both national and
international events that students of progressivism can read even today
with profit. It editorially analyzed the programs and legislation of the
New Nationalism and the New Freedom and usually was on the mark in
its assessments of Theodore Roosevelt, William Howard Taft, Woodrow
Wilson, Robert LaFollette, Tom Johnson, and Hiram Johnson. The
magazine's news columns kept abreast of developments in the labor
movement, particularly the affairs of the AFL, the IWW, and the Western Federation of Miners. Book reviews in *Wilshire's* were sophisticated
and by no means limited to works in social science or socialism. Interviews with prominent persons appeared regularly, the most publicized
being Wilshire's dialogue with John D. Rockefeller in 1903 on the trust
problem. A women's department was edited by Wilshire's talented wife,
Mary. Several works of both fiction and nonfiction, among them, Jack

London's *People of the Abyss*, first reached American readers in the pages of *Wilshire's*.

Gaylord Wilshire moved freely among New York's intelligentsia. Among his close friends were Anna Strunsky Walling, Rose Pastor Stokes, J. G. Phelps Stokes, Gelet Burgess, Julian Hawthorne, Richard LaGallienne, Eugene Wood, and Upton Sinclair. It was Wilshire who was mainly responsible for converting Sinclair to socialism. The author of *The Jungle* wrote of his first meeting in 1902 with the Socialist publisher at the home of George D. Herron: "One other guest appeared, a small man with a black beard and a mustache trimmed to sharp points, and twinkling mischievous eyes—for all the world the incarnation of Mephistopheles. . . ." Sinclair and Wilshire remained intimate friends throughout their lifetimes. "For years," Sinclair recalled, "we lived on the basis that when he had money he loaned it to me and when I had it, I loaned it to him. It was very helpful."

Wilshire both sought and obtained personal publicity, if not notoriety. Under the auspices of *The New York Times* he debated socialism with the English anti-Socialist writer, W. H. Mallock. He also engaged E. R. A. Seligman, professor of economics and president of the American Economic Association, in a Cooper Union debate. One Christmas night he delivered an impromptu speech from the audience of a New York theater after the star of the play, "The Battle," had criticized socialism in an after-curtain talk. He lectured at Socialist meetings at Harvard and Amherst under the sponsorship of the Intercollegiate Socialist Society. In 1902 and 1904, Wilshire ran for Congress on the Socialist party ticket with customary lack of success. Maxim Gorky's ill-fated visit to the United States in 1906 was made at Wilshire's invitation. Two years later, Wilshire was a leader of the New York antirent tenement strike. In free speech fights he courageously defended anarchists Emma Goldman, John Turner, and Carlo de Fornaro. Some Socialist critics sourly condemned such activities but they could hardly take issue with his objectives. What they didn't like was his style.

The year 1906 marked the high point in Wilshire's participation in the American Socialist movement. In the internecine conflict between revolutionary and reform elements of the Socialist party—never by any means mutually exclusive—he was identified with the conservatives, as were most of the other party intellectuals, and this despite his cataclysmic theory as to how socialism would eventuate in the United States. By the end of the decade, however, Wilshire was to become disillusioned with the Socialist party's failure to make significant gains through political means. For its part, the Socialist party looked askance on his growing sympathy for syndicalism (although he was not active in the IWW) and, even more to the point, the involvement of hundreds of Socialist "investors" in his gold-mining operations.

Wilshire had bought the controlling interest in a High Sierra gold mine in Bishop Creek, California, in 1906. Contrary to subsequent allegations regarding the venture by Wilshire's enemies in the Socialist party, the mine contained considerable, though not readily accessible, deposits of gold ore. To extract and refine it, however, required costly equipment running into tens of thousands of dollars. Wilshire, who had an unflagging belief in the mine, sought to obtain the necessary working capital from his subscribers to whom he held out the promise of quick and easy riches. At the same time, he pledged to put all of the profits which he personally earned from the mine into financing the magazine and other Socialist publications, including a proposed daily newspaper.

Most, though by no means all, of the purchasers of the Bishop Creek gold mine stock were Socialists who were not immune to capitalistic acquisitiveness. Criticism of Wilshire mounted in the Socialist press when dividends were not forthcoming. Prodded by Victor Berger and Thomas Morgan, the Socialist party officially went on record against participation by Socialists in gold-mining speculation, a resolution aimed directly at Wilshire. In 1910 the United States Post Office Department began an investigation of his mining enterprises which had spread to British Guiana. Charges of fraud, never proved, made headlines in both the Socialist and capitalist press. Wilshire, who was in England selling gold-mine stock, denied all accusations.

He did not, however, return to the United States until 1914 when war erupted in Europe. Meantime, the magazine continued to be published by Wilshire's faithful staff, although on a substantially modified basis. Wilshire's four years in London were busy and exciting. He and his wife rented the home of Prince Kropotkin in Hampstead and their Sunday afternoon teas attracted many of England's leading intellectuals and labor leaders. Henry M. Hyndman, of the Social Democratic Federation, attended regularly until he and Wilshire became temporarily alienated over syndicalism; by this time Wilshire had all but repudiated socialism in favor of syndicalism. Widespread labor unrest swept England and Ireland between 1910 and 1912, and Wilshire saw in it an imminent revolution. He spoke frequently at labor meetings and was a confidant of syndicalist leader Tom Mann. In the great 1911-1912 transport strike, Wilshire temporarily assumed editorship of *The Syndicalist* after its regular editor, American-born Guy Bowman, was imprisoned for an article calling on British soldiers not to shoot their workingmen "brothers." Upton Sinclair, also in England at the time, helped out as did Wilshire's European correspondent, Odon Por, who was to have a prominent role in Hungary's post-World War I Communist movement.

When Gaylord Wilshire finally returned to the United States at the outbreak of World War I, he had little or no money left and his only tangible asset, if indeed it could be so classified, was his California gold mine. The New York office of *Wilshire's Magazine* was closed and its final issue (February 1915) was published from Bishop, California. The magazine was a far cry from what it had been in its heyday and so, of course, was its circulation. In his last editorial, Wilshire called for immediate United States entry in the European war on the side of the Allies. While he considered the war a struggle between two failures, democracy and autocracy, he nonetheless could not contemplate defeat for Great Britian. When the United States became a belligerent in 1917, Wilshire was in the front rank of the superpatriots, criticizing "traitorous" antiwar Socialists and endorsing vigilante action against the war's opponents. He initially condemned the Bolshevik Revolution in Russia, although he later saw in the Soviet system the logical outcome of syndicalist theory. The immediate postwar world found him completely pessimistic if not nihilistic. He opposed Woodrow Wilson's League of Nations, and in 1920 voted for Warren G. Harding.

Almost as personally devastating to Wilshire as his eclipse in the public spotlight after 1914 was the fact that he had become economically dependent on his wife, who had returned to the United States in 1917 after studying for three years with C. G. Jung in Switzerland. Mary Wilshire was one of the first, if not the first, practicing psychoanalyst in southern California and she quickly had a thriving practice in Pasadena. The Wilshire home once again became a gathering place for local notables and visiting celebrities, among them Lincoln Steffens, Rebecca West,

Peggy Wood, Charmian London, Paul Jordan Smith, Emily Harvin, H. G. Wells, George Sterling, Charles Edward Russell, "Mother" Jones, Prince Hopkins, Upton Sinclair, and Julian Hawthorne.

Wilshire tried his hand at several different business enterprises with little success. He attempted a comeback in real estate, but nobody seemed to remember or to care that he had developed the Wilshire District. Nor did he fare better in marketing health food products. His efforts at speculation in international currency were hampered by lack of capital. Finally, there was still the gold mine; Wilshire was as convinced as ever that someday the mine would pay off and whatever little money he made, he sunk into it. In the end, he lost the mine and the considerable fortune which both he and other people had put into it.

Like his friend, Upton Sinclair, Wilshire was a health faddist and his career came to a crashing finale on the note of medical quackery. During the 1920s the country abounded with various kinds of electric health machines which purportedly could not only diagnose diseases but even cure them. Wilshire believed that radium carried with it the secret of good health and to this end sought to convert his Bishop Springs properties into a radium springs spa. This failing, he hit upon another idea: to infuse minute particles of radium into the human body through an electrically charged belt. Wilshire's Ionaco belt was introduced to the American public as a curative for almost every disease imaginable, including cancer, and it was not long before testimonials were received confirming its curative powers. Wilshire was equal to the occasion and a network of Ionaco agencies was set up in the country. Once again the money began to roll in.

But when the Rockefeller Foundation brought suit against Ionaco, the empire collapsed almost as suddenly as it had appeared. Gaylord Wilshire, whose own health had been failing, went with it. After an extended period of hospitalization he died of chronic cardiovascular disease and infectious arthritis on September 6, 1927, at the Hotel Westover in New York City. The "Millionaire Socialist" left an estate valued between $15,000 and $17,000; it was encumbered by liens far in excess of that amount.

Amherst, Massachusetts, 1969

The International Socialist Review
CHICAGO, 1900-1918

HERBERT G. GUTMAN

SOCIALIST and other radical movements have had a presence and an influence in other periods of United States history, but most historians agree that the Golden Age of American socialism was in those years spanned by the reelection of William McKinley in 1900 and the triumph of Warren G. Harding in 1920. That the Golden Age fell between two such symbols is an irony deserving little comment. In recent years, historians and others have quarreled vigorously over the causes and the precise timing of the decline of this Golden Age, but few have called the period itself into question. *The International Socialist Review* thrived through most of this period, and for all of its difficulties it was one of the few Socialist journals to span almost the entire era.

Some biographical facts and statistics are helpful. A ten-cent monthly magazine published by Charles Kerr, a Chicago Socialist publisher (and himself the son of a University of Wisconsin professor of Greek), *The Review* survived from 1900 to 1918. Algie M. Simons, a prominent Socialist intellectual and later the author of *Social Forces in American History* (New York, 1911), a significant and pioneering if quite narrow "economic" interpretation of American history, was its first editor and held that position until 1908. In these early years, *The Review* was filled with countless theoretical articles by American and European Socialists and reflected the rather moderate social-democratic perspective of Simons and other Socialists of the "center." Soon after its first issue, *The Review* had a circulation of four thousand, three-quarters of its readers being regular mail subscribers.

The developing divisions within the Socialist movement—factional splits over policies of all kinds that formed into shifting and complex "right," "left," and "center" groupings—affected the magazine, its editor, and its publisher. Editor Simons grew more "cautious" as publisher Kerr shifted to the "left." A conflict between them proved inevitable. Simons quit his post in 1908. After editing the magazine for a brief time, Kerr turned it over to Mary and Leslie Marcy. Mary was the more interesting of the two new editors. Her husband earned his reputation as a journalist, but Mary Marcy was better known. A few years before, she had worked as a private secretary to a major Chicago meatpacker, and at a time of great controversy over the "beef trust," she published the *Letters of a Pork Packer's Stenographer*. Not nearly as successful as Upton Sinclair's still unpublished *The Jungle* was to be, her work nevertheless gained Mary Marcy some reputation as a muckraker.

Under its new editors, *The Review* shifted its political orientation sharply toward the "left." It thrived and became the major organ of those Socialists critical of "reformism." Within a year, circulation increased three hundred percent. By July 1910, the monthly had 27,000 readers. Soon, its format took on the shape of a popular magazine, and theoretical matters aside, it published some of the most graphic accounts of the bitter industrial conflicts of that era. Paterson silk workers, Lawrence woolen workers, Louisiana timber laborers, Great Plains farm hands, Mesabi range miners—these among others—found their memorable conflicts recorded in the pages of *The Review*. In 1911, a more popular magazine—and a better written one—claimed more than forty thousand readers.

The Review was not without its Socialist critics. After 1908, moderate Socialists such as John Spargo complained of "the pernicious influence of *The International Socialist Review*." Robert Hunter was even more severe and penned a bitter characterization in 1911: "It has sneered at Political Action, advocated rival unionism, and vacillated between Anarchism and Proudhonism. The constant emphasis THE REVIEW lays on Direct Action and its apparent faith that a revolution can be evoked by Will or Force is in direct opposition to our whole philosophy." Worried over its seeming influence, Hunter and others like him even forced an official party investigation of Kerr and his varied publishing enterprises. Although the probe fizzled in its political intent, it did reveal that the ten or fifteen *Review* employees worked an eight-hour day, received time-and-a-half for overtime, and even a week's vacation with pay.

What matters in these brief facts is the simple recognition that *The Review* was hardly a neutral Socialist journal but rather a magazine with a distinct but changing point of view and therefore the object of much controversy within the Socialist movement itself. Its pages tell much of the depth of the many controversies that divided the Socialist movement in its greatest years. We learn a good deal from it about the conflicts among Socialists over immediate reform as opposed to a more revolutionary strategy. The struggle over a more flexible doctrine is detailed to excess, and there is much in the journal on the dispute over Socialist relations to the American Federation of Labor and the frequent but faulted efforts in that time to spark industrial unions, syndicalist organizations, and "dual unions." Not one of these issues was trivial to Socialists of that time, and yet it is altogether foolish to study *The Review* simply because it allows us to renew our acquaintance with the factionalism and disputes of a past era. "Most of all," David A. Shannon, author of *The Socialist Party of America: A History* (New York, 1955), has written recently, "historians of socialism have dwelt at some length upon bickering and conflict within the movement." Shannon adds intelligently: "These 'internal' histories of American socialism are often valuable for what they tell us about other things, but they fail to explain why socialism was never more successful in the United States than it has been."

Just as one strain in Socialist historiography has emphasized the movement's inner turmoil and dispute, another (more recent in vintage) has treated the movement—even in its "golden years"—as irrelevant to the mainstream of the national experience in the Progressive Era. Vigorously disputing so deterministic an emphasis, Canadian historian Kenneth McNaught has concluded:

American socialism in much of the recent writing becomes a monolithic concept with a fixed life of its own, a conceptual entity whose life was determined not by cumulative individual decisions but by the ghostly immanence of a host of socio-economic abstractions. Jeffersonian ideals, American dreams, Lockean underpinnings, and Algerism dictated that socialism could be in but not of American history.

Although they are very different in their perspectives, McNaught and Shannon nevertheless help focus attention on a proper conception of the significance of *The Review* in its time and as a lasting historical source. *The Review* is more than a relic of an irrelevant past or a nostalgic reminder of the vitality of a submerged, neglected, and quarrelsome radical tradition. It is an exceedingly useful historical record for those social historians concerned with understanding the successes and failures of American radicalism, the causes and consequences of American reform, the economic and social condition of American society before 1917, and the patterns of protest and acquiescence characteristic of a developed but imbalanced capitalist society.

American socialism and *The International Socialist Review* thrived together in a particular era. By 1894, the United States had completed its major phase of industrialization. In that year, the nation stood as first in the world in its productive capacity—far ahead of Great Britain, France, and Germany. And for the next quarter of a century, the United States entered a new phase of development, a time that marked the end of an old era and the start of a new one. Industrial power became centralized and rationalized; craft unionism was stabilized; bureaucracy became more characteristic of social organization; overseas expansion concerned politicians and businessmen; reform movements of a mature industrial society were felt on the local, state, and national level. Organization, centralization, and reform (both elitist and populist patterns of reform) characterized the entire era. So did profound social changes. The communications revolution flattened regional differences and saw the spread of modern ''mass'' culture. At the same time, the nation's population underwent profound ethnic changes that resulted from the massive migration of southern and eastern Europeans to the United States as well as the beginning spread of southern American Negroes to the north and west of the nation. Much in America changed in these years. Much of what is now called ''modern'' saw its roots in that time. And *The Review* lived through these changes—reflecting them and commenting on them in its own ways.

Careful study of *The Review* in the perspective of these and other significant changes should permit us to reexamine much that was relevant to the America of that time. If studied afresh, it might suggest new ways to examine more than the roots of Socialist disintegration in the war and postwar years. A modern examination of the contemporary Socialist critiques of progressive reform and corporate innovation, for example, is long overdue. More needs to be known about the reasons socialism appealed to so many of the young intellectuals in that era of reform. The relative success of the Socialists in such prewar craft unions as the machinists, and coal and metal miners, the brewery and quarry workers, and the men's and women's clothing industries needs further careful and comparative examination. The fact that the foreign-born grew more dominant in the Socialist movement after 1912 is noted by many scholars but not yet fully explained. The electoral successes of Socialist candidates have been recorded (in 1910, for example, thirty-three cities had Socialist mayors), but the day-to-day doings of these Socialist officeholders have not been systematically examined.

Much else remains to be explored in depth. Most important in many ways is the need for a critical and empirical study of the changing economic and social structure in the prewar decades. The pages of *The International Socialist Review* are indispensable for such work. The perspective of the men and women who filled its pages allowed them to open doors shut tight to persons of a less radical view. The Socialist perspective was not without its limitations, but it brought a particular view to bear on its contemporary world and that view ("ideology") shed light on what others saw dimly—if at all. Even though the quality of much of its prose seems wooden, and its theory simple and outdated, *The International Socialist Review* is a significant record of its times. It recorded that time from a particular perspective, vented a meaningful and often appropriate outrage and moral dismay, gathered unusual data, and pierced the optimism that saturated the more commonplace rhetoric of that transitional period in American history.

Rochester, New York, 1968

Socialist Party Monthly Bulletin
CHICAGO, 1904-1913

The Party Builder
CHICAGO, 1912-1914

JOSEPH R. CONLIN

ONE of the most striking facts about the history of the Socialist party in its Golden Age was the tolerance with which it carried on its internal affairs. There were plenty of squabbles, and, on occasion, one faction or another could and did win its way with a full complement of underhanded methods. But it is difficult to think of another organization of comparable size in which the dominant group did not seriously attempt to extirpate its opposition. That simply has not been the way of life on the American Left. But until 1919 the Socialist party was an organization which could tolerate differences from within. Only once, in 1913, was a high-ranking officer removed from his position for largely factional reasons. Even then there was no mass purge of his supporters, and his right to membership in the party was not really challenged.

This tolerance was reflected in the leadership's serious attempt to subject matters of policy to broad membership participation. The files of the national office were literally open as a matter of routine through the publication of the *Socialist Party Monthly Bulletin*. Founded in September 1904 as a means of promoting the second presidential candidacy of Eugene V. Debs, the *Bulletin* was preserved uncertainly after the election but then was established permanently as the national office's major means of communication with the rank and file. It appeared regularly in mimeograph or hectograph form until 1913. In 1907 and 1908 it was published weekly.

The Party Builder first appeared in August 1912 as a promotional squib for the party's lyceum program, a generally successful speakers' tour sponsored by the national office. Contracting membership rolls and revenues after the presidential election forced its merger with the *Bulletin*. The name of *The Party Builder* was retained (it had second-class mailing privileges while the *Bulletin* did not), but the character of the new publication was that of the *Bulletin*. Only a fraction of the journal was devoted to the lyceum bureau and this proportion gradually declined in favor of reports from other national departments.

This interesting source provides an insight into the practical, business-like approach to politics of the now dominant moderates. For all the ideological bickering, nothing seems better to illustrate the gap separating left- and right-wing Socialists in 1912 than their "style." An IWW organizer recalled that Vincent St. John, secretary-treasurer of the IWW in 1912, once dispatched him to a laggard local with a few oral instructions and a six-shooter. Big Bill Haywood, himself an able administrator, would file the day's receipts and memoranda in his hatband. How completely alien to this careless informality was *The Party Builder*'s comparison of the Socialist's task to that of a "commercial house"? The editor called upon

> fifty thousand socialists to spend, let us say, an average of twenty-four hours working in an educational propaganda campaign. That is 1,200,000 hours by competent working people. These working people would insist that their time is worth, at a low average, at least 25 cents an hour. . . .

And so on. Or, consider the unlikelihood of communication between the IWW's hobo organizers who rode boxcars to their revolutionary tasks, and lyceum speaker J. E. Snyder who castigated other speakers in *The Party Builder* for telling "a hard luck story of terrible conditions working for the Lyceum." "I weighed one hundred and forty-five when I left Chicago," Snyder wrote happily, "and one hundred and forty-seven when I got back."

It would not do to confuse style with substance and write off the post-1912 Socialist party as a collection of dilettantes who were not Socialists at all. But it would be a comparable error to miss the fact that it was a consummate middle-class party that published *The Party Builder*. And, whatever the gaucheries that punctuate *The Party Builder* (it does sometimes read more like a newsletter of a kaffeeklatsch than a revolutionary organization), the right-wing Socialists had a grip on a political fact of life that frequently eluded the left: that a movement which would win power must first demonstrate the legitimacy of its claim to govern. As national secretary John M. Work put it in *The Party Builder*, Socialists must "furnish the calmness, the precision, the positiveness, the aggressiveness, the constructiveness, the cool-headedness, and the self-possession" in a time when "everybody else is fuddled, confused and bewildered."

Unlike the dozens of Socialist dailies, weeklies, and monthlies, newspapers, magazines, and leaflets, *The Party Builder* was not a vehicle through which the Socialists attempted to make converts. It was not a propaganda sheet in which the party, like any aspirant, presented its best made-up and not necessarily most honest face. Rather, *The Party Builder* was a strictly *internal* newsletter, a means of information, communication, exhortation, consolation, and congratulation among Socialists already committed to the party. In this *The Party Builder* (and, of course, the *Socialist Party Bulletin*) was unique among Socialist periodicals. The four-, and later eight-, page newsletter included reports by the various administrative departments, messages from the neglected foreign-language federations, stenographic accounts of executive committee meetings, detailed statistics of gains and losses in membership, lists of locals and their resources, invaluable financial data, pleas for funds and members and a bit more zest in party work, and homey reports of local triumphs in Leonia, New Jersey, and Oak Grove, Louisiana.

It makes less exciting reading than the invective and jeremiads of the regular party press. It is also true that most of the information therein could be gleaned here and there from the back pages of the better-known Socialist periodicals. The recommendation of *The Party Builder* to researchers is that it is a veritable abstract of the essential source material. And it does provide that glimpse into how Socialists worked with one another which is at best obscure in journals such as the *New York Call*, *Social Democratic Herald* of Milwaukee, or even *The International*

Socialist Review. Finally, as an implement of the national office, *The Party Builder* provides a picture of the machinations of the party leadership to an extent elsewhere revealed only in private correspondence. *The Party Builder* read alone would leave the historian with a distorted conception of what the Socialist party was like. But the study of the SPA without it would be likewise incomplete.

Eynsham, Oxford, 1969

American Socialist

CHICAGO, 1914-1917

JEFFREY HEYNEN

THE *American Socialist* was the official organ of the Socialist party of America from 1914 to 1917. As such, it expressed the collective view of the party, giving Socialists a vehicle for expanding party membership and strengthening their doctrines. The paper thus served two main functions: the attraction of new supporters and the exchange of information among men already committed to the party.

Because its role was partly propagandistic, it did not serve as a forum for debate among Socialists and consequently does not exhibit analytic expositions of radical philosophies. On the contrary, the articles in this periodical are simple, straightforward, and appeal to a wide range of readers. In its small subscription price of fifty cents a year for fifty-two issues, the publishers attempted to capture the widest possible audience. Yet, while they hoped for a circulation of 100,000 copies a week, they never achieved this goal.

This failure does not detract from the value of the paper, however. One finds in these pages articles by the best-known and most influential Socialists of the time: Eugene Debs, Morris Hillquit, Charles E. Russell, A. M. Simons, and Jack London, to name a few. The contributions of these men are of the greatest interest for their impact on working-class readers.

Their arguments, in particular those of Debs, represent the opinions of many times more men than those included in the Socialist party, since many workingmen, though dissatisfied, were too timid to endorse Socialist doctrine. Herein, then, one finds a representation of the concerns of many, if not most, American workers—concerns about industrialism, plutocracy, unionism, reform politics, and, most important, war.

In skimming the pages of the *American Socialist*, one's first impression is likely to be of courage and dedication. The steadfast opposition to the world war in these pages is one of the finest legacies of the Socialist party and one of the most admirable developments of the period. That the paper's dates correspond to the dates of the war is no accident. It was established to fight against the impending war, and it fought this battle until it was suppressed in 1917.

The basic Socialist argument against the war appeared consistently in the weekly. This argument runs roughly as follows. Wars are evil but not wholly unnecessary events. In fact, all wars but those of the workers against the capitalists should be eliminated on humanitarian grounds. Yet, the best means to abolish wars is to eliminate the competitive and destructive capitalist system which foments them. Capitalism causes wars when industries produce more goods than can be consumed in the home market. This creates economic competition among nations for markets for their surplus production. Because capitalists control the governments of these nations, they employ political, as well as economic, means to ensure their prosperity. Hence, they create immense military establishments which in peaceful times serve as a threat to competitors, and which in times of war are used to eliminate competition entirely. Great national armies serve the capitalist class in another way as well, however, for they are means of both intimidating and killing off troublemakers in the working class.

Employing these arguments, Socialists called the war a "terrible world catastrophe" in which capitalists indulged in a "mass murder of European toilers." They proposed to bring the war to a close by starving it—i.e., by imposing an embargo on all American food shipments to Europe. And they hoped that nations would see the futility of their struggles and turn to socialism.

Although simple and straightforward, this argument was not wholly persuasive, for as the war proceeded it seemed to an increasing number of people that Germany was to blame, and was thus worthy of punishment. From the beginning, she appeared to be the most militaristic of the capitalist nations, and each year it became less easy to defend a neutral position toward her. In the spring of 1915 the "Lusitania" was sunk; in the spring of 1916 American shipping was attacked by U-boats on a large scale; and in the spring of 1917 the United States began war preparations, including the imposition of conscription.

The Socialist response was that Germany was wrong, but that "Prussianization," as it was called, was a universal phenomenon, forced on every nation by the dominant economic system. That Germany was more at fault than the others was not sufficient cause for American workers to fight German workers. This argument lost its force after some time, and by 1917 many Socialists were prepared to accept war against Germany as a means of ending war in general.

Hence, while the paper retained its antiwar position, the makeup of the Socialist party changed and some of the familiar bylines—those of A. M. Simons, Charles E. Russell, and Allan L. Benson, for example—no longer appeared. This change was a product of the St. Louis emergency convention held in April 1917.

At the convention the left wing of the party, led by Charles E. Ruthenberg, who was not associated with the paper, attacked the right wing, led by Morris Hillquit, who was very closely associated with the paper, on the issue of the war. Their conflict produced majority and minority reports. But since there was little difference between these reports, the conflict was probably more between the men than the issues. The outcome was an overwhelmingly antiwar vote. Yet the ultimate result was a loss to the party of its prowar members, and these unfortunately were most of its leaders.

Thus weakened, the party and its official organ were unable to withstand American war fever. In the spring of 1917 circulation of the paper steadily declined. The government began a policy of systematic harrassment of Socialists and prepared to silence the Socialist press. On June 30, the *American Socialist* was held up in the mail because it was claimed that the issue of June 16 had violated the provisions of the Espionage Act of June 15. The paper was subsequently denied second-class mailing privileges. This administrative decision on the part of the United States Post Office may have been unconstitutional, since it amounted to suppression of the paper without due process of law. When called to "show cause" why the decision should *not* stand, however, Morris Hillquit put up only a modest fight for the paper. Given the temper of the times, his choice to retreat rather than fight may have been wise. There was too little support to wage a major battle against press censorship.

Thus died the *American Socialist*, victim of a greatly superior force. The lively paper held to its principles to the end and deserves to be remembered for the bravery with which it stuck to an increasingly unpopular cause.

New York City, 1968

Part Three

WOBBLY PAPERS

THE Industrial Workers of the World (the IWW, or the Wobblies as its members were commonly known) was founded in Chicago in 1905. The group of unionists and radicals who created the organization was an incredibly diverse ménage, concurring in little else except their chagrin at the American Federation of Labor's monopoly of labor unionism in the United States. Some delegates conceived the new union as an adjunct of the Socialist party. Daniel De Leon and his followers, contrariwise, hoped the IWW would ultimately revive the decrepit Socialist Trades and Labor Alliance (the labor union wing of the Socialist Labor party). Still others were disillusioned with politics at least as much as with the AFL's conservatism, and envisioned the new organization as an independent, nonpolitical vanguard of Socialist revolution. While certainly sharing this ideal, components such as the Western Federation of Miners (WFM) would have been satisfied merely to extend the industrial organization of workers through the IWW, as the WFM had sought to do with its Western Labor Union and the American Labor Union. Finally, there were even some anarchists among the founders whose concrete plans remained far vaguer than their aspirations for humanity.

The general discontent with the AFL focused principally on three issues: the federation's conservatism and collaboration with capitalists; its adamant commitment to craft organization; and its refusal to organize the unskilled workers, who increasingly comprised the mass of the American working class. "We are going to get at the mass of the workers and bring them up to a decent plane of living," said convention chairman Big Bill Haywood.

> I do not care a snap of my finger whether or not the skilled workers join this industrial movement at the present time. When we get the unorganized and the unskilled laborer into this organization the skilled worker will of necessity come here for his own protection.

In fact, the first years of the IWW's existence were characterized by "raids" upon the AFL and, more notably, by factional fights which, given the wretchedness of the prize, must be counted among the most meaningless in the history of the American Left. By 1909, however, both the Socialists and the Socialist Laborites had given up trying to attach the union to their parties and had quit or been expelled. The nonpolitical unionists, led by Vincent St. John, a former WFM organizer, were in control. In 1909, a strike at the Pressed Steel Car Works of McKee's Rocks, Pennsylvania, and a successful Free Speech Fight in Spokane, Washington (to maintain propaganda rights among migrant workers who wintered there) demonstrated that the Wobblies were a viable hope for the unskilled factory workers and atomized wandering working force of the undeveloped West. Over the next few years, the union developed a national reputation and notoriety as a result of numerous strikes, including a dramatically successful one in Lawrence, Massachusetts (1912), and Free Speech Fights up and down the West Coast.

Beginning in 1914, IWW influence waned in the industrial centers, but a concerted organizational campaign among agricultural workers, lumberjacks, and western construction laborers brought in tens of thousands of recruits and seemed to establish the union as a permanent fixture in American labor relations. Success also brought enemies. And American intervention in the world war in 1917 presented them with their opportunity.

The IWW waffled on the war issue. Now under the leadership of Big Bill Haywood, the union hedged whereas the Socialist party, for instance, spoke stridently and loud. But northwestern log and lumber interests, AFL officials (worried by Wobbly competition), and antiradicals painted the union as unpatriotic and seditious. As a result, Justice Department deputies raided IWW halls throughout the country on September 5, 1917, and on April 1, 1918, the biggest of a series of trials of Wobbly leaders under the Espionage and Sedition Acts began in Chicago.

When one of the convicted leaders, Richard Brazier, was eventually released from Fort Leavenworth Penitentiary, he recalled his comrade Ralph Chaplin telling a federal official, "well . . . we are still here and the I.W.W. is still here." The law officer replied, "But it's not the same IWW" and Brazier commented, "No, Tom, it wasn't and it never was again. They had used all the forces of federal and state governments to crush us and they had succeeded, but it took all their strength and power to do it."

However valid Brazier's consolation, after the sedition trials the IWW was indeed changed. With so many of its officials under indictment it was forced to become virtually a legal defense association. The IWW was never really a union again but merely became another curious specimen on the fringe of American social movements. It survives in that guise to this day, maintaining its identity and deriving nourishment from its richly romantic history and legends.

While the Wobblies flourished, they were likely the most voracious readers that the American labor movement has ever known. In *The Casual Laborer*, sociologist Carlton Parker observed that

> considering their opportunity, the IWW read and discuss abstractions to a surprising extent. In their libraries the few novels are white-paged while a translation of Karl Marx or Kautsky, or the dull and theoretical pamphlets of their own leaders, are dog-eared. Few American analysts have realized what firmly-held traditions have been established throughout the working classes by the muckraking literature of the last twenty years.

Actually, the Wobbly newspapers were not so devoted to the abstract as they were concerned with organizational affairs and the news generally. But the IWW administration and numerous locals and local associa-

tions of Wobblies certainly supplied members with congenial periodicals. (Characteristically, one of the first actions of the IWW "local" in
the Cook County Jail during the sedition trial was to produce a handwrit-
ten, penciled organ, "The Can Opener.") Walter Goldwater cites eighteen Wobbly titles in his list of periodicals.

Industrial Union Bulletin
CHICAGO, 1907-1909

MELVYN DUBOFSKY

IN June 1905, more than one hundred individuals reflecting every nuance of American radicalism met in Chicago to declare total war on American capitalism. Resolving that "the working class and the employing class have nothing in common," they founded the Industrial Workers of the World in order to carry on their struggle against the established order. Created in the same year that revolution stunned Tsarist Russia, the IWW was born in a burst of optimism. After its blissful birth, however, the IWW existed perilously: internal dissension—not unlike the sectarian warfare common to other left-wing organizations—at times paralyzed it; secessionist movements took away its largest affiliates and the bulk of its membership; and the violent opposition of private employers, combined with governmental hostility, recurrently threatened its total destruction. Yet, somehow or other, the IWW maintained a precarious life.

The founders of the IWW had anticipated a day when American Federation of Labor affiliates would desert the house that sheltered them to seek more spacious room in the IWW's mansion. They expected skilled workers to unite with the unskilled in a common labor front based upon industrial unionism that would destroy American capitalism. But no AFL affiliates flocked to the IWW and few skilled workers evinced an interest in a united labor front. Indeed, the only IWW affiliate that resembled an industrial union and that included masses of unskilled workers—the Western Federation of Miners—seceded in 1907, taking with it the bulk of the IWW's membership. Precisely how the IWW leaders responded to this series of disappointments can be gleaned from a careful reading of the *Industrial Union Bulletin*.

First published on March 2, 1907, the *Industrial Union Bulletin* appeared on a regular weekly basis until August 8, 1908, after which it was published semimonthly until November 12, 1908. Between November 12, 1908, and March 6, 1909, the paper appeared only four more times, the IWW discontinuing publication with the issue of March 6, 1909. Published in Chicago and initially edited by A. S. Edwards, one of the IWW's founding members, the *Industrial Union Bulletin*, after Edwards' resignation as editor on April 25, 1908, was apparently edited collectively by the organization's general executive board, or at least the board members then resident in Chicago.

When the *Industrial Union Bulletin* first appeared in print, the IWW seemed on the verge of total collapse. At its 1906 convention, the organization had split in two, an insurgent faction through extraconstitutional means having successfully purged the officials elected at the 1905 convention. As a result of this 1906 split, two factions battled in the streets and in the courts for control of the organization, while the Western Federation of Miners simply withdrew from affiliation with the IWW. The victors at the 1906 convention themselves formed a shaky coalition, consisting on the one hand of the followers of Vincent St. John, formerly a prominent figure in the WFM, who were committed to direct economic, or trade-union, action as opposed to parliamentary politics; and on the other of the admirers of Daniel De Leon, one of the most dogmatic and controversial personalities in the history of American radicalism and the then unchallenged leader of the puny Socialist Labor party, who were dedicated to revolutionary political action. During its initial year of publication, the *Industrial Union Bulletin* highlighted the controversy raging between the followers of St. John and those of De Leon.

Indeed, for the period from March 1907 to August 1908, no better guide than the *Industrial Union Bulletin* exists to the IWW's evolving ideology. As pro- and anti-De Leonites debated their respective positions in the journal's pages, the ideological position of the IWW leaders came into clear focus. The contenders discussed a wide spectrum of questions, ranging from the proper relationship of the labor movement to political parties and legislatures, to the ability of trade unions to increase real wages, to the relevance of the Marxian analysis of social-economic change to the American system. Anyone seeking to discover the question and issues that most concerned American labor radicals early in the twentieth century would be hard pressed to find a source superior to the *Industrial Union Bulletin*. Anyone eager to understand the basis of the split between St. John and De Leon and also to comprehend the ideology, or lack of it, in the post-De Leon IWW can locate no better starting place than the columns of this paper.

From the first, the *Industrial Union Bulletin*'s reports demonstrated an obvious trend within the IWW away from the advocacy of Socialist political action and the dwindling support that De Leon and his Socialist Labor party commanded within the organization. Two of the IWW's most prominent ideologues of the 1908-1917 era—Ben H. Williams, editor of *Solidarity*, and Justus Ebert, a German immigrant and radical theoretician—first expressed their growing syndicalist commitment in the *Industrial Union Bulletin*'s pages. One-time supporters of De Leon and members of the Socialist Labor party, Williams and Ebert regularly vented their displeasure at De Leon's attempt to transform the IWW into an adjunct of the political party. They analyzed carefully, and at some length, the reasons why trade-union organization on an industrial basis and direct economic action at the point of production must necessarily precede working-class political organization or action. Most important, their analyses set the scene for De Leon's expulsion from the IWW at its 1908 convention, the only reports of which, in fact, appeared in the *Industrial Union Bulletin*. Interestingly enough, the convention struggle, as described in that journal, revealed the IWW's peculiar amalgam of intellectualism and anti-intellectualism. Although the *Industrial Union Bulletin*'s columns were ordinarily filled with abstruse treatises on economic and social theory written by self-proclaimed intellectuals, the debate between Vincent St. John and Daniel De Leon at the 1908 convention was printed under the titles: "The Worker (St. John) vs. the Intellectual" and "The Intellectual (De Leon) vs. the Worker." In a labor organization, the worker naturally triumphed.

The *Industrial Union Bulletin* also offers unmistakable evidence of other important trends in the evolution of the IWW. Unable to appeal successfully to craft unionists or to organize the skilled, the IWW of necessity sought different recruits, which it soon discovered among migratory and immigrant industrial workers. The western migratory, or freewheeling hobo, of IWW legend makes his first appearance in the *Industrial Union Bulletin* in the reports of Washington State organizer J. H. Walsh. Walsh recruited a delegation of western migratories, known to history as the "Overalls Brigade," that "rode the rods" east to the 1908 Chicago IWW convention. En route, "Brigade" members sang working-class songs of rebellion, which the *Industrial Union Bulletin* printed and which later became part of the now famous IWW *Little Red Song Book*. At the same time, stories published in the *Bulletin* described IWW efforts to organize immigrant industrial workers in such cities as Paterson, New Jersey; Lawrence, Massachusetts; and Schenectady, New York, where, perhaps, the first recorded sit-down strike in American history occurred.

In short, for students and scholars interested in discovering why the Industrial Workers of the World became increasingly syndicalist in orientation after 1907, and how and why American syndicalism assumed its particular historical configuration, the *Industrial Union Bulletin* is a vital and unsurpassed source.

Hadley, Massachusetts, 1969

Industrial Worker

SPOKANE AND SEATTLE, 1909-1918

MELVYN DUBOFSKY

PERHAPS the most famous and romanticized of all radical working-class labor organizations in American history has been the Industrial Workers of the World. When one thinks of the IWW and its members, one imagines a breed of labor radicals peculiar to the American West: freewheeling hobo workers, brawny lumberjacks, and tough hard-rock miners—rugged frontier individualists who mouthed the dogmas of Marx and Engels but who practiced the legendary six-gun justice and direct-action tactics associated with the American West. Too often, however, the myths linked to the Wobblies conceal and distort the actual history of the IWW and its role in the development of American radicalism. An excellent means by which to penetrate through to the historical reality beneath the layers of IWW mythology exists in the pages of the *Industrial Worker*.

For the years 1909 to 1918 the *Industrial Worker* is the most important single source covering the story of the western branches of the IWW. Published in Spokane and Seattle, Washington, the paper reflected the attitudes and the goals of those Wobblies who preached labor radicalism and proselytized for recruits among migratory farm workers, isolated lumberjacks, and militant copper miners. Its editors included some of the more notable western Wobblies, and its columns featured reports and analyses of radicalism by such prominent figures as William D. Haywood, William Z. Foster, and Elizabeth Gurley Flynn. From March 18, 1909, to September 4, 1913, except for the period February 5, 1910, to May 21, 1910, when repression by public authorities caused its editors to transfer publication of the paper to Seattle, the *Industrial Worker* was

103

published in Spokane on a regular weekly basis. In the summer of 1913, however, ideological conflicts among members of the paper's editorial staff and between the staff and the general executive board of the IWW resulted in the suspension of the *Industrial Worker*. This suspension of publication remained in effect until April 1, 1916, when it resumed weekly publication in Seattle as the official journal of the western locals of the IWW. It continued to be published weekly in Seattle until late 1917, when American intervention in World War I caused state and federal suppression of the IWW and intermittent seizures of its newspapers and journals, including the *Industrial Worker*, which appeared only irregularly after the September 1917 federal government raids against the IWW. It finally ceased publication with its issue of May 25, 1918, after which it could no longer obtain printers or maintain its special mailing privileges.

Most of the important developments in the history of the IWW were discussed in the columns of the *Industrial Worker*. A full-size newspaper, ordinarily running four to eight pages, it consisted of news columns largely concerned with IWW labor conflicts; feature stories and ideological treatises drawn from other radical publications (including European ones); exegetical contributions on Marxism contributed by such IWW theoreticians and immigrant intellectuals as Justus Ebert and John Sandgren; and a regular editorial page that included revealing rank-and-file letters to the editor, book reviews, and cartoons (Mr. Block, the IWW's cartoon caricature of the obsequious, hence stupid, wage worker first appeared in the *Industrial Worker*). Everything from the Wobblies' struggles for free speech to their bitter battles for industrial justice in McKees Rocks, Pennsylvania; Lawrence, Massachusetts; and Minnesota's Mesabi Range, as well as the organization's internal struggles over structure, tactics, and objectives, made its appearance in the pages of the *Industrial Worker*.

Because most of the IWW's fights for free speech occurred in the West, the *Industrial Worker* remains one of the better sources for comprehending the rationale behind those struggles and for evaluating the Wobblies' tactics. By following the battles in Missoula, Montana; Spokane and Aberdeen, Washington; and Fresno and San Diego, California, as they were described in the *Industrial Worker*, the student of American radicalism can consider some basic historical questions: What is the function and nature of passive resistance? What are its virtues and advantages? When does it cease to be an effective instrument of protest or resistance? To what extent have the dominant forces in American society responded to nonviolent resistance in a manner congruent with this nation's ostensible foundation on strictly defined constitutional procedures and a proper respect for the opinion of mankind? The history of the IWW's use of nonviolent tactics in the course of its free speech fights helps answer some of those questions.

The IWW's efforts to organize immigrant industrial workers in Lawrence and on the Mesabi Range, American-born migratories in the West, and black and white workers in the South also raise important questions that the reports published in the *Industrial Worker* help answer. The paper's detailed accounts of the Lawrence strike included a special Ettor-Giovannitti issue of July 25, 1912, which featured revealing biographical sketches of the two IWW leaders charged with conspiracy to commit murder as a result of their role in the Lawrence strike. Articles in the paper also analyzed at some length IWW efforts to integrate black and white Louisiana and Texas timber workers into a single labor organization: the Brotherhood of Timber Workers. Reading about these and other IWW attempts to organize the unorganized brings several questions immediately to mind: How did the IWW attract the interest of the unskilled immigrants and migratory Americans considered unorganizable by the American Federation of Labor? Why was the IWW able to organize the unskilled in times of crisis but unable to hold their allegiance over the long haul? Why did the American-born migratories and the lumberjacks of the West remain more loyal to the IWW than the immigrant workers of the Northeast and the Midwest? How did Wobbly organizers overcome, at least temporarily, racial prejudices in the Deep South? Partial answers to these and other questions can be derived from a careful reading of the *Industrial Worker*.

The *Industrial Worker* devoted equal attention to the IWW's internal ideological and structural struggles. In the fall of 1909, for example, the paper featured stories concerning the IWW's effort to obtain recognition from and admission to the International Federation of Trade Unions; these accounts sought to distinguish the IWW from the AFL on ideological and structural grounds. The IWW general executive board asserted, according to newspaper reports, that the Wobblies should be admitted to the International Federation because the IWW was the only American central labor organization that committed itself to socialism and that admitted all workers regardless of skill, nationality, or color. Within a year, however, the *Industrial Worker* carried reports that implied a division within the IWW concerning its relationship to the American Federation of Labor and to the international labor movement.

In 1910 both William Z. Foster and William D. Haywood went to Europe, where they observed other radical and working-class political and economic movements. As a result of their European experiences the two American radicals formed quite different impressions of the course that the IWW should pursue in the future. Their reflections on European working-class radicalism can be followed in a remarkable series of reports that Haywood and Foster wrote in 1910-1911 and that the *Industrial Worker* published. More than that, the divergent conclusions that they drew from their European journeys led the following year to an open split within the IWW. Foster returned to America committed to ending the IWW's existence as an independent labor organization in open competition for members with the AFL. In articles in the *Industrial Worker* and in a letter declaring his candidacy for the editorship of the paper on March 23, 1911, Foster suggested that the IWW disband as a labor organization, transform itself into a propaganda league, and that the Wobblies henceforward bore from within the AFL as a militant minority determined to transform the federation into a revolutionary industrial-union organization. For the next several months the Fosterites and the anti-Fosterites debated their respective positions in the *Industrial Worker*. From this controversy there emerged a relatively clear portrait of how most Wobblies viewed the function, purpose, and objective of their organization. The discussion, which demonstrated among other things Foster's lack of support within the IWW, explained the typical Wobbly's antipathy to the AFL and the reasons why he located the strength of American radicalism among the unorganized, unskilled, and marginal working classes.

No sooner did the Foster-induced controversy die than another ideological battle began to rage in the pages of the *Industrial Worker*. Walker C. Smith, the editor of the paper from February 1, 1912, to July 17, 1913, and a noted IWW pamphleteer, inaugurated in January 1913 a series of editorials that ran until April 24, 1913, and that discussed, in exceedingly laudatory and hyperbolic language, the tactics of sabotage. Precisely what the Wobblies meant by sabotage—a method of industrial warfare they dearly loved to expound—has never been clear, but what Smith believed it implied became only too evident for several important IWW leaders. The *Industrial Worker*'s editorial series appeared to give sabotage a violent, destructive connotation, and the IWW's leadership, already under considerable public criticism for the organization's allegedly violent methods, had no desire to give their enemies further ammunition. Hence, they strove to curb Smith's editorial proclivities and to redefine sabotage in terms that made it appear less destructive. These debates about sabotage cause the reader to inquire: Was sabotage central to the tactics and objectives of the IWW? Could sabotage be pacific and constructive, as Wobblies claimed? Or was it inevitably violent and destructive?

Inextricably associated with the issue of sabotage was another question that divided the IWW and ruptured the staff of the *Industrial Worker*: the problem of organizational structure. On paper, the IWW was a largely centralized labor organization with great power vested in its general executive board. In practice, however, owing to an insufficient number of permanent national officials and to the vast distances separating central headquarters from regional ones, most IWW locals went their own relatively independent ways. Thus, the general executive board's decision to eliminate the propaganda for sabotage appearing in the *Industrial Worker* and to remove Smith as editor in July 1913 brought the conflict over structure into the open. Smith and his supporters argued in favor of decentralization or, as they preferred to label it, rank-and-file or "participatory democracy." Their opponents favored a more centralized organization, though one that would still be democratically chosen and responsive to rank-and-file needs. This controversy dominated the western paper's columns in the summer of 1913 and was the issue that most immediately led to the paper's suspension of publication on September 4, 1913. This issue also raises a series of questions about the IWW that require answers: How far was decentralization an issue that divided Wobblies on ideological grounds? Was it true that westerners were the primary advocates of decentralization? Was decentralization, then,

largely a matter of geography? Did the question of organizational structure actually pit believers in "participatory democracy" against proponents of bureaucratic tendencies?

The *Industrial Worker*'s resumption of publication in April 1916
answers some of the questions about the decentralization controversy.
Ironically, Walker C. Smith and other advocates of decentralization in
1913 were by 1916 once again loyal Wobblies, loyal to an organization
now more effectively and centrally administered than ever before in its
brief history. The western paper reveals the new life breathed into the
IWW as a result of the firm leadership exerted by "Big Bill" Haywood,
who had become general secretary-treasurer in 1915, and the rising
demand for labor that resulted from war-induced increases in industrial
and agricultural production. The IWW's response to the exigencies of
war, its refusal either to combat or to endorse American intervention, and
its decision to carry on labor organizing and to wage industrial conflict as
usual despite the war emergency can all be followed in the *Industrial
Worker*. The last issues of the paper indicate an IWW desperately
struggling to survive the repression brought on by its wartime successes
in organizing lumber workers and copper miners, which had had the
practical effect of undermining the war-production effort. In the end, the
IWW, as a labor organization, never recovered from government suppression in the years 1917-1919, and the *Industrial Worker*, as the
official organ of the western locals of the IWW, ceased to exist.

Hadley, Massachusetts, 1969

Why?

TACOMA, WASHINGTON

1913-1914

DALE RIEPE

BETWEEN 1913 and 1914 *Why?* burned a message into the souls of western radicals and then disappeared. Published in Tacoma, it had close connections with syndicalism and anarchism, and sympathized with the IWW. It was edited first by Mrs. Frances Moore, later by S. Hammersmark, and finally by Eugene Travaglo. Little is remembered of these worthies, however.

Why? had as its motto: "No consecrated absurdity would have stood its ground if man had not silenced child's objection." Credits were seldom given the writers unless they had international reputation, but we can discern the educated brains of wits and scholars throughout. It is a critical and cerebral protest rather than the more militant cry to be found in most other radical journals in the first quarter of the twentieth century. Much less doctrinaire than the eastern radical journals, *Why?* has a tincture of transcendentalism as well as anarchism. The European Marxist tradition, so commonly revealed in the New York radical journals, is largely absent from its pages. Witness, for example, the January 13, 1913, issue, in which the editorial asserts:

> The rational function of society [is] to become a free association of producers and consumers where no one may feel moral or physical constraint, collective or individual. . . . To attain this end we must begin now to free ourselves from all germs of authority, and assert our individualities, our self reliance.

And as Emerson says in his essay "Self-Reliance," "Let each man do his

109

thing.'' This scarcely sounds like a gospel of Marxism or social democracy.

The publication of *Why?* occurred not many years after the strikes of the smeltermen in Tacoma and the sawmill workers of Portland, both directed, it is claimed, by the IWW. That organization's emphasis upon industrialism was finally to break through the concept of craft unions, recommending instead mass unions that could battle the pervasive power of capitalism. These collective unions were to consist of all wage earners in a single community. Both the editors and staff of *Why?* were sympathetic to this political and organizational direction. As they said in an early issue: ''Strike and the whole world strikes with you; vote and you vote alone.''

The pages of *Why?* reveal contempt for the sentiment of patriotism, which was considered to be an attitude ''maintained by school, religion, and a venal press, to suit the wishes of the government. . . . the police are always present . . . ready to grab anyone who has the hardihood or misfortune to yell something different from what has been prescribed by the authorities.'' Patriotism is revealed as a pretext to sanction military institutions required to safeguard privileges of wealth. To rid people of such a sentiment, the state must first be abolished because ''the state appears to us as an institution for the mutual insurance of the landlord, the warrior, the judge, the priest . . . to exploit the poor.'' ''The greatest fallacy of patriotism is that it makes us accept and endure certain wrongs that we would otherwise rebel against were they perpetrated by foreign tyrants.''

Law also is viewed with disdain. ''Men cannot be made virtuous by law, but they can be made vicious by it. They cannot be made honest by the law, but they can be made dishonest by it.'' Law promotes social inequality and the despoiling of the poor; it turns men into sycophants, jellyfish, and fawning menials through ten thousand avenues. The people never *make* the laws; they just vote for them. Intelligence and facts are needed more than law. Josh Billings is quoted as saying, ''I argue in this way: if a man is right, he can't be too radical; if he is wrong, he can't be too conservative.'' One should not feel personally injured when the law says, as a Seattle judge did, something as absurd as ''IWW members are not entitled to citizenship.'' One should realize that the judge's behavior ''is perfectly consistent with the ethics of his position . . . why expect legal recognition and consideration from the very institutions whom you despise and against which you have declared a bitter and relentless war? . . . Let's stand up like men and take our medicine; the Seattle judge has the goods on all of us.''

To the conservative, *Why?* offers the following anecdote:

> I stood in a soapbox crowd listening to a young fellow talk about freedom. A man at my side—a man of sixty and more—said to me resentfully: ''I was talking freedom long before that kid was born!'' This made me laugh. ''I say,'' I said, ''What are you after?, do you want freedom to be buried with you? Who's going to keep the ball rolling if the youngsters don't take it up?''

This incident is a fine example of the sympathy *Why?* shows throughout its issues to all forms of social protest, protest more populist and anarchist than Marxist or social democratic. A piece signed ''J. F. M.'' also demonstrates this well. ''If the Anarchist theory be not sound, it is a strange thing that all the facts of history go to corroborate it. It would be pretty hard to name a possible experiment in government which has not been tried somewhere. And every one of them has proved a fizzle and a failure.'' Can anything be done about it? No, ''the government superstition'' cannot be uprooted in an hour. There is no talk here of a dictatorship of the proletariat.

In the Bitter Bierce department one finds many acrimonious and sometimes witty remarks that give clues to the general outlook of the Pacific Coast radicals. The following examples are typical: ''Thirty-eight conductors on the Oregon-Washington Railroad have been dismissed for stealing fares. It doesn't pay to steal anything connected with a railroad—except the railroad itself.'' The next one is a bit more starchy: ''A dynamite explosion which wrecked a Harlem tenement house caused the death of four active revolutionists.'' Washington, D.C., was a target then as today: ''Now comes the Department of Labor with an alarming statistic to the effect that 300,000 babies less than one year old annually die in the U.S. mainly for economic causes. The interest displayed in behalf of these victims on the part of the above bureau is simply wonderful—since it can't do anything for them, it can at least count them.'' And for the gourmet: ''Sabotage—the only French dish not relished by American epicureans.'' It would be a novelty indeed if the do-nothing thinker were not praised: ''A philosopher is a genus homo who has grown so top heavy that he became weak in the vertebrae.'' Of the revolutionary it might often be said: ''A political radical is usually a man who wants to muss things up in the hope of establishing himself in circumstances sufficiently comfortable to warrant his becoming a conservative.'' And finally, concerning war, Thoreau is quoted as saying: ''It is impossible to instill principles in a soldier's mind without making him a deserter.''

When not attacking government and other large institutions, *Why?* took enough time to examine the Boy Scouts, evidently a favorite annual event among radical journals before 1941:

> The Boy Scout movement was originated by Ernest Thompson Seton . . . a man deeply interested in the life of the boys . . . who was wont to take a goodly number of them from the squalid and congested districts of our cities to his vast estate in New England. He was not a disciplinarian or a soldier, but a man of broad understanding who wanted the boys to revel in the wildwoods, close to nature.

But then General Baden-Powell appeared on the scene in Portland in the YMCA ''gymnasiums-for-soul-aviators'' and among the Scouts to devise ways and means to utilize Seton's excellent ideas ''to encourage a military training among the youths.''

Birth control was then, as today, a matter of grave concern. *Why?* asked, ''Is it immoral, is it obscene, to give to the enfeebled woman whose health, possibly whose very life, would be endangered by another pregnancy, the means of protecting herself against the brutality of a selfish husband, and to spare her to the children already born?'' The first argument is still considered useful, but the second and third are not much in evidence these days, although they seem no less valid or important.

A final word of wisdom for conservatives rounds out the hortatory material in *Why?*: ''Social unrest is not a disease but an indication of mental development. Verily discontent is mother of progress.''

Buffalo, New York, 1969

The Agitator

HOME, WASHINGTON, 1910-1912

The Syndicalist

LAKEBAY, WASHINGTON, AND
CHICAGO, 1913

MELVYN DUBOFSKY

MUCH of the history of twentieth-century American radicalism can be written in terms of the life and times of William Z. Foster (1881-1961). Indeed, Foster himself entitled one of his two autobiographical works *From Bryan to Stalin* (New York, 1937), for his political consciousness was first formed in the era of Bryanite Populism and his political odyssey ultimately carried him into command of the American Communist movement.

A child of Philadelphia's slums, Foster left home at an early age to follow a life of transient wage-work. After several years of beating about the country and shipping out with the merchant marine, he turned up in Spokane, Washington, where he encountered the Industrial Workers of the World during their 1909-1910 Spokane Free Speech Fight. Foster promptly became a fighter for free speech and a card-carrying member of the IWW. But after a visit to Europe in 1910-1911, he returned to the United States opposed to the IWW's dual-unionist approach to labor organizing. Unable to convert the Wobblies to his own tactic of "boring from within" the American Federation of Labor, Foster left the IWW in 1912 in order to found the short-lived Syndicalist League of North America. Only two years later, he became a member-in-good-standing in the Brotherhood of Railway Carmen, a conservative, craft-oriented af-

113

filiate of the American Federation of Labor. So well did Foster then adapt to the AFL's conception of the labor movement that Samuel Gompers, president of the AFL, placed Foster in charge of labor's attempt to organize the steel industry in 1918-1919. That effort, culminating in the Great Steel Strike of 1919, brought Foster to national prominence (some might say notoriety). Soon after the organizing campaign in the steel industry had collapsed and Foster had been repudiated by several AFL chieftains for his alleged radicalism, he moved completely to the political left, becoming a member of the American Communist party and, eventually, Stalin's most important and loyal American lieutenant. On three occasions—1924, 1928, and 1932—the Communist party chose him as their presidential candidate. And for the remainder of his life Foster served as the dominant figure in American Communist-labor circles. He certainly traveled a long way politically from the days of Bryan and populism.

The period of *The Syndicalist* (1910-1913) found Foster midway in his political odyssey; soon to depart from the IWW and to found the Syndicalist League of North America, he had not yet joined an AFL affiliate or committed himself to communism. Thus, *The Syndicalist* is valuable precisely for the opportunity it offers to analyze the evolving political and economic philosophy of a prominent American radical. Indeed, had Foster not been intimately associated with the journal, it would undoubtedly seem of slight historical interest.

First published in Washington State on November 15, 1910, as *The Agitator*, its place of publication was transferred to Chicago in January 1913, and its name changed to *The Syndicalist*. By 1913, Foster, as the self-styled secretary of the Syndicalist League of North America, supervised the journal's production and circulation from a Chicago office, while Jay Fox handled the editorial function from his Lakebay, Washington, home. Fox, like Foster, was a former Wobbly who had withdrawn from the IWW late in 1912. A tabloid-sized, four-page semimonthly, the paper became a monthly in August 1913, and finally expired with its September issue, as Foster's Syndicalist League simply faded out of existence. Aside from Jay Fox's front-page editorials and occasional lengthy contributions from Foster, the journal relied heavily on material drawn from other radical periodicals of the time and letters to the editor from a small circle of regular correspondents. Throughout its short life-span, *The Syndicalist* remained largely a pale imitation of the IWW's *Solidarity* and *Industrial Worker* and the Socialists' *International Socialist Review* and *New Review*.

During roughly its first year and a half of publication, when the paper still appeared as *The Agitator* and Foster and Fox were Wobblies, it functioned primarily as an unaffiliated IWW propaganda sheet. Most of its noneditorial matter concerned IWW free-speech fights and industrial conflicts. The editorials generally criticized the parliamentary "slow-cialists" in the Socialist party of America, who were sometimes accused of what later became known as "social fascism," and the class col-laborationists in the American Federation of Labor, attitudes clearly in line with IWW dogma. Yet there were already clear indications of the impending split with the IWW's approach. Where the IWW press stressed industrial unionism and disparaged notions that the Wobblies were anarchists, *The Agitator* more and more promoted the propaganda of anarchism and expounded a brand of anarchosyndicalism in which the anarchist component overwhelmed the syndicalist one. Indeed, the paper even asserted that anarchism represented the most perfect form of organi-zation. Mixed in with its political polemics were types of women's rights propaganda and pro-nudity pieces of a highly romantic and utopian nature unlikely to appear in sanctioned IWW publications. But as Foster drew away from the IWW and began to use *The Agitator* as an outlet for his views, the journal's tone changed. Anarchism became subordinate to syndicalism and the IWW became a target to present his own ideas about labor organizing and radical action. In April he inaugurated a series of articles on "Revolutionary Tactics." This series, which ran until July 1, 1912, criticized the IWW's alleged exclusiveness, called upon radical trade unionists to bore from within the American Federation of Labor, and advised Wobblies to become a French-style militant minority within the labor movement. Foster continued to dominate the columns of *The Agitator* in July and August 1912, writing a series of articles on syn-dicalism in France and then, on September 1, 1912, publishing a call for the formation of a new American syndicalist organization. Two weeks later, on September 15, *The Agitator* had apparently become the official sheet for Foster's Syndicalist League of North America.

Throughout 1913 the columns of *The Syndicalist* were filled with tirades directed against the Socialist party and especially against the IWW. Still opposed to parliamentary and electoral politics and favoring the direct-action economic methods associated with the IWW, Foster now asserted that direct action could best be accomplished within the AFL. Articles published in the paper also illustrated the strong influence that the French *Confédération Générale du Travail* had upon Foster's syndicalist ideology, while at the same time stressing the American radical's continuing commitment to industrial unionism in contrast to French labor's preference for craft unionism. Foster's and Fox's editorials and columns in *The Syndicalist* offer the student of American radicalism an excellent chance to compare the American and European versions of syndicalism and to understand why some Americans borrowed the French concept of the militant minority.

Hadley, Massachusetts, 1969

The One Big Union Monthly

CHICAGO, 1919-1921

GEORGE HARMON KNOLES

THE general executive board of the Industrial Workers of the World began publishing *The One Big Union Monthly* in Chicago, on March 1, 1919, and continued issuing the journal until 1921, when it was replaced by the *Industrial Pioneer* (1921-1926). The IWW revived the journal for a short time in the 1930s, when the general executive board initiated a new and short-lived series in December 1937. It was one of a number of organs issued by the IWW during the course of its history.

The Industrial Workers of the World appeared in 1905 as a revolutionary union dedicated to organizing the laboring men of the world into industrial unions, not only to wage the day-to-day war against the owners, but eventually to liberate the human race from the yoke of capitalistic imperialism and wage slavery. Initially socialist in its outlook, the IWW gradually fused current, and essentially European, anarchosyndicalist doctrines with a virile, indigenous commitment to the idea of industrial unionism.

Bitter internecine strife characterized the American Socialist movement during the 1890s. Two consequences of the struggle were the splintering of the Socialist Labor party (dominated by the abrasive and militant Marxian, Daniel De Leon), followed by the organization of the Socialist party under the leadership of Eugene V. Debs. At about the same time, the Western Federation of Miners emerged to a position of commanding leadership, partly as a result of the divisions within the ranks of the Socialists, and partly owing to its role in ten great strikes conducted during the decade following its organization in 1893.

In 1898 the Western Federation of Miners established the Western

Labor Union—later renamed the American Labor Union—which was Socialist, class conscious, and devoted to the principle of industrial unionism. Following the defeat of the steel workers' strike in 1901, radical leadership came to appreciate the grave weaknesses inherent in craft unionism. Increasingly, voices from the ranks of the disenchanted called for a new militant and aggressive union which would appeal to a larger segment of the laboring class than the conservative workers who made up the bulk of the unions affiliated with the AFL.

Responding to these calls, representatives of the Western Federation of Miners, the American Labor Union, the United Metal Workers' Industrial Union, and some other unions met at Chicago in 1905 and wrote a constitution for the Industrial Workers of the World. Prominent at the organizational meetings were De Leon, Debs, William D. Haywood, William E. Trautmann, and Vincent St. John. The convention adopted a preamble to its constitution which suggests aspects of the doctrine and mood dominating the organization. ''The working class and the employing class have nothing in common,'' the document asserted. ''Between these two classes a struggle must go on until all the toilers come together on the political, as well as the industrial field, and take and hold that which they produce by their labor through an economic organization of the working class, without affiliation with any political party.'' The authors of the preamble went on to decry the activities of the older unions which encouraged the workers to believe that they had interests in common with their employers. The only remedy for this sad condition was the establishment of industrial unions and, if need be, one big industrial union.

Fights over doctrine and tactics manifest at the founding convention continued to plague the IWW during the ensuing years. In 1906, the Western Federation of Miners seceded, leaving the more radical De Leon, St. John (now general secretary-treasurer), and Haywood in control. Two years later a struggle over whether the union should eschew politics, and concentrate on economic warfare looking to the destruction of capitalism and to the eventual industrial organization of society, led to the expulsion of De Leon's followers. De Leon, following a strict Marxist-Leninist line, had resisted the antipolitical tendencies inherent in the IWW movement, and urged that ''every class struggle is a political struggle.''

The IWW thus maintained the purity of its doctrine, despite losses in membership. Its principle of industrial unionism was America's contribution to revolutionary labor theory. As a later (1908) IWW preamble put it: "The army of production must be organized, not only for the everyday struggle with capitalists, but also to carry on production when capitalism shall have been overthrown. By organizing industrially we are forming the structure of a new society within the shell of the old." Syndicalist theory, imported from Europe with significant modifications, reinforced the antipolitical stance of the victorious majority. While it received these overseas infusions of doctrine, the IWW made use of only those features congenial to its constituents. Unlike the European syndicalists who looked forward to a new society of unstructured producers' units, the IWW envisaged a more thoroughly integrated economic order and a greater measure of social control over the diversified economic groups within society.

During its first decade, the IWW, never squeamish about the use of violence, came to epitomize the aggressive militancy of class warfare in America. It appealed to all workers to join the crusade against capitalism. It advocated direct action in labor disputes, arguing that collective bargaining led only to surrender to the demands of employers. It refused to participate in drawing up contracts for specified periods of time because such agreements shackled the laborers' hands. The IWW, under the aegis of "direct action," "sabotage," and the "general strike," conducted about 150 strikes in the years between its organization and the outbreak of the European War in 1914. The union actively campaigned against American entry into the war and refused to join the American Federation of Labor in a no-strike pledge.

The United States struck back at the IWW when it openly opposed the war. The government indicted 166 IWW leaders, arraigned and tried 113, and convicted 93, including Haywood. In the postwar years governments continued to prosecute IWW members, critically impairing the effectiveness of the organization. The appearance of the Soviet Union following the revolution of 1917 proved a more serious threat to the IWW than the prosecutions of domestic government. IWW leadership early sympathized with the Communist revolution, but it was not long before a violent controversy over the issue of economic *versus* political means of ushering in the new society threatened the integrity of the union.

At the same time, in 1919, many former members left the ranks of the IWW to help organize the Communist party of the United States, which then proceeded to fight for control of the revolutionary movement in the United States.

In 1920, the Third (Communist) International appealed to the IWW to abandon its traditional antipolitical posture in the face of the new revolutionary situation. Society could not wait, the Comintern argued, while the IWW formed "the structure of the new society within the shell of the old." The workers must seize political power, establish the dictatorship of the proletariat, erect a socialist state, and then gradually effect the communization of productive power. The state, meanwhile, would wither away as an engine of class domination. The IWW rejected the invitation to join the Communists, but influential members such as Haywood and William Z. Foster, along with many others, abandoned the IWW, and joined the Communist party of the United States.

The IWW probably reached the peak of its power and influence in 1912, when it enrolled about 100,000 members. Government pressure, along with the successful competition of the Communist party, severely crippled the union. Moreover, internal strife centering on doctrine, tactics, and structure sapped the organization's vitality. Although the IWW persists to our own day, its appeal since 1920 has been weak, except for a brief flurry during the depression decade of the 1930s.

The One Big Union Monthly may not be unique, since dozens of radical journals have appeared and disappeared over the years. One can find in its columns the familiar story of dedicated and aspiring devotees struggling to prevent the journal from expiring; there are plaintive appeals to news dealers asking them to pay up before bankruptcy overtakes the enterprise. The editor cordially invites would-be authors to accept the challenge to "enlighten the toiling and suffering bottom layer of humanity," payment to be in "love and gratitude." Here, too, are reports of intramural in-fighting. An announcement appeared in the January 1921 issue telling the readers that the general executive board had fired the editor who had held the job since the *Monthly*'s founding because he had severely criticized the Russian Communists and other revolutionary organizations for their propolitical biases.

On the other hand, the journal provides an insight into some of the peculiar views of the union, including some that reflect a palpable weakness of doctrine and strategy. For example, in a polemical article in August 1919, directed against well-wishers anxious that the IWW join the Socialist party, the editor explains the union's refusal to engage in politics by drawing upon the analogy of the chicken. When it's ready to be born after twenty days of incubation, the chick simply pecks a hole in the shell and is born. "No external help, no 'political action' is needed to release him. His own life force is sufficient. . . . So it will be with the taking over of the means of production. When the working class organization is ready to take over society, the taking over will be a perfectly natural process. To attempt the taking over before that time thru 'mass action' would be equal to social abortion. . . ."

The *Monthly* contains an abundance of material—news, reports, stories, editorials, cartoons—which affords the serious researcher an opportunity to explore what might be termed the mystique of the movement. Here he can acquire the "feel" of the IWW, the sense of excitement (and frustration) that suffused the crusaders for social justice as they preached, cajoled, taught, castigated, scorned, elucidated, pleaded, fought, perished.

Can it be said that the IWW contributed anything to the shaping of American radicalism? The answer is affirmative. For one thing, the IWW pressured the AFL to end its long-time, studied neglect of America's unskilled hordes of workingmen in the great and burgeoning mass production industries. Moreover, the IWW was the first major union actively to organize black workers in this country. Finally, the IWW bequeathed its peculiar brand of industrial unionism to the American Communist movement. The IWW constituted an American answer to revisionism within the ranks of the Marxian Socialists. Shunning all proposals to compromise in any way with the existing capitalist order in its economic or political manifestations, the IWW helped to keep alive a militant, uncompromising, radical revolutionary tradition in the United States.

Stanford, California, 1968

Industrial Pioneer

CHICAGO, 1921-1926

MELVYN DUBOFSKY

INDUSTRIAL PIONEER, published by the general executive board of the Industrial Workers of the World from 1921 to 1926, provides an excellent insight into the organizational condition as well as the ideology of a group that had once been the most radical and most feared labor organization in the United States. On the eve of American intervention in World War I, the IWW, an organization committed to revolutionary principles and dedicated to the establishment of a syndicalist society, appeared about to achieve an objective that had defeated other labor unions: the organization of migratory agricultural workers, lumberjacks, construction hands, and hard-rock miners into stable and effective industrial unions.

American participation in the war, however, doomed the IWW's activities to failure. In the interest of national security, the federal government (ably assisted by employers and state officials) broke IWW strikes, deported alien Wobblies, and prosecuted and imprisoned all prominent IWW officials and spokesmen. By the end of 1918, almost 200 influential Wobblies languished in prison, and the organization's strength among the workers it had previously represented had been destroyed, partly as a result of repression and partly as a consequence of government-compelled reforms in working conditions. Thereafter, the IWW could scarcely be considered a radical threat to America's security, and employers had no further reason to fear the Wobblies.

From 1920 to 1924, and for some years afterwards, three issues troubled the remnants of this once menacing labor organization: the status of its "political" prisoners (those members imprisoned by the federal government during the war, as well as the victims of California's repressive, anti-IWW criminal syndicalism statute); its relationship with the Communist party at home and the Profintern abroad; and the distribution of power within the IWW between centralists and decentralists, industrial unionists and anarchists. These, then, were the primary questions discussed in the *Industrial Pioneer*, a forty-eight page monthly, radical labor magazine that mixed didactic verse, moralistic short stories (perhaps best described as fables for the working class), typical IWW cartoons featuring bloated capitalists and bureaucrats, and proletarian art portraying brawny, virtuous workingmen with serious editorials and essays concerning industrial unionism, social theory, and Marxism.

The first controversy to dominate the *Pioneer*'s columns concerned communism. After the formation of the American Communist party in 1919 and the establishment of the Third International (Comintern) and its trade union component, the Red International of Labor Unions (RILU), the Bolsheviks invited the IWW to join both organizations. Wobblies split among themselves about how they should react to the Communist overtures. Some members maintained that the IWW should terminate its independent existence and ride the Communist wave of the future; the vast majority of Wobblies, however, preferred to remain true to traditional IWW principles. Still dedicated to syndicalism and to nonviolent direct action, they found distasteful a movement based upon absolute control of the state (the Bolshevik dictatorship of the proletariat) and violent seizure of power. Committed to the concept of industrial democracy, they viewed the Bolshevik principle of democratic centralism as alien. Opposed to all forms of coercion and bureaucracy, they rejected the new Soviet system.

These sentiments had been made evident in *The One Big Union Monthly*, and *Industrial Pioneer*'s immediate precursor, edited by John Sandgren, a Swedish immigrant syndicalist and prominent IWW ideologist of prewar vintage who, in the pages of his magazine, waged a bitter running battle against the Communists within the IWW. So vehement and personally acrimonious did Sandgren's editorials become that in 1921 the IWW suspended him as editor of the *Monthly* and changed the magazine's name to *Industrial Pioneer*. This, however, failed to still the ideological war then disrupting the IWW, for the new editor proved to be a Communist whose editorials and feature stories only served to embitter the non-Communist IWW majority. He, too, had to be removed as editor, and after his departure in 1922, the *Industrial Pioneer* assumed the form it was to retain for the remainder of its existence.

Dedicated to syndicalism and opposed to communism, the IWW, as reflected in the *Pioneer*'s pages, paid homage to Marx and Engels without subscribing to Soviet guidance. Although sympathetic to the Russian Revolutionaries, IWW writers, such as E. W. Latchem and Covington Hall (the latter was one of the organization's most prominent prewar poets and polemicists), asserted that other revolutions could not accord precisely with the 1917 Russian variety. Moreover, *nationalistic* Soviet policies should not be confused with internationalism, which would be nonsectarian, nondogmatic, and would include all workers, regardless of their political or religious beliefs. They also cited the Soviet example, as well as the rise of Italian fascism, to prove to American workers that political action resulted simply and solely in the substitution of one form of dictatorship for another. The *Pioneer* reminded its readers, as the IWW had been advocating since its creation in 1905, that the best route to revolution and to the establishment of a libertarian new society lay in the growth of mass industrial unionism and in the exercise of direct economic action at the point of production.

In line with traditional IWW ideology, the *Pioneer* from 1923 to 1924 stressed two themes: the necessity of mass industrial unionism and the need to organize the unorganized, particularly at a time when the AFL's membership was, in fact, declining. Articles were published to demonstrate the IWW's organizing opportunities in mass-production industries like steel and autos, where the craft unions had failed to open membership to the less skilled and to the nonwhite. One essayist even elaborated upon the profound importance of the northward migration of southerners, especially Negroes, white mountaineers, and Mexicans. He correctly observed that this population migration, quite rapid in the 1920s, imperceptibly yet irreversibly was altering the structure of southern society and its economy, and he also beckoned the IWW to organize these new industrial workers as they migrated north. Other essayists described technological innovations that affected the labor movement, and one writer, with truly remarkable foresight, prophesied the impact of the piggyback freight system upon railroads, over-the-road truckers, and shippers, and its consequent effect on workers in those trades. During 1923-1924, the *Industrial Pioneer* reflected the thoughts of radicals in an organization then attempting to organize the nation's least secure workers, and one which was probably more aware than the AFL of the basic social and economic changes transforming American society during the "Jazz Age."

After 1924, however, the nature of the IWW changed drastically, as did the tone and contents of the *Pioneer*. At its 1924 convention, the IWW split in two, a rupture from which it never recovered. Before then the IWW had been a propaganda group as much as, if not more than, an actual labor organization; after 1924 it became almost purely what some Wobblies had once labeled a "hot-air" organization. The pages of the *Industrial Pioneer* symbolized this change, for in 1925 and 1926, the last two years of its run, its columns were filled entirely with educational, historical, and philosophical articles that represented an amalgam of working-class intellectualism, pseudo-science, and didactic, though frequently objective, materialistic history. In addition, serious theater and book reviews became more common, as did fictional fables and proletarian poetry. Indeed, the *Pioneer*'s pages reflected the IWW's decline as a labor institution that organized workers and compelled employers to improve working conditions.

The *Pioneer*, however, illustrates considerably more than the IWW's decline as a labor organization; it also demonstrates the inner life and thoughts of a body of American working-class radicals who considered themselves to be self-taught intellectuals. Although few of the organization's prewar intellectuals—except Justus Ebert and Covington Hall—appear regularly in the magazine's pages, its editors and contributors amply show the IWW's unique intellectual tradition. A perusal of the *Pioneer*'s columns should lay to rest the notion that America's discontented masses—its Populist component—germinated the virus of anti-intellectualism in the United States. Indeed, this magazine proves the contrary: it suggests that Wobblies gloried in their intellectual pretensions and that they could cite Marx, Charles Beard, Lewis Henry Morgan, Franz Boas—even Plato and Aristotle—with the best and most pedantic of academics. The *Industrial Pioneer* illustrates, however, that Wobblies and other working-class radicals detested the sterile intellectualism that they associated with the academy and its staid defenders of the status quo. The *Industrial Pioneer* remains one of the finest examples of the poetry, prose, fiction, art, and socioeconomic analysis produced by self-educated, working-class radicals.

Hadley, Massachusetts, 1968

Industrial Unionist

PORTLAND, OREGON, 1925-1926

JOSEPH R. CONLIN

WHEN the IWW was founded in 1905, its organizational architect, Father Thomas Hagerty, designed a highly centralized union. Hagerty selected a series of concentric circles as the best graphic representation of his plan (Samuel Gompers called it "Father Hagerty's Wheel of Fortune"), with basic decision-making power residing in a central general executive board. This basic principle was maintained by Vincent St. John, secretary-treasurer of the IWW during its years of growth, and was strengthened by his successor, William D. "Big Bill" Haywood.

The centralized structure did not go unchallenged. The western wing of the union constantly agitated for and periodically attempted to effect reorganization somewhat along the syndicalist lines of the French *Bourses du Travail*, regional divisions of the *Confédération Générale du Travail* which maintained virtual autonomy in decisions affecting strikes and other tactical matters. The major crisis over the issue occurred at the union's 1913 convention when the decentralizers were decisively voted down.

The Wobbly decentralizers argued that different regions were dominated by different industries, each with its peculiar interests, characteristics, and points of vulnerability. Therefore, it followed that the local unions were better equipped than the general executive board—remote from the "firing line" in its Chicago offices—to disburse funds wisely, call strikes at the most opportune moments, and otherwise frame specific policies. There was, moreover, more than a pinch of anarchism in the reasoning of the jealously independent migrant workers who made up the faction. The migrants reveled in their mobility and considered that their

127

relative freedom from the restricting influences of home and family made them better revolutionists than the sedentary "home guard" which supported the centralists. Even before their unionization, the western migrant workers were accustomed to shrugging and "breaking for the high timber" when a job became oppressive. They were not likely to submit to anything smacking of regimentation in unionism either. Therefore, they suspiciously watched the emergence of a "pie-card" bureaucracy in the national office and exploded at the slightest hint of an authority not immediately under local control.

The centralists—frequently men like Bill Haywood with a background of long trade-union experience—thought that too much local autonomy led to wasteful and suicidal strikes for the most frivolous reasons. They argued that the central office knew best what risks the union could afford and what was feasible from the national viewpoint. The western faction's claim of revolutionary purity was turned against it by the centralists, who pointed out that the final strike for industrial democracy would be a general strike and that such a cataclysm would necessarily be coordinated from the center.

Despite his reputation as an erratic nihilist, Haywood was an experienced trade union bureaucrat and enjoyed tremendous prestige among the workers. As a result, he managed to contain the potential crisis as long as he was in Chicago. The rambunctious westerners grudgingly accepted centralization under his administration, but, as Paul F. Brissenden noted in 1919, they never wholly accepted the principle and the IWW was ever in danger of being "unscrambled."

World War I proved to be the catalyst in the process. Federal prosecutions of the IWW for sedition struck first at the central office. The great IWW trial in Chicago entangled one hundred of the union's principal leaders in a legal morass for three years and eventually sent most of them to prison. The IWW was forced to regroup as a legal defense organization; with the centralist leaders thus occupied, the initiative in union affairs passed to the westerners. Haywood, for example, spent most of 1918, 1919, and 1920 in jail or trying to keep out of it. Whether his prestige would have been sufficient in the postwar union to maintain a centralized IWW is moot for, when he fled to the Soviet Union rather than go to prison in 1921, he sacrificed any influence he might have had with the Wobblies. With Haywood and the other national leaders immobilized or discredited, the way was clear for the decentralists.

During the summer of 1924, five representatives of the western industrial unions called for a meeting of the general executive board. When the majority refused, the five met anyway and pretended to function as the whole. They were physically expelled from IWW headquarters at 1001 West Madison Street in Chicago and when delegates arrived in the city for the Sixteenth Annual Convention, they were confronted with the spectacle of two conventions, two headquarters, and two groups of well-known Wobbly leaders, each claiming to be the true IWW. After the initial confusion abated, it was clear that the majority of the union supported the legitimacy of the majority of the general executive board. But instead of capitulating, the five rebellious members published an "Emergency Program" and continued to function.

The Emergency Program (EP) was an unequivocal call for the decentralization and debureaucratization of the IWW. "The principal cause of the present trouble is the centralization of power at headquarters," the document read, and the EP's alternative was to turn power and finances over to the constituent industrial unions. Among other reforms, the splinter (soon known as the EPs by the IWW) called for the abolition of the posts of general secretary-treasurer, general organizer, and assistant secretary and the substitution for these executive positions of a "general supply clerk"—a purely administrative position. The EPs also called for an end to the IWW's Chicago and New York defense offices. These were remnants of the wartime prosecutions and many of the western Wobblies looked upon them, with some justice, as existing to provide sinecures for union bureaucrats. "They have long outlived their usefulness, if they ever had any," wrote James Rowan in the *Industrial Unionist* a few months after the split, "and have degenerated into mere bumming institutions. Defense, like organized charity, has become an industry with the prisoners as the raw material." This same resentment played a large part in the faction's espousal of decentralization. "Abolish profiteering by headquarters," Rowan wrote. In his IWW there would "be no jackpot at headquarters for peanut politicians to build up a parasitic machine to sap the energies of the industrial unions and sabotage the work of organization."

The Emergency Program had the support of large sections of four Wobbly industrial unions, located principally in the western states: the Lumber Workers, the General Construction Workers, the Metal Workers, and the Railroad Workers. The faction's most dynamic and best-known member was James Rowan. Chairman of Lumber Workers' Union 120 at the time of the split, Rowan was one of the last survivors of the prewar IWW leadership in the union's administration. He had first come to prominence as a result of agitation in Edmonton, Alberta, and had staked out his place in Wobbly hagiography by his leadership of the IWW's famous free speech fight in Everett, Washington, a confrontation which culminated in the "massacre" of November 1916. Rowan had truly risen from the ranks of the timber workers who formed the backbone of the IWW in the Pacific Northwest. He had remained on the "firing line" according to the Wobbly ideal and harbored a deep resentment toward those who compromised with the system (for example, those jailed Wobblies who solicited individual clemency) and those in the central office whom Rowan saw as desk-chair bureaucrats of the AFL type. Rowan was one of the five decentralist members of the general executive board who precipitated the split, and he became the prime mover in the establishment of the Portland, Oregon, *Industrial Unionist*, the organ of the EP faction.

Rowan played western Wobbly prejudices for all they were worth in the new publication:

> The present editor is one of your own type. He is a working stiff, accustomed to the same mode of life as yourselves. There is no halo around his head. He is not posing as an intellectual or leader. He does not believe in leaders and he is sure that the value of so-called "intellectuals" has been much overrated by the workers in the past.

The *Industrial Unionist* was published weekly for a little less than a year. It was a four-page sheet and, despite its factional purpose, was a fairly good labor newspaper. A surprisingly small part of it was given over to internecine bickering, usually no more than an article or two on the third page and almost never an editorial. The paper described itself as "a propaganda medium, one through which we aim to reach the unorganized workers," and the editors did display a remarkable resistance to the eternal weakness of American radicals for battling one another. The bulk of the *Industrial Unionist* consisted of straightforward prolabor accounts of union and radical news around the world. In retrospect, it is as comprehensive a survey of labor news during 1925 and 1926 as any paper of comparable size, including many of the more stable and better financed papers of the AFL.

It was a professional operation; the Wobblies had a compulsion to publish newspapers (one partial bibliography lists 66 periodical publications by the IWW between 1905 and 1919) and a positive knack for the craft. If the *Industrial Unionist*'s inevitable front-page cartoon fell below the famous high standards of other IWW publications and its factional articles were more tendentious than the norm in that tedious genre, its news reporting was quite good.

But neither the paper nor the EP faction lasted very long. The delegates who assembled at the Sixteenth Annual Convention in 1924 retained their poise and received telegraphed sanction as the genuine convention from 61 of 65 branches of the union. After haggling for over four weeks, they expelled Rowan's faction; chastised and removed from office the centralist leaders, Tom Doyle and Joe Fisher, for their part in the brouhaha; abolished the offices of general organizer and assistant secretary; and removed national administrative officials from the general executive board, reserving posts there for representatives of the industrial unions. The general spirit of Rowan's movement clearly permeated the membership—almost every one of the convention's reforms was in the direction of the Emergency Program. But Rowan and his followers had violated solidarity—and that was the cardinal Wobbly sin. An imprisoned Wobbly caught the spirit of the IWW's pique with his parody of the union anthem, "Solidarity Forever":

I must save the proletariat from the tactics of the stools,
The officials, Doyle and Fisher, they have broken all the rules,
And the forty-thousand Wobblies are a pack of — · — fools;
But the Injunction makes us strong.
      Second Jesus Jimmy Rowan,
      Second Jesus Jimmy Rowan,
      Second Jesus Jimmy Rowan,
      And Injunctions make him strong.

For their part, Rowan and his group called a "genuine" Sixteenth Convention at Ogden, Utah, which effected the Emergency Program and continued to publish the *Industrial Unionist*. Instead of depicting the EPs as a secessionist group the paper reported as if they were the authentic national organization, ignoring the majority IWW as if it did not exist. This was standard procedure for IWW splinters and rumps. When the first and only IWW president, Charles Sherman, was purged by the majority in 1906, he and his tiny coterie briefly continued to publish their *Industrial Worker* and maintained that they were "the real IWW." In 1908, Daniel De Leon and his Socialist Labor party followers were eased out of the union, but for six years maintained that they were the true Wobblies and that they had expelled "the bummery." The practice of claims to orthodoxy reached a new perfection when the Emergency Program group cavalierly ignored the organization it had left. Only in one or two accounts of refusals to compromise with the Chicago central office (represented as an established church's refusal to grant concessions to heretics) was the general silence broken—except in a sorry note in a corner of one of the late issues when subscribers' attention was "called to the fact that the Industrial Workers of the World have moved from their old headquarters at 1001 West Madison Street, Chicago, and are now located at 186 N. LaSalle Street. . . . No attention should be paid to any notices giving other addresses."

The *Industrial Unionist* was one of the few political periodicals ever to announce its own demise, perhaps because its publishers really did not anticipate a permanent closing. In June 1926, the editors announced a six-month "suspension" during which the paper's finances would be put in order. The precarious state of the movement is vividly illustrated by the fact that the *Industrial Unionist* went under for a mere $850 debt, most of it the printer's bill. (The editors took no salary.) Another EP paper, the *New Unionist* of Los Angeles, appeared erratically until 1930 when, according to John S. Gambs, membership in the group was down to two hundred. The EP itself endured until 1941, with Jimmy Rowan sticking it out with the same tenacity with which he led the Wobblies in better days.

The 1924 fiasco actually reflected the final convulsions of a movement already fallen on evil days. Robert S. Tyler writes in his *Rebels of the Woods* that "these bitter arguments of 1924 revealed unmistakably the kind of vicarious militancy that many Wobblies began to experience in mere talk. . . . The whole intense argument [was] a pathetic substitute for action.'' Indeed, it is interesting to note that the IWW's splits always occurred at times when the IWW was feeble and that the union always coped very nicely with its internal problems at times when it represented a significant force in American labor. Thus, the infant IWW, little more than a paper organization, split wide open on two occasions—in 1906 and 1908; these were the last significant schisms until 1924, well into the IWW's senescence. When the centralization issue came to a boil in 1913, the IWW was at one of its peaks of vitality and the question was adjudicated without loss of membership. Again, during World War I, centralist Haywood and decentralist spokesman Frank Little differed violently not only on organization but also on how best to react to the imminent American entrance into the war. Yet, with membership at an all-time high, with a prize worth fighting for, and with profound pressure on the union from without, both managed to stay in harness. Wobbly historian Fred Thompson described the split of 1924 as ''definitely the worst thing that ever happened'' to the IWW—but it seems more accurate to say that the Wobblies were far beyond their worst times in 1924. The centralization issue was as old as the IWW. The tug between the necessities of organization and the intense individualism of the western Wobblies also had a long history. Wartime prosecutions had thrashed and throttled the IWW, jailed its leaders, dispersed its membership, frightened recruits, hopelessly smeared its reputation, and thereby turned one of the most aggressive and extroverted social movements in American history toward introspection and a morbid concern for internal purity. Only 1,300 members voted in the referendum that expelled the EPs and the *Industrial Unionist* folded for the sake of a niggardly debt. The IWW was long past the time when the ''worst things'' could happen to it.

Chico, California, 1968

Part Four

JOURNALS OF THE BOLSHEVIK CRISIS

THE initial effect of American intervention in World War I was to unify and strengthen the Socialist party. Although some of its most prominent leaders, individuals such as John Spargo, William English Walling, and Algie Simons, broke with the party and supported the war effort, party membership held firm in opposition to the war and votes for Socialist candidates actually increased for the first time since the debilitating split of 1913. The party won 34 percent of the vote in a municipal election in Chicago in 1917, 35 percent in Toledo, and only slightly smaller percentages in other industrial cities. In the New York mayoralty race, Morris Hillquit won 150,000 votes, 22 percent of the total; ten Socialists were elected to the state's legislature.

But soon the war's more profound effects in Russia, in the Bolshevik Revolution, canceled out the party's apparent revival, neatly symbolizing the fact that, in the decades that followed, the American Left would be dominated not by a natively rooted movement but by foreign events and decisions.

It is ironic that the greatest single triumph in the history of world socialism should begin the destruction of socialism in America. But it is not difficult to understand why. Like radicals elsewhere, American Socialists were so electrified by the sudden success of previously obscure Russian revolutionaries that they began to anticipate a revolution at home which would catapult them to power. Substantial parts of the Socialist party became enamored of the Russian experience not only as an inspiration but as a blueprint. They became impatient with parliamentarism and an electoral strategy that yielded mostly minority votes in scattered cities. Did not the Bolsheviks come to power through a tightly disciplined, conspiratorial minority?

Moreover, many elements within the SPA became infatuated with all things Russian. Just as they came to look upon the Bolsheviks as their model, many American Socialists were quite prepared to defer not only to the Bolshevik rulers but also to Russian immigrants within the SPA, as if all Russians somehow shared a racial insight into successful revolutionism. The Russian immigrants and other Eastern Europeans in the party themselves came to accept this role and, through their largely autonomous "Foreign Language Federations," they exerted a large influence in party affairs. Strengthened in 1918 by an influx of new members, a phenomenon which itself was a consequence of the Bolshevik success, the federations grew increasingly restive under the old party leadership which they identified with lack of militance.

In fact, the established party leadership (now again known as the "right wing") was by no means hostile to the Bolshevik Revolution. Old party leaders like Victor Berger, Morris Hillquit, and Eugene Debs continued to defend the Russian coup and even its methods; the SPA applied for membership in the Third (Communist) International even after the split of 1919. But the old leadership insisted that what was appropriate in defeated and repressive Czarist Russia was not applicable in the victorious, prosperous, and stable United States. They continued to defend the parliamentary strategy on which the party had relied since its beginning.

During 1918, various "left-wing" propaganda groups sprang up within the party and, in February 1919, many of them convened and formed a left-wing party within the party, specifically designed to seize control from the SPA establishment. In April, they gained this control when left-wing candidates won an easy majority of the National Executive Committee. In one of the power contests, the old warhorse Victor Berger was defeated by the left-winger, John Reed. But the right wing set aside the committee election as fraudulent and proceeded to expel or suspend numerous leftists in the party, beginning with the Russian,

Polish, South Slav, Hungarian, Lithuanian, and Lettish Federations. Before the orgy was complete, an actual majority of the party had been ousted.

In June, left-wing Socialists met in New York City to plan strategy but themselves split on the question of whether to accept expulsion or to continue working to capture the party. The minority, the Russian Federation and an English-speaking fraction from Michigan, insisted on leaving and quit the conference already assailing not only the right-wing Socialists, but those "communists" who elected to make a last try at gaining the old party. In August and September, they met in Chicago and organized the Communist party. In the meantime, the majority of the left wing, led by John Reed and Benjamin Gitlow, was prevented from participating in the Socialist party convention and, almost simultaneously with the formation of the new Communist party, organized and launched their own new organization, the Communist Labor party.

For two and a half years, the Socialist, Communist, and Communist Labor parties warred among themselves, with further factionalizations, secessions, and realignments characterizing the period and setting the theme for the whole subsequent history of the American Left. Eventually, unity was achieved when the various Communists and a further leftist secession from the SPA formed the legal Workers party, and a secret, illegal, and largely inoperative underground party. But this was upon explicit instructions from the Soviet Union and upon no special initiative among the Americans.

Journals of a rather new sort played an important part in this controversy from its beginning. While factional disputes had periodically occupied Socialist journalists before 1918, their chief purposes had been news reporting and analysis, propaganda among the unconverted, regulation of party administration, and the like. With the very origins of the new left-right split, however, there appeared a spate of journals which were designed almost solely to battle other comrades. The propaganda committees within the party during 1918 concentrated primarily on producing their journals. When the left-wing conference of April 1918 formed its party-within-a-party, it also instituted an "official" organ. This phenomenon too augured much about the future of American radicalism. Never again would factional fighting and assailing heterodox comrades occupy so much of the radical editors' and writers' time.

Class Struggle

NEW YORK, 1917-1919

DAVID E. BROWN

CLASS STRUGGLE was one of a group of short-run, left-wing Socialist periodicals which appeared in the decade prior to the formal organization of the American Communist movement in September 1919. Each of these periodicals had a special significance by virtue of its articulation of the theoretical and tactical development of the left wing during this period, especially in regard to the crucial question of its relation to communism.

The estrangement of left-wing or "revolutionary" Socialists from the more successful moderate or "dominant" elements of the movement was not, however, precipitated by the formation of the American Communist parties. The history of that disaffection has its roots in the nineteenth century, centering around the attempted radicalization of the labor movement by Daniel De Leon and his coterie in the Socialist Labor party. The rift within the left wing itself, culminating in its decision to break with the Socialist party, support the Third International, and establish an American Communist party, began to gain momentum with the outbreak of World War I.

The war intensified the left wing's hostility toward moderate socialism and Socialist electoral politics, as the list of prowar Socialists continued to grow. In France, Holland, the United States, and especially Germany, the left wing attacked with mounting bitterness and disappointment both the Socialist legislators and party officials who voted for or approved the appropriation of war credits. For the Left generally, this signaled the long overdue demise of the Second International and helped to galvanize Socialist sentiment in opposition to parliamentarianism. In America, this meant promoting the call for a Third International and elaborating the Left's condemnation of the nonrevolutionary, right wing-dominated Socialist party.

The failure of Socialist parliamentarism at this time was seen by the left wing as symptomatic of the fatal dilution of revolutionary principles by the party, principles which the Left undertook to publicize with ever greater frequency and stridency. In the early stages of the war, Socialist elected officials were attacked from the Left—first for their ineffectuality in averting war and finally for their outright support of nationalistic belligerency. Later, the character of the attack changed as the war was seen as a lost opportunity to transform an imperialistic conflict into an international proletarian upheaval. But the war was only one issue.

As the pejorative vocabulary of the Left ripened to meet the demand, with terms such as "parliamentary cretinism" and "sausage socialism" gaining currency, the gap between the left wing and the much-scorned establishment Socialists widened. The critics did not limit themselves merely to castigating the moderates' conduct vis-à-vis the war or condemning incidents of cooperation with the capitalist state. They went beyond the (by now) conventional radical wing tactic of pressing for increased militancy—whatever that might mean for whichever radical wing. In fact, they began to develop a full-blown critique of moderate socialism which emerged with greater clarity as the final split approached.

Two journals played particularly important roles in the process of formulating and publicizing this critique: *New Review* and *Class Struggle*. The former provided a voice for left-wing theoreticians during the period immediately prior to America's entry into the war. Others, such as *International Socialist Review*, published left-wing materials, but not exclusively. *Class Struggle* alone served that purpose from 1917 until the founding of the Communist and Communist Labor parties in 1919.

In its pre-1914 phase, *New Review* echoed the latent revolutionary zeal and the dissatisfactions of the left-wing tendency within the Socialist movement. But just as the authors' subjects ranged widely, from standard political and economic analyses to art criticism and attacks on the reactionary character of the Catholic Church, so the underlying structures of the various arguments, as well as the tactical priorities which they expressed, lacked uniformity. That soon changed. The war allowed the left wingers to distinguish themselves as the most vociferous antiwar partisans. This, together with the corollary antiparliamentarism, initiated the crystallization of the left-wing critique. It also marked the beginning of an intensive process of self-definition whereby the Left not only severed its theoretical connections with "dominant" socialism, but gave notice to the more clear-sighted among its adherents that a fundamental reorganization of Socialist forces was obligatory and imminent. What form this would have taken in the absence of the Russian Revolution is, of course, debatable. In any case, the stage had been set. As the drama progressed, many of the actors who had played prominent roles in the earlier scenes were shown to be at best catalytic agents in the process of building what was soon to be regarded as an inevitable denouement.

Many of the themes which established *New Review* as an organ of the left wing were later adopted, refined, and, to an extent, dogmatized by the editors and writers of *Class Struggle*. Quite appropriately, chief among these was the view that a class struggle does indeed basically characterize the social, political, and economic relations within the capitalist system. Attempts to deny or amend this critical conceptualization could only result in faulty perceptions, tactical miscalculations, and the failure of socialism. Socialism could not be attained through reform. Neither could it be voted into existence at the polls. It would come as the result of the victory of the proletariat over the bourgeoisie; and since the "aristocracy of labor," the skilled rank and file of the American Federation of Labor, were victims of bourgeois ideology, the hope of the Socialist revolution lay with the unskilled—the unorganized, uncorrupted, but ultimately militant and class-conscious workers who bore the brunt of capitalist injustice.

It could be argued that by 1917 the entire body of left-wing principles derived from this belief in the reality of the class struggle. Internationalism, another major left-wing tenet, can be viewed as simply a recognition of the supranational character of capitalism, thus establishing an international proletarian brotherhood with a common interest in extending the class struggle beyond national boundaries. Hence, the left wing's rejection of any form of nationalism and their vicious excoriations of the nationalistic policies supported by social legislators.

Similarly, the espousal of industrial unionism was tied to a belief in the revolutionary potential of the class struggle. Spurning the Lassalean tactic of writing off labor unionism altogether, the left wing saw in labor struggles a breeding ground of revolution. Industrial unions would provide the organization and develop the class consciousness of the proletariat in preparation for the final blow against capitalism.

Certainly the record of Socialist political parties was unimpressive from the standpoint of a Socialist revolutionary. They had done little else than squelch proletarian militancy for a generation. And the "petty bourgeois laborism" of the AFL and the British Labour party offered scant encouragement. The IWW and the general strikes in France, however, demonstrated that the class struggle was still being actively waged, and with greater intensity than ever before. It remained to tap this source of energy and guide it toward the achievement of proper Socialist goals.

The debates over the relevance of syndicalism, and even of anarchism, accompanying this surge of interest in industrial unionism were particularly significant in that they pointed up the extent to which the left wing had become disillusioned with electoral politics. They sought to re-focus Socialist perspective away from narrow political action and on to the action of the masses and they denied the necessity of subordinating the conduct of union or other popularly based anticapitalist activities to the electoral interests of Socialist political parties. Although the lack of theoretical sophistication on the part of the syndicalists ultimately caused the left wing to reject them, the syndicalists' independence of formal political and organizational encumbrances made them very attractive.

Syndicalist successes infused the left wing with enthusiasm and served at once to stimulate interest in and add weight to the Left's cry for "mass action." Unlike the syndicalists, the left wing did not reject all forms of conventional political action or organization. It was rather a case of their reaffirming a faith in the revolutionary potential of the proletariat, and realizing that parliamentarism and laborism had flourished in the name of the proletariat while submerging their real interests and their revolutionary elan. The frequent accusations of opportunism were based on the view that Socialist politicos and union officials often achieved a measure of power and affluence by consciously or inadvertently deceiving their proletarian constituents while serving capitalist interests. If political action was to have any meaning at all, it would have to signify the conscious revolutionary action of the masses.

The great appeal of the near mystical notion of "mass action" rested largely on its promise of liberating the class struggle from the constricting hold of such organizations as the German Social Democratic party, the Socialist party of America, the British Labour party, or the AFL. Yet, this new burst of freedom for the proletariat was not to proceed untutored or unorganized. Enlightened revolutionary Socialists would take their places among the rising masses and guide them, as their class consciousnesses warranted, toward the final goal. As the end approached, it became increasingly important that the workers were organized along industrial lines, thus maximizing their solidarity and effectiveness. With such a concentration of power, the traditional conceptions of separate economic and political actions would necessarily lose their significance. Mass action, including all forms of proletarian activity, would dissolve those categories by relating all actions to a single revolutionary strategy.

This describes, in part, the conceptual path taken by a group of the most uncompromising pre-Communist Socialists. It was this group which responded most immediately and enthusiastically to the Russian Revolution, for they saw in it the realization of their revolutionary views. And it was this group, or a large portion of it, which sought to translate what they saw (or thought they saw) in Russia into American terms. It is no small irony, then, that the promoters of a kind of quasisyndicalist, proletarian spontaneity should be responsible for the creation of the American Communist apparatus, soon to be burdened by a top-heavy bureaucracy and consumed by myopic internecine conflict.

It is possible that this fate was foreseen by those secondary characters, mentioned earlier, who failed to follow their left-wing comrades into the Communist party. One can only speculate, or extrapolate from inconclusive evidence. In any case, there were those, like Louis Fraina, who saw in the formation of a Communist party the logical conclusion of years of left-wing oppositionism. Others, like Louis Boudin, simply did not appear for the final scenes. One could garner external evidence for an explanation of Boudin's—and others'—failure to "survive." Both Fraina and Boudin were quite at home in such journals as *New Review*; but it became increasingly evident that the alterations in the left-wing approach to revolutionary socialism which emerged in *Class Struggle* proved more and more unacceptable to Boudin, while Fraina continued to press forward.

The crucial difference between the two journals must be seen in terms of the gradual bolshevization of the left wing, a process which was reflected in the pages of *Class Struggle*. It is true that a residual populist syndicalism remained part of the left-wing orientation even after *Class Struggle* had been designated the official theoretical organ of the Communist Labor party in 1919. This was symptomatic of a remarkable diversity, among the various groups within the American Communist movement, in perceiving the nature and possible consequences of communism. The changes in the Left's revolutionary posture, which took place between 1914 and 1918-1919, were sufficient nevertheless to alienate the Boudins (or cast them into the already overcrowded historical dust-bin).

In addition to the increased emphasis on the class struggle, industrial unionism, and mass action, the change was marked most noticeably by an almost total absorption in the Russian, and later the German, Revolution. Large portions of several numbers of *Class Struggle* were set aside for the reprinting of "Documents for Future Socialist History." This served to record the progress and publicize the demands of the revolutionaries. The names of Lenin, Trotsky, Luxemburg, and Liebknecht began to appear with greater frequency than those of many of the regular American contributors. Equally illustrative is the editorial acceptance and increased use of the principle of proletarian dictatorship. Although never thoroughly explained, the term designated the necessity of destroying the bourgeois state and replacing it with proletarian instruments of power wielded by workers' councils.

Probably the most significant change in the attitudes of the left wing, as they moved toward independence from the Socialist party, was their evaluation of the recuperative powers of capitalism. Immediately before the war and during its early stages, Fraina, an editor of *New Review*, expressed a prevalent belief that capitalism would experience considerable growth and development following the armistice. By 1917, Fraina, then an editor of *Class Struggle*, expressed the growing conviction in the left wing that the war represented the last stages of a crisis-ridden, imperialistic capitalism. The revolution was imminent. "Socialist reconstruction" could no longer be thought about in terms of long-range, pre-revolutionary tactics. It was no longer appropriate for the revolutionary Left to hedge against capitalist recovery, avoiding direct preparations for *la lutte finale*. Thus the left wing moved with apparent inexorability toward the founding of an American Communist movement, leaving many of the more cautious, or more skeptical, comrades behind.

It is not my intention to impose an artificial order on the antecedents to the birth of American communism, but, rather, to illuminate certain aspects of the larger context so as to place *Class Struggle* meaningfully within it. Consequently, the formal organization of the Left Wing Section of the Socialist party reported in *Class Struggle* should not be seen as "an inevitable first step" toward communism, although it does appear in retrospect to have been a necessary one. The illustrations cited earlier, intended to give some idea of the ideological composition of the left wing, should not suggest, moreover, that this development can be explained simply in terms of an intellectual evolutionary process. The accumulation of a body of analytical and tactical tools commensurate with the emergence of a Communist organization was both cause and effect. The complex interrelationship between the relevant ideas, events, personalities, and historical accidents is not, of course, beyond comprehension. It has been admirably delineated, in fact, by Theodore Draper in his *Roots of American Communism* (New York, 1957). The error lies in forcing these factors into a lineal pattern of historical and intellectual inevitability.

My purposes in this essay are, in any case, much more limited. I have noted some features of that segment of left-wing socialism, best exemplified in the pages of *Class Struggle*, which helped to precipitate the organization of American communism. I have underscored the influence of foreign revolutionary developments in the American movement. Finally, I have sought to sketch the distinction between the pre- and postwar views held by the left wing. In that *Class Struggle* figured prominently in all of these important developments within the pre-Communist Left, it must be considered among those documents essential to a thorough understanding of American radicalism.

Potsdam, New York, 1968

The New York Communist

NEW YORK, 1919

JAMES WEINSTEIN

FOR the Socialist movement in the United States, as for that of Europe, the Russian Revolution was experienced as a profoundly contradictory event. The first successful Socialist revolution would, under any circumstances, have been a joyous happening and would have exercised a powerful influence on the thinking and subsequent actions of various parties throughout the world. Coming as it did in the midst of World War I, at a time of the collapse of the Second International after almost all the European parties failed to oppose the war, it was like a bolt of lightning clearing the skies of disillusionment and despair. That the Revolution occurred in the most reactionary and backward of the major European nations was a further source of inspiration—particularly for those Socialists who, like virtually the entire party in the United States, had opposed the war. In the eyes of these Socialists, the Bolshevik triumph justified their adherence to principle and renewed their confidence in the face of wartime persecution and repression.

Yet, within two years, the Socialist party of America had split over questions growing out of the Bolshevik seizure of power and the formation of a new International. Superficially, the divisions in the American party paralleled splits that had fractured almost all of the European parties a year or more earlier. The reality, however, was substantially different. In Europe, particularly in Germany, continued support for the wartime governments meant support for military intervention against the Revolution. In the United States, because those who remained in the party opposed the war, such was not the case; Socialists here were no part of the governing system. More clearly than in Europe, the 1919 breakup of the

American Socialist party was an early effect of the operation of the *law of uneven development* with respect to the Russian Revolution. Unlike the stimulating effect of the 1917 Revolution on the world Socialist movement, particularly in the preindustrial East, the Revolution's occurrence in an industrially and culturally backward country tended to retard the development of Socialist theory and practice in the advanced industrial nations.

In Europe, this tendency was obscured by the reactionary role played by the majorities in all the Socialist parties but the Italian. When war had come to Europe these parties had failed to live up to their earlier commitment to international working-class solidarity. Having immersed themselves in the day-to-day functioning of the trade union movement and in the narrow reforms of parliamentary politics, the various parties had been incapable of resisting either the patriotic appeals of their bourgeoisies or the practical concerns of their trade union base. All had supported the war; many had taken posts in their respective governments. Their attitudes not only toward the war, but also toward the Soviet government and the prospect of revolution in Western Europe, led inexorably to splits in these parties.

The Socialist party in the United States also relied heavily on its work within the trade unions, and the predominant tendencies were toward a narrow parliamentary perspective. Yet the American party was spared the fate of its European counterparts, partly because it had three years to discuss the question of support for the war before the United States became involved, and partly because the party was less successful in the unions than were the European parties, and therefore had less at stake in splitting with prowar unionists. Then, too, the party in the United States still viewed electoral activity primarily as an opportunity for education and agitation. Most European parties had large parliamentary delegations and a heavy stake in maintaining them; the American party had elected only two congressmen, one in 1910, the other in 1914 and 1916. In short, relative lack of success in modes of work that led away from the development of mass Socialist consciousness enabled the American party to remain truer to Socialist principles in time of crisis.

In any case, the Socialist party as a whole condemned the entrance of the United States into war, urged an immediate end to hostilities based on a program of no indemnities and no annexations, and actively agitated against the war as one of imperialist rivalries in which the working class had no real interest. The Russian Revolution was no more a divisive issue than the war; the wartime experience had led the entire party closer to a reassessment of its parliamentary perspective and trade union strategy. Neither reassessment was seriously undertaken, however, because of the split in the American party and the consequent formation of the Communist party and Communist Labor party in September 1919. The split did not occur, as it had in Europe, over the question of support of the war and opposition to the Soviets. Rather, it was over the perspective of the Third International, which was organized in Moscow in January 1919. That perspective grew out of the general belief among Socialists before 1917 that the Revolution would occur in an advanced industrial nation, and that socialism was impossible in a country that had not passed through a prolonged period of capitalist accumulation and industrialization. Lenin concurred, but he argued that the Bolsheviks could *begin* the European revolution by seizing state power in Russia, although the revolution could not survive without revolutionary governments in the West coming to their aid. Thus, the new International was organized on the principle of immediate insurrection in the West. And since the Russian Revolution could not survive without aid from the West, any party that lacked a program of immediate insurrection was defined as objectively anti-Soviet, regardless of its professions of support and solidarity.

As G. Zinoviev wrote in the first issue of *The Communist International* (May 1919), "the dictatorship of the proletariat is the order of the day throughout the civilized world." Two years later Zinoviev spelled out what this meant: those who joined the "Army of Revolution must adopt as their program the program of the Communist International—open and revolutionary mass struggle for Communism through the dictatorship of the Proletariat, by means of the Workers' Soviets." To achieve this, all adherents of the International must "create a strongly centralized form of organization" and "a military discipline." Party members "must be absolutely subject to the full-powered Central Committee of the Party," and must "sever all connections with the petty bourgeoisie, and prepare for revolutionary action, for merciless civil war."

Those in the United States who were to remain Socialists (or drop out of Socialist politics) would not accept this program. To them it was clear that the war had consolidated the hegemony of the American corporate bourgeoisie and strengthened its position vis-à-vis the European imperial powers. "Revolution in Russia," Victor Berger wrote to Morris Hillquit, had been one thing. Russia was "a beaten country," both economically and militarily. By 1917 her first line of military forces was destroyed and the second line was "honey-combed with propaganda." Furthermore, the Socialists "absolutely controlled the trade unions and the landless, starved and hungry peasants had no other place to go than to the Bolsheviki."

"None of these conditions prevail in America," Berger observed. On the contrary, the war, and the Wilson administration's inclusion of labor representatives on government boards for the first time during the war, had "strengthened capitalism, reaction, and *treason* within the *working class*. We can learn from the Bolsheviki," Berger concluded, but "we cannot transfer Russia to America."

Berger's analysis complemented that of Rosa Luxemburg, who warned against taking the Bolshevik experience in backward, pre-industrial Russia as a Socialist model for the West. It would have been demanding the superhuman from Lenin and his comrades, she wrote, that amid the ruin and isolation caused by the war and Allied counter-revolutionary intervention, they should "conjure forth the finest democracy, the most exemplary dictatorship of the proletariat and a flourishing socialist economy." Under the circumstances the Bolshevik achievement was magnificent. The danger began, Luxemburg insisted, "when they make a virtue of necessity and want to freeze into a complete theoretical system all the tactics forced upon them by these fatal circumstances, and want to recommend them to the international proletariat as a model of socialist tactics."

Unfortunately, the International did what Luxemburg warned against. It insisted on the universal validity of programs and policies that emerged from the specific historical circumstances of the Russian Revolution. The first of these policies was that of immediate insurrection, which the Bolsheviks saw—in a sense correctly—as necessary to the survival of their own revolution, but which was impossible in the United States and most of Europe. Later, starting as a tendency under Lenin's leadership and becoming the rule under Stalin's, the policy of the International became an increasingly direct reflection of Russia's process of industrialization under party guidance and of her problems as a national state.

This process created a series of false issues which retarded the development of a Socialist movement in the United States and Western Europe. Beginning with the issue of immediate insurrection, support for the International's policies was equated with support for the Soviet Revolution. Those who became Communists increasingly glorified the evolving Soviet policies and achievements of the period of primitive Socialist accumulation. Those who remained Socialists increasingly defined their own politics in terms of opposition to the Soviets. Eventually, they too began to act as if they believed that the Soviet experience was all that socialism could be. Thus creating a Hobson's choice, they abandoned a serious approach to Socialist revolution in the United States and became nothing more than ideologues for the reformers. In short, the impact of the International was to divert the American Socialist movement (as well as the European) from its primary postwar task, the extension of Marx's theories of capitalist development into the epoch of advanced corporate capitalism and the building of a movement for postaccumulation socialism.

The most obvious example of the mechanistic and ahistoric mimicking of Bolshevik experience in the United States was the adoption of what came to be known as the Leninist party. The Leninist form of party organization was developed in Russia in order to enable Socialists to function under conditions of illegality and Czarist repression. Its two main features were democratic centralism—a top-down, semimilitary process of decision-making—and the concept of a vanguard, which did not mean simply the most advanced political force, but was used to signify a small, elite cadre, a mobile political force, as opposed to a mass or popular party such as those in Western Europe and the United States. At the time of its adoption Lenin explained the necessity for this form of party organization under the harsh conditions of Old Russia. He made it clear that the new form was not abstractly desirable, but made necessary under circumstances that did not allow a party publicly to reveal its identity or to agitate and educate openly for socialism among the masses. Under bourgeois democracy—and, Lenin expected, after a successful revolution—such a party would give way to a more democratic and, therefore, preferable form.

After the Revolution, the Bolsheviks believed, the Leninist party would no longer be necessary; first, because the dictatorship of the proletariat would change the state from a dictatorship of a minority (the bourgeoisie) over the majority (the proletariat) into a dictatorship of the majority over the minority, and second, because with the completion of the process of accumulation, the general technical proficiency of the masses, and the development of new institutions of Socialist self-government, the state itself would dissolve and the party along with it. This process clearly implied a steady debureaucratization and a raising of the level of popular education and culture at least to that of the party cadre, thus eliminating it as an elite. The Soviets were to be such a transitional state, Lenin wrote in April 1917. They were ''a higher type of democratic state,'' which as Engels observed in discussing the Paris Commune, was ''no longer a state in the proper sense of the word.'' The Soviets, like the Commune, would smash the ''machinery of oppression'' of the bourgeois parliamentary republic—the army, the police, the bureaucracy—and permit ''direct participation in the *democratic* organization of the life of the state from the bottom up.'' This kind of government would mean that reforms that had ''not absolutely matured both in economic reality and in the minds of the overwhelming majority of the people'' could not be introduced.

This development, of course, was dependent upon Socialists taking power not only in Russia but in other more highly industrialized countries. As late as February 1922 Lenin proclaimed ''this elementary truth of Marxism, that the victory of socialism *requires* the joint efforts of workers in a number of *advanced* countries.'' Yet, by that year, with the Civil War over, it was clear that there would be no ''help from the West'' in the form of other revolutions. Isolation and the immense weight of Russia's terrible backwardness now had to be faced. By the early period of the Civil War, the Soviets had ceased to function as Lenin had hoped in the euphoria of 1917. Because of the low level of education among the masses, Lenin wrote in March 1919, ''the Soviets, which according to their program were organs of government *by the workers*, are in fact only organs of government *for the workers* by the most advanced section of the proletariat, but not by the working masses themselves.'' By the end of the Civil War the situation was even worse. Large sections of the working class had been destroyed, either as casualties in the war or through dispersal back into the countryside following the destruction of their factories. Instead of having full democratic participation by workers and peasants, the party alone exercised power.

What of this party? Was it to become less hierarchical and centralized now that the authority and power of the bourgeoisie had been destroyed? That, of course, had been the theory before 1917, based on the expectation of revolution in a country with an adequate economic infrastructure and cultural level. In fact, in order to defend its very existence, the Russian party moved in the opposite direction. As Trotsky pointed out, the demobilization of the five-million-man Red army after the Civil War played a large role in the formation of the new bureaucracy. The victorious army commanders returned to civilian life to assume leading posts in the local Soviets, the economy, and in education; everywhere they introduced the mode of leadership that had assured success in the Civil War. Further, the number of Bolsheviks and educated workers was so small that there were not enough to fill even the major portion of industrial management and governmental posts. Instead, the party had to recruit large numbers of former Czarist bureaucrats. By 1922 Russia was governed by a few thousand Bolsheviks at what Lenin called ''the summit of the power structure,'' with hundreds of thousands of former Czarist functionaries at the base and middle levels. These people, of course, had little or no loyalty to socialist ideals, and although they proved loyal to the regime, their ideas and modes of work were profoundly antidemocratic. The Bolsheviks were in a small minority even in the governmental structure.

A centralized, semimilitary party (which maintained as much internal democracy as was possible under the circumstances) had been necessary to function under Czarist repression. During the Civil War, in the face of White armies equipped and aided by the major Western powers, a stricter centralism became imperative—although even then discussion within the party continued within the limits imposed by military necessity. Prohibition of factions and of discussion of fundamental problems—the monolithic party—came only after the war. As Moshe Lewin points out, ''the constantly alarming nature of the situation and the extension of the state of emergency required a constant mobilization of the cadres, their transfer from one front to another, or from a military task to an economic one, and vice versa. No democratic procedure would have made these solutions possible. These methods, which were sanctioned in no way either by theory or by statute'' became the reality of party life. Sincerely believing in the dictatorship of the proletariat, the Bolsheviks first saw the substitution of party for class rule as an unfortunate expedient that would disappear when the workers were organized in the large factories. The continuation of the Leninist party into the post-Revolutionary period was neither anticipated nor desired.

And yet an unwanted and hopefully temporary expedient within Russia became, through the mediation of the International, a model for Communist organization throughout the world. In the East, particularly in China, this development advanced the revolution because the kinds of problems facing revolutionaries there were in many respects similar to those existing in Russia. But the model was also imposed on Communist parties in the highly integrated bourgeois democracies of the West, where the results were negative, except in those parts of Europe under fascist occupation during World War II. This happened partly because Russia's example of successful revolution was so powerful and partly because the task of developing Socialist strategy appropriate to advanced corporate capitalism was so difficult. Had the prewar Socialist party in the United States developed a theory and strategic response to corporate liberalism, the relationship of Russia (through the International) to the American and other Western parties might have been less one-sided. But the old party was not able to do that, even though its wartime experience (the expulsion of Socialist councilmen in Cleveland in 1918 for voting against war bonds, the refusal of the House of Representatives in early 1919 to seat Victor Berger, the expulsion of five Socialist assemblymen from the New York Assembly in 1920) pointed up the limitations of its parliamentary perspective.

In this respect the left wing of 1919 had made a significant advance, based in part on its comprehension of the Bolshevik Revolution. That advance, hazy though it was, was the concept of mass action, which, according to the leading left-wing theoretician, Louis Fraina, implied ''the end of exclusive concentration on parliamentary tactics.'' Its value was that it redefined political action, which in the old parlance simply meant electoral activity. Mass action, Fraina explained, meant bringing ''mass proletarian pressure on the capitalist state'' by shifting the center of activity from the parliaments to the shops and the streets, making parliamentary activity only one phase of mass action. Understanding and sharing Lenin's vision of the Soviets as a transitional form of the state, Fraina wrote that such a form had been implied in the revolutionary industrial unionism of the IWW, of which he had been a member. But in the IWW the idea of a transitional state had never been developed. The IWW had no theory of the state or of a highly integrated economy. Fraina was now concerned with these questions because of the Revolution, which, along with its opposition to the war, had brought him back into the American party in 1917. But Fraina's thinking was original and advanced, and in the left wing he stood almost alone in that respect.

That this was so is reflected in the brief life of *The New York Communist*, organ of the Left Wing Section of the Greater New York Locals of the Socialist party, which was published in early 1919. At that time the left wing in Boston had already been publishing *The Revolutionary Age* for several months as the official organ of Local Boston, the first major local to be won by the left wing. After the formal organization of New York's Left Wing Section, John Reed and others tried to have *The Revolutionary Age* transferred to New York. But Fraina (the editor) and his comrades refused the offer and on April 19, 1919, the first issue of *The New York Communist* appeared—with John Reed as editor, Eadmonn McAlpine as associate editor, and Maximillian Cohen as business manager. Identifying with Fraina and his Boston paper, *The New York Communist* started out as a more or less temporary affair, and, as anticipated in the first issue, published only until the national Left Wing Conference met in New York on June 21, 1919, and made *The Revolutionary Age* its official organ.

In the short span of ten issues *The New York Communist* demonstrated a self-confidence appropriate to a rapidly growing trend and to a group still caught up in the euphoria of the successful revolution in Russia. Reed and his colleagues viewed the Socialist party moderates as consistent supporters of "liberal state capitalism" as a result of their commitment to parliamentarianism. Although they did not yet attack the old party leadership as prowar, they did tend to equate it with European social democracy, which, Reed wrote, was "as responsible for the war as Wilhelm."

Clearly, the New York left wing anticipated a continuing upsurge of revolutionary sentiment and consciousness among American workers. With thousands of Socialists and IWWs in prison, *The New York Communist* opposed participation in a planned amnesty convention, writing that the time had come for Socialists "to withdraw from active cooperation in reform movements, and to devote their energies to organizing the proletariat so as to make its strength felt directly—which will do away with the necessity for Amnesty Conventions.'' In this, Reed was echoed by Fraina, who wrote that while the party's center proposed ''cooperation with bourgeois and essentially reactionary organizations in Amnesty Conventions,'' the principled way to proceed was through ''a mass political strike to compel the liberation of our imprisoned comrades.'' Two weeks later, without seeing the implications, *The New York Communist* reported a series of attacks on May Day parades by mobs of soldiers, sailors, and police, and explained that in Europe similar parades had not been attacked because there the working class was too well organized.

While the left wing in New York, as throughout the United States, became more and more caught up with the insurrectionary perspective of the new Communist International, the old leadership of the Socialist party reacted to the wartime repression and postwar antiradical hysteria by appealing to traditional American democratic rights and liberal values. Thus, at the same time, each wing of the Socialist movement exhibited one side of the polarity that has characterized the movement as a whole since World War I: in its *revolutionary* phase a resort to abstract revolutionary appeals; in its *popular* (defensive) stage a falling back on the dominant liberalism. As later events would demonstrate, neither side had developed significant new politics; they were simply out of phase with each other.

Beyond this, *The New York Communist* was caught up in the turbulent events of the spring of 1919, particularly the struggle for control of the Socialist party organization. That story—the expulsion of 40 percent of the party membership by the old National Executive Committee, the refusal of the New York Local to recognize the left wing, the Left's confidence that it represented a large majority of the membership—is well known. The short life of *The New York Communist* is no indication of failure or collapse. Quite the contrary, it came into being to serve a specific purpose. It served that purpose and ceased publishing at the peak of enthusiasm within the left wing of the old party.

San Francisco, 1969

The Revolutionary Age

BOSTON AND NEW YORK,

1918-1919

MARTIN GLABERMAN AND GEORGE P. RAWICK

THE history of the formation of the American Communist party is embodied in the brief life of *The Revolutionary Age*, and many of the problems of American communism are reflected in this journal. Founded in 1918 as the organ of the left wing of the Socialist party, *The Revolutionary Age* was first published in Boston, then a stronghold of the foreign-language federations that were the backbone of the left wing. Later the journal was moved to New York.

The editor of *The Revolutionary Age* was Louis C. Fraina. At that time, and for a short period thereafter, Fraina was the leading theoretical and political figure of the Socialist Left and of the early Communist movement. As a result of difficulties that were in part personal and accidental, he disappeared from the scene for a number of years. He reemerged in the 1930s as Lewis Corey and produced some interesting work as an independent Marxist. His early difficulties, however, resulted in his being expunged from all official Communist histories.

Together with Fraina were most of the leading figures of the left wing. The managing editor was Eadmonn McAlpine. Among the contributors were John Reed and Jay Lovestone. On the controlling board were C. E. Ruthenberg (who was the leading figure in the young Communist party until his death in 1927), Benjamin Gitlow, and Bertram D. Wolfe. Gitlow, Wolfe, and Lovestone were associated in 1929 with an entirely different *Revolutionary Age*, which was the first organ of the Lovestone group at the time of its expulsion from the Communist party.

Associated with the American editors of *Revolutionary Age* was Sen Katayama, the Japanese Communist, then in his declining years and living in the United States. Among those whose articles appeared in its pages were Chicherin, the Soviet foreign minister; Bukharin; and, most notably, Lenin, whose "Letter to American Workers" first appeared there.

The kinds of problems that plagued the young Communist movement were reflected in *Revolutionary Age*. It was entirely concerned with European news and events. Revolutionary events in Russia, in Germany, and in Europe generally were its overwhelming concern. While this of necessity would have to be a major concern of any left-wing revolutionary newspaper or journal, it could not legitimately exclude all American events without considerably distorting its character as a national organ. It was an English-language journal and yet the majority of its editorial board was foreign-born and primarily concerned with events overseas. It is not too much to say that their belief in and support of an American revolution, while genuine, was, on the whole, abstract and relegated to some distant future. Their belief in a European revolution was concrete and immediate.

A similar orientation applied to the theory of the new movement. Fraina was the leading theoretical figure and at the time the most prominent spokesman for the Socialist Left. If he had any organizational leanings or capacities he, and not C. E. Ruthenberg, undoubtedly would have become the first head of the united Communist party. Yet Fraina was not a profound theoretician on the level of many in the European Socialist and Communist movements. Lenin, Plekhanov, Luxemburg, Bernstein, Kautsky, and some others towered above him. It is not at all a matter of comparing lists of attainments; it is simply the theoretical poverty of American socialism and communism. Although there was some excellent political journalism in *Revolutionary Age*, nowhere did it (or its antecedents or successors) reach the levels of seriousness or originality of some of the European Marxist journals.

It was an inevitable consequence that the theory of fledgling American communism was substantially a European theory. American society was not subjected to the searching analysis that the European Marxists directed at their own countries. This further intensified the dependence of the editors of *Revolutionary Age* on European Marxist theory. As far as European Marxist practice was concerned, the pull was even stronger. It was the pull of the Russian Revolution, a successful proletarian revolution in a world they viewed as one of death and reaction. Compared to that, there did not seem to be any urgency in reporting the activities of American workers.

Most historians of the period credit the European orientation of the early years of American communism to the great weight within the movement of the foreign-language federations. An examination of the significant facts, however, would seem to indicate that this was not an objectively necessary relationship. While it is true enough that most of the editors of *The Revolutionary Age* were foreign-born and included several who directly represented foreign federations (such as N. I. Hourwich and G. Weinstein), the journal was effectively edited by what was essentially the American wing of the Socialist Left. John Reed, C. E. Ruthenberg, Wolfe, and Fraina himself, in the initial split in the left wing which led to the short-lived formation of two Communist parties, leaned toward the American-oriented Communist Labor party.

But what is more significant is the role played by the foreign-language federations. The Lithuanian federation dominated the left wing for a while, and was gradually replaced by the Russian organization, which gained in membership and influence as a result of the Russian revolution. But this need not have led to the virtually exclusive discussion of European matters.

What is rarely recognized is the fact that for a period of years following 1908 the majority of the American industrial working class was foreign-born. And the majority of these were among the newer immigrants who were represented in the Socialist federations, immigrants from Eastern and Southern Europe. It seems reasonable to assume, therefore, that a concern for foreign-born workers did not at the same time have to alienate the leftist Socialists and Communists from American problems. It could very well have had the opposite effect, of immersing the Left in the mainstream of American working-class activity. What was involved, apparently, was not the nature of the membership of the new Communist organizations, but the nature of the leadership. In part it was the leaders' orientation toward Europe and European politics. In part it was also the fact that an orientation toward American workers and American politics most often meant an orientation toward traditional union organizations such as the AFL. And this resulted in reaching for the native American, relatively skilled workers who were found in those organizations, and ignoring the unskilled foreign-born workers who could be found in their own organizations and in the unorganized mass-production industries. The inability of the Socialists to relate to the immigrant workers inevitably carried over to the Communists. The foreign-language federations were not organs of working-class struggle. They were more like fraternal organizations whose politics were oriented toward the old country.

This contradiction was never recognized and so could not be grappled with. The result (and, to some degree, the cause) of this contradiction can be seen in the pages of *The Revolutionary Age*. But it was expressed in the relative narrowness of the journal, in its self-imposed limitations.

In 1919, with Fraina still as editor, *The Revolutionary Age* became the national organ of the newly organized Communist Labor party. This did not result in any broadening of the journal's interests or concerns. In September 1919, the two factions of American communism united into a single organization. *The Revolutionary Age* was replaced by *The Communist* as the official party organ. Fraina remained as editor of *The Communist*. He was given what amounted to the second-ranking post in the united party, that of international secretary and editor of party publications. Ruthenberg was made national secretary.

Despite its limitations, which were really part of the Communist movement as a whole, *The Revolutionary Age* had an independence and a verve, a liveliness and a freedom, which did not last very long as characteristics of Communist organs.

Detroit and Rochester, Michigan, 1968

The Socialist

NEW YORK, 1919

JOSEPH R. CONLIN

THE Russian Revolution could have been a tonic to the American Socialist movement, but it proved rather to be a fatal poison. Instead of invigorating the Socialist party of America through its inspiration, the Revolution led many American radicals to conclude that the Bolsheviks had drafted a universally applicable blueprint for Socialist victory and had to scrap any contradictory ideas they had previously held. The Left Wing Section of the party, which developed around this principle, soon set out to remake the SPA in the Bolshevik image and, in doing so, helped to tear the once-significant organization to pieces.

Since the Bolsheviks had taken power in Russia through a forceful *coup*, the Left Wing Section expected socialism to come to America in one fell swoop also, and insisted that the party abandon its parliamentary tactics and "immediate demands." The Bolsheviks had operated underground, so their American disciples were drawn away from the SPA's traditional openness to the romance of conspiracy. And since the Bolsheviks had triumphed after a split in the Russian Socialist movement, the left wing resolved that a split of the SPA was not only not undesirable but a positive, progressive step.

The Left Wing Section was literally a party within a party. It had its own program; it collected dues, authorized locals, and published its own newspapers. Factionalism in the SPA was nothing new. But the highly formal organization of the left wing's campaign and its explicit avowals by the spring of 1919 that it planned to expel right-wing elements were innovations.

Also new was the nature of the left-wing press. Previous Socialist

159

publications had paid plenty of attention to internal disputes and had usually taken sides in them. But they continued to serve some other principal purpose, generally the winning of converts to socialism. The new organs of the Left Wing Section, however—*The Revolutionary Age* of Boston, John Reed's *New York Communist, The Ohio Socialist* of Cleveland, and a half dozen others—were devoted almost entirely to factional purposes and to waging the Comintern's "merciless fight" against right-wing comrades.

The right wing—those Socialists not unfriendly to the Bolsheviks but committed to a parliamentary program and not sanguine about imminent revolution—did not let the attacks go unanswered. They controlled the party administration and much of the established party press. In the most critical theater of the battle, New York City, where Left and Right were about evenly divided, a group of right-wingers actually organized a counterpart to *The Communist*, a purely factional organ designed in this case to clear the decks of the leftists. This was the deliberately and defiantly named *Socialist*.

Its contributors (there was no editorial board as such) were not anti-Russian by any means. But they clung to the SPA's traditional methods and demurred at the Left's implicit argument that Bolshevik methods were applicable in America. They abhorred the Left's organization-wrecking program to the extent that they were themselves willing to tear the party apart.

The Socialist's most effective polemicist was Louis Waldman, a lawyer of some celebration within the party who hammered indefatigably at the weaknesses in the left-wing manifesto. Waldman traveled from local to local in his efforts to keep them in line, and he delivered numerous speeches on the subject of the left wing, many of which were printed in *The Socialist*. Another in the circle was state party committeeman David P. Berenberg, who was the first to move actively for the expulsion of left-wing locals as early as April 13, 1919, a week before *The Socialist* first appeared. Abraham Beckerman, a Socialist leader in the International Ladies Garment Workers Union, was an early opponent of the left-wing program and served as *The Socialist*'s "business manager" and coordinator.

The motives of the publishers were mixed. On the one hand, parts of

Waldman's and Berenberg's writings are thoughtful, telling, and even temperate critiques of the left-wing manifesto. They and their associates had seen established party tactics prove successful in the past, and they sometimes vaguely perceived the irrelevance of Bolshevik methods to American conditions. On the other hand, a left-wing triumph within the party would have meant at least the removal of the right-wingers from their organizational positions. There is more than a little of the old-fashioned spoils fight in *The Socialist*'s campaign and more than a few party hack-types associated with it. As right or as wrong as *The Socialist* might have been in its reasoning, it was the voice of an entrenched old guard. This came out clearly enough in August Claessens' satire of left-wing demands:

> All members of over 30 years' service in the movement must be speedily oslerized.
> Members of 20 years of service must be expelled.
> Those of 10 years' service should be recalled from all offices and committees.
> Members of 5 years' standing should be suspiciously watched.
> They show signs of persistency, therefore reaction.

There is no doubt that *The Socialist* resented the impudence of the party's young Turks.

The Socialist was ad hoc by definition, aimed solely at discrediting and emasculating the Left Wing Section in New York City. It was first published in late April of 1919, shortly after the Left's overwhelming victories in a party referendum and its election of twelve of fifteen National Committee seats and four of five international delegacies. As *The Socialist* inveighed, the party's right wing was acting. It nulled the election and expelled the 6,000 members of the Michigan party and the seven foreign-language federations (20,000 members), which had made the victory possible. The purge would continue until actually more than half of the party had been cast out. But the effect of the campaign was clear by the middle of June: the right wing would control what was left of the organization. *The Socialist* folded happily by the end of the month, its purpose served. Indeed, it is difficult to think of any other American

Socialist periodical that had as complete a success as *The Socialist* and its left-wing counterparts. They set out to split the party, and they did so in grand style.

It would be a foolish enterprise to deal out blame for the split of 1919. It was an event as predetermined as the Communists of 1919 believed their Revolution to be. The left wing of the party was swept up in near hysteria by the Russian excitement with men of the caliber of Louis Fraina, Bertram Wolfe, and John Reed enamored of a program that was utterly unrealistic in the United States. And the party's right wing clung doggedly to the puny prize of organizational control in a manner that reduces Michels' "Iron Law of Oligarchy" to the absurd.

If there was no delineable sin, however, there was a clear penance. The membership of the unified SPA in January 1919 was 110,000. Two years later, the right-wing remnant of the party had 11,000 members. The left wing's Communist party fared worse; its 1921 membership was about 10,000. The once significant American Socialist movement fell to this sorry state for many reasons. One of them is that an aggressive, outgoing movement turned to fratricide and alienated those comrades more interested in effective action. As a major voice of one of the contending factions, *The Socialist* is a valuable source for understanding the split. It is also, curiously, a neglected one. Although both of the students closest to the dispute make considerable use of *The Socialist*'s left-wing counterparts, neither even mentions *The Socialist*.

On May 17, the editors of *The New York Communist* put out a bogus issue of *The Socialist*. The concept of the twit bears the stamp of *Communist* editor John Reed but its satire seems rather too heavyhanded for much of it to have issued from his pen. The imitation presented a variety of parodies of typical *Socialist* articles, including "Another" speech by Louis Waldman delivered at Madison Square Garden on April Fool's Day. The genuine *Socialist* minutely described the perpetration of the hoax in its edition of June 4.

The incident is hardly important in itself. What it reveals, however, is the extent of bitterness with which the two factions fought their battle. What might have been a good prank falls ponderously flat. And the real *Socialists*'s reaction was hopelessly priggish. Its contention that the purpose of the hoax was profit is apparently serious. And, *The Socialist* went on, "Every word of the fake issue was written in what appeared to be a careful attempt to fool the unthinking into believing that they were reading a copy of the real thing,'' a statement that belied *The Socialist*'s low opinion of its readers' intelligence. ''It is a depressing new chapter in the Socialist history of this country,'' the editors continued, noting as the only bright spot the fact that Comrade Bertha Mailly was practically prostrate with grief in the knowledge that the Rand Book Store had unwittingly sold copies of the phony issue that were planted there. (Comrade Mailly returned all of the misspent nickels.)

There was a depressing chapter in the history of American socialism being written, surely enough, but it was not this silly episode. It was the whole phenomenon of 1919.

Eynsham, Oxford, 1969

The New Justice

LOS ANGELES, 1919-1920

JOSEPH R. CONLIN

AMERICAN news reporting of the Russian Revolution and Civil War was woefully distorted. The press inflated the excesses of the Reds and either ignored or played down the atrocities of the Whites. The papers distorted the nature of the allied intervention in Russia, misrepresented the progress of the war, and pictured the Bolshevik leaders as scarcely human. The language of *The New Justice* in describing the situation was flamboyant, but its assessment was not inaccurate: the columns of "the capitalist newspapers . . . were flooded with a deluge of falsehoods that turned them into fathomless morasses of mendacity in which the truth could be hit only by accident."

In part this situation reflected the general American inexperience in foreign correspondence and the journalistic difficulties inherent in the chaotic Russian scene. But the distortion also represented a conscious policy of the American press to propagandize rather than to report on all things socially radical. The policy was perfected in the smears of the Industrial Workers of the World before World War I, and the press went fairly berserk during the war itself. This mood carried beyond the armistice in its application to the Russian Communists.

There were exceptions; the Bolsheviks had some friends in influential positions. A few large newspapers attempted to make sense of the Revolution, and some liberal periodicals, such as *The Nation, New Republic*, and *Dial*, spoke up on behalf of the Soviets. But these were the anomalies. The major burden of combating the diabolical image of the Russian Revolution devolved on the small American Left.

The radicals were willing. American Socialists reacted almost unanimously with enthusiasm to the news of the October Revolution. Themselves discouragingly harassed during the war, the Socialists were happy to share vicariously in the Russian coup. By 1920, some American Socialists and Wobblies began to sour on the Bolsheviks, but in the meantime, they defended the Revolution to the full extent of their resources. This they did primarily through reporting pro-Bolshevik news in the established Socialist press, and in some cities, they founded new journals avowedly devoted to the defense of the Russians. The fortnightly *New Justice* was one of these ad hoc ventures, the work of a group of "friends of the Russian Revolution" in Southern California. Los Angeles in 1919 was no hotbed of radical activity, so that the city's regular press took some note of the novelty in the midst. The *Citizen* represented the new magazine as a misguided but dangerous spokesman for Lenin and Trotsky. W. J. Ghent and a number of other old-Socialists-become-anti-Communists published an anti-Bolshevik sheet called *The California Commonwealth*, which was in part a response to *The New Justice*. And the rarely outdone *Los Angeles Times* went so far as to call the journal "the organ of the Los Angeles Bolsheviks."

In fact, *The New Justice* was the voice of no organization, least of all the American Communist parties, which had not even been founded when the magazine was first published. Its overlarge editorial board (sixteen persons) was a ménage too diverse to agree on much more than the idea that the Revolution deserved a chance to survive. Calling themselves "Socialists," the editors considered *The New Justice* to be "a radical magazine." And they printed many of the sort of articles typical of the Socialist magazines of the day, on topics ranging from the Seattle General Strike to "Socialism in Old Norse Legends." But the general tone of *The New Justice* does not quite fit in with the uncompromising, even arrogant, tenor of most of the contemporary Socialist publications—and this despite the editors' obvious effort to sound just so. One of *The New Justice*'s five purposes was vaguely stated as "Industrial Democracy, Social Justice, Unity of the World's Workers." But the first four included nothing to which any genuine libertarian could take exception: self-determination of nations, honest journalism, amnesty for political prisoners, and restoration of civil liberties abridged during wartime.

It is instructive that the editors rarely abused President Woodrow Wilson. When Wilson was attacked, it was as a betrayer of principles rather than as a natural enemy. And when *The New Justice* listed political prisoners like Emma Goldman, the "leader of militant anarchism," and Big Bill Haywood, the "leader of militant industrial unionism," it included Roger Baldwin as the "leader of militant Americanism, if you please." The *Los Angeles Times* to the contrary notwithstanding, these were not steely Leninists, but liberal, basically unrevolutionary humanitarians. Their self-stylization as Socialists is less important than the numerous points on which they differed from other Americans of that persuasion.

In its analysis of the war, for example, *The New Justice* does not voice the usual radical account of high finance and munitions manufacturers beaming over wartime profits. Coeditor Clarence Meily thought that there was "no doubt that the war, with its fearful destruction of wealth, its enforced socialization of industry, and its revolutionary aftermath, has plunged international capitalism into a profound panic. 'Never Again' has become its motto." The reasoning is hardly unique in the history of Socialist thought, but it was peculiar among American radicals in 1919. The idea that the war had progressive side effects—"socialization" in this case—is, nevertheless, reminiscent of contemporary liberals of *The New Republic* stripe.

The thrust of *The New Justice*'s pleas on behalf of the Bolsheviks is also worth noting. The magazine did not seek to picture the Russian Communists so much as the universal saviors of the working peoples as it attempted merely to assert the acceptability, the legitimacy, even the dull respectability, of the Revolution. In his regular department, "The Truth About Russia," J. H. Ryckman collected information correcting specific distortions in the conservative press, documents demonstrating the reasonableness of the Bolsheviks in their foreign relations, and a pot-pourri illustrating Soviet cooperation with organizations such as the Red Cross, the YMCA, and the YWCA. The low-keyed approach was calculated to demonstrate that the Bolsheviks were not quite beasts. In one issue, *The New Justice* presented a quite unsatirical appeal to American business:

There was a market, one of the richest and most inexhaustible in the world, which belonged almost of right to the United States, which was begging for American goods, and glorying in what it thought was American friendship. That market was Russia.

Not that "radicals" should mourn the lost opportunities of American imperialism, the editors added lamely. Still, proviso or not, it was the sort of argument that John Reed, Louis Fraina, or Max Eastman could not have conceived.

The magazine's attitude toward fellow American Socialists comes close to scorn. This is more strident in the final issues, but is present even in the first, when *The New Justice* gloated over how "professional" agitators were left dumb struck and impotent in the face of a strike they thought impossible. Even more remarkable in an ostensibly Socialist publication is *The New Justice*'s nearly complete unconcern with Socialist party affairs, although the months when it was published were the most tumultuous and critical in the party's history. A "Left Wing Section," veritably a party within a party, had developed around the intention of capturing the entire organization and remolding it along Russian Communist lines. This program included a purge of right-wing elements, but the right wing acted first and expelled a large number of left-wing locals. One contingent of the excommunicants organized the Communist party. Another made a final, futile attempt to capture the Socialists and then formed their own Communist Labor party.

But these most remarkable events went all but unnoticed by *The New Justice*. In August the magazine took passing note of the "regrettable controversy" among the comrades. Two months later it commented in exasperation that the split was "too deplorable to be amusing and too preposterous to be taken seriously."

The fact is that *The New Justice* took it seriously enough. It was relatively silent only because the editors were mystified by the heated ideological debate within the party. "Practical issues unite people," they stated curtly, "while theoretical issues divide them." And, as the Socialist-Communist Left dissipated into a tangle of gaggling cults, *The New Justice* editors drifted into issue and action politics. In 1920, they cooperated with the Labor party's attempt to fuse Socialists, trade unionists, and liberals in accordance with the British precedent. *The New Justice* was quite as confident as the Leninists that some sort of social upheaval was imminent in 1919. At one point, it urged workers to forget "economic criticism" and start learning the techniques of industrial administration. But where the American Leninists prepared for the catastrophe by purifying the cadres of future power, *The New Justice* hastened to broaden the "revolutionary" movement. The new Communists were drawn toward conspiracy and the romanticism of underground operation; *The New Justice* represented the old social democratic ideal of an open party. While both right- and left-wing Socialists were hell-bent on the expulsion of deviants, *The New Justice* set as its "special desire, the winning over of non-radicals who are inclined liberally."

The oddity of the magazine's position partly accounts for its demise less than a year after its founding. On the one hand, most Socialists were uninterested in its line. On the other, it could be successfully red-baited by shrill newspapers like the *Los Angeles Times*. In addition, *The New Justice* never quite managed to establish the distinct personality that is the *sine qua non* of any successful publication. Not that it served no purpose. To the extent that it was read, it helped to counter the distortions of Russian news in the regular press. But this was an essentially negative function on an issue that aroused little enthusiasm in the country at large and required no belaboring among Socialists.

The magazine might have survived as the focus of progressive political action on the West Coast if its editors had pursued the goal with any tenacity. But they vacillated too long between the idea of serving a sectional purpose and heady notions of a national role. As a result, their coverage of West Coast radical news was at best spotty. For example, there is practically nothing in these pages on the trial of the Wobblies at Sacramento or the Tom Mooney case, which was to loom so large as a rallying point in the region in the future. In this direction, too, *The New Justice* proved inadequate.

All of which boiled down to the familiar financial crisis. *The New Justice* missed its September 15 issue and announced in October that it would become a monthly. The editors stated candidly that the journal had appeared that month thanks only to a fortuitous subvention and that "unless a plan of adequate support of the magazine is promptly put into effect, this issue will be our last." *The New Justice* needed 5,000 subscriptions at $1 per year to pay for itself; it had only 500. Or, the magazine could survive with twelve contributions of $5 each month. The

November issue was brought out with half that many donors. There was no December number, and the tone of the final *New Justice* in January 1920 was one of stupefied despair. The federal government had deported 249 Russian radical aliens on December 21, 1919. New York Communist organizations had been raided as early as November, and on January 2 and 5, 1920, the famous raids on radical headquarters all over the nation were staged by Attorney General A. Mitchell Palmer. The editors of *The New Justice* simply did not know what to say. They were individuals with a consummate faith in the essential benignity of American democracy. They felt that only lies stood between the Russian revolutionaries and the sympathy of the American people. They thought that an equitable social order was little more than a matter of time and education. So the cynicism laid bare by the Palmer raids was a cruel blow. The editorial on the subject is literally dumfoundedness in print. Even if its finances had been sound, it is difficult to imagine *The New Justice* surviving the end of that bizarre year.

Eynsham, Oxford, 1969

The Workers' Council

NEW YORK, 1921

JOSEPH R. CONLIN

LIKE many radical periodicals, *The Workers' Council* had a short life. Founded as a biweekly, it actually published only ten numbers between April 1 and December 15, 1921, with one long hiatus during the summer. It was staid in appearance and style, featured cartoons after the manner of Robert Minor's in *The Masses*, and printed speeches by the revolutionary leaders of the Soviet Union.

But the columns of *The Workers' Council* were primarily devoted to events within the little world of American radical politics. The journal's specific purpose was to win the Socialist party of America to affiliation with the recently founded Third or Communist International (Comintern). Its publishers included some Socialists who were apparently part of the party establishment. J. Louis Engdahl, for example, was editor of the SPA's official organ, *The Eye Opener*. Alexander Trachtenberg, a veteran of the 1905 Russian Revolution, was prominent in the affairs of the Rand School, the SPA's "academy." William F. Kruse was head of the party's youth section, the Young Peoples' Socialist League. Others were Benjamin Glassberg, a New York City schoolteacher; Moissaye J. Olgin, a popular Jewish writer; and J. B. Salutsky, editor of the radical Jewish weekly, *Naye Welt*. All were at least personally connected with the party's Jewish Federation and, organized after mid-1920 as the Committee for the Third International, they comprised the SPA's left wing.

The nature of their organ, *The Workers' Council*, must be seen against the background of the American Socialist movement's organizational history between 1919 and 1921. The story is a fantastic tangle of competing parties, sometimes with the same name; myriad factions within parties; legal and illegal organizations; expulsions, secessions, and fusions. Theodore Draper remarked trenchantly in *The Roots of American Communism* (New York, 1957) that anyone not "slightly confused" by the course of events "cannot be sure that he has fully recaptured the Communist atmosphere in this particular period."

The SPA emerged from World War I in one piece but divided within itself. The party's traditional right-left division was based on questions of trade unionism, parliamentarianism, and the "immediate program," but the distinctive dimension of the postwar split was the product of the Russian Revolution. Just as the prewar party Left had been attracted to the Industrial Workers of the World by the union's aura of excitement and dramatic strike victories in cities such as Lawrence, Massachusetts, the postwar Left looked worshipfully to the more formidable Russian Bolsheviks.

The Revolution worked magic among American Socialists. For two decades they had poured their souls into the struggle against capitalism with precious little to show for their efforts. Although they had elected a thousand public officials, "Socialism" remained an abstract as vaporous as it had been on the day the SPA was founded. By 1917, American Socialists were in the habit of living with the prospect of a long and tedious struggle.

Then overnight arrived the news from Russia of a revolution engineered by a few revolutionaries as obscure as the American Socialists! Vladimir Ilych Lenin's name was hardly known in the United States. Leon Trotsky was personally known to New York City Socialists—as an anonymous tenement dweller who, like themselves, passed whole nights in seemingly trivial discussions about founding weekly newspapers. After 1917 it was not possible to see any revolutionary act as trivial. Nor did it seem preposterous to wonder hopefully who would be the "American Trotsky" and the "American Lenin."

It would be difficult to overstate the Revolution's psychological impact on American left-wing Socialists. Their awe extended beyond the Bolsheviks to Russian immigrant members of the SPA to whom they humbly deferred as if, by virtue of national origin, the Russians possessed special revolutionary wisdom. But the Revolution's ultimate effect on American Socialists was neither harmless nor silly. Deference to Russian immigrants evolved into obeisance to the directives of Moscow. Much of the SPA's left wing, moreover, concluded that the Bolshevik revolutionary pattern provided a scientific guideline for Americans: thus, because the Russian Revolution had been accomplished by violence and at one fell swoop, the left wing reasoned that Americans must do the same and confirmed their contempt for parliamentarianism and "immediate programs"; the Bolsheviks had operated underground, so their American imitators assumed a conspiratorial air; the Bolsheviks had managed their revolution only after a split in the Russian Socialist movement, so the SPA's left wing resolved that it too must divide the party.

There was indeed a split but it originated with the right wing. After the left wing elected a majority of the party's National Executive Committee in 1919, the Right claimed fraud, nulled the election, and in late May expelled some 26,000 left-wing members. Within six months the minority right wing read out of the party about two-thirds of the total membership. Such a remarkable manipulation was possible only because much of the left wing was happy to be expelled. In September 1919, they organized the Communist party (CP) in Chicago. A second section of the left wing ventured a final attempt to capture the SPA but, after prompt failure, organized the Communist Labor party (CLP).

This was not the end of the Communists' fragmentation. One splinter of the CP bolted in 1920 to form the Proletarian party. Another, led by C. E. Ruthenberg, split and for a month led a separate existence using the same name, the Communist party. From that point the trend was to reunion. Ruthenberg's group joined with the CLP in May 1920 under the name of the United Communist party. A year later, under pressure from Moscow, this UCP and the CP allied as the Communist party of America.

All this left within the SPA only the traditional right wing and the group which would publish *The Workers' Council*. This rump of the left wing agreed with the secessionist Communists on most points. That is, they scorned the right wing's parliamentarianism and "immediate program" and they advocated affiliation with the Comintern. But they stopped short of leaving the party in 1919. They had been in the party longer than many of the Communists (the Russian Federation, for example, had not been founded until 1915), and retained strong attachments to the old warhorse of American socialism. Several of the reduced left wing, like Engdahl and Kruse, also held important organizational positions, which they were reluctant to give up. More important, they were not so uncritical of the Bolsheviks as were the American Communists. Trachtenberg applauded the liberal March revolution in Russia and briefly remained skeptical of the Bolsheviks even after they seized power. Olgin's *Soul of the Russian Revolution*, published in 1917, took an anti-Bolshevik position.

Even after the Bolsheviks won their admiration, the SPA Left balked at accepting without reservation the Comintern's prescriptions for proper American revolutionary methods. At the 1919 Socialist convention, their minority resolution that the party affiliate with the Comintern pointed out the difference between Russian and American conditions. Finally, the left-wing Socialists still hoped to capture the SPA. It was no pipedream: even after the expulsion of 1919, the Left's minority resolution to affiliate with the Comintern won a party referendum over the right wing's more equivocal policy.

But circumstances during 1920 and 1921 dashed the hopes of the SPA Left. Banking on the new Communist parties in the United States, the Comintern brusquely rejected the SPA's application for membership in 1919. Within the party the Left grew more amenable to Bolshevik demands while the Right gravitated toward an independent course. At the 1920 convention the left wing moved for unconditional affiliation while right-wing leader Morris Hillquit proposed affiliation with certain conditions. When Hillquit's policy carried the party, Engdahl, Kruse, Trachtenberg, Olgin, Glassberg, and Salutsky organized the Committee for the Third International.

The Committee and the formally independent *Workers' Council* occupied a position midway between the majority Socialists and the Communist parties. Criticisms of the SPA dominated the journal's pages during the first half of the year. The party's failure to affiliate with the Comintern, the *Council* argued, was a tragic blunder. If American conditions were indeed unlike the Russian, it was also true that Soviet Russia had challenged world imperialism and was harassed by the capitalist nations simply because it was a proletarian state. American

Socialists must not abandon this marvelous phenomenon. "Let Russia lead the way," one writer rhapsodized,

> Let the American workers realize that Russia's fight is their fight, that Soviet Russia's success is the success of the laboring people the world over! Hail Soviet Russia, the first Communist Republic, the land of, by and for the common people. . . . Comrades in America, watch the bright dawn in the East; you have but your chains to lose, and a world to gain.

But, especially in its final issues, *The Workers' Council* was also harshly critical of the American Communists. The fundamental point of friction was the Communists' tenacious insistence that Bolshevik methods could be fruitfully employed in the United States. At the end of 1919, the two Communist parties had retreated underground, dissolving their public organizations and regrouping as an illegal party. *The Workers' Council* demanded an open, legal party. While the Communists claimed that the Palmer Raids of 1919 necessitated a conspiratorial organization, the *Council* group attributed the move to an adolescent "atmosphere of revolution and romanticism that the Russian upheaval had generated." The journal pointed out that governmental persecution of radicals had eased and argued that secret organizations were incapable of converting the masses. Evincing the group's roots in the formerly heterogeneous Socialist party of America, *The Workers' Council* warned that an illegal organization prevented healthy dialogue within the revolutionary movement. A conspiratorial party by definition required iron discipline and "To demand unswerving allegiance to a set of doctrines that tomorrow may prove false, encourages unthinking slavish obedience," no manner in which to liberate the oppressed of capitalism.

Along with the Jewish Federation, *The Workers' Council* quit the Socialist party when the convention of 1921 made it clear that the party would remain independent of the Comintern. The journal then directed its attention to organizing, in league with the Communists, an all new, legal party. During the last week of December 1921, *The Workers' Council*, the Communist party of America, and several other groups met in New York City and established the Workers' party. The new organization represented a theoretical victory for *The Workers' Council*. The party adopted as its own the journal's prospectus of September 15, 1921, with the exception that an ostensibly controlling illegal organization, the Communist party of America, continued to exist. Even it was scrapped in April 1923.

It was not, of course, the little periodical's juggernaut logic which persuaded the Communists to reverse their position of two years. The key to that step was the American publication, in January 1921, of V. I. Lenin's *"Left Wing" Communism: An Infantile Disorder*, and the directives of the Third Congress of the Communist International. With these events Moscow declared that the worldwide revolution was not imminent and that it was disastrous for revolutionaries to act as if it were. This decision forced the CPA to adopt an immediate program, emerge from underground, and fuse with groups like *The Workers' Council*, which the party had shortly before castigated as reactionary. But the Workers' party was not simply a Russian creation. *The Workers' Council* group had preached what became the Workers' party line in 1919 and 1920 while Lenin supported the American Communist line. Throughout 1921, *The Workers' Council* was published to the same effect, seizing on Lenin's analyses but not deriving from them. In a sense, the group secured in the Workers' party the sort of organization into which, until mid-1921, it had tried to convert the SPA.

The journal may also be read as the last realistic attempt in the United States to reconcile the old social democracy with the new communism. James Weinstein writes in the *Decline of Socialism in America*,

> Programmatically, the formation of the Workers' Party meant a full cycle return to the Socialist party position of 1919. The new party's program omitted all reference to the dictatorship of the proletariat, to workers' Soviets, to violent revolution; instead of calling on workers to seize power immediately, it included a set of limited immediate demands.

The difference was that the American Socialist movement was by 1921 irrevocably split.

The journal folded with the formation of the Workers' party. As

Theodore Draper points out, "at the first sign of the willingness of the official Communists to come up for air, *The Workers' Council* lost its reason for existence." It had won both its legal party and Comintern affiliation. The Revolution would be a stickier problem.

Chico, California, 1968

Part Five

PUBLICATIONS OF
THE SOCIALISTS

AFTER the expulsions of the Communists in 1919, the Socialist party moved into a decline from which it never recovered. In the presidential election of 1920, Debs polled 915,302 votes, a larger figure absolutely than that for 1912, but only 3.5 percent of the total compared to 6 percent in the earlier year. Moreover, much of this total was decidedly a sympathy vote, personal homage to Debs who was imprisoned for his opposition to the war throughout the campaign. It was not so much a "radical" vote at all. The party's membership continued to decline even as the election was contested.

Additional desertions to the Communists during the early 1920s further reduced the party. In 1921 membership dropped to 13,484 and in 1922 to 11,277. In Oklahoma, where the party had been proportionately strongest, there were only 72 dues-paying members in 1922 and 14 in 1924.

In 1924, the Socialist party supported the presidential candidacy of Senator Robert M. LaFollette who also ran as the candidate of the Conference for Progressive Political Action, the CPPA or, as it was most commonly known, the Progressive party. LaFollette won 4,826,471 popular votes (17 percent) and the electoral votes of Wisconsin. But it is difficult to assess how much of this came from the Socialists. In a state like New York, where LaFollette's name appeared as both "Progressive" and "Socialist," the greater number of LaFollette votes was registered in the SPA's column. But Socialist candidates for other offices in the state did considerably worse. Historian Kenneth MacKay has estimated that the party actually accounted for 1 million of the old Progressive's votes but, in view of its continued decline after 1924, this may be overgenerous.

The fact is that with the exception of Socialist-governed municipalities like Milwaukee and Reading, the party simply found little audience in the era of Coolidge prosperity. Only with the ascendancy of Norman Thomas to party leadership and the unsettling onset of the depression did the party show new vitality. But the new Norman Thomas socialism was not, like the party of Debs, rooted in the working classes. Rather, labor-oriented supporters continued to fall away from the party and it came to be characterized by its support from intellectuals and liberal professionals, notably progressive Protestant ministers.

Still the party did recover. After a first nadir in 1926-1928, membership increased and, in the 1932 presidential election, Norman Thomas won 884,781 votes. But, in Thomas' phrase, this revival was but "an indian summer." When Franklin D. Roosevelt's New Deal accomplished many of the "immediate demands" in the Socialist platform, both distinguished patrons and anonymous members left the party. In 1936 the Socialist vote declined to 187,342 votes and, shortly after the election, membership fell to less than 7,000, less than the party had in 1901. By 1950, Thomas urged that the party recognize that it had no electoral role to play and that it should no longer run a national slate. To this advice he appended his own refusal to be a candidate again. The party directorate overruled him and nominated a lawyer from Reading, Pennsylvania, Darlington Hoopes, for president; he received only 20,000 votes, fewer than the Socialist Laborites and even the Prohibitionists. Finally, the most enthusiastic comrades were prepared to acknowledge their party's irrelevance.

The Socialist party failed for many reasons. The general national prosperity, native conservatism, the tenacity of the two-party tradition, the Socialists' popular identification with communism (despite the party's unstinting efforts to demonstrate its dissociation) all worked to turn a once vital movement into just another of a dozen erratic sects. To other American radicals, the party came to be regarded as, at worst, an active agent of capitalist reformism and, at best, as a society of pleasant, innocuous, and ineffective do-gooders. As Thomas himself phrased it in connection with the SPA's opposition to World War II, the Socialist program seemed to amount to nothing more than a "general condemnation of wickedness." What vitality remained among organized American radicals in the 1930s and 1940s rested with the Communists and the Communist sects with their labor affiliations or with, at least, their revolutionary fervor. To Norman Thomas, in accounting for the failure of his cause, "what cut the ground out pretty completely from under us was this. It was Roosevelt in a word. You don't need anything more." But that postmortem does not explore the implications of the fact that an ostensibly Socialist movement was therefore, by self-definition, undercut by a reformist legislative program. The old SPA of Berger, Hillquit, and Debs had ceased to offer a genuine alternative.

New Day

CHICAGO AND MILWAUKEE,

1920-1922

PAUL M. BUHLE

IN historical retrospect, the title of the periodical *New Day* is a bitterly ironic comment on the period of its existence. For the heroic era of American socialism had passed, and the remaining faithful already edged toward despair. Not that the popular basis for Socialist agitation had simply and easily ceased to exist. From every indication, the election of 1920, in which Socialist party candidate Eugene Debs received over a million votes, marked a continuation of popular Socialist consciousness. But it also marked the disintegration of the Socialist impetus in a nationally organized form, and the rapidly growing inability of organized radicals to forge or recreate a link with the mass of the American people.

Less than two years earlier, the Socialist party seemed to be emerging strengthened from a world war that it had opposed in the United States almost singlehandedly. Although it lost—temporarily, its adherents believed—much of its rural, small town, and official labor support, it seemed vindicated in its warning against the fruits of Woodrow Wilson's war policy. More important, it had added to its ranks a solid base among foreign-speaking workers, then the bulk of the industrial working class. Yet government repression, in the form of harassment of Socialist periodicals especially, had hurt the Socialists; and the raids, deportations, and mass trials following American entry into the war had cut into the fabric of their program for social transformation. Certainly, it was far more difficult by 1920 than a decade before to believe a government that repressed its leftist critics would ever peacefully accede to the establishment of a cooperative commonwealth. And worse, the accumulated frustrations with the leadership of the Socialist party fed the fires of

180

internal rebellion set off by the Russian and German revolutions and the movement toward the establishment of Communist parties the world over. Thus the task of destruction begun by the government was completed by bitter factionalism, and by the time *New Day* was founded, the Socialist party was torn asunder, discouraged, and unable to either reestablish the old course or chart a new one.

The staff members of *New Day* were a significant reflection of the experience, and the limitations, of the paper and the party. Begun in Chicago as successor to the national office paper, *The Eye Opener*, its first editor was William Feigenbaum, a second-line functionary imported from the daily *New York Call*. While putting together *New Day*, Feigenbaum simultaneously served as editor of the National Office Press Service and of the weekly national magazine, *The Socialist World*. The business manager was J. Mahlon Barnes, a Socialist leader of Samuel Gompers' cigarmakers' union in the 1890s, former national secretary of the Socialist party until a morals charge drove him to resign from office, and originator of the idea of a "Red Special," the famous campaign train in which Debs toured in the 1908 and 1912 campaigns. Like many of those who remained behind when the Communists split from the Socialist party, Barnes was of a conservative persuasion, a longtime antagonist of Debs (whose nomination for president Barnes opposed repeatedly), and purportedly one-time "boss" of Pennsylvania's previously powerful Socialist organization.

When in mid-1921 *New Day* was removed to Milwaukee for financial reasons, its editorship passed to Frederick Heath, another longtime Socialist. Heath was a significant figure in the Milwaukee Social Democracy, a leading tendency within the Socialist party for "constructive socialism," and held in high esteem for its success in sending Victor Berger to Congress and in electing a Socialist municipal government in 1911. Although Barnes had been closely allied with Berger since at least 1905, Heath had actually been converted to socialism by the former school teacher in 1898 from a Fabian Club in Milwaukee. Down through the succeeding years, Heath had served as Berger's lieutenant in his role as editor of the Milwaukee *Social-Democratic Herald* and state party official representing Berger's point of view when the latter was in Congress. Heath was also a Socialist leader of the Milwaukee Federated Trades Council, as well as the Wisconsin State Federation of Labor, until the war detached the American Federation of Labor nationally from the Socialists' influence. Throughout its Milwaukee period, Berger's editorials were a most prominent feature of *New Day,* offering a particular set of political attitudes that, due to the decreasing amount of resistance to them within the Socialist party, represented the party's general stance much more so than in former years.

It announced in its first issue that *New Day* was "published exclusively for the propaganda for Socialism." When the Socialist party continued to falter, the paper added an occasional discussion of the party's internal affairs from the pen of Victor Berger. But as the paper curtly reminded its readers, while commenting on the Communist papers' penchant for factionalism, *New Day* generally hoped to lay theoretical questions to rest and speak to non-Socialists, the unconverted. A regular contributor for one period was the beloved Oscar Ameringer, the "Mark Twain of American Socialism," who reflected that although there were as many varieties of Socialists as Protestants in an Indiana county seat, all Socialists had at least some "common delusions" about human betterment—or so *New Day* continued to hope. It was in this ecumenical spirit, especially during its Chicago days, that *New Day* published articles by such notable left-wing Socialists as Kate Richards O'Hare and friends of the party who had not yet become Communists, such as future Communist party leader William Z. Foster.

New Day's greatest single task was to serve as a general agitational sheet for the 1920 presidential campaign. Over the years, the Socialists had been driven from concentrating on the issue of socialism itself, to antiwar activities and the defense of free speech and free assemblage as the national *foci* of their campaigns. The party's 1920 assault on repression was symbolized by its choice of candidate for president, Eugene Debs, who remained behind prison bars in Atlanta, Georgia, for the wartime charge of "sedition." Apparently Debs' prominence during the campaign was inversely proportionate to his actual physical presence, for he became more than ever before the party's link to hundreds of thousands of organizationally unconnected sympathizers with the Socialist cause. "DEBS IS WATCHING," *New Day* warned editorially. "LET US MAKE GOOD."

From his cell, Debs was permitted to write press releases, which were certainly the most poignant—and possibly the most sentimental—articles published in the newspaper. He poured into print his capacity for love, which he was not free to express in his famous oratory. To the workers, Debs offered his career of self-sacrifice:

> I have seen you blacklisted and your children starved because you refused to be a dog; I have seen you a tramp, an outcast, sharing your crumbs with your pal in rags; I have seen you in jail, beaten by a brute into insensibility in the name of the law; I have seen you in the penitentiary, a branded convict, shorn of every right to be a man, and everywhere my heart has been with you; everywhere I have felt the hunger pangs, the biting blasts that you endured; everywhere I felt the blows that fell upon your body and the bullets that pierced your body; everywhere you were my brother and I loved you, and never in my life have I loved you as I love you now, behind these walls. . . .

In a special message to children, he spoke of the "Carpenter comrade of ours who was crucified at Jerusalem by the capitalists of His day," and His love for children. The White House had no lure for him, Debs commented, for he would "rather be with the least of you in the humblest cottage or the meanest tenement, with your arms about me, than be in the White House surrounded by fawning sycophants and posing as a wise and mighty ruler of the people." To the women, he confessed in a series of messages related to the first national election with female suffrage, that "no true man can think of his mother as other than perfect," and every good husband envisioned his wife just as on the day "when she was in the bloom of beauty and first won his heart." The nineteenth-century vision of the family, the traditionalist attitude toward children, the fundamentally Protestant position on the class struggle—all these were Debs' last bursts, through *New Day,* of an energy that was rapidly fading, from the party as well as from Debs' worn body, in 1920.

That year Debs' faith and courage were the spirit, if not nearly all the strength, of the Socialist party. Not free to campaign with his beloved rhetoric, Debs was more than ever before pictured in Christ-like terms, as in the poetry of Covington Hall, or likened to John Brown by the preelection crowd in Reading that sang again and again, "Gene Debs' body lies in a prison cell, but his soul goes marching on!" When a bomb was exploded on Wall Street, Debs ironically commented that had he been loose, he might have been arrested, but behind bars he had a perfect alibi. His comment was typical of the Socialists' difficulties, if not their humor, reflected in the *New Day*'s pages. The physical threats, which by 1921 grew into kidnappings of featured speakers Ida Crouch Hazlett and Kate Richards O'Hare by American Legion-inspired crowds, were already ominous. Vice-presidential candidate Seymour Stedman managed to lead a parade in Oklahoma only after bluffing the sheriff with his credentials to speak as a lawyer before the Supreme Court. From any perspective, the campaign of 1920 was at least one of the most difficult in the party's history.

And yet, with the million votes garnered for Debs and Stedman, the campaign seemed at first a success. *New Day* praised the activists as that "little band of comrades, sadly depleted but never discouraged," setting out to "do the work that had been done in the past by well nigh ten times their number," and against all odds had "won" at least a moral victory. Within a year, *New Day* urged patience at the slowness of the pace of socialism's successes, reminding readers that because of the kept press, most workers were "practically brainwashed to think the way their oppressors want them to think." It would take time, for "the turning of a people into a democracy is a slow process, all considered."

As membership continued to trickle away, as young people were drawn, if to politics at all, to the Communist rather than (or even from) the Socialist party, the distress grew increasingly harder to conceal. Victor Berger, who had once been recalled from the party's National Committee for a purported compromise with a Republican candidate for a local Milwaukee office, a violation of the Socialist party's constitution (Berger denied the charge and was eventually returned), now boldly revealed this strategy for Socialist rejuvenation. The United States, he noted, was "the only country in the world where the Socialist Party according to its old rules could not join in any coalitions with another political party." The result, he held, was that the United States was "the only large country in which the Socialist Party has not gained a strong place nationally." At first, Berger looked to the model of the British Independent Labour party, a body that, by retaining its autonomy within the larger Labour party, had managed to give great theoretical influence to socialism, and weight to itself, in British politics. Like other right-leaning Socialists, he took the ILP rather than the Bolsheviks as the paradigm of future American radical politics. He scorned cooperation with Robert LaFollette, the Republican Progressive from Wisconsin, and sought to work within a new and independent farmer-labor coalition. By 1922, LaFollette's stock had risen as the Socialist cause slumped, and the Wisconsin Social Democracy supported the senator for reelection, with the eventual hope of detaching him and his radical following from the Republican party. Thus, the way was paved for the campaign of 1924 when the Socialists all but liquidated their infrastructure for the benefit of the Progressive party.

Thrown back on increasingly scarce resources, the party and *New Day* could only muster courage and hope. In 1922, the "free speech" issue was still alive, but logically appealed more to big-city liberals than to farmers or workers. *New Day* hammered incessantly on the subjects of open-shop drives, stagnant wages, and rising prices for the consumer. Farmers, whose economic position nationally was declining in the 1920s, were offered special appeals, but without noticeable effect. And former Socialists, of whom there were certainly hundreds of thousands, were persistently called upon to galvanize their ranks and return to the fold. As elsewhere, *New Day* cried in the wilderness.

What remained, as Socialists turned back to their old style of agitation—with constantly decreasing returns—was a profoundly *moral* vision of America and of the future. Perhaps Vida Scudder, a professor at Wellesley and author of *Socialism and Character*, put it best when she called socialism "a rational idealism . . . a heroically disinterested passion for justice." For her, socialism was not egotism but its opposite, the only potentiality for the worker to acquire altruism by being shown group ideals through his experience in the class struggle. To "lift the laborer out of his apathy and give him the inspiration of the hopes and duties of a larger cause," to offer the middle class a "wise comprehension of the laws of progress" according to the Socialists, to create a society where classes would be abolished, these were the aims of Miss Scudder and *New Day*. When the 1920s turned a blind eye toward the call for a reawakened idealism, the last card for Debsian socialism, including *New Day*, had been drawn and played.

Madison, Wisconsin, 1969

Socialist World

CHICAGO, 1920-1926

American Appeal

CHICAGO, 1926-1927

JAMES B. GILBERT

THE decade of the 1920s was a period of severe decline for the Socialist party. It was splintered by defections to the Communists, often ignored because of a general decline of interest in radicalism, and toward the end of the decade, bereft of two of its most important leaders, Eugene V. Debs and Victor Berger. In the 1920s Socialists could no longer count upon impressive electoral showings, although there remained isolated pockets of Socialist strength in Wisconsin, New York, and Pennsylvania. The party's activities were no longer of much importance to the American intellectual community, which had once considered the Socialists to be an important force struggling for social transformation and reform. Yet the Socialist party was alive (if somewhat nostalgic about its successful past), and it continued to print important newspapers and journals. In the most superficial sense these magazines chart the decline of the Socialist party, measure its sinking fortunes, and record efforts made to revive it. But for the Socialist movement, the period of the 1920s was far richer than the party's obvious failures would suggest, and the periodicals published were more fascinating than a muted reflection of former brilliance. The Socialists were a significant force in the LaFollette presidential campaign of 1924, and during the whole decade their views on American labor and world politics continued to be incisive and important.

One of the most important journals of the Socialist movement was the *Socialist World,* founded in July 1920 (superseding the *Young Socialist's Magazine*), and transformed, in January 1926, into the *American Appeal,* which then continued publication into 1927. As an official publication of the movement, the *Socialist World-American Appeal* was deeply concerned with party matters. During its first years under the editorship of William Feigenbaum, former Socialist member from Brooklyn of the New York State Assembly, Otto F. Branstetter, National Executive Secretary of the party until 1924, and finally, from 1924 to 1926, under Bertha Hale White, the succeeding National Executive Secretary, the journal printed a number of official party documents and discussed important internal developments affecting the movement. A thorough reorganization of the paper in 1926 made Eugene Debs editor, with Murray King managing editor. When Debs died in 1926, King continued as editor with the addition of Harry Laidler, of the League for Industrial Democracy, as feature editor. So the editorial staff of the journal remained until it was absorbed into the *New Leader* in 1927.

The several changes in editors and the serious reorganization and reappearance of the *Socialist World* in 1926 under a new name, the *American Appeal,* demonstrated the movement's search for a serious mass readership. The journal thus gradually widened its early perspectives because of the need to attract new readers, and printed more news and feature stories. As an official organ the magazine began to report on developments in the party to its membership; by 1926, the party hoped to revive the Socialist movement using the *Appeal* to spearhead a membership drive. The Socialists hoped to recreate a mass radical movement modeled after the former successes of the party. To do this they called upon Debs to be editor, and they patterned the paper after *Appeal to Reason,* the very popular Socialist publication that appeared before World War I.

In the early 1920s, when the *Socialist World* was most concerned with narrow party matters and was printing the minutes of the National Executive Committee of the party and official party documents, it was still involved in fascinating and important events of the day. The paper was generally favorable in 1920 to the Russian Revolution (with important reservations, of course). Gradually, it became disenchanted with the Soviet Union and bitter over its struggle with the American Communists, a chapter in the history of American radicalism which is well documented in the magazine. The magazine printed the proposed resolutions and minutes of discussions considering affiliation with the Communist Third International. When the Communists made impossible demands upon the Socialists, which amounted to an attack on the party and a personal swipe at Socialist leader Morris Hillquit, plus requirements that the party accept almost absolute direction from the International, affiliation became impossible. Interest in the Soviet Revolution then lagged, and the journal assessed its position and admitted some of the disastrous effects of the internecine war on the Left. The solution, the party found, was either to form an independent labor party or join with non-Socialist, liberal elements such as the American Federation of Labor, the railroad brotherhoods, the remnants of prewar Progressive reform elements, Social Gospelers, and other independent radicals. It was this latter course which the Socialist party pursued.

For three unsuccessful and ultimately frustrating years, the party worked with the Conference for Progressive Political Action (CPPA), a broad group of liberal organizations. When the CPPA supported Robert LaFollette of Wisconsin for president in 1924, the Socialists aided him, and the *Socialist World* closely followed the election. It even printed a bitter debate between Communist William Z. Foster and Eugene Debs over the LaFollette candidacy; Foster charged that the Socialists had given up all claim to radicalism and Debs defended his party's action. The Socialists withdrew their support of the CPPA in 1925 when the organization failed to create a permanent third party. It was at this point that the Socialist party and its publication, the *Socialist World,* reached their lowest ebb.

There had been lighter moments for the party and the journal from 1920 to 1925 when immediate political concerns did not preoccupy Socialists. The *Socialist World* printed occasional poems and book reviews. In a membership drive in 1921, the party had offered a new Dodge touring car to the local that signed up over 2,000 new members, and a series of lesser prizes, such as watches and books, were offered as rewards for obtaining new members. Much space in the magazine had also been devoted to an amnesty drive to free Eugene Debs from federal prison, where he had been committed during the Wilson administration. Reports on the struggle of the labor movement to resist the open shop drive after World War I also filled the columns of the journal. Important, too, were the speeches of Socialist Congressman Victor Berger, which the magazine reprinted.

By June 1925, a decision was made to alter the format of the magazine and to invest greater hopes in it as the center of a propaganda drive to rebuild the party. Four principles guided the creation of the revised journal: it would revive, and hence hope to share in, the former success of the *Appeal to Reason*; it would be less a house organ of the Socialist party and would aim its appeal more directly at the American working class; it would be published weekly and therefore would appear frequently enough to comment on current events; and it would have Eugene Debs as editor. "The *American Appeal* will strip wrongs naked," the Socialists proclaimed; "it will lash mercilessly, explain simply. . . ." It promised to be a "weekly propaganda Socialist paper, with Eugene V. Debs as editor in chief, a major enterprise in the present awakening and rapid upbuilding of the American Socialist movement."

In preparation for the appearance of the new magazine, the *Socialist World* suspended publication in July 1925, while the party organized an "Appeal Army" (reminiscent of the old group organized around the *Appeal to Reason*), which hoped to build circulation to 100,000 readers and bring new members and sympathizers into the party. To aid the "army," the revamped magazine featured articles by Norman Thomas, Carleton Beals, and Anna Louise Strong; a feature column by Harry Laidler; a series of "Letters to Judd," in which Upton Sinclair explained the necessity of socialism; and a series of articles on the Soviet Union by Otto Bauer. Special news sections, such as "Sparks and Flashes from News of the Week," collected bits of important or striking news. A column by Debs was an important part of the publication, and even after his death in late 1926, his brother, Theodore Debs, continued a column about the great Socialist leader's thought. Important, too, were the magazine's discussions of American relations with Mexico when war seemed to threaten between the two nations in the late 1920s.

Despite some initial success, the *American Appeal* failed to play a major role in reviving the Socialist party; it could not create the wide and loyal readership its prewar counterpart, the *Appeal to Reason,* had once enjoyed. By the middle of 1926, the editors began to discuss circulation problems and the failure to achieve a readership of more than 20,000. By

1927, plans were made to merge the paper with the *New Leader,* published in New York City. This union was significant because it reflected the journal's difficulties in achieving a solid foundation in the movement, and it indicated the shift of the party itself to the eastern part of the United States. Many of the writers for the *Appeal* appeared in the *New Leader,* but in the main the magazine's efforts to be the center of a revived party had failed.

The changing editorship, the shifting tactics, and the uneven fortunes of the *Socialist World-American Appeal* illustrate the mechanical side of the decline of the Socialist movement during the 1920s. Beyond this, however, the journal provides an important view of American thought during the 1920s, different from the bland utterances from Washington, the official scandals, or even the cutting interpretations of H.L. Mencken. The magazine kept its attention on issues such as "100% Americanism," amnesty for political prisoners, labor conditions, the rise of fascism, theoretical and practical divisions on the Left, and the Bolshevik Revolution. The *Socialist World-American Appeal* did not save the Socialist movement from decline, but then perhaps nothing could have accomplished this at the time. Yet the journal was a significant publication; it recaptured some of the excitement of the prewar days and suggested, and in some sense even contributed to, the revival and redirection of the Socialist party in the early 1930s.

College Park, Maryland, 1968

The Intercollegiate Socialist

NEW YORK, 1913-1919

The Socialist Review

NEW YORK, 1919-1921

Labor Age

NEW YORK, 1921-1933

HERBERT G. GUTMAN

THE 1920s were not a good time for American radicals. In his outstanding history of the American worker between 1920 and 1933, *The Lean Years,* Irving Bernstein tells us why. He also reminds us of much forgotten in the mythic idealization of the Jazz Age. "The symbol for the twenties," Bernstein notes, "is gold." Charles and Mary Beard, for example, entitled their beginning chapter on that era "The Golden Glow." Bernstein offers a different perspective: "For the great mass of people . . .—workers and their families—the appropriate metallic symbol may be nickel or copper or perhaps even tin, but certainly not gold." Reviewing in detail the immediate years before the Great Depression, Bernstein advises that "the interplay between illusion and reality is a key to the period." Certain magazines published in the 1920s remain basic sources for exploring that relationship. Liberal weeklies such as *The Nation* and *The New Republic* head any such list. So does *Survey,* a weekly often remembered just for its advice to "social workers" but actually a rich mine for social historians. The monthly *Labor Age* belongs with those better known weeklies. More specialized, more radical, and less well-edited, it is a basic source for understanding the seamy underlife of the Jazz Age as well as a little-recognized but steady stream of radical social commentary and criticism. In addition, *Labor Age* and its editors are a crucial link between the socialism of Progressive America and the more complex radicalism of the New Deal era.

A few months before the Great Crash, labor economist William M. Leiserson privately fumed over the failures of organized labor. He had good reason for his muted despair. The decade had seen a drop in trade union membership, from 19.4 percent of the labor force in 1920 to only 10.2 percent ten years later. More than this, the golden decade of American capitalism had seen a hardened social conversation develop among the top national leadership of the American Federation of Labor. This process caused and also reflected much else.

The 1920s were not friendly to social experimentation and radical politics. Industrial unions such as the United Mine Workers of America fell into disarray. Powerful collective bodies were lacking among workers in most mass-production industries. The triumph of the American Plan meant little more than a mixture of company unions and welfare capitalism. Politics celebrated little more than the triumph of crass materialism. The corporate society of the 1950s and the 1960s made its greatest advances in that decade after World War I. Modern America was born during World War I and came to a hasty maturity in the 1920s. Organized labor seemed asleep in these years. And that lull disturbed those who quarreled with the underlying assumptions that sustained the New America. "What the labor movement . . . now needs is a lot of strong criticism showing up their weaknesses and their stupidity," complained Leiserson a few months before the Great Crash. "That is the only way . . . in which they can be awakened and stimulated to perform the functions . . . which they ought to be performing." Those who edited and wrote for *Labor Age* did not need such advice. For nearly ten years, they had played that role—as critics of the New America and especially of its hardened labor establishment.

Published between 1913 and 1933, *Labor Age* spanned two critical decades in twentieth-century American labor and radical history. It started soon after Woodrow Wilson went to the White House and just before progressivism was to flower fully. Its last issue went to press shortly after the beginning of Franklin Roosevelt's first term and while the nation still lived in the pit of the Great Depression. In its first issue, Ellen Hayes, a Wellesley College professor, expressed a moral outrage that would repeat itself in other ways for the next twenty years:

> They who reach forth strong hands to grasp the cup that holds the wine of life are esteemed the fittest for its enjoyment. They may be over-fed, over-clothed, over-housed, over-opportunitied, and it is quite in accordance with the nature and order of things, even though this over-living costs others the primary necessaries of life. On the other side in the great social alignment are those who perceive more or less distinctly the worth and rights of every human being.

She wrote for the magazine when it was called *The Intercollegiate Socialist* (1913-1919). It next appeared briefly as *The Socialist Review* (1919-1921). Its major span was under the name *Labor Age* (1921-1933). It shared common personnel under all three titles, but when it became *Labor Age* its focus shifted, as did its importance. Over its entire life, the magazine bore witness and gave testimony to the collapse of the pre-1920 Socialist movement, the growing conservatism of trade unionists such as Samuel Gompers, William Green, Matthew Woll, and John Frey, the despair and isolation of their radical critics, and finally to the breakdown of the new capitalism itself between 1929 and 1933.

The Intercollegiate Socialist (and its successor *The Socialist Review*) differed from *Labor Age,* had importance of its own, and deserves brief note. Harry W. Laidler edited it for the Intercollegiate Socialist Society. That it served as the Society's major publication is reason enough for it to retain importance to students of American society and culture. The Intercollegiate Socialist Society brought together older Socialists and younger critics of pre-World War I capitalism and liberal reform. Its members included a veritable *Who's Who* of significant American social critics and theorists as well as writers and artists. Some had already achieved importance, but others would emerge between 1920 and 1940 as major social critics. ISS members included Thomas Wentworth Higginson, Clarence Darrow, William English Walling, Benjamin Flower, Jack London, Morris Hillquit, John Dewey, William J. Ghent, Florence

Kelley, Roger Baldwin, Randolph Bourne, Paul Blanshard, Bruce Bliven, Paul Douglas, Morris Ernst, Lewis Gannett, Freda Kirshway, Alexander Meiklejohn, Broadus Mitchell, A. J. Muste, Selig Perlman, Vida Scudder, Charles Steinmetz, Ordway Tead, Walter Weyl, Norman Thomas, and Bouck White. To write of American social thought in these and later years without considering these men and women is to write of a foreign country.

Its first issue suggested the range of *The Intercollegiate Socialist.* Although it contained a poem by Arturo Giovannitti, then in an Essex County, Massachusetts, jail, in the aftermath of the 1912 IWW Lawrence textile strike, the magazine was directed more toward intellectuals, students, and Socialists than toward trade unionists and workers. The same issue contained "theoretical" articles by Upton Sinclair, William English Walling, and W. J. Ghent. An essay came from the pen of Lester Frank Ward, the father of American sociology whose theoretical works had matured during the Gilded Age. The magazine followed its early position, promising in Laidler's words to shed " 'light, more light' on the meaning of the world-wide movement for industrial democracy known as Socialism." The second issue printed a little known essay by historian Charles A. Beard, "Why Study Socialism." Other early issues included a significant special supplement by Walling entitled "Who Gets America's Wealth?" (December 1915-January 1916). But *The Intercollegiate Socialist's* greatest value lay in what it recorded about the Socialist dispute over the World War I. Even articles by Karl Kautsky and Keir Hardie fall away in importance when compared to the special supplement (April-May 1917) entitled "Socialists and the Problems of War. A Symposium." It need only be noted that, in addition to Walling, the contributors included Randolph Bourne, Walter Lippmann, Scott Nearing, Algie M. Simons, and John Spargo.

Labor Age drew some of its writers and much of its spirit from *The Intercollegiate Socialist,* but it represented a quite different emphasis. Full and quite useful details concerning *Labor Age,* and the events that led to its birth and that explain its importance, appear in James O. Morris, *Conflict Within the AFL, A Study of Craft Versus Industrial Unionism,* 1901-1938 (Ithaca: Cornell University Press, 1958, especially pp. 86-135). What follows draws heavily from that account. Concerned largely with the struggle within the AFL over the craft union as an appropriate response to modern technology and business organization, Morris gives careful attention to the "labor progressives" of the 1920s. *Labor Age* was their magazine, and it is the major source for understanding their role inside and outside the formal labor movement. Such men and women as fit under the rubric "labor progressives" opposed the dominant AFL strategy in the 1920s, which Morris properly characterizes as hoping "to promote organization through union-management cooperation and to convince businessmen, politicians, Legionnaires, other groups, and the public in general that organized labor was a 'respectable,' 'patriotic,' and 'American' institution." The AFL national leadership had numerous critics within organized labor. Between 1919 and 1923, for example, the leaders of fifteen state AFL federations and twelve national unions favored more "aggressive" policies, including "amalgamation" and industrial unionism. From among them and the radicals (mostly Socialists) outside the unions came the Workers' Education Bureau of America (1921), Brookwood Labor College (1921), the Labor Publication Society and *Labor Age* (1921), and, finally, after severe conflict with the national AFL leadership, the Conference for Progressive Labor Action (1929). Early cooperation between the "labor progressives" and the conservative AFL national leaders in adult workers' education was doomed to failure. The critics from the Left worried men like William Green and Matthew Woll, and conflict seemed inevitable. Morris carefully describes these troubles over adult education, and especially the growing mistrust of Brookwood by the AFL national leaders that finally sparked a rupture between the federation and "labor progressives" such as A. J. Muste.

The Labor Publication Society and *Labor Age* grew increasingly dissatisfied with and critical of national AFL leadership and policies. *Labor Age* regularly revealed these disagreements. At its start, the Labor Publication Society, which sponsored *Labor Age,* included on its Board of Directors old ISS members and other Socialists and radicals outside the formal trade union movement, among them Florence Kelley, Harry Laidler, Louis Budenz, Elizabeth Gurley Flynn, Roger Baldwin, Stuart Chase, Anna Strunsky Walling, and Muste. But the LPS represented more than this small group. It also included Progressives, many of them Socialists, within the trade unions. Its president was James Maurer, the

Socialist head of the Pennsylvania Federation of Labor, and its vice-presidents included Amalgamated Clothing Workers of America leader Joseph Schlossberg, and Thomas Kennedy, the secretary-treasurer of the United Mine Workers of America. Others on its Board of Directors included the editors of *Headwear Gear* (J. M. Budish) and *Justice* (Max Danish), as well as the presidents of the International Upholsterers' Union and the International Brotherhood of Firemen and Oilers, the vice-president of the International Brotherhood of Electrical Workers, and the vice-president of the New York State Federation of Labor.

From its start, *Labor Age* made clear its differences with the national AFL leaders. It promised to be different from its predecessor and from contemporary trade union and radical periodicals. Unlike *The Socialist Review*, Harry Laidler insisted, *Labor Age* would give "far more attention . . . to the problems of labor unions." The journal promised to "fill a well-defined need" and present "a viewpoint distinct from the interests of any party or section." In its first issue (which included a typical range of articles on trade activities and strategy as well as on labor conflicts by such writers as Baldwin, Powers Hapgood, Danish, Budenz, Maurer, Solon De Leon, Leo Wolman, Stuart Chase, and Paul Blanshard), the editors assured readers they would report and interpret "up-to-date happenings from the battle-line of the struggle" and would bring together in one place information scattered in hundreds of specialized labor and radical journals. *Labor Age* set out its objectives plainly. "The goal of the American labor movement," it stated, "lies in the development of a system of production for service instead of for private profit." It favored "independent political movements" and "worker's educational efforts."

Especially after 1926, such an emphasis caused increasing conflict with the AFL national leadership. The conservatism of Green, Woll, and Frey did not help matters. Nor did their suspicion and concern regarding the influence of the "labor progressives." The rhetoric of Muste, Budenz, and Laidler dominated the pages of *Labor Age* and grew increasingly critical of the labor establishment. Their radicalism questioned official AFL policies, favored organization of the mass-production industries, and urged attention to groups (including women and Negroes) bypassed by the craft unions. *Labor Age,* James Morris concludes, "developed arguments which were not in any substantial ways improved upon by the labor insurgents of the 1930s.'' Needless to say, the dispute over Brookwood deepened the wedge between the AFL and the "labor progressives.'' Some trade union supporters quit the Labor Publication Society as *Labor Age* turned more bitterly against the AFL and its dominant outlook and policies. Muste and others finally formed the Conference for Progressive Labor Action in 1929, and together with Maurer, James Oneal, and Norman Thomas, they pressed fruitlessly during four years of depression against both AFL policies and Communist efforts. The AFL dismissed its critics as a "group of professional tingling souls who dream of a labor party,'' and Communist William Z. Foster condemned the CPLA as the "little brothers of the big labor fakirs.'' *Labor Age* grew more partisan and sectarian. But it resisted its critics from the Right and the Left and continued to appear for another five years before it was buried in an already crowded cemetery filled with countless defunct labor and radical publications.

For several solid reasons, however, it retains its life for scholars and students of twentieth-century American radical and labor movements. In it lie buried countless clues to aspects of the 1920s not yet studied. Fine journalism fills many of its pages with details about neglected strikes and lockouts. One learns much about men like A. J. Muste and Louis Budenz, who became even more important after *Labor Age* perished. Articles on labor racketeering in the early 1930s continue to command attention, and so do pages of depressing but instructive prose about the conditions of working people between 1929 and 1933. The magazine contains a running and often stringent and angry critique of welfare capitalism as well as of faulted AFL policies. There also are many excellent photographs of working-class life, including some otherwise inaccessible work by Lewis W. Hine. Most of all, the pages of *Labor Age* afford us a perspective on the 1920s that is quite different from the one that dominates most historical literature. Socialism faded from the mainstream of American life in the 1920s, but the Socialist editors of *Labor Age* recorded aspects of that mythicized world that escaped the attention of Americans drowned in bathtub gin and deafened by Chicago jazz.

Rochester, New York, 1968

American Socialist Quarterly
NEW YORK, 1932-1935

American Socialist Monthly
NEW YORK, 1935-1937

Socialist Review
NEW YORK, 1937-1940

DAVID HERRESHOFF

A TRIO of Left Socialists, all of them active in the workers' education movement, started the *Socialist Review*. Anna Bercowitz and David P. Berenberg were with the Rand School, and Haim Kantorovitch was with the Workmen's Circle High School, when they discovered they shared a desire to bring out a Marxist theoretical magazine for the Socialist party. The editors conceived of the magazine as answering a need which they felt had existed in the Socialist party since the Communist split of 1919, and spoke of it as a successor to *Class Struggle* (1917-1919), a magazine in which Louis C. Fraina and Ludwig Lore rallied Socialists to the Bolshevik Revolution and ultimately to the Communist Labor party. From the first volume onwards they proceeded in the conviction that "the movement, insofar as it wishes to be more than an expression of aimless benevolence, must be based on [Marx's] theories, at least until a better set of theories is advanced." (Vol. I, No. 4, Fall 1932).

In the second year of its publication the *American Socialist Quarterly* became the official organ of the Socialist party. This adoption is a sign of the party's leftward drift during the 1930s. That drift received its principal impulse from the shattering of the great reformist Social Democratic movements in Central Europe. "Everywhere," writes Kantorovitch in 1934, "the feeling is growing that the Socialist movement cannot, after the tragic experiences in Germany and now in Austria, remain 'just as it was.' The year of revolution and counter-revolution, the advent of fascism, have left their mark on the Socialist movement. The number of Socialist voices demanding a revision of Socialist tactics, a restatement of Socialist principles is steadily growing" (Vol. III, No. 1, Spring 1934). The volumes of this magazine record many such voices in that part of the Socialist party between Norman Thomas and the spokesmen of the Trotskyist faction in the party, Max Shachtman, Felix Morrow, and James Burnham.

Characteristic Left Socialist responses to the New Deal are on view in the magazine in articles by Berenberg. In the first months of the New Deal, Berenberg remarked on a growing Roosevelt myth and predicted that "It will not be long before all the blessings of nature will be attributed to him," and that in the event of any substantial recovery from the depression, "the myth will live long that it was the measures of the Roosevelt administration that brought it about" (Vol. II, No. 3, Summer 1933).

In 1937, he asserted that the United Auto Workers' sit-down victories were due to the intervention of Roosevelt and Governor Frank Murphy of Michigan, but warned that "Unions that win strikes mainly by government pressure become prisoners of the government, if the government is not entirely their own" (Vol. V, No. 9, February 1937). The unresolved problem posed for Socialists by the growing Roosevelt myth was how to win American workers away from the New Deal. It brought Norman Thomas to a stark questioning of Socialist hopes during the Recession of 1938: "If we cannot win the workers now, there is no particular reason to think we can do it in some future emergency. Is not the present crisis bad enough to 'start them broad awake'?"

The socialism of the American Jews who edited the magazine was decidedly non-Zionist. Kantorovitch himself was an ex-Zionist who left the Paole Zionist and joined the Socialist party in 1926. The relatively small space the magazine devoted to the Palestine question afforded expression to attitudes which were indeed predominantly anti-Zionist. A position paper published in 1936 asserted that Palestinian Arabs feared that "the small Jewish minority, supported by hated English imperialism, is about to conquer their lands" and warned "against the continuation of the chauvinistic policies of the Zionists of all kinds in Palestine." It urged that "in no case, should this immigration be utilized to deepen the chasm between the Jews and Arabs in Palestine" (Vol. V, No. 6, August 1936).

Other issues examined and debated in the magazine included the relationship of Left Socialists to Communists, to Trotskyists, to Old Guard Socialists, and to proletarian literature. On the last-named topic the voice of Kantorovitch dominated. Kantorovitch was an editor of V. F. Calverton's *Modern Quarterly* in addition to being on the editorial board of the *American Socialist Quarterly*. In the latter magazine he argued against the Communists' campaign for proletarian literature. He denied that any major writer in the Communists' camp was a maker of proletarian literature. "To demand from Sherwood Anderson proletarian literature is neither wise nor just. The problem for the Marxian critic is not how to make naturally non-proletarian writers become proletarians, but to interpret the American writer from a Marxian standpoint, to find what Plekhanov designated as the sociological equivalent in artistic creation" (Vol. II, No. 2, Winter 1933).

With the death of Kantorovitch in 1936 and the departure of the Trotskyists from the Socialist party in the following year, the contributions of such younger Left Socialists as Gus Tyler grew in prominence. Tyler warned Left Socialists of the rise of a "new layer of trade union petty bureaucrats in the party [who] are the intransigent pressure group for a reformist line of practice in America." At the same time he decried the Trotskyists as sectarians whose "only rationalization . . . for their present splits, and further splits, for their present weakness, is the mystical notion that the masses will unquestionably flock to them at the right moment, if they have the perfect program." Tyler summoned "consistent Marxists *to combat right wing capitulation and left sectarianism with equal vigor*" (Vol. VI, No. 2, September 1937).

The suspension of the *Socialist Review* in 1940 was symptomatic of the weakened condition in which the Socialist party found itself as it entered the 1940s.

Detroit, 1968

Challenge!

NEW YORK, 1943-1946

MILTON CANTOR

CHALLENGE was the periodical of the Young People's Socialist League (YPSL), organized in 1912 as the youth section of the Socialist party. The league had been formed as a political instrument to provide a "socialist education for young people" and to serve as a cultural and fraternal agency for Socialist youth. It had marked time in the 1920s along with all radical youth organizations. But in the 1930s, a time of fear and hope, it had helped mobilize campus sentiment against militarism and fascism and had a considerable influence upon America's political and intellectual life during the depression. Certainly it was the premier Socialist youth group, tending to dominate the Student League for Industrial Democracy (SLID) college chapters, especially those located on large urban campuses.

The three tumultuous wartime and postwar years (1943-1946) of *Challenge* may seem less exciting than those of the New Deal, but in retrospect they are at least as crowded with memorable deeds and momentous issues. Moreover, they contributed mightily to shaping both the course of events and the climate of opinion for decades to come.

By its prominent role in opposing Hitlerism, in promoting peace "strikes" on college campuses, and in supporting labor's demands, the league provided valuable shaping experiences for many undergraduates as well as for those who would be postgraduate liberals, intellectuals, and trade-union leaders—that is, for the articulate spokesmen of postwar society. As such, it probably was more influential than the Socialist party, which did not function as an organizational training ground for those coming to maturity. Besides, the party itself had been torn apart by factionalism in the early 1930s. Its lacerating polemics and internal warfare were capped by the grievous election setback of 1936, which saw the Socialist vote generally plummet, and it had shown little vigor as late as Pearl Harbor. These observations also were applicable to the Yipsels, particularly in the mid-1930s' quarrel with Trotskyist youth members. But the league rebuilt itself after this faction departed, and Socialist students were a vital and positive force in the student movement of the late 1930s. Frequently quarreling among themselves, to be sure, and with other radical blocs, the Yipsels nonetheless often joined with them —driven into a loose and temporary community by poverty, the social crackup, parlous economic conditions, menacing overseas developments, and high moral purpose.

Ruptures were produced by the Oxford Pledge (an English import pledging its adherents to pacifism; they would under no circumstances "fight for God and country"). Although this pledge was endorsed by a pacifist minority among undergraduates, including some Socialists, the student movement of the prewar period was becoming increasingly politicized. It was being transformed into a political instrument for preparing undergraduates for a crusade against fascism. When overseas hostilities finally broke out, this movement itself became one of the first casualties of the war. The Yipsels lost their peripheral support (in the Youth Committee Against War) and mass base—what with a quiescent labor force, a university community more remote and secluded than ever, and military conscription that took their best organizers and most eloquent speakers out of circulation.

The destruction of the Socialist party as a political entity was also complete by the outbreak of war. Its members now belonged to an alienated and isolated sect—soured outsiders who analyzed a situation that they could neither condone nor control. Norman Thomas, their titular leader, had long opposed preparedness and conscription, which view, to be sure, the Communist party shared until the German invasion of Russia. But the Socialists never made the turns and tergiversations of the American Communist party. Depending on one's view, they were more doctrinaire or more consistent. Hence they reiterated their opposition to the war, even directly after Pearl Harbor, when Socialist delegates, assembled in annual convention, resolved that the party does "not give . . . [its] blessing to this war—or any war—as the proper method" for achieving its objectives. Delegates to the 1944 Socialist national convention adopted a comparably worded resolution and a platform that demanded "an immediate political peace offensive based on the offer of an armistice to the people of the Axis nations." Indeed Socialists throughout the conflict protested against it, gave the American war effort only equivocal and vague support, and offered a program sufficiently flaccid to encompass Thomasite pacifists and both antiwar and prowar advocates. Thomas himself had surrendered his religious pacifism, but his position on war was tainted and ambiguous, and he even rejected "so negative a slogan as unconditional surrender." Small wonder then that the Socialist party ceased to exist in these years; or that the Communist party, on the other hand, found prestige in its identification with the Soviet Union and the tough resistance of the Russian people.

Socialism in America had almost touched bottom in June 1943, when the first issue of *Challenge* appeared. This issue set the tone for the periodical's brief and frenetic existence with its fearful announcement about the coming of American fascism and its attempt to maintain orthodox Socialist ties with the working class. Its warning that the nation's campuses were being militarized was one more manifestation of that continuing YPSL antagonism to ROTC, which so preoccupied the radical student imagination in the 1930s. Regarding socialism and the working class, it is significant that the Communist and Socialist positions sharply contrasted to John L. Lewis' strike activities. Proclaiming the war to be a democratic crusade, Communists were eager to subordinate, if not abandon, their long-run objectives in the interest of Allied victory. Consequently, they eagerly endorsed the no-strike pledge and actively sought to discourage strikes. Understandably, therefore, they vehemently turned on John L. Lewis, a hero of yesterday, who maintained that the right to strike existed, even in wartime, and called for a miners' walkout in 1943. Lewis, in Earl Browder's view, was nothing less than an accomplice of the Nazis, and his attack on the no-strike policy a victory for Hitler. *Challenge,* in sharp contrast, lionized the striking miners, in uncompromisingly militant tones reminiscent of all radical publications, including Communist, of the 1930s. And in later issues, its Yipsel editors would condemn the National Service Bill, a labor draft measure, again markedly different from the Communist party which demanded all-out mobilization for war production.

Strikingly dissimilar responses were also apparent on two additional issues that absorbed radicals in June 1943, issues that would remain visible for the life of *Challenge*. The YPSL had been longtime champions of civil rights, and so were its publications. The first number of *Challenge* urged justice and equality for the Negro, supporting A. Philip Randolph's march on Washington movement as part of a global protest against the "white imperialist world." But the Communists saw grave danger in the refusal of Negro leaders to suspend, for the duration of the war, their struggle for elementary justice for black America. Randolph's movement utilized "justified grievances," party spokesman James Ford stated, "as a weapon of opposition to the Administration's war program." No such viewpoint appeared in *Challenge*. Rather, in its three-year existence, the journal featured continual attacks on Jim Crow, came out in support for those who protested discrimination in army camps, and clamored for a permanent Fair Employment Practices Commission and equal rights.

Unlike the Communist party, as has been suggested, Socialists underwent no startling political transformation. They did not become overnight devotees of the USSR or of American overseas policies. They shared the Trotskyist view that the global conflict was between competing imperialists, and that there was little to choose from among Russian, German, British, and American manifestations. *Challenge,* like the Fourth International of the Socialist Workers party (SWP), continually reminded its readers that war under capitalism was endemic, that imperialism dominated both belligerent camps, and that superprofits, greater political power, and territorial aggression were the goals of all the warring nations. If anything, Trotskyists were more forthright than Yipsels in support of the Russian war effort, desite their hatred of the "Stalinist clique" in Russia and of the American Communist party. *Challenge* never made the sort of direct plea for support of the USSR that appeared in SWP periodicals. Rather, from its first number, it exclusively stressed the "degeneration of the Russian Revolution as criminal and tragic" and rejected any attempt "to palm off moral acceptance of Stalinism." So did the Trotskyists, to be sure, but they invariably balanced such comments by pleas for support of Russian military efforts, something that *Challenge's* editors neglected to do.

For the rest, Yipsels shared a view of international events common to the Left generally. They displayed, from *Challenge*'s first number, a vital concern for the "international Socialist movement," and publicized—especially in an irregularly featured column, "Around the World"—new and radical parties, reorganized unions, and agrarian revolutionaries, putting the most optimistic gloss upon such reports. "Workers Revolution Sweeping Italy," "British Workers Defy Labour Heads," "Courageous French Socialists Still Fight On" were typical of the deceptive captions that warmed and inspired Yipsels readers, who in wartime more than ever before possessed the temperament of banner carriers, purists of lost causes. Inevitable, too, were mindlessly sanguine reports on German anti-Nazi youth activities, self-serving and delusive commentary about radical demonstrations in Milan, and reminiscences about the Spanish Civil War that were exhumed for faithful readers who were reminded not to forget the Spanish working class. There were also articles directed to British Prime Minister Clement Attlee, urging him to provide a sanctuary in Palestine for European Jews, and vignettes that recorded the facts about "starving millions in India," who, as *Challenge* subscribers were told, were under "the iron heel, not of the Nazi over-lords, but of the British." On a more positive note, Yipsels could read of the encouraging activities of their brothers overseas and of the need to work for a "people's peace"—a term employed before Earl Browder appropriated it for the Communist party platform.

Like Norman Thomas, the editors of *Challenge* also criticized the indiscriminate bombing of German cities, which was interpreted as bombing the German working class, and Allied insistence on uncondi-tional surrender of the Axis nations. Like the entire non-Communist Left, the editors never forgot that there were two Germanys and two Italys; and they identified with the workers, as distinct from the "ruling class," which also knew no frontiers. They then came to the inevitably reasoned and orthodox proposition that workers, indeed the "common people" everywhere, should "join hands across the boundaries, across the battle lines" in the belief that, if they did, "the world will be ours."

From this point, however, the Yipsels went on to conclusions regarded as disastrous on both the Communists and the Roosevelt adminis-tration—namely, that Allied efforts to impose a "harsh and crushing peace" must be rejected. And in a significant paragraph, *Challenge*'s editors joined warmly sympathetic commentary on "the war-weary

Germans'' to the plea that they be permitted to escape forced labor in
Stalin's ''construction battalions.'' Further passages highlighted the contrast between ''a miserable and anguished people'' and the aggressive
demands of a number of nations, including Poland and Czechoslovakia,
''now closely allied to Russia.'' Joseph Stalin was inseparably linked to
Roosevelt, Churchill, and other ''imperialist'' rulers as part of a conspiracy to thwart socialism and an aspiring working class. As *Challenge* increasingly emphasized, Stalin was ''boss of a world terror and
propaganda apparatus.'' Thus the Yipsels joined other non-Communist
radicals, notably the Trotskyists—both Shachtmanite and Cannonite
wings—and De Leonites, in expressing a single obsessive article of
faith—namely, hostility to ''Stalinist terrorism.'' As in the 1930s, Russia
still hung over their lives like Spanish moss, and antagonism to her
allegedly lethal designs would bloom in the hothouse atmosphere of the
postwar decade.

Foreign affairs, while a source of brooding concern, were hardly of
exclusive interest to YPSL readers. On the domestic scene they continually arraigned President Roosevelt for sponsoring the Smith Act, especially its implementation in the Minneapolis SWP case, and for ''crack-
ing down'' on wage earners by means of War Labor Board and Office of
Economic Stabilization decrees. Such decrees, *Challenge* editorialized,
in effect repudiated Roosevelt's near-unanimous labor support in the
1944 presidential campaign. Yipsels, by these articles, attempted to be
both revolutionary and reform-minded. Like the Socialist party itself
—and the Communist, for that matter—they were proud of their
''realism'' and of their nonsectarian attitudes, as distinct from the
Socialist Labor party, for example, which, in their view, refused to help
reform capitalism and to support strikes and other union activity. But
Yipsels were uncomfortably aware of their vulnerability to the charge of
being ''social democrats.'' For the league, indeed for nearly the entire
Left, reform versus revolution posed an historic and irreconcilable dilemma, papered over by bravura rhetoric to the effect that ''between the
whirlpool of compromise and the rock of perfectionism, the Young
People's Socialist League shall sail their ship of socialism.''

Their words, formulas, and protestations notwithstanding, Yipsel
editors gravitated inexorably toward the ''bourgeois parliamentarianism'' they scorned. They appealed for the end of the poll tax,

exposed injustices practiced against ethnic minorities such as Mexican-Americans, encouraged radical youth to join the Montgomery Ward picket line, and when the war ended, urged presidential amnesty for conscientious objectors. "The Summing Up" (and, later "YPSL News") reported monthly on membership activities across the country—for example, YPSL picketing of receptions for foreign dictators; or in support of Negroes arrested for union work; picketing of an American Youth for Democracy (AYD) meeting in behalf of universal military training (UMT); and efforts of high school or college league members in providing Socialist study groups on campuses.

Challenge persistently demanded that radical youth be mobilized for an assault on poverty, conscription, and war—that stubbornly resistant trinity of evils which seemed most menacing in the early 1940s. To that end, they rejected—as a choice between tweedledee and tweedledum —both major party candidates in 1944 and sought to advance the Socialist party presidential and vice-presidential designates, Norman Thomas and Darlington Hoopes. The YPSL election program contained no surprises; indeed, it had been reflected in the year-long emphases in *Challenge* on opposition to peacetime conscription and elimination of Jim Crow in the army. The former had a growing urgency, as the war neared its end; by September 1946, Yipsel energies centered upon ROTC and UMT, which seemed to have an axial role in America's militarization. Segregation in the U.S. Army lost its force as an issue after the war, job discrimination replacing it as a major concern of league members. And added to these postwar demands were those for an across-the-board wage increase of 30 percent, abolition of "slave-labor" measures, and legislation that would meet the threat of unemployment—increase of unemployment benefits, nationalization of idle production facilities, and educational subsidies for unemployed youth.

Challenge was naturally preoccupied with league affairs, and it extensively reported YPSL conventions and delegate-approved platforms, chief among them being opposition to American imperialism, the struggle for civil rights, and alliance with the working class. Every convention identified with the European wartime underground, with colonial peoples engaged in struggles for national liberation, and with radical minorities; and in the opaque and traditional language of radicalism proclaimed,

"We will fight side by side with them." Countless delegates looked across the seas for the generational support they needed, and created a mystique—that of a single organism, an international of Socialist youth—which they invested with moral color and a high emotional charge.

Naturally, all Communist students would be excluded. Young Communist League (YCL) activities in this country were of more than peripheral or academic interest to readers of *Challenge*. Long before the rising hate-Russia crusade had reached its apogee, even during the grand political *amour* between Russia and the United States, Socialists had concluded that it was impossible and impermissible to work with Communist-inspired or Communist-led groups. Like their parents, Yipsels declared war to the finish on the YCL, which, they claimed, was trained in totalitarian methods. When the league changed its name to American Youth for Democracy (AYD), *Challenge* concluded that nothing else had changed, and the new organization came under sustained and violent emotional attack. Recurrent editorials exposed the continuity of personnel and policies involved in the renamed organization and claimed that both old and new groups revolved around the interests of Stalin's regime. AYD appeals for closer Russian-American collaboration and for a Second Front had been, it was claimed, the twin focal points of YCL activities. As for its call for universal military training, the journal editors noted that AYD shared this egregious opinion in common with the villainous *New York Daily News*. Other youth groups were dismissed with insouciant disregard—with the Yipsels in effect preempting the field of student radicalism. Only the YPSL, *Challenge* continually reaffirmed, was youth's agency of social resurrection; only it maintained a principled dedication to Socialist goals.

The end of World War II brought disillusionment with it, owing in part to the devastation of human values, the use of the atomic bomb, and the uncertainties attendant upon the transition to a peacetime economy. Having condemned saturation bombing during hostilities, Socialists (as well as Dwight Macdonald and SWPers) also denounced the Hiroshima and Nagasaki bombings. Such weaponry, they said, invited the punishment of the gods. Confronted by man's possible extinction, Yipsels invoked the standard argument that war itself must be eliminated. To that end, the economic and political system that was at the root of international conflict also had to be extirpated, and, predictably, the alternative was a Socialist society.

Of greater concern to *Challenge* were the economic problems posed by military victory. Its editors shared the overshadowing domestic fear that beset the nation in 1945. Due to Truman's inadequate preparations for economic readjustment, it seemed likely that a catastrophic postwar depression was impending. Such a fear was very widely held. After all, factories had to be reconverted. Government wartime expenditures of $100 billion had come to an end. Demobilization was proceeding, war plants were closing, and millions of defense workers and returning veterans were pouring into the labor market. *Challenge* adumbrated, clearly and shrilly, the nation's anxieties. Its editorials seemed grimly realistic in their forecasts of depression, of massive unemployment, and of another WPA. Equally realistic were its demands for Negro rights, for the nation had remained generally insensitive and uncommitted to the black man's cause.

The end of hostilities, in sum, was a time of mingled joy and uneasiness for the nation. *Challenge*'s editors, similarly, found their carefree faith in science destroyed by atomic fission though, unlike many of their countrymen, they retained their faith in progress and in mass movement. But the immediate future did look ominous—even for youthful readers of *Challenge*. The Greek guerrilla forces of EAM, the National Liberation Front, were being destroyed by a United States-supported military campaign, which was denounced in the journal and which also contributed to the Communist party's change to an anti-American posture. (Needless to say, Communists did not appreciate equal editorial time lavished upon condemnation of Soviet occupation policies in Eastern Europe or upon sympathy for "lovers of freedom for the anti-Nazi underground" and for the German people as a whole.) Neither did the non-European world scene provide a basis for optimism, what with the British practices in Palestine and India, French attempts to crush a nationalist uprising in Indo-China, and the Dutch seeking to do likewise in Indonesia.

Nor were domestic conditions and developments a source of pleasant contemplation. *Challenge* catches the ambience of this postwar America in every issue. Witness, for instance, the seeming unwillingness of the Truman administration to fight for housing, benefits for labor and the poor, and for civil rights. The Yipsels, it followed, with some justification and with great moral indignation, could propose the only possible panacea, and one in which they still retained a heuristic absorption —namely, abolition of the "profit system." There were lesser priorities as well, all of which carried over from the prewar and wartime years: end imperialism, support democratic working-class organizations in every country; civil liberties for all minority groups; inviolability of unions; free universal public education regardless of race or creed; elimination of racial discrimination and segregation; equal rights for women.

Apparently nothing had changed. The life-span of *Challenge* had symmetry, ending where it began. History swept in upon the monthly and without editorial recognition or consciousness, which customarily is the death sentence of a radical publication. But *Challenge* never became entirely useless or sterile—possibly because the past that enslaved it also saved it from extinction—because its tradition of radicalism, of naysaying, continued to give it vitality. In any event, the monthly never—like Dwight Macdonald, for example—chose the West in any unqualified way; it never wholly abandoned the old political orientation; it never turned away from the Socialist desideratum, the example of the Soviet Union notwithstanding; it never became skeptical about the future of socialism and grasped this goal with that fiercely proprietary spirit exhibited by all American radical periodicals and organizations.

Amherst, Massachusetts, 1969

Part Six

THE COMMUNIST PRESS

THE two American Communist groups which were founded in the wake of the Bolshevik Revolution were united in the Workers party in 1922. The merger took place after impatient orders from the Comintern, a fact that set the principal theme for the history of communism in the United States. Ever after, the party's policies on virtually every question it faced (including, for example, the question of race in the United States) were not formulated on the basis of a study of conditions or even by an independent application of Marxist principles. Rather, such policies were determined by the Soviet-dominated Comintern which was not only generally ignorant of American circumstances but almost explicitly arrived at its conclusions with only Soviet interests in mind.

American Communists as well as those from other nations were painfully aware of the criticism that they were mere lackeys for the Russian state. But, retaining their conviction that the Russian Reds were actually building a new society, American Communists were able to construct the perfectly feasible rationale that what served even the foreign policy of the workers' state served the cause of world Socialist revolution. However, as revolutionary idealism in Russia gave way to the mundane exigencies of statecraft or, as other analysts would see it, as communism was "Stalinized," the interests of the USSR frequently bore little relationship to the most fundamental ideals of socialism. Indeed, Soviet interests could and did undergo lightning-quick shifts and even complete reversals—to all of which the U. S. Communist party was expected to respond.

The classic example of these policy shifts was the Nazi-Soviet Pact of August 1939, which meant the termination of Soviet propaganda against fascist Germany and, for American Communists, literally meant an overnight switch from support of antifascist liberals to attacks on them as at least as bad as the Nazis. In the party line on American foreign policy, the Communists and their periodicals switched with equal suddenness from "collective security" to isolationism. And this was only the profoundest of the reversals. Throughout the 1930s, 1940s, and 1950s, the CP was obligated by its premises to make similar if less momentous twists. Irving Howe and Lewis Coser relate an incident in the party's Lovestoneite factional fight of 1929 when Robert Minor delivered an article to the *Daily Worker* headlined "Lovestone Backs Bukharin." When, that same night, Lovestone denounced Bukharin, "Minor rushed in, breathless and distressed, shouting, 'Stop the press!' " He then modified a few words in his article, reversed its meaning, and ran it the next day titled "Lovestone Denounces Bukharin."

Decisions made in Moscow on American party policies often had such ridiculous effects. The Comintern would sometimes issue policy directives on matters such as race which were neither related to Soviet interests nor based on an understanding of American conditions. Rather, such rulings were based on a purely theoretical, even absolutely abstract, divination. It is not difficult to understand why the Soviets resorted to such tactics. It is equally clear that the easy acquiescence of the American party resulted in the debilitation of the party's effectiveness and appeal. The CP simply was less relevant to the United States than the old SPA or IWW had been.

Through the 1920s, American communism exerted minimal influence in American life. The prosperity of the middle class, the hostility of libertarian Socialists and Progressives, the antipolitical cynicism of the intellectuals, the ennui of the most exploited groups in America, the conservative defensiveness of the organized labor movement—all served to isolate the party from its most likely allies and sources of support. Little more than a sect, the CP haggled within and busied itself with ideological hairsplitting and organizational trivia. Looking outward only to the Kremlin, the Communists virtually lost sight of American conditions and, in the factional competition that seems inevitable when no real work is being done, they vied obsequiously for the favor of the Comintern legates and tried to secondguess rival comrades as to the Comintern's next directive. Reflecting this desuetude, the party's candidate for president in 1924, William Z. Foster, received only 33,000 votes (although it was undoubtedly a short count); in 1928, Foster polled 48,000.

In the depression election of 1932, Foster received 103,000 votes—a disappointing figure to the party but a considerable increase over 1928, and one which was complemented by considerable local gains. (In California alone, one popular candidate received 80,000 votes.) More important, new directions taken in the 1930s, again coming from Moscow, opened up a "Red Decade" for the Communists, a "golden age" of influence comparable to the old SPA's apogee during the 1910s. The party attracted numerous distinguished artists, writers, and intellectuals for at least brief periods. Energetic and selfless Communist organizers helped to build from scratch and continued to lead many of the new industrial unions of the decade. These included the National Maritime Union, the Transport Workers Union, the United Electrical Workers, and others. Communists and fellow-travelers such as Wyndham Mortimer were important leaders in the United Automobile Workers and occupied important positions in the CIO's national office. Len DeCaux, a radical journalist with close and obvious ties to the CP, edited the *CIO News* and enjoyed the confidence of John L. Lewis.

But the extent of Communist influence was illusory even during the Red Decade. The party's appeal to the literati was as a symbol and was therefore shallow. Like perhaps all bohemian radicalism, the communism of the intellectuals was ephemeral and dilettantish. Even when an individual commitment ran deep, the patent "clientship" of the party leadership to the Comintern and the party's frequently undemocratic, and even sordid, tactics quickly soured such converts. By the time of the Nazi-Soviet Pact, most of the party's celebrities had already deserted the party.

In the labor movement, the Communist party was likewise not as well-established as it sometimes appeared. The problem was, first, that most CP union leaders continued to be enamored of conspiracy or were so uncertain that class organization would indeed unfailingly lead the workers to communism that they kept their affiliations and their beliefs a closely guarded secret. So, in the 1940s, anti-Communist rivals for power could easily red-bait them and oust them from their positions with membership support—even when (which was almost typical) the Communist union leaders had never done anything to or with their unions but render solid (and conservative) trade unionist services.

With the breakup of the wartime Soviet-American alliance and the onset of the Cold War, governmental tolerance of Communists quickly evaporated and the Soviet-directed party itself moved from its Popular Front line to blanket hostility toward American institutions. The party's union base was eroded within a few years, while aging and postwar prosperity chipped away at the once respectable membership figures. When McCarthyism and general acquiescence in the harassment of Communists finished their work in the 1950s, the party became the weakest of the radical sects. Somehow, it continued to survive into the 1960s. (Some suggested, only half-facetiously, that the party survived only because so many of its members were FBI agents who paid their dues religiously.) Spillover from the New Left probably reinvigorated the Communist party in the 1960s but, to most of the young activists in that tumultuous decade, "*the* party" that had loomed so large in the imagination of their radical forebears had become the greatest of jokes.

Communist International
NEW YORK, 1919-1940

WITOLD S. SWORAKOWSKI

THE official organ of the Communist (Third) International, the periodical entitled *Communist International*, published during 1919-1943 in several languages, is one of the most important primary sources for the study of the international Communist movement and the activities of the organizational apparatus that inspired and directed this movement after World War I.

Despite this importance, scholars and writers who have produced hundreds of books and articles on the subject in the past fifty years have only rarely referred to the contents of this periodical. The reason is very simple: not a single library in the United States—nor, as a matter of fact, in the entire world—has a complete set of the English edition of the *Communist International*. A few American libraries do have complete sets of the much broader Russian edition, *Kommunisticheskii Internatsional*, but they can be used only by a comparatively small number of students and scholars who have an adequate knowledge of the Russian language.

The second reason for the limited use of this periodical by scholars and students is the lack of cumulative indexes for the entire runs in particular languages. Starting in the 1930s the publishers provided yearly subject and country indexes, but these are far from adequate or exhaustive. In order to satisfy the needs of students and scholars, cumulative indexes for the various editions should be prepared and published. But this undertaking is not possible until complete sets of the four main language editions are available. Certainly, the Russian edition is available in a complete run, and a cumulative index for this edition could be prepared. But this edition comprises 542 numbers in over 450 issues, with a total of about 37,000 pages. The indexing of a publication of these dimensions is a gigantic and costly undertaking that has little chance of finding a commercial publisher because of the comparatively small number of prospective users and buyers. This could be undertaken only with the financial assistance of a foundation. Attempts of the Hoover Institution in past years to obtain this support failed because the cost was considered to be disproportionately high in comparison to the limited number of beneficiaries of such indexes. Nevertheless, this writer has worked for several years in his free time on a cumulative index to the Russian and English editions. If the English edition of the *Communist International* could be completed, the work on the index would progress much faster.

Here the difference between the contents and research importance of the *Communist International* and the *International Press Correspondence,* the so-called *Inprecorr,* should be clarified. At its founding in 1919, the official organ of the Executive Committee of the Communist International, the *Communist International,* was intended to spread in four of the most widely used languages (Russian, English, German, and French) the ideology, strategy, and tactics of the "Weltpartei," the worldwide "international communist party" which was to lead the way toward a global soviet republic. It was also to include the announcements and instructions of the Executive Committee of the Comintern. Immediately after publication it became the gospel for party members and "activists," which in the Communist jargon included sympathizers and unaffiliated followers of communism in all countries.

However, the third congress of the Communist International, held in Moscow in June-July 1921, changed the task and character of the official journal. The second congress, held in Moscow in July-August 1920, adopted the well-known "Twenty-one Conditions of Admission to the Communist International," which became the organizational basis of the Comintern and imposed "democratic centralism" as its dominant concept. The third congress had the task of discussing and establishing the organizational structure of the member-parties, their tasks and methods of operation, and also the mutual relationship between the member-parties and the executive agencies of the Communist International. It should be kept in mind also that during the eleven months between the second and third congresses radical changes had taken place in the revolutionary potential and expansionist possibilities of international communism.

In early August 1920, the Red Army was victoriously advancing through Poland, and it seemed only a matter of weeks before it would be able to join the revolutionary German proletariat in establishing a German soviet republic in the heartland of Europe. Revolutionary movements in France, Italy, and other Western European countries also seemed to herald the victory of the "Weltpartei," at least in Central and Western Europe. Thus, the Russian Communist leadership at the second congress of the Comintern was overconfident of its approaching victories. But a few days after the second congress was terminated, the Red Army was decisively defeated at the gates of Warsaw and the Communist advance into Central Europe was definitively stopped. Then the March 1921 Communist uprising in Germany, which was to accomplish the revolution without the help of the Red Army, failed dismally. The May elections in Italy gave almost ten times as many votes to the Social Democrats as to the Communists. In France adherents of the Communist International, seemingly quite strong in 1919 and 1920, were still unable to split the old Socialist party. All this showed beyond a shadow of a doubt that the belief of Lenin and his Communist associates, at the time of the second congress, that the proletariat in Central and Western Europe was eager to repeat the "Russian October," was wishful thinking. Hence, the third congress was given the task of elaborating the organizational basis for a new Communist assault with the intention of conquering the wavering proletariat.

In his report to the third congress (July 10, 1921) on the organization of the Communist parties and on the organization of the Communist International, the German Communist Koenen referred briefly to the draft of the "theses" to his report, which devoted much space to the party press. Accepting the opinion of his Russian mentors, Koenen assured the congress that "the best means for the organization of broad masses in communism is the press." The theses on "The Organization of the Communist International," adopted on July 12, in a chapter entitled "On the Party Press," contain the following recommendation:

3) In order to promote this welding together of all the National Sections into a single International Party the Executive should

publish a newspaper in all the important languages of Western Europe. This paper would be able to direct the ever increasing growth of communist ideas; and further by supplying reliable and uniform information would serve as a basis for active work in the various Sections.

The obvious purpose of the new "newspaper" was the "welding together" of all the Communist parties of Western Europe into a unified tool of Moscow's policy. (Another "welder" of a totalitarian movement, Adolf Hitler, invented perhaps a better word for this procedure—*Gleichschaltung*.) Thus was born the *International Press Correspondence,* or, as it became broadly known, the *Inprecorr,* a new mouthpiece of the Communist International, published since September 24, 1921 in German and, starting a week later, in English and French.

Inprecorr appeared more regularly, first as a weekly, and later, for some time, twice a week. It provided the Communist and pro-Communist press with current information on political events and economic developments, paying special attention to news about the workers' movement and to information on Comintern meetings. It printed some speeches and resolutions of Comintern congresses and plenum meetings before they were available in comprehensive editions. However, its information and evaluations of political and economic matters were slanted and unreliable. Perhaps the best known boner pulled by *Inprecorr* was its announcement of the death of Mao Tse-tung. It seems that in recent years the Soviets would prefer to forget *Inprecorr,* since the article on *Inprecorr* that appeared in the first edition of the *Bolshaia Sovetskaia Entsiklopediia* has been omitted from the second edition.

There is still another interesting incident that reveals details about the *Communist International* which were not contained in the protocols of the third congress of the Comintern. The jubilee issue of the *Communist International,* published on the occasion of the tenth anniversary of the founding of the Comintern, contains an anonymous article about the journal and its ups and downs during its first ten years. It mentions that the third congress of the Comintern had decided that the journal "would in future be devoted only to questions of theory, tactics, and organization." Furthermore, at the time of the third congress in 1921, it was announced that the *Communist International* would appear regularly as a monthly. Eight years later the author of the aforementioned article complained:

> The promise made of the regular publication of the "C.I." was not then kept, and this was partly due to the fact that after the appearance of "Inprecorr" the "C.I." was, for a time, pushed rather into the background. The jubilee number which appeared on the fifth anniversary of the Comintern . . . contained a number of contributions concerned with the Comintern celebration . . . but nothing, not even a notice, on the five years existence of the journal, on its work and tasks.

The above article dealt with the *Communist International* in general but had the Russian edition primarily in mind. In those years the "Old Series" of the English and German editions were complete translations of the Russian edition, with certain delays on some articles because of evident difficulties with the translations, particularly with the English one. Thus, the irregularities of the appearance of the Russian edition were mirrored in the English edition.

As can be seen now, the limitations imposed on the journal in 1921 in connection with the appearance of *Inprecorr* were only temporary. When the struggle between Trotsky and Stalin began after Lenin's death and the Comintern was dragged into that struggle and went through its first "Trotsky crisis," the Stalin forces in the organization became aware of the need for a broader explanation of the ideological aspects of this struggle to the comrades abroad. The Comintern's journal, which in the meantime had become obligatory literature for all party leaders and *apparatchiks* in the foreign parties, became the obvious means of transmitting the Communist ideology to the foreign parties. This is the explanation of the start of the English edition of the "New Series" early in 1924.

Naturally, the reorganization of the English edition was again a reflection of the changes in the Russian edition. Starting with January 1925, the Russian edition appeared regularly as a monthly, with the number of pages of the issues growing from month to month. The English "New Series" followed suit: in 1925 there were eleven issues and in 1926 it continued as a monthly, although at irregular dates. In September 1926, the Russian edition was published as a weekly, and the English edition, starting with 1927, became a bi-monthly journal and continued as such until August 1935. But during this entire period, the number of issues each year was always less than twenty-four. In September 1935, the English edition returned to monthly publication and remained so until its liquidation by the Moscow leadership in December 1939.

This fluctuation in the frequency of publication of the *Communist International* in all four language editions reflected the development of the internal struggle in Russia for Lenin's legacy. The years 1925-1936 marked the period of the most intensive struggle, starting with the Trotsky crisis and ending with Stalin's victory, crowned by the Stalin constitution for the USSR. These were also the years when the leadership in the Comintern changed twice (Zinoviev replaced by Bukharin late in 1926, Bukharin replaced by Molotov early in 1929), and when Stalinists were being imposed as leaders in foreign parties.

Furthermore, one should be aware of another peculiarity of the English edition of the *Communist International*. From the very beginning the "New Series" was printed in England (London and other places). But starting in January 1934, another English-language edition was printed in New York. The numeration was identical, and in the beginning so was the cover, with prices in pence and cents. Later the covers were different, and each edition became easily identifiable. However, any doubts as to the place of printing can be clarified by checking the bottom of the last page, where the name and location of the printer are indicated.

The December 1939 issue of the English edition of the *Communist International* does not contain an explanation for, or even mention, the closing down of that edition. Like many things and persons in the Communist orbit, the official organ of the Comintern simply disappeared. There is no question that this was Stalin's decision. It fitted his foreign policy of that time. He faithfully kept his economic obligations resulting from the commercial treaty with Nazi Germany that paved the way toward the Molotov-Ribbentrop agreement of August 23, 1939. But at the same time he did his utmost to keep open the wires to London and particularly to Washington. After the disastrous effects on the Communist parties in England and the United States of the Molotov-Ribbentrop agreement and of the aggression against Finland, Stalin could hardly help these parties by continuing overt Comintern activities in those countries. Hence, the liquidation of the official organ of the Comintern in the English language became meaningless for the work of the ruined parties. But at the same time it reduced the complex of friction with both governments. The liquidation of the English edition of the *Communist International* as a gesture of noninterference in the internal affairs of England and the United States became a harbinger of the dissolution overnight, in 1943, of the Communist International as an expression of Stalin's readiness to appease the Western democracies at the expense of the *lavochka*.

In 1940 Earl Browder, the leader of the Communist party of the United States, was permitted to publish twelve issues of the *Communist International* in New York, but the old subtitle, "Organ of the Executive Committee of the Communist International," was replaced by "Edited by Earl Browder." Thus, the publication containing the translation of a limited selection of articles from the Russian edition became an "American publication," without reference to the Moscow organization and its official organ.

Stanford, California, 1968

The Worker

CLEVELAND, CHICAGO, AND

NEW YORK, 1922-1924

Daily Worker

CHICAGO AND NEW YORK,

1924-1958

HARVEY A. LEVENSTEIN

"YOU must raise ten quick for E Daley to secure fifty quotation stop." Thus read the cryptic cable from the Communist International which arrived in the office of the Workers party of the United States in November 1921. The Comintern was offering to provide $50,000 in seed money for the founding of the "English daily" if the Workers party could raise $10,000, one of the earlier instances of the matching grant idea later so popular with the Ford and other foundations.

From the very beginning of the Communist movement in the United States then, the need for an English-language organ had been obvious. The membership of the new Workers party, later the Communist party of the United States, was overwhelmingly foreign. It could hope to go nowhere in the United States until it rid itself, and communism, of the "foreign" taint. Indeed, Lenin himself, at the Third Comintern Congress in mid-1921, had emphasized this point to the American delegates, urging them to establish an English-language daily as soon as possible.

The party was publishing an English-language weekly, called *The Toiler*, in Cleveland, but this was clearly inadequate. The paper was moved to New York and its name was changed to *The Worker*. But the new *Worker* was still a weekly, and thus was regarded as merely the forerunner of better things to come. Its very first issue, in February 1922, proclaimed: "This, the first edition of *The Worker* is the advance agent of the *Daily Worker*."

Even with the Comintern's generous offer, it proved difficult to raise the resources necessary to change to daily publication. Indeed, it proved much easier to accept $10,000 offered in a previous section of the telegram to found *Freiheit*, the Yiddish daily which would compete with the Socialist *Forwartz* for that section of the immigrant market.

Ironically, the existence of the *Freiheit*, and other Communist foreign-language dailies, eventually provided a basis for the creation of the English daily. By the fall of 1923, the disparity was becoming an international embarrassment. Gregory Zinoviev, head of the Comintern, led off a new campaign for the daily. "It is a most deplorable fact," he wrote to the foreign-language federations of the Workers party, "that against some ten foreign-language communist dailies there is not a single English communist daily in America. Every comrade whose heart beats for the sake of communism must and certainly does deplore this fact and realizes that until the Workers Party has at least one English daily with a wide circulation it will not be able to reach sufficiently wide masses of the American proletariat."

The foreign-language federations, which still comprised the large majority of the party, were each assigned quotas. By early 1924, they had raised the $100,000 deemed necessary to launch the new journal. It was a substantial achievement for a party that could not have counted more than 15,000 members, and, one that, as Zinoviev stated, was already supporting ten other dailies to boot.

The first issue of the *Daily Worker* received some free advance publicity from an unexpected source. Ever on guard against the dangers of the prairie fire of bolshevism, threatening to engulf the world, the State Department had alertly obtained a translation of a letter by Zinoviev, published in *Pravda*, addressed to readers of the new daily. Secretary of State Charles Evans Hughes distributed a translation of the letter to the press, announcing that this meant that a dangerous new paper would soon be on the streets. He was almost scooped, however, for just three days earlier, the *New York Times* had reported virtually the same news, in a small article on the Workers party Convention which misinterpreted Zinoviev's letter.

Finally, on January 13, 1924, in Chicago, Illinois, the first issue of the much-anticipated newspaper rolled off the presses. Tabloid sized, the headline, in characteristic fashion, predicted imminent doom for some enemies of communism: "BANKERS SEEK TO PROP TOTTERING GERMANY" it drooled. One knew at a glance that their chances of preventing the collapse of the rickety structure were slim. The lead editorial, on the front page, confidently declared that the new daily was "the forerunner of more revolutionary dailies in other parts of the country," a prophecy not to be fulfilled for over twenty years, and then only temporarily.

Thus, in the midst of its characteristic financial shortages and incessant optimism, the *Daily Worker* began its long and varied journey as probably the most important single publication in the history of radical journalism in the United States. Born in debt, it remained a financial drain on the Communist party throughout its life. Indeed, from all reports, it was continually the party's largest single expense. Yet, as every Communist was to recognize, it was, until the very end, well worth the money. Although its deficits were frequently bemoaned, rarely was the expense questioned, for Lenin and Zinoviev were right: a party which could not produce a daily newspaper in the language of its own country, giving its own version of the events of the day, could have little claim to being the party that would soon take power there. When, ultimately, daily publication was abandoned, it meant the abandonment, by the party, of the last wispy hopes of assuming power.

From its inception, control of the *Daily Worker* was recognized as crucial by any group which hoped to control the party. The newspaper was the main source of theoretical analyses and party documents for most members. Until 1935, and especially during the later 1920s, Comintern cables to the party were often printed *in toto* by the paper, allowing all members to judge their relevance and meaning. Its editorship and direction, therefore, were more often decided by the outcome of internal party political struggles than by any more mundane journalistic or commercial considerations. This was especially true of the 1920s, when the party went through its most unruly period of factionalism and internal struggle. In 1923, no sooner had the weekly *Worker* been moved from Cleveland to New York, the stronghold of the Charles Ruthenberg faction, when that faction lost its control of the party. The party's National Office and the

Worker were then moved to Chicago, power base of the archrival William Z. Foster faction. There, a compromise was reached whereby control of the paper was supposed to be shared by the two factions, which would also share control of the party. This agreement broke down in August 1925, when the Foster faction gained the upper hand. In anticipation of this rise to power, a group of Foster supporters, armed with pistols, occupied the paper's offices for thirty-six hours, holding off the attempts of Ruthenberg supporters, including the coeditor, to enter. Finally, the Comintern intervened, restoring co-control.

In 1926, the contending factions again reached a standoff, with a tie vote in the Central Executive Committee on the Ruthenberg group's proposal to move the offices of the party and the *Daily Worker* back to New York. The matter was again placed in the lap of the Comintern, which decided in favor of Ruthenberg. Thus, by January 1927, the editorial office of the paper was back in New York, where it was to remain. Thereupon, the party and the paper settled down to a less tumultuous, if not less factional, existence.

The Great Crash and the ensuing depression should have inaugurated a rapid escalation in the readership of the *Daily Worker*, but, if the figures it reported are to be believed, its circulation remained remarkably steady from 1926 to 1935, rising very slowly from 28,500 in 1926 to 30,390 in 1932 to 30,959 in 1935. Of course, the figures it reported are not necessarily to be believed. Not being in the competition for advertisements from Ivory Snow, Chevrolet, and the other major advertisers, its circulation figures did not need to be verified by guardians of the advertising agency dollar such as the Audit Bureau of Circulation. It could report any figure it cared to, thumbing its nose at those who would not dream of advertising in it anyway. The paper was therefore often accused of inflating its reported circulation to exaggerate its support. It is likely, then, that the 1926 figure was highly inflated. During the 1930s, the paper seems to have developed a propensity to submit ever more credible circulation claims, until 1938, when, with the party approaching one of its peaks of strength, the *Daily Worker* still claimed a circulation of 30,598. Although this was not the peak circulation ever claimed for the *Daily Worker* (it claimed 48,601 in 1940, but a rapid decline to a claim of 22,000 in 1944 throws this in doubt), it was probably the most accurate estimate. It is likely, therefore, that the *Daily Worker* experienced a slow but steady rise in circulation in the early 1930s and reached its zenith in the later 1930s and 1940.

It was during the period of the Popular Front, beginning in late 1935, that the *Daily Worker* metamorphized into more than a daily version of many of the other radical journals whose news consisted almost entirely of strikes, lockouts, and the imminent collapse of capitalism. With the new line, adopted to woo Socialists, liberals, and other antifascist non-Communists into an alliance, came a new emphasis on communism as an ideology "as American as apple pie." In the words of Earl Browder, who rose to leadership and came to symbolize the new line, communism was "twentieth-century Americanism." With the new line, there also came a new editor, Clarence Hathaway, who was to retain that post until 1939. For the *Daily Worker,* this meant two things: First, a softening in the sectarian jargon, the hardbitten, obscurantist language of the Third Period, underground, revolutionary party and the attempt to adopt a breezier style, simpler and more direct, calculated to appeal in a new way to the "working stiff," the "man on the street." Gone, for instance, were the interminable, heavy, epistles from the Comintern and the party executive. In came features like political cartoons, lampooning the politicians of the day. Second, the field of interest and coverage of the paper expanded greatly, as the party admitted that there were a variety of aspects of American life which were worthwhile thinking about, amusing oneself with, and plunging into. To accommodate the growing number of "features" it wished to publish, a weekly edition was begun in 1935. Soon, entertainment coverage was expanded, books and novels were being reviewed, and radio programs were being commented on. In early 1937, one of the paper's most popular features, a sports page, was begun.

Ironically, the shift to a breezier, more catholic format and the down-playing of party directives and Comintern analyses was also a function of the shift from the relatively wide-open (though ostensibly more secret) debates and quarrels of the 1920s to the increasingly secretive attitude towards party decision-making of the Stalin era. During the 1930s, the *Daily Worker* ceased being what it had been in the 1920s: the party's chief theoretical organ. Whereas during the 1920s the party workers often looked to the *Daily Worker* for the latest Comintern directive, the im-plementation of which would be debated at the next party meeting, as the party grew more Stalinist its debates grew less public, and its decision-making more centralized. The theoretical articles, or at least the complex explanations of the reasons for party policies, tended to be published in separate party journals, primarily in *The Communist* (later *Political Affairs*). The *Daily Worker* was aimed at the lower echelons of party members and nonmembers, those who could not be expected to understand or be interested in the *real* reasons for party policies or in overly complex explications of party policies. For them, it was enough to try to instill in them some elemental ideas: class consciousness, hatred for "the bosses" and fascism, sympathy for "the workers," "underdogs" like Negroes, Spanish Loyalists, and antifascists throughout the world.

It is from this vantage point that the *Daily Worker* of the Popular Front era holds most of its interest for the historian and scholar. It is the best record we have of how complex matters were explained to the party faithful and fellow-travelers, those who participated little or not at all in the interminable wranglings over the real issues of tactics and strategy that occupied those in the loftier quarters of party power. We know now, for example, that the news of the Nazi-Soviet Non-Aggression Pact of 1938 hit the party like a bombshell, causing all sorts of questioning, misgivings, and self-doubts among those in important party positions. A reading of the *Daily Worker* for that period betrays not the slightest hint of this. The pact is accepted, after the fact, as the most natural thing in the world—indeed, as a masterstroke of Soviet diplomacy. The same applies to the subsequent shift back from the strategy of accommodation with Germany and condemnation of Franklin D. Roosevelt as an imperialist "war-monger." After the shock of the German invasion of the Soviet Union, the paper reversed itself with hardly a word of explanation, aside for the occasional note that the invasion had changed the nature of the war from what it had appeared to be earlier. By late summer of 1941, the paper was embarking on crusades such as the heartrending one to revenge the loss of lives of the poor sailors who went down with the *U.S.S. Reuben James*, torpedoed in the North Atlantic while tailing a U-boat, radioing its position to British destroyers rushing to move in for the kill. The campaign to ensure that the nation did not forget the *Reuben James* must have seemed ironic to many readers, for the paper itself was providing an amazing display of amnesia. Had the unlucky ship gone down a few months earlier, the hardy tars aboard her would have been branded as poor dupes of imperialism.

When the United States finally entered the war, the *Daily Worker*'s reporting of the war became much like that of most other newspapers, generally accepting Allied press releases at face value, incessantly optimistic, always seeing the light at the end of the tunnel. It had a bit more practice than most of its capitalist counterparts at this type of reporting, for it had been covering the civil war in Spain in considerable detail from 1936 to 1939, announcing a plethora of climactic Loyalist victories at first, tailing off into the usual brilliantly executed strategic withdrawals. When the Japanese invaded China, it had further outlet for fertile imaginations. ''CHINESE PLANES SINK FIVE JAPANESE SHIPS: ONE AIRCRAFT CARRIER IS SUNK IN YANGTSE IN RAID ON NAVAL CONCENTRATION; INVADERS REPORTED WITHDRAWING.'' read a typical headline in 1938. It is doubtful, of course, if a single shot was fired in anger from a Chinese plane during the entire year, let alone one that hit its target, but this type of exaggeration was certainly not the sole province of the *Worker*. As a glance through the war reporting of august newspapers such as the *New York Times* would show, all newspapers are prone to this type of reportage, slaves as they are to the government press release and their own wishful thinking.

Naturally, the *Worker*'s war reporting tended to glorify the Red Army and devote proportionately more space to the Eastern Front in Europe than did the capitalist dailies. But this can be regarded as a more accurate reflection of the real balance of importance of the theatres than that of the regular daily press, which led the American public to believe that campaigns such as those in North Africa, Sicily, and Italy, essentially side shows, were of equal importance to the massive, decisive engagements in the Soviet Union. Lest the *Worker* be accused of not being patriotic enough, it should be pointed out that it is difficult to think of a journal that was more patriotic, more proud of the G.I.'s, more enthused about the latest weaponry developed by the massive war machine, and all the workers sweating on its assembly lines, than the *Daily Worker*. Indeed, even before Pearl Harbor, during the latter half of 1940 and 1941, pictures of the latest aircraft, ships, and weapons, accompanied by War or Navy Department blurbs extolling their speed and/or mighty devastating power, were a regular feature of the paper.

Although, for the most part, it relied on the standard wire services for its war news, the *Worker* did develop alternate sources of news. Using

Communist G.I.'s, writing back from their remote posts, and the network of exiled Communists and other antifascists from the occupied countries, it was able to supplement the wire services with coverage more sensitive to the growing nationalist sentiments in much of the world. This was especially true towards the end of the war, and especially so of South Asia, the CBI (China-Burma-India) theater.

While war reporting and foreign news tended to dominate the paper in the years 1935 to 1945, domestic politics were certainly not ignored. Because it could not hope to be comprehensive in its reporting, the paper tended to emphasize a few main themes and topics. First, perhaps surprisingly, there was substantial coverage of the game of politics, of the predictions about whether FDR would run for a third term, whether Willkie could woo away the industrial states of the Northeast, and so on. Then, there was always considerable detailed coverage of selected labor conflicts, the CIO, and the course of legislation affecting labor in Congress. Also, there was usually a daily article or two on the latest pet reform that the party had undertaken to support, varying from the prewar antilynching bill, through opposition to the Taft-Hartley "slave labor" bill, to the drive for Medicare in the 1950s. Finally, there were frequent stories dealing with New York City politics, with detailed analyses of the positions of and fortunes of, first, the New York state and city Communist party organizations and, subsequently, the American Labor party.

The economic reporting of the paper was one of its weaker aspects, but this was a function of party policy, which generally supported liberal Democratic economic policies while claiming that they were merely patching up the leaky capitalist vessel. This was difficult to communicate in individual articles on specific economic issues, so the main devices for making this point were glowing articles on the Soviet Union's victory over depression and deprivation. "RAIL WAGES GO UP IN USSR AS U.S. WORKERS FIGHT CUT" read a typical headline in 1938.

The sports page was the part of the paper with by far the most zest. Like hundreds of other dailies, each day it published a drawing of a leading baseball player or other athlete, with a capsule biography and cutish little cartoons of highlights of his career squeezed around him. Distributed as it was by United Features, it could in no way be considered radical propaganda. Like the other mass dailies of the time, boxing received extensive coverage, but perhaps even more so in the *Worker*. Boxing was the one sport which was integrated, where black competed with white, and it provided an outlet for zealous integrationists to wax ecstatic over the achievements of black athletes. Joe Louis, naturally, was the apple of the *Worker*'s eye. If that atheistic journal could possibly have done so, it would have begun a campaign for his immediate sanctification by the Catholic Church after he defeated the pro-Nazi German Max Schmelling in 1938. But the *Worker* sports page was almost equally breathless over every major fight that took place. When one of the last great Jewish hopes, Barney Ross, faced Henry Armstrong, a fine black boxer, in May 1938, with the aging Ross' welterweight title on the line, *Worker* sports reporter Abe Newman clearly faced divided loyalties of a sort, but knew who had to win. His prediction was written in typical *Worker* (and *New York Daily News*) sports page style:

> The classy welter champ from the windy city will be in there throwing leather with both fists until he goes down before ''Hurricane Hank,'' but the windup figures to find Armstrong crowned world's welterweight king. Fifteen is a tortuous distance for a vet who has been kicking around in the manly art of modified murder as long as Ross has.

The *Worker*'s only continuous story cartoon was run on the sports page. Called ''Little Lefty,'' after its cleancut adolescent hero, for a long while it featured the adventures of ''Professor,'' a scrawny, intellectual little boy with amazing boxing skill. At one point, unable to lure ''Professor'' away from his obsession with reading long enough to train for his crucial upcoming fight with ''Blinky Bloat,'' the big, fat villain, ''Peanuts,'' Lefty's ever-present black friend, gets the bright idea of taking Professor to the Charles Ruthenberg library, ''treasure house of books by, of and for the labor movement.'' There, they get him to train by lifting his heavy ''beloved books.'' Not too surprisingly he wins the fight, ensuring that the gate receipts are donated to ''the kids of Spain and China.''

The *Worker* sports page should not be dismissed too lightly. Aside from being the equal of most other New York dailies in breezy analyses of the Dodgers' latest confrontation with the Giants, it did something they consistently failed to do: it raised the issue that everyone else swept under the rug, the race issue. The *Worker* was likely the only nonblack daily in the country that consistently reported scores and news from the Negro Baseball League. In the late 1930s, it had a regular column, written by Bill Mills, a Harlem journalist, on black activities and achievements in sports. Perhaps most important, and least remembered, is its continual campaign for integration in professional baseball. The campaign finally bore fruit at least in part because of the persuasive pressure *Daily Worker* sports editor Lester Rodney was able to exert on Brooklyn Dodger General Manager Branch Rickey to give Jackie Robinson the chance to break the color barrier.

The entertainment section of the *Worker* tended to be much duller and more awkward than the sports page. Stalin and other Marxist theorists had written much more about the proper attitude towards the arts than they had about boxing and baseball. Entertainment reviewers found themselves correspondingly more restricted. This was especially true of the poor souls who had to review the long succession of lightweight Hollywood movies churned out in the 1930s and 1940s, the swashbuckling adventure stories, the flimsy love stories, starring luminaries such as Douglas Fairbanks, Jr. and Danielle Darrieux, with only the occasional Paul Muni thrown in, like a tantalizing life-preserver to a Marxist film critic drowning in a sea of trivia. The *Worker* reviewers could not simply ignore Clark Gable and concentrate on urging the workers to see *Lenin in October, Pugachev, Young Pushkin,* and other worthy Soviet films a second and third time. America was movie-mad, and reviews had to explain *ad nauseam* why it was mad about the wrong movies. For example, in a typical article previewing an upcoming international film festival in New York in 1938, *Worker* movie critic David Platt, not surprisingly, found the Soviet films to be the ones most worth looking forward to. "You will note," he wrote, "that the most exciting films on the above list are those with social content." He explained:

Films are unthinkable without the masses. It is almost impossible to make a decent motion picture without taking into consideration the masses engaged in the production of the film and the masses who will eventually constitute an audience for it. Unlike certain ivory tower books and paintings, films are not made for one or two people to see. . . . There is no such thing as "pure entertainment" in a film.

Even the most innocuous of Hollywood and British films reflect the
petty aspirations and complexes of a class. . . . The average motion
picture today solves most of its problems by the exercise of pure,
unadulterated love. Love conquers all. There is nothing higher. It
even solves union troubles and questions of war and peace. So they
tell us.

As the above passage may illustrate, the general level of criticism in
the paper rarely reached the heights that Marxist criticism was capable of.
Rather, it tended to be formula criticism, repeating hackneyed saws
which were oversimplifications of some of Stalin's less interesting ideas
on socialist realism.

Yet, the entertainment page was not without redeeming features. Like
the sports page, it was one of the few in white America which was
continually conscious of the social aspects of its topic, especially those
aspects which bore on racism and discrimination. For example, the same
David Platt, reviewing David Selznick's hit movie *Duel in the Sun* a
number of years later, wrote, "[It] is a degrading film. Not since *Gone
With the Wind,* which also came out of the House of Selznick, have we
seen such a display of chauvinism toward colored people." Calling the
movie a harbinger of the growth of fascist thinking in Hollywood, he
attacked the way Jennifer Jones, playing a part-Indian, was degraded and
called "Papoose, Half-Breed Squaw, Bob-Tailed Half-Breed, Min-
nehaha, Tamale, Pocahontas," and similar epithets. "The chauvinism in
Duel in the Sun," he continued, "extends to the Negro maid played by
Butterfly McQueen who evokes laughter every time she opens her mouth
to speak." He also pointed out that Jennifer Jones was doomed to die in
the end because the Production Code forbade Charles Bickford, Joseph
Cotton, and Gregory Peck, all of whom lusted after her, from marrying
her. Not until after blacks and other minority groups had begun their rise
from powerlessness would other white entertainment critics become as
sensitive to racial stereotyping and slurs as was the *Worker* in the 1930s
and 1940s. This is not to say that the *Worker*'s sensitivity was always
well-placed and its attacks always justified. But at least it noticed. This
put it far above most of its competitors.

Even at its peak circulation, in the years just before America's entry in
World War II, the *Worker* was far from self-supporting. Advertisements

were sparse and paid few of the bills. Needless to say, the *Worker* was not a mainstay of national advertising campaigns for automobiles, canned soup, and the like. Rather, in the late 1930s, it had to rely on a few want ads, usually offering rooms to let, and a considerable number of ads for left-wing camps and resorts—Camp Unity, Hilltop Lodge, Camp Nitgedaiget, Avanta Farms ("Dairy and Vegetables on Premises. Bathing, Tennis, Basketball, Ping Pong. 5 Per Cent of Profits to Daily Worker"). For a while a weekly "Where to Dine" section seemed to do well, with a marked preponderance of advertisements from Chinese restaurants, perhaps reflecting more the heavily Jewish membership of the CP in New York City than auguring a Red future for China. By 1947, although circulation had dipped somewhat, ad revenue had picked up a bit, with the addition of a sizable business and professional directory, touting everything from electrolysis to undertaking, but heavily weighted towards services in the needle trades.

But ads were never enough, sales were never enough; direct subsidies from the party were necessary to keep the paper afloat. The paper usually ran at least $50,000 in the red, as it were, the figure increasing to over $100,000 in the postwar years. Fundraising campaigns to defray the *Worker*'s deficit were an annual event, indeed, a continuous event. Party members were urged to contribute a day's pay, and often more. Opponents of the Communists in unions charged that unionists in Communist-dominated unions were forced to contribute to the *Worker* and *Freiheit*.

The party was never satisfied with this deficit and devoted much time and effort to trying to expand circulation. Members were exhorted to sell subscriptions to the paper at their workplaces and in their neighborhoods. In the 1940s, "Red Sundays" were begun. Teams of *Worker* salesmen would blitz neighborhoods, selling it from door to door. If they could not enroll subscribers to the *Daily*—and this was always the most difficult thing to do—then they tried to sell the weekly *Worker* alone. The campaigns met with some success. While *Daily* circulation declined from 48,601 (likely inflated) in 1940 to 22,000 in 1944, the circulation of the weekly *Worker* held steady at around 72,000, the management reported.

This was still not enough. In 1945, launching a massive drive to expand circulation, party leader Earl Browder said: "We are only playing around with the *Daily Worker* until we have given it a minimum circulation of 100,000 copies a day. To set this goal of 100,000 circulation is merely to reach those workers with whom we are already in contact. Until this goal is reached, we must declare that the circulation of the *Daily Worker* is the weakest sector in our battlefront.''

The entire party apparatus was to participate in the drive. Each unit of the party (the so-called ''cells'') was to have a member whose duty it was to increase the paper's circulation and distribution. Each section and each district of the party had a *Daily* representative. ''These comrades are primarily responsible for seeing that the *Daily* is sold in correct quantities in their territories,'' said the party, perhaps ominously.

The emphasis on selling the *Worker* was not merely the result of a desperate urge to balance the budget. Left-wing organizations tend to take money-losing publications for granted. Increasing sales of the *Worker* were important because it was the main organ for expanding the influence of the party among the unconverted. Thus, Browder's magic number of 100,000 circulation was not the ''breakeven'' point. It is doubtful if anyone ever seriously calculated where that would be. It was a political, rather than an accounting, calculation that led to setting that figure as a goal. ''We look upon Sunday mobilization not only as a means of selling papers, but as a means of getting the Party into the homes of the community,'' wrote a Harlem leader.

The dual nature of the drive to expand the *Worker's* readership, the combination of economic and ideological motives, is illustrated in an instruction booklet given to solicitors. Visit the workers' homes, the canvassers were admonished; that is the best way to get *permanent* new readers. Don't simply say ''Do you want to buy the *Daily Worker?*'' they were warned; use a sales speech designed to show them how they will benefit from it. The following sample speech was provided, with the suggestion that relevant issues be substituted for the mythical unemployment insurance bill:

I want to speak to you about the Workers' Unemployment Insurance Bill, now in Congress. If this bill is passed, every member of your family will receive insurance for the period he is out of work. It means $10 a week for each working member of your family and $5 in addition for each dependent, child, or invalid. The bill is now in Congress because of the efforts of workers all over the country acting through their organizations, the Unemployment Councils. The bill is pigeonholed in Congress now, but you and I can wake up the Congress and force action by demanding that they pass the bill. Here is a copy of the Workers' Unemployment Insurance Bill as it is now in Congress.

To understand it better, you should read the *Daily Worker*, which carries news almost every day about the fight for the bill; it tells you of the struggles of the working class to obtain *real* unemployment insurance.

The canvasser would then proceed to explain the *Worker* more fully. If the canvassee would not lay out the 18 cents a week for home delivery of the *Daily*, an attempt would be made to have him subscribe to the weekly, then appearing on Saturdays, for $1.50 a year.

As for street sales, party militants were encouraged to purchase white sweatshirts with a hammer and sickle and "DAILY WORKER" emblazoned in red on the front and "RED BUILDER" on the back, and to station themselves in front of factory gates (or, if the workers worked in an intimidating atmosphere, down the block) or at strategic street corners. To sell effectively on the streets, party newsboys and newsgirls were told, one must develop an effective shout. A sample shout was: "Read the Daily Worker! Only workers' newspaper. Police attack Detroit strikers! Seattle workers demand general strike! Read about Chinese Red Army victories! Read the Daily Worker!"

Another tactic for spreading the good word had dubious environmental effects. "Readers of the *Daily Worker* should not litter up the city's ash-cans with the paper," read the edict. "Copies should be left on the street cars, on busses, on subways or ferry boats. A worker may pick up the discarded copy and suddenly find for the first time the paper he has long been wanting."

Despite the herculean efforts to break the 100,000 mark, by 1947 the paper reached a plateau far below it, one from which the journey would be all downhill. The irony is that the downward slide in circulation had nothing to do with the quality of the paper.

The relationship of the paper to the party bureaucracy, and especially the party leadership, had always been an anomalous one, one that caused repeated problems. Most of the members of the editorial staff were party members, as were some, but by no means all, of the production workers. Few of them, however, were in leadership roles in the party. How, then, was the paper to accurately represent the party line on all major issues of the day, every day? The only certain way to accomplish this would be to have the paper written and edited by the party Politbureau, the committee that ran the party on a day-to-day basis. This was clearly impossible. The alternative was never totally satisfactory. The editor-in-chief of the paper was usually chosen from the top party officialdom, on the basis of political, rather than journalistic, criteria. It was sheer accident that Clarence Hathaway, editor from 1935 to 1939, happened to have considerable journalistic talent. The choice of Earl Browder, already party leader, as his successor showed that journalistic experience or talent meant nothing to the party leadership. The chief function of the editor became to act as a go-between between the Politbureau and the paper, bringing the party's general stance on various issues of the day to the editorial meetings of the paper. During the war, Browder's position became totally titular, and the function of chief go-between was taken over by Louis Budenz. The party Politbureau would meet on the ninth floor of the building on 14th Street that housed the party organizations and Budenz or whoever else served that function would then come down to the *Worker* offices, on the eighth floor, and assemble the top editors of the paper to thrash out an approach to the day's news that would conform to the outlines from above.

These meetings, which involved intense discussions of the paper's approach to the whole range of complex domestic and international issues, required a type of Renaissance man to ride herd on the discussion. Budenz came nowhere near this ideal and commanded little respect among the staffers. The person who really ran the paper, although not officially on the editorial board, was Jack Stachel, a top party leader who also attended both the meetings upstairs, on the ninth floor, and those on the eighth floor.

But neither Budenz nor Stachel was a newspaperman, and the great majority of the staffers, whatever their origins, were now thinking of themselves as professional newspapermen. They were becoming almost as interested in and as committed to their profession as they were to the party. Restiveness with Budenz' leadership was reaching an explosive stage when he left the party in October 1945. Significantly, the growing friction between him and the party leadership had little to do with his ineffective performance as *Worker* editor. Despite the attempts of *Worker* staffers to have someone more competent in journalism appointed to the editorship, he was replaced by Morris Child, a party organizer from Illinois with no journalistic talent or interest.

Child's editorship was a minor disaster, and he managed to ride herd over his sullen staff for only a little over a year. Finally, in the summer of 1947, the Politbureau chose a man whom the staffers welcomed as a breath of fresh air. John Gates had no journalistic experience either, but at least he was young (34), intelligent, charming, and the party's bright up-and-comer. An officer in the International Brigade in the Spanish Civil War at a tender young age, he had just been demobilized from the paratroops of the U.S. Army after World War II and had become a leader in the party's veterans organization. He was welcomed with open arms by most of the staff, learned the trade quickly, and became known, along with Hathaway, as one of the two editors in the *Worker*'s history who managed to successfully combine both journalistic and political leadership.

But Gates was placed aboard just as the ship was beginning to flounder. The Cold War was refrigerating rapidly, and the party was about to be virtually destroyed in the process. Along with it would go the *Daily Worker*. After the fiasco of the Wallace campaign in 1948, the expulsion of the Communists and fellow-travelers from the CIO, the Hiss Case, the ''fall'' of China, and finally, the Korean War, it became positively dangerous to be a member of the party. The Truman administration had begun an intensive persecution of Communists in the United States. It became risky to be seen with a copy of the *Worker*. Gates, as editor, was imprisoned for four years in 1950, along with the other top party leaders convicted under the Smith Act. One cannot even say that he was released too late to halt the precipitous decline of the paper, for even the best edited and written paper in the world would have folded by the late 1950s if it bore the *imprimatur* of the Communist party of the United States.

The pattern was set soon after World War II, when the *Worker* began to lose readers to *PM*, the New Left-liberal daily begun in New York by Marshall Field. Aside from being a larger, more comprehensive paper than the *Daily Worker,* it was more comfortable to be seen with in the subway. *PM* folded in 1948, but a new ''progressive'' weekly, the

National Guardian, had just come on the scene, siphoning off much of the *Worker*'s fellow-traveler audience. The appeal of the *Guardian* over the weekly *Worker* increased in direct proportion to the upsurge of anti-Communist hysteria in the late 1940s and early 1950s.

But the final blow to the *Daily Worker* came, perhaps with some kind of poetic symbolism, amidst the same kind of factionalism into which it had been born. Nikita Khrushchev's revelations of the crimes of the Stalin era, his confirmation of all the worst rumors of Stalin's demented anti-Semitism and the slaughter of virtually a whole generation of old Bolshevik revolutionary leaders, had led to a great upheaval within the party. The Soviet invasion of Hungary had exacerbated the split. John Gates had emerged as the leader of the "liberal" (according to its opponents) faction, and was accused of using the *Daily Worker* for his own nefarious political purposes.

The *Daily Worker* had been the only Communist newspaper to print Khrushchev's speech in its entirety in June 1956, publishing the version circulated by the State Department. Gates had thought this a valuable contribution towards encouraging open debate of the issues, the type of "de-Stalinization" Khrushchev seemed to be encouraging. But Khrushchev had also warned against making the revelations public, against "washing the Party's dirty linen in public," as he phrased it. The publication of the speech aroused a furor within the party and gave Gates' opponents among the "Old Guard" a chance to have him repudiated. Led by aging William Z. Foster, they accused Gates of encouraging the "liberalization" of the party in the worst sense of the term: turning it towards bourgeois liberalism, which meant capitalism and imperialism. The publication of the speech swung to their side a crucial ally, the general secretary of the party, Eugene Dennis, the leader of the group in between the two rival factions. When Dennis sided with Foster in a National Committee vote to censure him, Gates handed in his resignation. But the leadership was leery of provoking the open fissure this could cause. The resignation was rejected, but the battle grew even more intense.

Finally, in November 1956, Gates clearly overstepped his bounds. The *Daily Worker* condemned the Soviet intervention in Hungary. "The action of the Soviet troops in Hungary does not advance but retards the development of socialism because socialism cannot be imposed on a country by force'' began the editorial.

Gates' editorial exemplified the anomalous position of the *Worker* and its ambiguous relationship to the party. His condemnation of the invasion was published the day after it occurred, before the party leadership had a chance to formally decide on its stand. Clearly, the paper was becoming an organ for expounding Gates' views rather than those of the party. Gates seemed to be carrying liberalization to its ultimate conclusion in the newspaper field. He was acting as if he were the courageous independent editor of a bourgeois liberal paper, editorializing according to the dictates of his conscience rather than those of the owner. Gates' neck was saved, temporarily, only by the fact that the party leadership was badly divided over what position to take regarding Hungary, but he had provided his enemies with crucial evidence of his irresponsibility.

During the next months, the attacks on him by the Foster group increased in intensity and venom. He and the *Daily* were accused of being soft on Israel and too tough on Egypt. Gates, in his autobiography, recalled a partial list of the things which Foster called him: ''right-winger, Social Democrat, reformist, Browderite, peoples capitalist, Trotskyist, Titoite, Stracheyite, revisionist, anti-Leninist, anti-Party element, liquidationist, white chauvinist, national Communist, American exceptionalist, Lovestoneite, Bernsteinist. . . .'' Gates' problem was that the very things he was protesting had already driven many of his supporters and potential supporters from the party. The people who left the party over Khrushchev's revelations, Hungary, and Israel were not deterred from doing so by a few *Daily Worker* editorials. Those who remained found the editorials infuriating.

One of the last straws for Gates, and the *Worker,* came in the spring of 1957, when he defended the publication by *Mainstream*, the Communist cultural journal, of an article by Howard Fast, the last of the great writers to leave the party. The article outlined Fast's reasons for disillusionment with the party and called the Soviet system ''totalitarian socialism.'' Led by Negro leader Benjamin Davis, the Foster faction accused Gates and the *Worker* of not denouncing Fast violently enough. They were also charged with not covering Egypt favorably enough and of being infected with ''Jewish bourgeois nationalism.'' The ensuing months were occupied by an unsuccessful struggle to wrest control of the paper from Gates by appointing an executive editor more responsive to the national leadership to work with him. The group led by Dennis was now aligning itself increasingly with the Foster group, becoming impatient and disillusioned with Gates, waiting to strike a final blow.

Meanwhile, the paper was sinking rapidly. Most of the *Daily*'s readership had always been concentrated in the New York metropolitan area; it was in this area, primarily among Jews, that the party was experiencing its greatest defections. Readership dropped from 10,000 to around 5,000 and there seemed to be no way of pulling out of the nose-dive.

The futile attempts to save the *Daily* came, and failed, rapidly. In September 1957, the *Daily Worker* announced a reduction in size from eight to four pages. The weekend *Worker* would now be published on Friday instead of Saturday. There would be no paper on Saturday. "Frankly," said the statement, "we have reached the bottom." Party membership had dropped drastically from 17,000 to 10,000 in the past year, and circulation had plummeted almost as drastically. Advertising revenue was virtually nonexistent and publication costs had risen sharply. The annual drive to raise $100,000 to cover the paper's deficit had failed miserably, netting only $45,000. If the size and frequency of the paper had not been cut, the deficit would have reached $250,000. As it was, even with the cutbacks, it would be necessary to raise an additional $100,000. The disastrous decline in the fortunes of the paper, said the announcement, was the result of both the internal crisis in the party and the "sharp harassment of the Left in the Cold War decade," an analysis that, in retrospect, appears substantially correct.

But it would have been inappropriate for the *Daily Worker* to quietly slip beneath the surface. It did not die without a struggle. Gates held on, and tried to keep the paper alive. It seemed to be the last hope for forcing a change in the direction of the party, for rallying the forces of "liberalization" for a last attack on the old Stalinists and their allies. He clung to his position as editor-in-chief and fought until the end. Finally, it became apparent that the only way to silence Gates would be to silence the *Daily Worker*. On December 22, 1957, the National Executive Committee of the party voted to suspend publication of the paper, replacing it with a weekly. Gates appealed to the full National Committee and lost. He argued that the *Worker* was still viable, and was eminently salvageable.

He had noticed jumps in circulation when it dared to print the truth, before it was muzzled by the Foster group. "The *Daily Worker* is not dying a natural death," he argued. "It is being murdered."

But saving the *Daily Worker* on Gates' terms would have meant the repudiation and overthrow of the Foster group and their allies, the middle-of-the-conflict group led by Dennis. The National Committee refused to do this, and Gates soon resigned as editor and as a member of the party. Shortly thereafter, on January 13, 1958, exactly thirty-four years after it first appeared, the last issue of the *Daily Worker* appeared on the subway, bus, and ferry seats of New York City.

Hamilton, Ontario, 1973

Young Worker

CHICAGO AND NEW YORK,

1922-1936

DALE RIEPE

YOUNG WORKER was nearly unique in enjoying one of the longest lives of all the radical journals published in the United States in the past seventy-five years. Begun in 1922 with the declaration that youth "steps forward upon the arena of the Class-Struggle, and intends to stay there till the end," it ended in 1936 with the warning that the impending world war would not bring back prosperity because "war is only a capitalist way out of the crisis."

Harry Gannes, the editor, raised the question in an early issue, "Can the children of the petty tradesmen, shop keepers, bureaucratic hangers-on of the capitalist state and the bourgeoisie become revolutionary?" This seemed highly unlikely because the "idiotic" school system prevented future intellectuals from experience of life; instead it inculcated the ideals laid down by the ruling class. An example of this is the promotion of drill-like sports. What is needed, Gannes believed, is a method to neutralize the banal influence of the intellectuals on the students.

Young Worker was staffed with many writers who have passed into oblivion. Some were local reporters giving out information about the nearby Civilian Conservation Corps camp food, or about lighting and other conditions in a textile factory in Lowell, or about the prevalence of child labor at a canning factory in Imperial Valley. Some of the names appearing frequently were Harry Gannes, Martin Abern, I. Ginsberg, E. Elston, and Max Shachtman. Occasionally Max Lerner or Nat Kaplan would contribute. Rarely could one find an article by Lenin, Trotsky, or Paul Lafargue. Besides the usually serious if not grim tone of the monthly issues, there was also a burst of humor or satire. Chlipke Poor usually provided this touch in such moralistic articles as "How Mr. Kayle Killed His Conscience." The story tells of Mr. Kayle, a wealthy big business-man, who reads *The Mediator*, another radical journal of the day, so that he can get a conscience. But his conscience, after he gets it, bothers him so much that he is reduced to reading Einstein, the Bhagavadgita, and the third volume of *Capital*. Despite these, his conscience still hurts. Finally, he makes the supreme sacrifice by freeing 1,000 slaves from employment in his factory and presenting a moveable desk globe to a hungry child. Another spoof by the same writer is entitled "A Heavenly Interview." God is asked, "Was Noah's Ark built by union labor?" God's parting advice is that men should not worry about such evanescent things as child labor and unemployment, because these problems are as *nothing* com-pared to what is yet to come. "The only thing to do," God says, "is to forget your troubles by working hard." Later, a humor column was begun which contained notes like the following:

> A nifty Sheik
> Is this boy Francis.
> He knows no Marx,
> But how he dances.

New dance steps were the rage in 1924 because Red says: "Norah: 'What do you think of the Radical Movement?' Dumborah: 'I think the police ought to stop those dances.' " Sports reporting sometimes provided a light touch, as in the story headlined "Communist Youth Beat Interna-tional Soccer Champs." The Karl Liebknecht soccer football team "beat the bourgeois team with ease."

For reportage of then-existing conditions, *Young Worker* is probably unmatched. It had a wide range of correspondents who covered every section of the country. They were devoted to bringing the poignant facts of the suffering youth to the attention of the readers. Theoretical issues such as the relation of labor power to wages and surplus value are encapsulated in headlines such as "You Give Your Boss Free Six Hours of Labor Daily." Instead of excursions into Socialist theory, the editors, including Gannes, hammered home the lessons of conditions of young workers in Macon or Port Townsend.

Articles analyzing the role of organizations in the support of capitalist ideology found the YMCA and YWCA favorite targets. It was pointed out in a 1922 issue that the YMCA, with assets of 100 million dollars, spent forty-five million a year to help fit young boys into the system without a whimper. It was alleged that the YWCA attempted to win as many students as possible away from sympathetic support of the Soviet Union. A list of board members of the YWCA included Mrs. Rockefeller; Mrs. Speer, ''whose husband helped dope millions''; Mrs. George Davison, wife of the president of Hanover Bank and Trust Company; and Mrs. Finley, first vice-president of the American Red Cross, ''which is starving the farmers in the south and west and discriminating against negro workers.'' The Boy Scouts are seen as ''the white guards of international capitalism.'' In Germany it was the young cadets, students, and boy brigades, *Young Worker* points out, who were instrumental in crushing the Spartacists. In England the Scouts aid in strike-breaking. In the United States Scouts are useful in intimidating workers into the acceptance of lower wages and slavish working conditions. That is why the capitalist class is heart and soul behind the Scouts. The Scouts motto, ''Be Prepared,'' really means ''be prepared against a working-class uprising.''

The biggest problem for *Young Worker,* according to its editor, was to raise the level of class consciousness, for ''the United States is the most highly industrialized country in the world. And yet . . . the American proletariat has the least developed class-consciousness of any proletariat the world over.'' Some of the reasons for this, besides the mobility of the workers, waited upon the analyses provided in the 1960s by Goodman, Harrington, and Marcuse.

Young Worker differed from most other radical journals in its time by being (1) youth-oriented, (2) reported and written by youth, (3) more adventuresome in format and features, and (4) more conscious of other than economic effects in the process of alienation. This may seem odd to say, because economic statistics abound on most pages. But these statistics are merely the base of sociological and psychological stories of privation. In short, *Young Worker* is an important source for future studies in American alienation during the closure of the system into militarized monopoly capitalism.

By 1932 the tone of *Young Worker* became more urgent and militant. Food appeared to be rotting in capitalist warehouses while Americans starved. Christmas Day 1932 found Chatham, Michigan farmers without enough food to maintain substandard calorie intake. Speculation on the theme of starvation led the editor to publish an article entitled "How to Starve Scientifically, with the help of the U. S. Children's and Home Economics Bureau in Washington." Things were everywhere getting worse in 1932 and in many places did not improve until American entry into World War II in 1941. Michigan labor camps closed down while Bethlehem and McKeesport Tin Plate Company buncoed workers by laying them off and then rehiring them at lower wages. Ford Motor Company closed plant after plant, and in order to discourage rising dissidence, even the Social Problems Club of DeWitt Clinton High School was closed in New York City. A bright spot for those who still had a little money was the Red Star Restaurant at 49 East 12th Street in New York, which advertised "Good Proletarian Food at Proletarian Prices." A six-course lunch was thirty-five cents, and a seven-course dinner was fifty cents. If one considers bread and butter to be a course, then it is not impossible. In those days one could not find the soup for the oyster crackers.

There are few more fascinating or more realistic sources of American social history than those found on the pages of fourteen years of *Young Worker*. They catch the vitality of the embattled youth attempting to hold its own against an embittered and decaying system.

Buffalo, New York, 1969

Labor Defender

CHICAGO AND NEW YORK,

1926-1937

Equal Justice

NEW YORK, 1937-1942

MILTON CANTOR

THE International Labor Defense, which was founded in 1925, held its first national conference in Chicago on June 28 of that year. The delegates in attendance voted favorably upon a motion "for the publication of a magazine as soon as the organizational basis of the ILD was strong enough to support it." *Labor Defender* became the ILD's official voice in January 1926. Considered with its successor, *Equal Justice,* it was unique among periodicals espousing radical causes in that it had a comparatively long life, some sixteen years. Otherwise, *mutatis mutandis,* it was very similar to other voices of American radicalism —hortatory in tone, lacerating in its polemics, indulgent where Russia was concerned, susceptible to Communist argument and influence, and expressing the American conscience at its best.

Labor Defender/Equal Justice was Chicago-born, at a time when the old moral idealism had been shattered, the old prewar faith eroded, when racial and labor violence reached a new high for the twentieth century. This was, paradoxically, a period of crisis and consensus, of controversy, and of great material prosperity. The story has been skillfully described elsewhere—of how World War I had profoundly affected the old social order. Population grew by seventeen million in the 1920s; the balance of economic and political power shifted to the cities; and the increase in national wealth was phenomenal. But this wealth continued to be unevenly distributed, and the laboring poor remained as poor as ever, a large and seemingly irreducible segment of the population.

American labor felt the full impact of these changes in the old order. The immediate postwar period was a time of testing and of crises, what with nearly a million men on strike in 1919 and the defeat of the great steel strike in the following year. The Industrial Workers of the World (IWW), that highly publicized and greatly feared order, was being smashed on the rocks of repression, and ultimately was eliminated as an effective instrument of the hopes of the unskilled and unorganized. Irreplaceable though it was, the IWW was partly supplemented by William Z. Foster's Trade Union Educational League (TUEL), organized in 1920, which served as a coalescing and directing agency for revolutionary unionism and as a militant educational bureau. But with the gradual emergence of the Workers (Communist) party from its underground existence, the TUEL—more often than not ineffectual—slipped from prominence, and the party became the major force among the unskilled and in those industries traditionally receptive to IWW organizers and ignored by the AFL.

Communist organizers in the labor movement had to make their way against both the passivity of labor and the prejudices of nearly all Americans. The decade of the 1920s found American labor, the beneficiary of steady employment and rising wages, increasingly timid and troubled. Despite a marked national increase in union membership, the heavy goods industries remained relatively unorganized, and, furthermore, employers appeared determined to restore working conditions to *status quo ante bellum*. Hence the 1920 drive of the National Association of Manufacturers for the "American Plan"—that is, the open shop—and the industrial warfare that ravaged coal fields and mill towns in this decade.

Finally, it must be remembered, these were the years of the Palmer raids and of the chauvinism that produced the Sacco and Vanzetti case. John Reed was dead and so was the old *Masses*, killed by a federal judge, and even right-wing labor—now stripped of wartime government protection—was naked to its enemies and greatly weakened. Given the celebrated affluence of the decade, it is understandable that revolutionary unionism should fall completely short of its basic goals. Understandable,

too, was the violence that greeted its attempts to organize certain industries and that made the industrial violence of the 1920s so reminiscent of
the prewar scene.

This scene was steadily available to the readers of *Labor Defender*,
some 14,000 by March 1928 (according to the monthly's count); and they
must have been touched and aroused by the sense of being lost in a
newsreel archive. Such was one purpose of *Labor Defender*—to evoke
the "rich traditions of former struggles" in order to tap emotions and to
build a militant labor organization. Consequently, the monthly presented
articles on the Haymarket "martyrs," the lynching of Frank Little, the
Homestead strike, *inter alia*. Big Bill Haywood's "electric figure," and
heroic Wobbly exploits in the 1912 Lawrence strike and elsewhere, were
constantly recalled in an attempt to identify the ILD with a heritage of
labor radicalism and to see it as conservator of the revolutionary tradition.

That such an attempt meant approval of a strain of romantic anarchism
escaped the ILD, though it fell increasingly under Communist party
influence. *Labor Defender*, to be sure, was hardly Communist-led at the
outset. Its national committee suggested something of the wide range of
radical styles possible in the mid-1920s, for its members included Wobblies, Socialists, trade unionists, former anarchists, and a sprinkling of
Communists—with Eugene V. Debs, Upton Sinclair, Scott Nearing.
William Z. Foster, Robert Minor, Benjamin Gitlow, Max Bedacht,
James Cannon, and Ralph Chaplin chief among them. Indeed, the ILD
boasted that its national executive committee included a wide spectrum of
political and nonpolitical opinion.

Like the columns of nearly all radical journals, those of *Labor Defender* saw only parlous social and economic conditions and, moreover,
observed them in terms of moral antinomies. The heroes were those
unions and union members that maintained the hallowed tradition of
labor militancy or that expressed faith in a Socialist *ex machina*. The
villains were employers, Klansmen, and local and state officials who
were seeking to destroy union organizing drives, and whose antilabor
practices produced the inevitable *cri de coeur*. Hence Angelo Herndon
and J. B. McNamara were deified, while Tom Girdler and American
Legionnaires exhibited the unmistakable stigma of villainy. It follows
that *Labor Defender* gave over its pages to ILD activities, particularly
those of legal defense and "for release of class war prisoners." It

publicized the efforts of ILD attorneys who were counseling alleged violators of criminal anarchy and criminal syndicalist laws. Witness, for instance, *Labor Defender*'s repeated attack on the Flynn Act, Pennsylvania's state sedition statute, under which—in the argot of radical journalism—"workers have been arrested, manhandled, tortured, confined."

Possessed of a simplistic understanding of social and economic realities, *Labor Defender* inevitably limned a state of industrial conflict and characterized the ILD as "labor's shield." It would protect the unorganized and unskilled, those "who fall into the legal clutches of the enemy," and those besieged by "the open dictatorship of the bourgeoisie." To the vocabulary of warfare, *Labor Defender* added a smattering of Marxist rhetoric, seeing the national scene in terms of class struggle and the increased pauperization of the working class. But it also betrayed the influence of Zinoviev's 1921 ukase of a popular front by continually emphasizing that the ILD was officially "nonpartisan" and "nonpolitical," acting in behalf of *all* who struggled "for a better living," and that *Labor Defender* "has opened its pages to all class conscious workers regardless of their political affiliations."

Such words and protests notwithstanding, *Labor Defender* remained faithful to labor radicalism, especially to the Wobblies. There were, for example, frequent articles about James B. and John J. McNamara, the confessed dynamiters of the *Los Angeles Times* Building who had gone to prison in 1912. Duly recorded conversations with them became part of the monthly's inspirational rhetoric. Readers of *Labor Defender* were also continually reminded of the plight of Warren K. Billings and Tom Mooney, both of whom had been imprisoned as a result of their alleged participation in the 1916 bombing attack on the San Francisco Preparedness-Day parade. Both men were well-known trade unionists, and Mooney was also a Wobbly, sufficient reason for ILD interest in what was described as "the outstanding case of class persecution in America at the present time." The Mooney-Billings case, therefore, became representative of all the instances of "class injustice," and I use representative in this context not to indicate the average but the paradigmatic. The prisoners were, it follows, "convicted by the testimony of perjured witnesses"; they were victims of a "diabolical conspiracy"; they remained in "indomitable spirit," *Labor Defender* assured its readers, though it anxiously noted their greying hair and failing health; and the ILD would "conduct its fight [for them] in every corner of the world." As part of this fight, the ILD mobilized its 20,000 members (which it claimed by 1928) into an army of campaign workers, seeking parole for the two imprisoned labor martyrs.

Like the IWW itself, the ILD was powerfully drawn to the cause of the unskilled and unorganized, reacting with special passion to the issues that troubled them. Consequently it featured an article by William Haywood—a decade after the event—on the 1919 "Centralia Tragedy," and ceaselessly urged freedom for the seven IWW members who were still behind bars. "My heart bleeds for my brothers in Walla Walla," declared one contributor. Another, visiting them in 1928, comforted *Labor Defender* readers by finding that "the Centralia prisoners have borne their martyrdom with a soldier's spirit." A third, investing this issue with the same high emotional charge, urged ILD members to "bring together all the power at our command to force the release of our noble brothers."

The ILD also adopted the cause of Sacco and Vanzetti with the same fiercely propriety spirit. It exhorted its followers and the labor movement as a whole to support these "frame-up" victims against "the vultures of capitalism." Sacco and Vanzetti thus became archetypal figures for the ILD—essential elements in radical iconography—and *Labor Defender* was pledged to work devotedly in their spirit, which was always identified with the larger issue of freedom for all "class victims."

These victims were largely the ignorant and the friendless, men and women now swept into the darkened corners of labor history. They were unnamed Passaic workers sent to prison by "the textile barons" because, *Labor Defender* claimed, they joined a Sacco-Vanzetti protest meeting; nine furriers who raided a "scab shop" in Mineola, Long Island; one Edward Horacek, unsuccessfully defended by ILD lawyers; three Portuguese anarchists in Fall River, Massachusetts; IWW deportees in New York; striking taxi drivers in Boston; an ILD attorney accused of violating the Pennsylvania antisedition law; a "Philadelphia militant" who was arrested on an Amalgamated Clothing Workers picket line and whose ILD defenders needed funds. At times, to be sure, these defendants were shaped into prominence by the ILD and by *Labor Defender*, which recognized the importance of publicity and mass pressure campaigns, and by a virile fraternity of their ideas and language. That these ideas amounted to little more than an *ex parte* case for an imprisoned worker, that this language was polemical and unsubtle to a remarkable degree, seemed wholly irrelevant. What appeared overwhelmingly urgent was that every effort be made to free "class-war prisoners," or at least to provide aid and comfort, and the letters of imprisoned labor radicals—on display in "Voices from Prison," a regular feature of *Labor Defender* gave touching testimony to ILD efforts. Nor did the ILD and *Labor Defender* limit their support to individual victims of state repression. Declaring war *à outrance* against American capitalism, they defended American labor in some of its most memorable battles. The bloody and bitter Passaic strike was an object of passionate concern, and for compelling reasons: the strike occurred simultaneously with the first issue of *Labor Defender*; it was the first major strike led entirely by the Communist party, which had begun to see new possibilities in the labor movement; and it had the usual accompaniments—injunctions, invaded union halls, and police who attacked strikers with clubs, water hoses, tear gas, and guns, and who made nearly a thousand arrests. The ILD's response was vigorous and not limited to legal defense of arrested strikers. It would support those imprisoned "for the crime of wanting to live," and, by giving the workers moral support, make "them feel that they are not alone in the fierce fight against the brutal attack by . . . the tyrannical ruling class."

Labor Defender's compulsive moral fervor splayed over half a hundred causes. Witness, for instance, the assessment of Chicago's Packingtown workers, whose condition was found to be no different than when Sinclair wrote of them in *The Jungle*. Or the description of sweatshop conditions in New York's garment industry. *Labor Defender* supported the Needle Trades Workers Industrial Union (NTWIU), that short-lived, Communist-led attempt at dual unionism, sponsored mostly by Ben Gold's furrier workers. It condemned "Schlesinger's company union [ILGWU], the police commissioner, and the lying and slanderous capitalist press," as well as police brutality, broken picket lines, and the thousand arrests of the 1929 strikers.

Labor Defender survived into the 1930s as the ILD house organ. It proudly observed, in January 1930, that the ILD "is now defending nearly 1,100 workers against capitalist justice." Its national officers remained on the lecture circuit in behalf of "class-war prisoners" and the "frame-up system." Its pages continued to be crowded with ILD activities: the endless mass meetings, the frequent bazaars and other fund-raising devices, the prison-relief fund campaigns, the work of ILD branches (which occupied a regular column, "Organizational Notes"), the catalogue of "capitalist justice" in state after state, the letters from prison, the leaflets and pamphlets that supplemented *Labor Defender* (and which took the form of legal primers on the rights of arrested workers, descriptions of chain-gang life, and hagiographic case studies of prisoners being assisted by the ILD), reports on the number of new recruits, the continuing fight for constitutional rights—which *Labor Defender* found to be "one of the glorious pages of history"—the signed articles by Vito Marcantonio, president of the ILD, that denounced vigilantism, a near-obsessive concern of many contributors to the monthly.

The change of title that occurred in January 1938 was no more than that: *Equal Justice* maintained the policies of its predecessor. Vigilantism, for instance, continued to be a favorite target of obloquy, deplored now in the late 1930s, when practiced against members of the Union of Mine, Mill and Smelter Workers. The arrest of striking miners produced a characteristic statement of support; that is, "drive fascist-vigilantism" out of California. Concern for civil liberties also continued. The exultant announcement in *Labor Defender* (of August 1937) that the Indiana supreme court freed Paul Butash of the charge of incitement to insurrection (comparison to the Herndon case was inevitable)—"We Win the Butash Case"—was matched by an article in *Equal Justice* (May 1939), "We Win the Strecker Case," which described how ILD counsel, representing Joseph Strecker before the U.S. Supreme Court, had successfully blocked his deportation. Anita Whitney's exposure, in April 1929, of the blatantly antiunion motives behind California's deportation proceedings was matched by an *Equal Justice* editorial in March 1939 issue defending Harry Bridges, then in danger of being deported by "witch hunters and red baiters." Now the enemy was Michigan's Black Legion, the Tampa klansmen, the Hague machine in Jersey City, and vigilantes who "terrorized" Westville, Illinois workers, Yuma County, Arizona lettuce growers, and CIO organizers in Mississippi.

There still were old causes to be trumpeted, chief among them being the chain-gang practices, Tom Mooney's "years of living death," the countless "political" prisoners. But these were joined by new issues and heroes, such as the Scottsboro Boys, whose freedom became an *idée fixe* of the ILD. Indeed, the ILD transformed their case into one of its major causes, having entered the proceedings at the outset. It mobilized a national publicity and fundraising effort in behalf of the nine defendants, and gave them maximum exposure in the columns of *Equal Justice*. ILD activities became part of a new emphasis on civil rights, and the journal reflected greater concern for the Negro's plight than did *Labor Defender* in the 1920s and early 1930s. It presented many more instances of race discrimination and brutalities practiced against black men. It ran articles telling of outrageous jail terms given for petty infractions; it described the treatment of the Negro in burgeoning southern industry; it publicized lynchings by itemizing the annual record—complete with names and dates—of those Negroes who were shot, hanged, burnt alive, beaten, castrated, and otherwise mutilated; it chronicled the ILD's efforts in support of federal antilynching legislation; it presented the story of prison conditions on Georgia and Virginia chain gangs; it approved President Roosevelt's executive order banning discrimination in defense industries, and the Justice Department's antipeonage efforts.

Reflecting the enlarged scope of ILD activities, *Equal Justice* set forth the record of pro- and antilabor laws on both state and federal levels. This record—compiled by the ILD's legislative bureau—was accompanied by appeals that readers support or campaign against a particular measure. In this manner readers were alerted to the Smith Act and the Los Angeles antipicketing ordinance (which was part of "a gigantic conspiracy by corporate wealth to deprive labor in California, Oregon, Washington of its right to organize").

But the legislative bureau did not limit itself to labor measures; it concerned itself with civil liberties generally. Indeed, this area took on an expanded importance by the late 1930s, with the ILD focusing its attack on state measures to legalize wiretapping, to prohibit mixed marriages, to create "Little Dies Committees"; on federal attempts to deport Communists or veterans who fought for Loyalist Spain; and on federal laws such as the Hobbs Bill, which would have established detention camps. It excoriated the "red baiting, labor baiting" Dies Committee in a number of articles and editorials. Finally, the legislative bureau also advanced a positive program of legislation, which included repeal of various state criminal anarchy and teacher oath laws, passage of laws prohibiting lynchings, strengthening of antidiscrimination statutes, and elimination of the "third degree." And, of course, the program included bills that would forbid arrest for picketing under disorderly-conduct laws, prevent discrimination against strikers on relief, curb the use of the National Guard in strikes, and outlaw "strikebreaker agencies."

Equal Justice persisted in waging relentless war against those agencies and officials charged with violating labor's rights—from Martin Dies to "neck-tie" parties for union organizers, from antileaflet laws in Illinois and California (challenged by the ILD) to sheriff-led mobs which attacked striking miners in these same states, from arrests without warrant to the forced "exile" of strikers from Nevada City, California. Readers of *Equal Justice* were refamiliarized with stories common to the 1920s: "Goon squad attacks" on Chicago's stockyard workers; "horror regimes" in various prisons; the fight to free McNamara ("the caged eagle"), Tom Mooney, and the Scottsboro Boys; the ILD Problem Clinic, which helped uncompensated victims of industrial accidents or those threatened with deportation; the successful struggles in Oregon —for Dirk DeJonge, for those arrested without warrant, for those accused of violating criminal syndicalist legislation; ILD-organized protest demonstrations against lynchings in Florida; ILD-assisted defendants in Chicago leaflet-distribution cases; ILD lawyers who counseled those arrested in a Brooklyn shipyard strike. *Equal Justice* ticked off the account, city by city and state by state. In the course of its exposés, it ran the rhetorical gauntlet, describing police brutality and business-police collusion in the freewheeling style of its predecessor.

Supplementing these horror stories were *ex parte* attacks on persons and organizations which, while not directly related to labor, had become favorite targets of liberal and radical opinion in the late 1930s: Herbert Hoover and his "millionaire cabinet"; the American Legion's activities in the cause of "world fascism"; the Ku Klux Klan ("the Knights of Fascism") which, it was prophesied, would be swept aside "together with their imperialist masters" by the working class; the anti-Semitic Silver Shirts; a variety of hate-sheets including, as was to be expected,

Charles Coughlin's *Social Justice*; the "copperhead" Charles Lindbergh, especially after his notorious Des Moines speech.

Finally, *Equal Justice* increasingly stressed overseas developments. Not that *Labor Defender* had been deficient in this area. It had unceasingly warned its readers that events abroad had taken a menacing turn, threatening to the working class everywhere and to world peace as well. There were continual tocsins, such as the Matteotti trial in Italy, the "white terror" in the Balkans, the mass arrests of peasants and workers (invariably "anti-Fascist") in Bialystok, the "proletarian political prisoners" in Germany, the 1923 Hamburg revolt, the Chilean dictatorship, the bombardment of the Karl Marx Hof in Vienna, the Canton uprising, and the savagely repressive regime of Premier Tanaka in Japan. Additional articles featured ILD efforts to free Béla Kun in 1928, Max Shachtman's national tour to educate Americans about Far Eastern affairs, and "American imperialism" in Venezuela, Guatemala, and Nicaragua.

But, as the clouds of war darkened over Europe and Asia and as Hitler's forces grew stronger and bolder, *Equal Justice* displayed even greater concern than its predecessor with overseas affairs. Criticism of imperialist endeavors in South America correspondingly slackened, as the monthly gave full and passionate treatment to those developments in Europe and Asia that so seared the radical conscience. The threats to human liberty seemed more imminent and menacing than ever: the Szanto-Vagi trial in Budapest, "class persecution" in Greece and the Balkans, "brutal oppression" in Poland. *Equal Justice* carried articles urging international solidarity with the Chinese people, denouncing the Koumintang's devolution from a revolutionary body to "an organization . . . of Chinese bourgeoisie," and pleading for a boycott of Japanese silk. "All the women in the National Office of the I. L. D.," boasted one editorial, "have been wearing lisle since the boycott began."

The Spanish Civil War brought a real ordeal of the spirit to liberals and radicals alike; and *Equal Justice,* as was customary with such periodicals, identified Republican Spain with democracy and with resistance to fascism. A constant flow of anti-embargo appeals came from ILD headquarters. In the columns of *Equal Justice* the Spanish Loyalists were depicted in heroic terms—a radiant and unbeatable people who, with fists invariably clenched, gallantly cried, "No pasarán." American volunteers who fought and died for the Loyalist cause were also drawn larger than life, and their efforts surely gave a strong emotional life to the radical readership of the monthly.

The tendency to convert concrete developments into moral and ideological problems, which was so evident in everything that appeared in *Equal Justice*, is most clearly seen in commentaries on the rise of Hitlerism. Attacks on fascism were made with compulsive moral fervor because of the equation of fascism with evil. *Equal Justice*, to its great credit, immediately recognized the new German regime for what it was. Greatly alarmed, it decried Nazi brutalities against *all* those opposed to Hitler, whatever their political or religious affiliation. It savagely denounced the arrest of Social Democratic unionists as well as of Communists, Catholics, as well as Jews, the Gestapo's activities in the Sudeten, and the "hideous betrayal" of Czechoslovakia. It warned that Hitler was "the chief enemy of world peace," pressed for a boycott of German goods, and observed that the ILD was among the first to protest Nazi pogroms. The journal repeatedly reminded readers that Marcantonio wired appeals to Franklin Roosevelt and to the State Department urging action against Hitler, or assistance to political refugees, or international cooperation with all antifascist nations, in the belief that Hitler "cannot crush the whole world beneath his heel if the forces of progress and democracy unite today in a firm front against him."

This essay has been devoted to tracing the record of the ILD, and especially the two monthlies that expressed it. It is easy to pick at them, just as it is to criticize most radical publications. They tended to frequent vulgarization of complex issues; to heavyhanded, prolix, didactic, sentimental, and often sensational language; and to neglect of those events that reflected adversely upon their political commitments, such as Trotsky's downfall, the great purge trials, the Russo-German Pact, and the POUM (Worker's party of Marxist Unification). But there were virtues to accompany these defects; and one should recall not only the opaque language, so typical of political journalism, and the persistent avoidance of embarrassing turns in Communist tactics, not only the *ad hominem* attacks and the incompetencies of the old Left, but also the very real achievements, especially the efforts of *Labor Defender* and *Equal Justice* to hammer home the significance of fascism and depression to Americans, and to organize campaigns against them, and the activities of

ILD and Communist field workers—at New Bedford or with the National Miners Union and National Textile Workers Union—and the heroism and self-sacrifice which they displayed and which no amount of political denigration could dismiss. These activists were repeatedly beaten by company police and armed vigilantes: some were killed during strikes, and others were imprisoned for long terms on false charges; all of them worked without pay or at subsistence wages. On balance, the ILD and its monthly journals exerted a positive influence on American life. They recapture the freshness, the enthusiasm, almost the innocence, of earlier decades. They recall us to our best traditions and to our humanity.

Amherst, Massachusetts, 1968

Party Organizer

NEW YORK, 1927-1938

PHILIP TAFT

BY 1927, when the *Party Organizer* was established, the Communists had emerged from the underground where the postwar Palmer anti-Red Raids had sent many of the leaders. The Workers party had been established as the legal arm and "Communist" had been added when antiradical sentiment began to recede. The Aesopian name was soon changed to Communist party of the United States of America. The party had also temporarily ended several years of factional controversy during which those unwilling to submit to "iron discipline" had left or had been forced from the ranks.

The *Party Organizer*, published for the next ten years, was not intended for general circulation. It was issued for "Party functionaries so that the National Organization Department will issue instructions and give assistance . . . in the Party campaigns. The 'Party Organizer' is not a mass organ. It is for the Party membership." When the leaders became aware that it was being circulated among nonmembers, an order was issued that "the practice of selling it to non-Party workers must stop." While the directive denied that the *Party Organizer* contained confidential or conspirative information, it noted: "We must, however, differentiate between agitational and propaganda literature for the masses and inner-Party literature for Party members written for the purpose of improving the Party." The magazine is an indispensable source for discovering the programs and policies of the party. The usual jargon and tone typical of other Communist publications are generally avoided. Its purpose is not conversion of unbelievers, but increased effectiveness. With an occasional exception, the unsigned articles are directed to improving the efficiency of the organization and the success of the campaigns in progress. The second issue (April 1927) emphasizes the need for concentrating attention upon training nuclei and fraction ''secretaries and active workers in the districts, sections and sub-districts.'' Articles on how to influence large groups on behalf of the party, or on how to run a meeting, are printed alongside instructions to concentrate upon campaigning for a labor party. How to establish and operate a shop paper is a recurring theme.

A review of the *Party Organizer* tells us the particular areas and plants to which party activists are asked to direct their major attention. No effort is made to hide shortcomings or failures. A constant complaint is the high membership turnover, and suggestions for reducing the outflow are continually discussed. The *Party Organizer* can therefore provide a limited check of the claimed successes which are found in other Communist publications. Reference to specific campaigns conducted by the party are frequently given, and party members are told when and how to promote them. In 1928, party members were urged to give first priority to promoting the anti-administration campaign in the coal miner's union, and to raise funds for a conference to launch an opposition to that organization.

Beginning in 1928, an increasing number of articles stress the importance of establishing party nuclei in factories, especially the large ones in Ohio and Michigan. Advice on campaigns in the textile industry and how to conduct open-air meetings and study circles is also given. The *Party Organizer*, from 1929 on, gives increasing attention to the duty of party members to join trade unions and to become active in them. Details on specific behavior in these organizations are also offered. For example:

> Communist members of each union . . . must be united into a Communist fraction and conduct active fractional work. . . . The policy pursued in every union is determined by the Party Committee. The fraction is the instrument of the Party in carrying out this policy. The fraction can only make decisions insofar as they refer to applying the policy of the Party as already decided upon by the Party Committee. . . . The decision of the Party Committee must be unconditionally carried out by the fraction. Candidates for all conventions, committees, etc. shall be nominated by the fraction execu-

tive and approved by the proper Party Committee. If necessary, the Party Committee itself can nominate its candidates.

This type of directive did not appear in literature published for general circulation, and the value of the *Party Organizer* is in revealing aspects of policy which are not publicly discussed or acknowledged. The affiliation of several thousand Communists with the trade unions made it necessary to convey this order through semisecret channels.

Interspersed among articles on how to handle finances and work in mass organizations are discussions on recruiting and the relations of the member to the party. In March 1931, the central committee said: "Refusal to act in accordance with the line laid down by higher specific committees of the Party, or refusal to carry out specific decisions and instructions issued by the leading committees within their respective jurisdictions, are absolutely impermissable."

Articles in 1931 and 1932 deal with work in mass organizations; extending influence to small towns; and how to act under arrest, stabilize finances, conduct antiwar demonstrations, and develop shop nuclei. Several articles appear on organizing war and heavy industries, and how to work among the unemployed. The recruiting of Negroes into the party is urged with greater frequency in the early 1930s and continues thereafter. How to improve agitation is another topic which is periodically examined. Special stress is placed upon infiltrating particular large plants, and the manner by which success can be achieved as illustrated by the experience of others. Shop papers put out by party activists are examined, and there is frequent discussion of how to make these publications more attractive. How to win the confidence of workers in the shop, and the art of concentrating upon certain plants are gone over a number of times. The articles seek to go from the general to the particular, and illustrations from experience are frequently given to show how grievances in plants can be utilized to gain influence for the party.

Throughout 1933, the winning of "key workers in key industries" is given attention, and instructions on how to promote the "united front" against war and in favor of unemployment insurance are also published. Information on how to avoid arrest and the safeguarding of membership lists and records from police seizure is given in another article. A number of strikes are discussed, and advice is also offered on how Communist minority blocs can operate within unions without arousing opposition. Recruiting of strike activists into the party is another favorite topic, they and the young being prime targets of Communist recruiters.

The first Roosevelt administration opened possibilities of organizing millions of workers into unions, and a number of issues devote space to directions for concentrating major attention upon particular plants in industries which appear promising to Communist penetration. Over the entire period of publication the recruiting and fluctuation of membership are given periodic attention, and members are advised on methods by which recruits can be kept in the party.

Housekeeping topics are not avoided. Advice on how to keep financial accounts and hints on effective expenditures and dues collections appear. Shortcomings in methods and failures in specific situations are continually examined, and advice is offered on how to avoid future failures. Effective methods of distributing literature, penetrating Negro groups, establishing shop newspapers, capitalizing on grievances, training "Communist cadres," writing a leaflet, organizing a shop meeting, an election rally, or a class on Leninism, are all analyzed and members are urged to heed them. The aim is to make the activist more efficient in work within the party, and also within nonparty groups in which he may be operating.

The pages of the *Party Organizer* are almost completely free of denunciation of opponents or exaggerated claims. The ten years in which the *Party Organizer* was issued was a period in which the Communist party enjoyed its greatest influence in the United States. It is one of the important records of party activity during this time, and one that no student can overlook.

Providence, Rhode Island, 1968

Student Review

NEW YORK, 1931-1935

GEORGE P. RAWICK

STUDENT REVIEW was the monthly organ of the National Student League between December 1931, and October 1935. The National Student League was the agent of the Communist party and the Young Communist League on American university campuses in the 1930s; it was strongly centered in New York City with smaller units elsewhere. Among the editors of *Student Review* were Theodore Draper, who was later to break with the Communist party and become the major historian of American communism, and Donald Henderson, then a young instructor at Columbia University, later to become president of the Farm Equipment Workers of America.

In general, the contents of the *Student Review* paralleled that of other Communist periodicals of the same period. The Communist International was in its so-called "Third Period" when it called for immediate revolution everywhere and considered all non-Communist Socialists to be "social fascist," that is, while subjectively Socialist, objectively they served the purpose of the fascists. Thus, for example, *Student Review* characterized the Socialist League for Industrial Democracy and its Student Council as "social fascist."

In the pages of the journal in 1932, 1933, and 1934, strong emphasis was placed on the most violent struggles in the United States: coal mine strikes in Harlan County, Kentucky, demonstrations of the unemployed in dozens of cities, near-violent demonstrations of students at the City College of New York against the policies of its president, and reports of farmers' unrest. Significantly, there was relatively little about the stirrings among workers in auto, steel, and rubber, out of which would come the Congress of Industrial Organizations. The Communist students had no more relationship with these events than did most other sectors of American socialism and communism.

There was considerable emphasis in the journal on the development of something called "proletarian culture" in art and in literature. One can discern, however, a certain reluctance on the part of the editors of the journal to accept fully this "prolecult" approach to the arts. In this way, and in others, *Student Review* indicated that there was at least some degree of deviation from the hard and fast Communist party line within the National Student League.

Until 1934, *Student Review* generally parrotted the hard Communist line in relationship to the struggle against fascism and Naziism. Only through a Communist victory, which would include the defeat and destruction of the "social fascist" social democrats, could there be a victory over Hitlerism and other fascist manifestations. But in 1934, there began to be a shift in emphasis on this subject in the pages of *Student Review*. The editors of *Student Review*, in daily contact with the Socialist students from the Student League for Industrial Democracy, had begun to find less and less reality in the doctrines of the theory of "social fascism." They discovered that there were many in the Student League for Industrial Democracy with whom they could work, and that it was pointless to attack these as "social fascists." There began to be seen in the pages of *Student Review* reflections of united front activities with SLID members on various campuses in the New York City area. In so doing, the National Student League and *Student Review* anticipated by many months Dimitrov's speech at the fifth congress of the Comintern in late 1934, which heralded the abandonment of the third period "social fascist" line and the development of the Popular Front, that is, the united struggle of all left-wing and Progressive forces against fascism and the consequent abandonment of the call for the Socialist revolution.

In the transitional period of late 1934 and 1935, the *Student Review* laid heavy emphasis on antiwar and antifascist activities, including the organization, with the SLID, of massive antiwar demonstrations.

Thus, by late 1934, the stage had been set for the first open, united front activity with the SLID and the eventual merger of the two organizations in late 1935 and the creation of the American Student Union, which was to emerge as the most significant agency of the Popular Front in the United States.

Rochester, Michigan, 1968

Joseph Clark writes of *Student Review*:

Perhaps the 1930s will not seem so different or so distant after a reading of *Student Review*. The span from first issue to last takes us from the end of 1931 to the spring of 1935. As the magazine of the National Student League it ceased publication when it attained a major objective—merger of the NSL with the Student League for Industrial Democracy, to form the American Student Union.

Here is the voice of the New Left of the 1930s, or of that part of the student Left dominated by the Communists. Oddly enough, to this participant in that student movement, whose children have grown up in a vastly different world, whose ambience is the New Left of the 1960s, re-reading the magazine brought with it a shock of recognition. I refer not to nostalgia, but to how reminiscent this is of *today's* portside politics. Indeed, *plus ça change, plus c'est la meme chose,* since the similarities between Old Left and New Left are so startling. We'll note the differences, too, but the similarities seem to tell us that each generation of youthful activists must make its own mistakes, even when they are the same mistakes made by earlier generations.

Take two fundamental *Student Review* attitudes which are, essentially, also positions of the New Left. One, that the source of all malaise, all evils and wrongdoing, is the capitalist-imperialist system, *our* social system; and the corollary, that the old system must be overturned, dug out, root and branch. Second, that the major foe is liberalism and that the concentrated wrath and fire of the youthful revolt must be directed against those who would reform the system, those who seek social change through moderate political action; and the corollary of *that* position, that issues are raised not to be decided, since the worse things are, the better the chances of revolutionary change. Civil rights leader Bayard Rustin aptly described this as the philosophy of ''no win.''

"Tragedy of a Liberal" is the characteristic title of a review of Lincoln Steffens' autobiography, in an early issue of *Student Review*. Though the reviewer is disappointed that "the real message of the Revolution failed to penetrate" to Steffens, he is happy about one conclusion which the great muckraker did arrive at: "that representative government in any real sense was a myth." We'll find similar conclusions today in the ranks of Students for a Democratic Society (SDS) and in magazines such as *Ramparts*.

Readers of *Student Review* might wonder how the National Student League ever acquired a measure of influence on campuses in many parts of the country, considering its sectarian attitudes. Thus, in an early issue the Socialist party is condemned, and along with it, the Socialist-minded League for Industrial Democracy, for calling on the American government to oppose the Japanese invasion of Manchuria. And an open letter to seventeen Chinese students at Columbia University berates them for volunteering to return to China to fight Japan. (Even indirect support or reliance on either capitalist government—U.S. or Chinese—was anathema.)

But the discerning reader will appreciate how much appeal there was to idealist and forward-looking students in actions such as the delegation that went to embattled Harlan and Bell counties in Kentucky. Steffens' harsh judgment about the myth of representative government had considerable truth in the coal-mining counties of Kentucky; the Bill of Rights was as repugnant and alien to the sheriffs and their deputies who did the mine-owners' bidding in those days as the *Communist Manifesto*. And John Dos Passos wrote in *Student Review* that he felt the actuality of the American Revolution in the Kentucky mining regions.

While the Communist leadership of the National Student League was always seeking to impart the "deeper political significance of the issues" as they might arise on campus, students responded to the real issues themselves. Thus, when Columbia University suspended Reed Harris, editor of *Spectator*, the National Student League organized protests and a student strike; Reed Harris was reinstated. If the Communists won a small measure of influence among college students, they were ably assisted by the Harlan County sheriffs who brutally broke strikes, and by college administrators who curbed the freedom of college editors. The

Communists had the wit and the guile to champion the cause of free speech even though their ideology bound them to a suppression of freedom as ghastly as any imposed in modern times.

In at least two respects the Communist student movement outmaneuvered the more moderate Socialist Student League for Industrial Democracy. From the very beginning the National Student League emphasized very real, immediate demands and issues. These ranged from academic freedom (of which there was a greater scarcity in the 1930s than in the 1960s) and opposition to high fees and tuition (in the midst of a raging depression), to lower prices for milk in school cafeterias and better conditions for student-workers. The League for Industrial Democracy tended to stress the larger social issues of the day. And secondly, the Communists discovered the power of "unity" as a watchword against reaction. Early in the 1930s, even before the signal came from Moscow for a united front, and later, for "organic unity" with the Socialists, the Communist student leaders were urging a merger of the National Student League and the Student League for Industrial Democracy. The Socialists often found themselves on the defensive in this situation, and when the American Student Union was born the Communists achieved a "higher" synthesis by dominating the new organization.

I remember quite vividly the long negotiations between committees of the NSL and the SLID about the terms of the merger. Along with other NSL leaders I was utterly sincere about the need for wider unity, and there were tears in my eyes when I finally agreed that we would give up the name of our organization.

In at least one respect the Marxist Left of the 1930s had more evidence to support its position than ever before in the history of Marxism, at least since the middle of the nineteenth century when Marx was pouring over the Blue Books in the British Museum. The depression and mass unemployment made much of what we read in Marx's *Capital* seem very prescient. Perhaps this circumstance explains an important difference between the student Left of the 1930s and that of the 1960s. While both Old and New Left may have made liberalism the enemy, and while both may have given up the possibilities of peaceful progress and reform, there are few signs that the New Left today has a blueprint of the future as the Communists had in the 1930s. Millions of unemployed, ten, twelve, even fourteen million workers out of jobs, with no unemployment insurance, was certainly evidence of how poorly the system was working. Surely in a society of production for use and not for profit, where the means of production were collectively owned, this could never happen. Proof? We had it! Look to the Soviet Union, where they have labor shortages, not unemployment.

Lincoln Steffens had gone to the Soviet Union and brought back the stunning message: "I have seen the future, and it works." And student delegations, encouraged by the National Student League, traveled to the promised land; what they saw shocked some of them, but they continued to believe and spread the gospel, as reported in *Student Review*. Eyes that were prepared to see no evil saw evil, but failed to report it, and those, like myself, who heard it, refused to believe the evil. One of the Columbia students who had been to Russia in 1932 was on the same boat on which I was returning from the Amsterdam antiwar congress that summer. To this day I remember the shock and disbelief I felt when he said, quite casually: "There's famine in the Ukraine, people are dying and being killed by the thousands in the collectivization campaign." That part of what he discovered in Russia never appeared in *Student Review*. I never really believed it until I read that incredible comment of Stalin to Churchill, about how many peasants "were wiped out" in that four-year period of the early 1930s; "ten million," Stalin told Churchill. (Winston Churchill, *The Hinge of Fate,* New York, 1950, p. 498.)

It's hardly possible for any section of the New Left today to offer the Soviet Union as the wave of the future or as a model for the present. Some in the New Left have seen something of a model in Che Guevara's Cuba, or in Regis Debray's fantasies; but these are mainly dreams of revolutionary ecstasy rather than blueprints of a new society. And though ideology creeps in upon the New Left it is not (at least as yet) the deadening, all-embracing ideology which made a secular religion of what had once been Marxism.

It may be that in every era when critical issues cry out for solution in a democratic society, there will be division between those who envision apocalyptic, revolutionary solutions, and those who seek practical reform and change. The very big question raised in the 1930s was whether our system could eliminate large-scale unemployment and end the depression that had darkened the land. The issue was decided in favor of reform, mainly through the New Deal, with an assist from a renascent labor movement. Many who participated in the struggles of the 1930s have learned another lesson—that the need for reform and change is never-ending. One transformation, even one revolution, hardly ever suffices. The greatest test of a democratic society is its ability to change and make continual progress; and it seldom comes easy.

Participants in the student Left of the 1930s lived life intensely; they enjoyed the battles; they were part of a brotherhood of like-minded persons. They were beckoned by false visions, but, as Wordsworth once noted:

> Bliss it was that dawn to be alive,
> But to be young was very heaven!

New York, 1968

Student Advocate

NEW YORK, 1936-1938

GEORGE P. RAWICK

AT the end of 1935, the pro-Communist National Student League merged with the Socialist Student League for Industrial Democracy to form the American Student Union. The National Student League's organ, *Student Review*, was merged with *Student Outlook*, the SLID publication, to form *Student Advocate*. The leading figures in the American Student Union, James Wechsler from the National Student League, and Joseph Lash from the SLID became the main editors of *Student Advocate*. They both agreed that the major aim of the American Student Union and of *Student Advocate* was to support a collective security foreign policy, that is, the unity of the Soviet Union and the Western capitalist democracies in the struggle against fascism and Roosevelt's New Deal at home.

The American Student Union and *Student Advocate* were probably the most important Popular Front enterprises of the 1930s. They were so successful in merging Communist, social-democratic, and liberal points of view as to appear as liberal publications and organizations without any Marxist or Socialist content. Although many of the most important leaders of the American Student Union and editors of *Student Advocate* were members of the Communist party and the Young Communist League, or were perfectly willing to work with them, the ASU public image and impact was liberal and pro-New Deal.

The New Deal itself fully recognized this and utilized the American Student Union and the pages of *Student Advocate* as propagandists for President Roosevelt's policies. Mrs. Eleanor Roosevelt became the champion of the American Student Union and of the *Student Advocate* editor, Joseph Lash. Leading American Student Union officials often were guests at the White House and were consulted on matters dealing with youth; in the activities of the federal government's National Youth Administration, the American Student Union had an official and important position on the National Advisory Committee of that agency.

The pages of *Student Advocate* from February 1936 to March 1938 read like the official news releases of New Deal agencies. Moreover, they acted as a special lobby for the New Deal youth program, the Civilian Conservation Corps, and the National Youth Administration, but most particularly the latter.

In the first part of 1938 *Student Advocate* was abandoned, as the Popular Front in the United States moved to disband any institutions that might be seen as conflicting with or disagreeing with the New Deal. It was obviously felt that *Student Advocate* provided too close a link with that period of the American Student Union's history when it was presumed to be a united front of Socialists and Communists. The new American Student Union, which was to be purely liberal in its public appearance, no longer needed this publication.

Two last points. The main significance of the American Student Union and *Student Advocate,* from a point of view other than that concerned with policy-making, was the fact that, through the manipulation of the Communist party, these organs became conveyor belts that carried young Communist and young Socialist students from these commitments to the official liberalism. The function of the ASU was therefore not that of making Communists out of liberals, as has been charged by many, but precisely the opposite. It made liberals out of Socialists and Communists.

Thus, it was no accident that both former Communist James Wechsler and former Socialist Joseph Lash, the editors of *Student Advocate,* were to refuse to go along with the Communists in the American Student Union when the latter sharply abandoned the collective security line at the time of the Hitler-Stalin pact in late 1939. (Wechsler became the liberal editor of the *New York Post,* and Lash a journalist for that paper.) Wechsler, Lash, and hundreds of others demonstrated that their participation in the American Student Union and *Student Advocate* was based no longer on the tactical needs of the Communist party and the Soviet Union, but upon genuine advocacy of the New Deal at home and collective security abroad.

The American Student Union and *Student Advocate* were not simply somewhat isolated parts of the American Left; they were part of the mainstream of official governmental and political life. This fundamental experience of an entire generation of young liberals was to leave its indelible mark on the development of American liberalism. The fact that American Student Union leaders were welcome in the White House is a mark of the transition from that stage where American liberalism was a main part of a dissenting tradition to its becoming the center of the establishment.

Rochester, Michigan, 1968

Joseph P. Lash writes of *Student Advocate:*

Re-reading *Student Advocate,* which I had not done for almost thirty years, was like re-visiting an old love. She had been hard to get along with and in the end she had betrayed you, but in retrospect the misery and anguish seem less important than the glory and high romance of those days. Perhaps it was because we were young, could believe, and were committed.

We loved the good and hated evil, brimmed with energy and soared on the wings of our hopes. We also thought of ourselves as an army—"the armies of progress are marching/ At the fascists they are hurled," we sang as we paraded proudly and defiantly on May Day.

I tell you when a man's young
He should have the full strength of an angry love. . . .

one of the undergraduate contributors to these pages wrote. His name was Richard Rovere and the lines catch the spirit of those who were young at that time, and of these pages.

The *Student Advocate* was successor to two other radical student magazines. One, the *Student Outlook,* was the voice of the Socialist-oriented Student League for Industrial Democracy. I had been its editor. For two issues we called it *Revolt,* but even in the turbulent days of bank closures, farm holidays, and bonus marches, that proved too lurid a title for students who had to hawk the magazine on the campus, so we shifted to the more neutral designation, *Student Outlook*. The other predecessor of the *Advocate* was the magazine of the Communist-oriented National Student League, the *Student Review*.

In Christmas week 1935, the two left-wing student groups, together with some independent liberal clubs, combined to form the American Student Union as a campus Popular Front against war and fascism. James A. Wechsler, young, brilliant, combative, formerly editor of the *The Columbia Spectator,* was designated by the National Student League as editor of the *Advocate*. To balance the masthead politically I was designated as associate editor, largely to safeguard the Socialist investment in the enterprise. I turned out to be a wretched guardian, because a couple of years later I went over to the Communist side. I intrude this autobiographical note only because readers will find the journal lively, well-written, surprisingly free of political sectarianism, and genuinely reflective of what was taking place on the campus. That was largely the result of Wechsler's inspired guidance, his talents as an editor, and his wide ranging interests.

The magazine was a departure from the heavyhanded and solemn punditry that usually passed for journalism on the Left. Wechsler published articles on undergraduate sports, how Vassar girls snared their men, as well as an eyebrow-raising series on sex problems. Some of the more solemn left-wing thinkers thought the last was carrying the Popular Front approach too far. But all the articles had some political angle and those on sex were billed as part "of a broader effort by students everywhere to shed the cloak of hypocrisy and deceit so rampant in our society today." The fact that the author was a reputable public health official and a Negro also helped to deter those who thought we were confusing radicalism with bohemianism.

As one goes through these pages it becomes apparent that the new student Left of the 1960s is not too different from the old. No doubt others writing in this book will be quoting the old maxim that those who fail to read history are condemned to repeat it. I would hope that the youth of the 1960s would take a look at *Student Advocate*, for I think our experience in the 1930s has some relevance. For one thing, we felt Armageddon to be just as imminent as the 1960s do. It was the justification of our zealotry, of our compromises with truth, and sometimes, even with decency. Yet we survived those dangerous years and would have been better off with less fanaticism and fewer compromises with the dogmatists. It should also be noted—in our favor—that difficult as those years were, especially after Munich, the Moscow trials, and the fall of Republican Spain, we did not try to escape into drugs and nihilism.

Like the 1960s, we went after the campus establishment, as is evident in the series on college presidents called "Academic Napoleons." We demanded that students be given a voice in the shaping of curriculum and disciplinary decisions. We harried the ROTC with the same ferocity that the 1960s go after recruiters for the CIA and Dow Chemicals. Peace was the overriding, obsessive preoccupation of the 1930s as it is of the 1960s. We were partisans of the Oxford Pledge not to support the government in any war, and our annual student strikes were said to be dress rehearsals of what we intended to do if and when our government did declare war. "I hope they mean it," one principal is quoted in these pages as saying. "I want to believe that upon the declaration of war one million young men will march singing into the internment camps."

We were never put to the test because by Pearl Harbor most of us had abandoned the Oxford Pledge. We began to do so with the outbreak of the war in Spain. Because of Spain, the 1937 peace strike was a divided affair, with the isolationists and pacifists holding fast to neutrality, while the rest of us insisted that there was no contradiction between the fight for peace and the militant defense of Loyalist Spain against the fascist aggressors. Our feelings were not dissimilar to those felt in June 1966 when many of us who opposed the war in Vietnam found ourselves cheering on the Israelis.

Stimulating and informative as these pages are, there is a grimmer side to them. In the first issue of the *Advocate*, Wechsler bravely wrote that the magazine was appearing "in an hour when independent thought and endeavor are being curtailed on every side. So terrifying is the onrush of reaction, so bold are the exponents of the goose-step that the need for an uncensored fearless student journal seems self-evident." The sentiment was grand, but we were hardly exemplars of freewheeling journalism, pursuing the truth no matter what the cost to vested interest.

There is a noticeable blandness about these pages. The disputes that were tearing apart the Left go unmentioned. There is no word adverse to the Soviet Union, little honest debate of the problems that were confronting the Left. In an early issue the president of the National Student Federation of America is denounced as a careerist and opportunist for calling the American Youth Act unrealistic. Yet two years later the left-wing sponsors of the Act were themselves amending its provisions in line with suggestions from officials of the Roosevelt administration. We did so because we now wanted to help rather than harass the New Deal. FDR was no longer "the friend and ally" of the Liberty League, yielding to "right-wing pressure on every crucial issue," as we wrote in March 1936. Our new evaluation of Roosevelt was sound. Our amendment of the Youth Act made sense in terms of creating jobs for young people. But the change in policy was never frankly and honestly debated in these pages nor was it ever made clear that a primary motivation for the shift in policy was the Popular Front policy of the Communists, a policy that reflected Moscow's desperate search for allies against Hitler.

We were fearless paladins of the truth when it came to the world outside of the Left; we were little better than apologists when it came to the Left itself. Wechsler, a spirited man who valued his independence and freedom, broke away in 1937 and I followed him two years later, at the time of the Nazi-Soviet pact.

And yet I would not want anyone to be deterred by our experience from political involvement. With all their disappointments and abominations, the 1930s for many of us still represent a shining moment in our lives. We *did* try to make this a better world. And a surprisingly large number of us are still trying to do so.

New York City, 1968

Champion of Youth

NEW YORK, 1936-1937

Champion Labor Monthly

NEW YORK, 1937-1938

MARTIN GLABERMAN AND GEORGE P. RAWICK

CHAMPION OF YOUTH, published from 1936 through 1938, was an organ of the Young Communist League during the height of the "Popular Front" period of the Communist movement. The last two issues that were published (Vol. 3, Nos. 9 and 10, in August and September 1938) carried the name *Champion: Labor Monthly*, but neither content nor orientation was changed.

The political basis for *Champion* and the Popular Front was set forth at the seventh (and last) congress of the Communist International. In 1934, as a consequence of Hitler's victory in Germany and the changing relationship of forces among the nations of the world, the Soviet Union undertook a new foreign policy directed at making alliances with the relatively democratic powers of the West against the rising threats of Germany and Japan. In August 1935, the seventh congress of the Comintern was held to formalize the new line and to impose it on all the Communist parties.

The resolution of this congress on "The Offensive of Fascism and the Tasks of the Communist International in the Fight for the Unity of the Working Class Against Fascism" indicated a departure from the earlier ultra-Left Communist line. One clause asserted:

. . . without for a moment giving up their independent work in the sphere of Communist education, organization and mobilization of masses, the Communists, in order to render the road to unity of action easier for the workers, must strive to secure joint action with the Social-Democratic Parties, reformist trade unions and other organizations of the toilers against the class enemies of the proletariat, on the basis of short or long-term agreements. . . .

Champion, a popularly written and presented magazine, was one of the most thorough reflections of this attempt to create the widest possible people's front of liberal democrats, union leaders, Socialists, and reformers "in the struggle against fascism."

Edited for most of its existence by Morris Schnapper, *Champion* did not acknowledge its Communist sponsorship. It attempted in both format and contents to emulate the popular journals of the period by devoting considerable space to visual material. The illustrations seem rather primitive today, but they are no more so than, for example, the illustrations found in *Liberty* magazine, the Macfadden publication of the same period.

The program of *Champion* was minimal and couched in patriotic American terms. It called for the building of a United Youth League of a vaguely liberal nature, as well as for a Farmer-Labor party. (Governor Floyd B. Olson, the Farmer-Labor governor of Minnesota, wrote an article for the first issue.) *Champion* called for production for use and not for profit, a Socialist formulation that was in vogue during the depression years. It also called for racial equality, stating that this was "the American dream." It declared that the drive to war was produced by financial powers such as the House of Morgan. The language of analysis of *Champion* was more Populist than Marxist. Its critique of capitalist society was based more upon the actions of individual men and the institutions they headed than upon the Marxist "laws of motion" of capitalist society.

Champion published articles by a significant cross section of American liberals, although in some instances these writers only had answered a questionnaire. Paul de Kruif, Langston Hughes, Granville Hicks, John L. Lewis, Budd Schulberg, Frances Gorman of the Textile Workers Union, Robert Morse Lovett, Oswald Garrison Villard, Harry Elmer

Barnes, Walter White, Mark Starr, and Sinclair Lewis were some of the more prominent names that were featured in the magazine.

Champion also published sports articles written by such people as John R. Tunis and Nat Holman, the City College of New York basketball coach. Muckraking articles were leavened with occasional articles on sex, short stories, and the like. But news of labor struggles and articles by labor leaders were the mainstay of *Champion*.

In the last year of its existence, 1938, the format of *Champion* changed to a more conservative layout featuring less display artwork. A cartoon by William Gropper became a regular feature, but the range of contributors and advisory editors remained the same—a broad spectrum of liberals, leavened by prominent Communists such as Angelo Herndon and Joseph Starobin. A feature called "Ringside" replaced the miscellaneous news items, although the nature of the material did not change. Spero Galanopulo replaced Morris Schnapper as editor. A page that had been devoted to the Civilian Conservation Corps camps was replaced by a column on Social Security news. In addition, columns on radio and camera appeared. An occasional column named "Miss America" concerned itself with recipes and the news of young women.

The specific aims and policies of the Young Communist League found their way into the paper somewhat obliquely. This was quite different from the Communist practice before the Popular Front. *Champion* had been preceded by the *Young Worker*, published from 1922 to 1936 as an avowed organ of the Young Communist League. It was a harsh, party-line magazine that emphasized class struggle in strident tones. Although the tone of *Champion* was a manifestation of the change in the party line, it did not reflect any change in organizational policies or structure in the Young Communist League. The People's Front policies that the new journal embodied did not imply a lessening of the discipline and rigidity of the Communist movement. They were, rather, intended to make it possible for the YCL to function as a tight-knit group in the broader arena of Popular Front coalitions. For example, in the same period members of the Young Communist League faced expulsion if seen talking to members of Trotskyist youth organizations.

The broad liberalism of the Young Communist League and the editors of *Champion* was rather onesided and narrow. While politically loose and diffuse and able to appeal to a broad spectrum of even nonradical opinion, it was at the same time organizationally narrow and tied to the Communist movement. Buried in the back of most issues were brief news items about the internal organizational life of the Young Communist League and the Communist party. For example, *Champion* would inform the public of forthcoming conventions of the Young Communist League and other YCL activities. The magazine tried to retain a façade of objectivity by also including reports of other groups, such as the Methodist youth.

This complex relationship of avowedly loose, liberal politics with centralized, tight internal discipline was typical of the approach of the Communist movement in the Popular Front period and, indeed, accounts for much of its strength and impact during the 1930s. Young Communists, like their elders, could function as liberals in liberal organizations and movements by openly sharing liberal politics while gaining control over such groups by tight, disciplined organization.

Detroit and St. Louis, 1969

Young Communist Review
NEW YORK, 1936-1940

The Review
NEW YORK, 1940-1941

Weekly Review
NEW YORK, 1941-1943

IRVING KATZ

THE *Weekly Review*, sponsored by the Young Communist League of the United States, began publication in September 1936, as a monthly under the title *Young Communist Review*. It became a biweekly, *The Review*, in February 1940, changed to the *Weekly Review* in August 1941, and expired in July 1943. Just as the Young Communist League was intended to be a junior division of the Communist party, its journalistic organ was expected to interpret the "party line" to young Communists. From first issue to last, *The Review* faithfully mirrored its senior colleague, the *Daily Worker*, heaping lavish praise upon the Soviet Union—a land where a Communist party, as "an instrument of the working classes," had established control of a state operated by and for the masses.

The American Young Communist League was formed at an underground convention in New York City in April 1922, four years after the founding of its Russian counterpart, the "Komsomol." Members were to be between the ages of fourteen and twenty-three; at the latter age they could be graduated into the regular Communist ranks. "YCLers" did not automatically hold party membership, though many regarded themselves as belonging to both organizations simultaneously. For those under fourteen, the party established the Young Pioneers of America, whose summer camps and local branches were designed to counter the attractions of the Boy Scouts of America, which the Communists attacked as a "direct organ of the capitalist class used to poison the minds of children." Following the Russian example, national YCL conventions would ceremonially admit Young Pioneers into the YCL as a result of their coming of age and having completed a specified period of "training."

Though the YCL was supposed to recruit its supporters from the "working youth," who would actively engage in trade union organization and participate in strikes, most of its members were in fact students, whose connection with the proletarian struggle was either vicarious or, through their parents, indirect. Yet, as long as the Communist party emphasized "direct participation" in the fight against "bosses" and "imperialists," YCLers felt uneasy as full-time college students, though some rationalized their campus life by constantly arguing with peers and professors. YCLers also found time for extracurricular rallies and demonstrations in public squares and solicitations for strike and bail funds.

In view of the League's heavy concentration of student members and spurred on by directives emanating from Georgi Dimitrov's Communist International (Comintern), American Communist leaders saw clearly by the 1930s that schools, not factories, were the most fertile sources of YCL strength, and they shifted their focus accordingly. By the eve of World War II, most major American colleges and universities had clubs affiliated either with the YCL, the Communist-controlled National Student League, or the sympathetic American Youth Congress. John Gates became a YCLer by virtue of his membership in the YCL-affiliated Social Problems Club at New York's City College. James A. Wechsler was recruited during his Columbia University days by a zoology instructor. Thomas Merton had a brief stay in the YCL while at the same campus. Among high school youth, David Greenglass joined the YCL's Lower East Side (Manhattan) chapter because its handball team had a vacancy he was anxious to fill. Seymour M. Bakst was invited to join a

YCL-backed choral club, and he found it "very easy" to become a YCL member.

In September 1936, following a Young Communist International pronouncement that made the establishment of a youth press mandatory for all countries, the YCL brought out the initial issue of the *Young Communist Review* for present and potential members. The stated editorial purpose was to popularize "policy, tactics and educational problems among our membership and masses of youth." To make certain that this purpose would not be left to chance, the *Review*'s editorial writers and contributors were generally seasoned YCL organizers, publicists, and administrators. For example, Joseph R. Starobin, Joseph Clark, and Claudia Jones had all been active in local and national YCL functions before each took over *The Review*'s editor-in-chief position.

Starobin, a YCLer at New York's DeWitt Clinton High School, had quickly risen to a leadership post in CCNY's Social Problems Club. Clark, a Communist since 1929, had been an official in the National Student League, a YCL organizer in Detroit, and state secretary of the New York YCL. Miss Jones, a British West Indian by birth and a stenographer by training, had served as chairman of the New York State YCL and as regular columnist for *The Review* long before her tenure as chief editor. Among the contributors were such future Communist party leaders as "Johnny" Gates, who had withdrawn from CCNY to become a full-time YCL organizer among Ohio steelworkers and would soon fight for the Loyalist government in the Spanish Civil War; Gilbert ("Gil") Green, a native of Illinois, national president of the YCL and a presidium member of the Communist-inspired World Congress of International Youth; Henry Winston, who had made the leap from Hattiesburg, Mississippi, to the post of YCL national administrative secretary; and Max ("Mac") Weiss, suspended from CCNY in his senior year for editing an unauthorized campus publication and already a veteran member of the YCL national council.

In addition to editorials and news articles, the staff periodically inserted "regular features" into *The Review*. Ostensibly designed to be "interesting and informative" to the average reader, sophisticated contemporaries could have only found them limited in their *Weltanschauung*, stifling in their conformity, dull in their predictability, unintentional in their humor, and outrageous in their distortions. Dave

Richards' occasional quiz, "How Much Do You Know?", intended to serve as a pedagogical tool, must have confused readers by its dialectical nit-picking.

The prevailing international Communist stand urging an "antifascist people's front," particularly in regard to the Spanish Civil War, received primary attention during *The Review*'s early period. Leftist groups which responded negatively to such appeals for a broadbased coalition as the Socialist party and its youth affiliate, the Young People's Socialist League, were branded "Trotskyists" and linked to the "reactionary plotters" being purged and executed in Moscow.

The Nazi-Soviet Pact of August 23, 1939, and the Anglo-French declaration of war against Germany following Hitler's attack on Poland nine days after the pact, signaled a new Communist approach to European and American affairs. In view of the shifting tides of Soviet diplomacy, *The Review* necessarily practiced editorial legerdemain in order to maintain adherence to the "orthodox" party line. The bellicose antifascist editorials of the Popular Front period gave way to a virtual pacifism; the war between Nazi Germany and the West European "bourgeois democracies" was stigmatized as an "imperialist conflict" and of no concern to the national interests of the United States. To avoid expected confusion within and possible defections from the YCL, the editors felt compelled to remind readers that

> as in every other phase of Y.C.L. work, the changes in the international situation altered the character of this month's *Review*. That is as it should be, we think. It would be a sorry magazine, indeed, if we were still . . . writing in a language that [has] wrong meanings today.

This new "character" would stress the YCL "stand against war" because of the growing "danger of American involvement on the side of the British and French imperialist circles." With calculated candor, the editors even confessed that articles originally planned for readers before the summer's developments were "out-of-date" and in need of obvious revision. The Socialists, whom YCLers had earlier tried to woo as desirable allies in a joint front, were now beyond the pale, denounced as "social-fascists" for their castigation of the 1939 pact and for their support of the Western democracies. Even the administration of President Franklin D. Roosevelt, discreetly applauded by *The Review* during the 1936 election campaign, was subjected to ridicule and contempt for expressing concern over the possible fate of Hitler's opponents.

Whereas *The Review* had earlier used illustrations from American history to justify this country's incessant opposition to antirepublican forces throughout the world, the magazine now praised those historical figures who had stubbornly opposed the nation's involvement in "unjust" wars, from the New England dissenters of 1812 to the pacifists and isolationists of 1917. The American tradition, if it held any meaning at all, clearly favored peace and nonintervention. "The Yanks Are *NOT* Coming" became an oft-repeated slogan in *Review* pages and at YCL meetings.

Such reversals of opinion apparently perplexed many *Review* subscribers, and by early 1940 the editors took steps both to correct the discontented and to mollify them. The February 1, 1940 edition announced a shift to biweekly publication, explaining that "history races ahead so swiftly these days it's not easy to keep your bearings. To steer a straight course you've got to know where you are at all times." A month between issues was too long a stretch of time for *The Review* to promulgate each fresh change or revision in the party line. Not trusting that more frequent publication alone would quiet the restive, the staff also decided upon a livelier format. A slogan under the masthead—"The Truth Shall Make Youth Free"—parodied incongruously both the New Testament and the anti-Communist publisher William Randolph Hearst. Columns on such youth-oriented topics as movies, radio, sports, YCL club news, jazz, and girls were promised as standard fare. Gradually, almost imperceptibly, *The Review* muted its shrill assaults on Roosevelt and, acknowledging its sizable readership on college campuses, began to devote more attention to student conflicts with educational authorities.

The summer of 1941 raised further havoc with *Review* content; even a biweekly could become obsolete immediately amid the lightning pace of historical events. The June issues, for example, continued to articulate the party line laid down two years earlier, scolding the Roosevelt administration for convoying aid to the Allies (mainly Great Britain), albeit on a relatively minor scale. *The Review* gave ample space to a forthcoming American Youth Congress convention and endorsed and reprinted an AYC petition, scheduled to be passed around at the meeting, warning the

President: "Get this straight. . . . Common sense tells us to get our country out of this war and to keep it out. We are opposed to convoys."

Then, on June 22, the news burst upon American Communists that Hitler's armies had invaded Soviet soil. The very next issue echoed yet another new line, as martial front-page headlines screamed: "SUPPORT USSR'S FIGHT AGAINST THE NAZI WAR." The succeeding edition declared that "Fascism Must Be Destroyed" and that the United States must give "full aid" (not mere convoys) to the Soviet Union, England, "and all nations who fight against Hitler." Roosevelt's announcement that his government would also extend material assistance to the Russians was deemed to be "in accord with the deepest desires of American youth." Outsiders might label *The Review*'s altered policy "hypocritical," but Carl Ross, an earlier member of the journal's editorial board and the YCL's national executive secretary, justified the new stance on the ground that "the entire character of the war had changed." As late as the December 9, 1941 issue (prepared before the United States entered the war), Claudia Jones was still patiently explaining to bewildered readers why the "bourgeois democracies" suddenly became worth saving. Before June 22, 1941, the European conflict had been only a predatory war between two rival imperialist powers; after the German invasion it became "a people's war." Following such an about-face, it was a relatively small change for *The Review* to hail the Boy Scouts as heroes in the nation's preparedness and defense efforts.

The August 18, 1941 issue began *The Review*'s third and final phase; it became a weekly and remained so until the end. Sobered and even a bit apologetic by the new turn of world affairs, the YCL decided that even two weeks between issues of "America's leading antifascist youth magazine" would not suffice to keep readers abreast of the new, "correct" interpretations. Behind the *The Review*'s rhetorical façade, the editors revealed another and more pressing reason for going weekly. Funds were needed to help the party, and doubling the number of issues to the same list of subscribers would increase income, and might even double it.

As a result of the Japanese attack on Pearl Harbor on December 7, 1941, and the ensuing German and Italian declarations of war against the United States, *The Review* adopted a strong tone of American nationalism. Even the class struggle took second place to an Allied victory. Heroes of the American Revolution were held up as forerunners of the nation's "traditional" policy of aiding democratic forces around the globe. Young Thomas Jefferson became the eighteenth-century version of a YCLer as leading Communists, conveniently ignoring the Virginian's ownership of Negro slaves and his perennial fear of centralized power, proudly claimed "special kinship" with this champion of "self-government for the masses." Max Weiss, who succeeded "Gil" Green as national YCL president, praised this *Review* habit of presenting items on American history.

After a short absence, popular features returned to *The Review*'s pages. There were poetry contests in which items with such titles as "Browder is our Leader" were awarded prizes. Chapters of a new serial, "The Vanishing Footprints," appeared, which the editors hailed as a "humdinging proletarian mystery" and which included among its chief characters a murdered union president, a union organizer, a union secretary, and a union newspaper editor. Even that staple of the American tabloid—the comic strip—found a home in *The Review*. Labeled "Production Yank," the strip pictorialized "a regular guy who knew his job and gave it all he had," just as YCLers were to do. To *The Review*'s credit, and regardless of YCL motives, the sports columns persistently reminded young readers that excellent Negro athletes were denied the right to participate as professionals in most organized sports.

The Review's demise in mid-1943 was due less to a falling off of subscribers than to an American Communist party plan to dissolve, at least on the surface, both the Young Communist League and its parent. Party leader Earl Browder interpreted the Comintern dissolution of May 1943 as pointing the way for emulation by national Communist parties and their constituent bodies. In September, Weiss announced that the YCL was considering a proposal to change its name and broaden its membership base. A month later, a special YCL convention met in New York City to celebrate its twenty-first birthday and, accompanied by a snake dance, the chanting of "Solidarity Forever," and the singing of "The Star-Spangled Banner," the League went "out of exsitence." The following day, over four hundred delegates selected an organizational name without "Communist" in the title—"American Youth for Democracy"—and appointed ten veterans of the "deceased" YCL to serve on a temporary presidium. The AYD survived until 1949, when the

Communist party dissolved it, too, and directed the members to join the Young Progressives of America or the Labor Youth League. By the 1950s, the latter two had also disappeared from the American scene.

In addition to its primary function as a medium through which to interpret the party line in words and ways palatable to young people, *The Review* also seemed to serve as a training school for future journalists with the Communist party. The United States government deported Claudia Jones to her native West Indies after World War II, but Starobin, Clark, and Gates were graduated to more responsible capacities. Starobin moved on to the *New Masses,* where he was foreign editor until 1942, at which time Louis Budenz hired him for the *Daily Worker.* Starobin was soon designated the *Worker*'s foreign editor, but disenchantment with Stalinism in the Russian and American parties led him to leave the party in late 1953 and to give up his editorship the following year. Clark, after winning a Silver Star for gallantry in action while in the Army, joined the *Worker* in 1946 and became a foreign correspondent stationed in Moscow. Gates was elected to the Communist party national committee during his Army service in 1945. Two years later, he became editor-in-chief of the *Worker.* With time out for serving a three-and-one-half-year prison term after his conviction on charges of teaching and advocating the violent overthrow of the federal government, Gates occupied that post until 1958. By then, rumbling within the Communist world over the revelations of Stalin's crimes (made louder by the use of Soviet force in Hungary) led Clark and Gates to resign from both the *Worker* and the party.

Bloomington, Indiana, 1968

National Issues

NEW YORK, 1939

HARVEY A. LEVENSTEIN

NATIONAL ISSUES was a rather remarkable journal. Published monthly in 1939 by the National Committee of the Communist party of the USA, it strongly resembled the liberal *New Republic* and *Nation* of the time not only in format, but in editorial stance as well. It is perhaps the epitome, if not the high-water mark, of the Popular Front line in the United States.

In August 1935, the Communist International, in its seventh congress in Moscow, had responded to the rise of fascism in Europe and the expansion of Japan in the Orient by calling for the Communist parties of the world to take the lead in forming "antifascist people's fronts." Whereas previously the Communists had called for united fronts of workers against fascism, their policy had precluded working with non-Communist organizations and had centered around wooing workers into Communist-led unions and the Communist party. The "Popular Front" line not only allowed the Communist parties to cooperate with non-Communist parties and organizations, it positively admonished them to seek out formal ties with their previous rivals for the hearts of the proletariat: the Social Democratic parties, the reformists, and the pacifists. Indeed, any group that appeared to be moderately progressive and that did not consistently attack the Soviet Union was to be courted into forming a broad political grouping whose main stance would be antifascism.

In the United States, the new line proved to be a mixed blessing for the Communist party. In spite of the International's protestations of its worldwide relevance, the new line was obviously oriented toward Western European political conditions, where the main allies in the alliance were to be the Socialists. In the United States, an alliance with the Socialist party of America, even weaker than the Communist party, proved to be not only impossible to effect, but, more important, meaningless and powerless. Thus, the party was forced to turn to the motley collection of groups supporting the New Deal.

The CPUSA pursued the new line with characteristic zeal. A myriad of antifascist front organizations were set up to alert liberals to the growing worldwide threat of fascism. Earl Browder, the leader, set out to change the image of the party from that of something secret, revolutionary, and foreign. Communism became "Twentieth-Century Americanism." Party members were admonished to support the progressive and antifascist forces in America. They were now to participate in forming "people's fronts" in all types of organizations and on all levels of government.

In theory this sounded fine, but in practice, problems arose. How was one to tell exactly who was progressive and who was not? What were the criteria for being antifascist? Which measures wending their way through the labyrinth of Congress should one write one's congressman to support or oppose? Communists were now expected to have opinions on a whole range of political issues, from the most sweeping foreign policy issues to the most petty questions surrounding municipal budgets, and they were expected to be able to argue them convincingly. Neither the party nor its members could now take refuge in denunciations of the "contradictions" of the system, predicting its imminent downfall, and dreaming of the utopian system that would follow. The party now began to participate openly and responsibly in local politics. Indeed, by October 1938, the New York State Committee had sufficiently mastered the intricacies of municipal finance to send a representative to the New York City budget hearings. He called for a not-very-revolutionary increase of $16 million in the $155 million capital budget and, moreover, showed how this could be done without increasing the mandatory debt limit.

National Issues was founded around this time, not as a "front" magazine published by a progressive-sounding organization controlled by the Communist party, but as an official organ of the CPUSA. Its function was obviously twofold. First, it would give direction and depth to the opinions of party members and "fellow travelers" on the important national issues of the day. In the same way that the *New Republic* and the *Nation* told liberal readers, in depth, who was really liberal and why, so *National Issues* would tell its readers who was really progressive and why. Second, it would help to promote the broadbased coalition of Communist and reformist forces that the Popular Front line aimed for. The congressional elections of 1938 brought sharp reversals for Franklin D. Roosevelt and the New Dealers. It was very likely that Roosevelt would not seek a third term and the Democratic convention would fall into the hands of conservative Democrats. There would then be a good chance of a mass defection of New Dealers from the Democratic party playing an active role in it. *National Issues,* by demonstrating the reasonableness of the CPUSA, its sophisticated, realistic appraisal of national politics, and its consistent support for the progressive wing of the Democratic party, would help forge the basis for the new coalition.

Alas, the high hopes of the founders were not to be realized. In August 1939, the party was badly shaken by the signing of the Soviet-German Non-Aggression Pact. The September issue of *National Issues,* which had been ready to go to press with an expanded review of the legislative record of the Seventy-sixth Congress, contained a hastily written editorial in defense of the Soviet action and a transcript of a radio speech on the topic by Earl Browder. An October issue had been planned, but the new events in Europe forced a rapid, agonized reassessment of the CPUSA's position with regard to Roosevelt and the New Deal. If it was to continue in existence, *National Issues* would have to accomplish a complete about-face in its line with regard to Roosevelt's foreign policy. Whereas it had previously supported the halting efforts of the administration to combat "fascist aggression" in Europe, it would now have to attack them. In addition, it would have to adopt a much more critical stance toward New Deal domestic measures. This would also involve highly complex, and highly embarrassing, changes in position with regard to the myriad of legislative proposals upon which it had already advised its readers in detail. Certainly, it would be much more comfortable simply to allow the journal to disappear quietly from the scene.

But we know enough about the rapidity with which other organs of the CPUSA, such as the *Daily Worker,* accomplished the about-face to know that the discomfort and complexity of the shift could not have been the only factors involved in the death of *National Issues.* Although the

CPUSA's true financial status at the time is difficult to decipher, throughout the summer of 1939 it had been issuing urgent appeals for funds from its members and sympathizers. It simply cost much more to run the new type of "responsible" political party, with its open conventions and many publications, than it did to run the party of the 1920s, when shabbily dressed members of the "vanguard of the proletariat" could meet secretly in New York apartments and circulate mimeographed polemics. *National Issues* was an expensive magazine to produce. It had no advertising, and it is doubtful if its circulation ever reached the level where it paid for more than a small fraction of the cost of production. Even the *New Republic* and the *Nation*, with their much larger circulations, found it difficult to survive without financial support from either well-heeled owners or readers. Thus, it appears that *National Issues*, founded in imitation of liberal, capitalist journals, died for rather mundane, capitalist reasons.

Although its life was short and its influence in its own time not too important, *National Issues* has become a valuable source for historians of the New Deal, labor, and communism in the United States. Its detailed spelling out of the CPUSA stand on virtually every major piece of legislation, its lists of which congressmen the CPUSA supported and opposed, its articles outlining the Communist position on everything from the Wagner Act and the CIO to welfare programs and the Ludlow Amendment, make it an important and convenient resource for anyone doing work in this period.

New York City, 1969

Clarity

NEW YORK, 1940-1943

MARTIN GLABERMAN AND GEORGE P. RAWICK

CLARITY was the theoretical organ of the Young Communist League (YCL), edited by Max Weiss, from 1940 to 1943. It was announced as a bimonthly in its first issue (April-May 1940), but thereafter was actually published quarterly. It is a typical example of Communist, Liberal, and Left youth publications of that period.

The first year of publication of *Clarity* was during the period of the Hitler-Stalin pact, and the magazine reflected faithfully the vigorous antiwar stand of the Communist party of the USA. During the first year of publication, there were articles such as "Youth Reject Roosevelt Program" by Gil Green, "American Youth in Struggle Against Imperialist War" by Carl Ross, and "Negro and White Unity Against the War" by Henry Winston.

Following the German invasion of Russia in June 1941, there was a complete about-face in *Clarity*. The very next issue after the invasion —Volume 2, No. 2, Spring 1941—consisted of the reports to a national YCL meeting that presented the new prowar policy to the organization. The lead article was the speech of Robert Minor, acting secretary of the Communist party, "Continued Political Struggle Against Hitler by Military Means," which implied that there was some kind of nonmilitary struggle against Hitler during the period of the Hitler-Stalin pact. All the big guns of the YCL—Gil Green, Henry Winston, John Gates, and Joe Clark—were directed toward presenting the new line.

The titles of the articles in the issues that followed exemplified a complete switch in the policy of the magazine. "War Service Through the Young Communist League" by Frank Cestare, "Notes on Apprenticeship for War Production'' by James West, ''Keep 'Em Floating'' by James West, and similar articles were dedicated emphatically to increasing war production. Combined with these practical guides were more traditional political polemics defending the new prowar policies.

The tightly disciplined nature of the Young Communist League organization, which *Clarity* reflected and developed, made the 180-degree turn in policy in June 1941 starkly visible and easily documented. In the article by Henry Winston, the leading Negro functionary in the Communist party, in the first issue in 1940, before the German invasion of Russia, the basic theme was an unremitting struggle for Negro rights through the policy of opposing the movement of the Roosevelt administration toward involvement in the war: ''. . . the fight of the Negro people for full citizenship rights, and for civil rights assumes added importance today when the Roosevelt-Wall Street forces are driving toward war.''

After the invasion of Russia, the tone and content were reversed. Winston, in the article ''Negro Rights and the Anti-Hitler War,'' in the Winter 1942 issue, wrote:

> This failure to see the paramount importance of the anti-Hitler struggle, expressed in a tendency to place the struggle for Negro rights as something separate from or even in contradiction to it, necessarily also led to a lack of understanding as how to integrate the Negro people into the war effort. It is clear that the full mobilization of the Negro people to support the war was not yet fully achieved before December 7, and was still a major task confronting the anti-Hitler forces.

Winston argued that the attempt to involve Negroes in the military forces and in war production was the way to get Negro rights.

As time went on, the tone of *Clarity* became more patriotic. During the war there was popularized among Negroes the slogan of the Double V: victory against Hitler and victory for Negro rights. Most Negro leaders, even the most conservative, placed equal emphasis, at least in words, on both aspects of the slogan. But *Clarity* refused to modify in any way its total devotion to the prosecution of the war. Thus Eugene Braddock, in the Summer 1942 issue, wrote:

For our country, also, there is a great lesson. Fourteen million loyal patriotic American Negro citizens stand as one in their desire to give their all to their country in this great war of united nations against fascist slavery. . . .

Whereas the sentiments expressed by the "Double V" slogan represent the desires of the Negro people, the slogan itself tends to separate the problems of the Negro people from the problems of the oppressed masses in other parts of the world; thus, through this separation the fight for Negro unity and for Negro rights is weakened.

What was true of the change in policy on the Negro question was also true on other matters. Roosevelt was no longer a warmonger, but a champion of democracy. From militant labor struggles the turn was made to unremitting hostility to strikes of any kind for the duration of the war. Even in its organizational details and development *Clarity* reflected the changed national policy. At its inception, *Clarity* was called the "Theoretical Organ of the Young Communist League" and was published by the YCL. With the change in policy and the desire to work toward a broader appeal, the Spring 1942 issue (Volume 3, No. 2) was called "A Magazine of Youth Devoted to Marxist-Leninist Theory and Practice." Although there was no change in direction, policy, or format, the organizational connection with the YCL was further concealed by the statement "Published by New Age Publishers," which was a general agency for Communist party publishing.

Even this orientation, however, was ultimately considered much too narrow and radical. In order to mobilize the broadest possible elements of the population in a coalition that would unstintingly support the war against Germany and in defense of the Soviet Union, *Clarity* in 1943 was abandoned, and the organization for which it spoke was dissolved. During Christmas week a convention of the Young Communist League voted to terminate its existence. In the same hall on the following day the founding convention of the American Youth for Democracy was convened, with many of the same delegates but with all formal ties to the Communist movement severed. Eleanor Roosevelt was the keynote speaker.

Clarity, as a youth journal, was completely subordinate to the Communist party in all policy matters. This relationship was not a specifically Communist characteristic. A similar relationship was true in all Socialist or Marxist organizations of the period, even in liberal organizations. The right of the parent-adult party to determine policy for its youth sections was not challenged anywhere. Moreover, the practice of strict organizational discipline, in which minority views were not allowed public expression, was general on the Left, although the Communist party and its affiliates probably had less internal democracy than did other groups.

Clarity, a typical left-wing youth periodical of the period, was the theoretical organ of the Communist party's youth, the Young Communist League. Yet there was little theoretical discussion in its pages. It was, rather, an instructional manual, basically pedagogical in nature, designed to explain the current political line to the members and sympathizers of the Communist youth movement. In carrying out that function it perfectly represented the structure, methods, and policies of the Communist party of the USA.

Detroit and Rochester, Michigan, 1969

World Survey

NEW YORK, 1941-1942

WALTER GOLDWATER

NOT long after the signing of the Hitler-Stalin pact in 1939, the Soviet leader decided that the Third (Communist) International had outlived its usefulness as an instrument of Soviet foreign policy. The two important publications promulgating the international revolution were *International Press Correspondence* (usually known as *Inprecorr*), and *Communist International*. Both of these were published in several languages, and had been distributed throughout the world for many years—*Inprecorr* since 1921 and *Communist International* from the time of the establishment of the organization itself in 1919. *Inprecorr* had changed its name to *World News and Views* in 1938, and became quite innocuous from 1940 on; *Communist International* was deprived of its subtitle "Organ of the Executive Committee of the Communist International" with the last issue of 1939, and ceased publication altogether at the end of 1940.

As in the case of *Inprecorr*, however, it was thought unwise to stop publication abruptly, so a new magazine in name, though not in content or format, appeared for the first time in April 1941, with the name *International Review*. Two objections were found to the new name: the word "international" lost its charm after the German attack on Russia in June 1941, for it became important that no internationalist or radical taint should touch the magazine, whose emphasis was largely on Russian matters; and the American distributors, who apparently had not been consulted, informed their employers abroad that the name would lead to confusion with another magazine of the same name, which had been published for some three years but had ceased publication in 1939. This was a Left-Socialist periodical, and was bitterly anti-Communist. The third issue therefore appeared with the milder name *World Survey*, a modification that corresponded in kind to the earlier change from *Inprecorr* to *World News and Views* and the change from *Soviet Russia Today* to the current *New World Review*.

Of the two magazines, only seven numbers appeared, with dates but without numbering, and they are interesting mainly as a reflection of the change in emphasis during this crucial period (antiwar until the attack on Russia, then strongly prowar). The last number appeared in June 1942, when the Communist war effort in the United States had become total and the magazine would have served no useful purpose in that context. Nothing of a similar (international) nature appeared again until after the war, when the Cominform (Communist Information Bureau) paper, *For a Lasting Peace, for a People's Democracy* began publication in Yugoslavia.

Readers of *World Survey* will find the articles hackneyed, trite, and repetitive, but they do contain the gist and the form of Communist propaganda: the exaggerated statistics—"2,000,000 workers are languishing in Franco's jails"; the exhortation—"The struggle is flaring up with a force to strike terror into the hearts of the Nazis and their henchmen"; and on every page high praise for the glorious Stalin. The student may easily wonder who could have read this, who could have borne it; but party members and fellow-travelers did indeed bear it, and certainly would continue to bear it and revel in it to the present day if it were demanded of them. A dispassionate reading, however, will establish one fact clearly: the end of the magazine *Communist International*, like that of the parent Communist International itself, came not with a bang but with a whimper.

New York City, 1968

U. S. Week

MILWAUKEE AND CHICAGO,

1941-1942

STANLEY SHAPIRO

BY 1941 a good number of American radicals had traveled what Louis Fischer called the "road to Kronstadt." Just a decade earlier the depression had spurred a generation of political idealists into alliance with the Left. There they had found—and created—an exhilarating spirit of hopefulness and common struggle. But the sectarian arguments of the 1930s, the Russian betrayals of faith, especially the purge trials and the Nazi-Soviet pact, together with the good works of the New Deal, dissipated that eager spirit. Depression radicals painfully realized, as Alexander Berkman had discovered in the Bolshevik suppression of the Kronstadt revolt, that the Left could practice callous, expedient politics and a self-seeking will to power. That revelation soured all but the diehards. Whatever the reason, whatever the "Kronstadt," by World War II most radicals felt "a sense of having touched something unclean."

The rise of fascism in Europe revived American radicals. The specter of Hitler's armies, "goose-stepping automatons in green . . . their legs shooting out like pistons," quickened the democratic ardor which had been the source of radical protest all along. This time the cause was not bread; it was the very "soul" of man that stood in doubt. Radicals rallied to the defense. The historic mission of America was rediscovered. American values were reaffirmed. Granville Hicks led the way in 1938 with *I Like America;* in 1939, Lewis Mumford published *Men Must Act;* and in 1940, Waldo Frank offered an inspirational *Chart for Rough Water*. All three authors had been allied with the Communists in the 1930s.

The democratic or reformist Socialists, who had been in bad odor during the depression, were strengthened by European developments, too. While the Socialist party was immobilized by the conflict between its antifascist and antiwar policies, the moderate Socialists, who had warned of the dangers of totalitarianism (of the Right and the Left) and who had urged a decent respect for liberal traditions, took an interventionist position. These gradualists earlier had approved of the New Deal's direction and now actively supported the administration's policy of collective security. From their point of view, the benefits of a "people's war" outweighed the dangers of an imperialist war; Adolf Hitler was clearly a more terrible menace than Kuhn or Loeb. After the invasion of Russia in June 1941, the moderates were joined by the Communists so that only a handful of radicals stood apart from the patriotic coalition.

This strange coalition of gradualists and Communists formed the staff of *U. S. Week,* a periodical of some eleven months' duration, beginning with the passage of Lend-Lease in March 1941 and ending in January 1942, just after Pearl Harbor. The magazine was sponsored by the William E. Dodd Foundation "to foster and forward the Jeffersonian democratic ideals" of the ex-professor and ambassador to Germany.

In some ways *U. S. Week* was a standard radical journal: its format resembled the *Nation* and *New Republic*; it carried no advertising; it depicted itself in opposition to the "Goliath of distorted, censored news." The fellow-traveling New York daily, *PM,* provided most of the magazine's information and the majority of its reporters. Associate Editor Richard Boyer had been *PM*'s foreign correspondent; Leo Huberman, author of the *Labor Spy Racket* and national affairs editor of *U. S. Week,* had been a labor reporter for *PM*. They joined Doris Berger, daughter of Wisconsin Representative Victor Berger, who was installed as editor; William E. Dodd, Jr.; and Martha Dodd's husband, Alfred K. Stern, who was a member of the antiwar American Peace Mobilization. Donald Ogden Stewart, Hollywood writer and former chairman of the Communist-dominated League of American Writers, and his wife, Ella Winter, added literary luster.

The journal advocated the standard variety of liberal and radical causes. It stood for the protection of civil rights at a time when America was condoning alien "detention camps" and wiretapping, and enacting antistrike laws. It assailed Jim Crow while the southern system of segregation was still intact. It exposed anti-Semitism. (Its fastidiousness was occasionally quaint. In April 1941, *U.S. Week* reported: "Americans last week celebrated Easter or Passover, according to the dictates of their consciences.") The most fearful domestic enemy of course was big business, the more so since it was consolidating its economic position under the cover of patriotic service. The magazine generally favored nationalization of industry and the creation of a mass labor party.

But *U. S. Week* also deviated in some respects from the typical radical magazine. There *was* something fundamentally Jeffersonian and homespun in its democratic faith, in its sense of optimism and confidence in "the people." Its description of the national mood after the passage of the Lend-Lease Act was characteristic: "Americans last week worked and played, laughed and cried, and said their say on all public questions. Whatever the future might bring, they felt hope and strength in themselves, remembering the words of Ma Joad: 'We're the people, and the people keep on coming.' " Oddly enough for a radical weekly, its varying position on intervention almost perfectly paralleled changes in public opinion. And, finally, the journal was remarkably free of sectarian jargon and logic. When participation in the war virtually put an end to politics, *U. S. Week* stopped publication.

The "people's peace" that *U. S. Week* hoped for did not materialize after the war. Indeed, the dangers posed by fascism in 1941 seemed wonderfully simple and immediate compared with the massive intractability of the Cold War. Some of the contributors to *U. S. Week* made one more attempt to reshape the world in 1948 through the Progressive party. When Wallace failed, signaling the eclipse of postwar radicalism, they either withdrew from politics or went underground. In 1957, Martha Dodd Stern and Alfred K. Stern, accused of espionage against the American government, fled to Czechoslovakia.

Detroit, 1968

Part Seven

PERIODICALS OF
THE SECTS AND
SPLINTER GROUPS

THE oldest radical sect in the United States is also the nation's oldest radical party. The Socialist Labor party emerged from the proceedings of a merger convention of "three pygmy Socialist organizations" held in Philadelphia in the centennial year of 1876. An inconsequential, largely foreign membership party until the ascendancy of Daniel De Leon to its leadership in the 1890s, the SLP first flourished when De Leon emphasized the need to "nativize," but it also suffered from De Leon's authoritarian commitment to a rigidly defined official ideology. De Leon's truculence on matters of doctrine (and his own personal dominance) led to numerous expulsions and secessions. The most important of these occurred when the "kangaroo" faction led by Morris Hillquit of New York City took an important part of the party's membership out of the SLP and, eventually, into the Socialist party of America.

After the founding of the SPA, the SLP showed a remarkable organizational integrity. But the party was never, after the 1890s, more than a mildly troublesome sect. For the period after De Leon's death in 1914, in fact, it may be more accurate to describe the SLP as a "cult." While it continued to run slates of nominees in every election for which it could qualify, the party's chief function (through its long-lived organ, *The Weekly People*) seems to have been a pious preservation of De Leon's thought and writings. An able journalist, De Leon is still featured conspicuously in every issue of the SLP's widely distributed periodical.

Curiously, along with the party's remarkable survival in the face of isolation, the SLP has sustained practically none of the repression and governmental harassment that has at least periodically colored the story of every other American radical group.

The Socialist party of America was relatively unmarred by sectarian spinoffs. When individuals broke with the party, it was as individuals rather than as aspiring new leaders. Indeed, it was the party's first real sectarian crisis that ended the important phase of its history. The Communist party, on the other hand, born in this crisis, spun a history that can be seen as a sequence of fractionalization, internal scheming, and splintering. Tiny but cohesive factions moved into and out of the CP during its formative period. When the party took shape much under the direction of Soviet interests in the late 1920s, the splits followed Russian divisions rather than particularly American questions.

Thus, on October 27, 1928, James P. Cannon, Max Shachtman, Martin Abern, and a few other disciples of the disgraced Trotsky were expelled from the Communist party, as Trotskyists were being ousted from Communist parties throughout the world. A few years later, Shachtman and Cannon formed the Socialist Workers party, which itself became the lushest seedbed for splinter groups. So fractious were the Trotskyists that the tiny SWP suffered more subdivisions during the 1930s—and through the 1950s and 1960s as well—than the Communists did.

Instrumental in ousting the Trotskyists in 1928 and himself a master of factionalism, Jay Lovestone and his "Right-deviationist" Lovestoneites, including Bertram Wolfe, were eliminated from CP councils during the summer of 1929. Lovestone's *denouement* had little relationship to American Communist questions; rather, it reflected Stalin's attacks on Nikolai Bukharin in the Kremlin power struggle. The Lovestoneites organized their own "Communist party, USA (Majority Group)" but it apparently never won more than a few hundred adherents and did not, like the Trotskyists, continue to function for very long.

Factionalism did not just debilitate the pretensions of American radicals to power; it also fatally crippled the nature of radical propaganda and, of course, the chief agency of that propaganda, the journals. The concern of sectarian editors turned more and more toward swatting heretical and schismatic comrades and less and less toward the construction of a viable movement. Sectarian rhetoric was alternately pathetic and ludicrous. In 1936, when a tiny group of Trotskyists, who were too inconsequential to affect much of anything, even temporarily, entered the Socialist party, CP leader Earl Browder solemnly warned the Socialists: "Be careful, you are about to swallow a deadly poison, which we know from sad experience. Better prepare an emetic, for surely you will soon be in convulsions from severe political disturbances." Concern with such matters was as central to life on the American Left, and to the editors of the radical organs, as rumors of a secret romance were to a Ladies' Tulip Guild.

The People

NEW YORK, 1891-1899

The Weekly People

NEW YORK, 1899-1900

Daily People

NEW YORK, 1900-1914

Weekly People

NEW YORK, 1914—

THOMAS WAGSTAFF

THE WEEKLY PEOPLE has been the official organ of the United States' most persistent and consistent radical sect, the Socialist Labor party, for more than seventy-five years. It achieved its greatest influence and acquired its permanent character during the two decades before World War I, the "Golden Age" of American socialism. During that period, *The People* and its brilliant and quixotic editor, Daniel De Leon, made major contributions to the development of American radicalism. *The People* outlined and interpreted the main body of Marxian Socialist thought, and anticipated and discussed several of the major tactical problems that have continued to plague every effort to construct a viable Marxist movement in America down to the present time.

At the same time, the SLP and its journal displayed a sectarian contempt for popular American culture and historical traditions, an arrogant political elitism, and an increasingly abstruse theoretical dogmatism. It was eventually isolated entirely from the main currents of American radicalism, and became and remained a mystic and impotent cult. This fate presaged the sad history of American Socialist movements during the major part of the twentieth century.

The Socialist Labor party was formed in 1877 by a group of German Marxist immigrants after a series of struggles among Marxists, Lassalleans, and Bakuninists had fragmented the original Socialist International. For the next fourteen years, the party remained the property of the German-speaking Marxists. In 1890 when Daniel De Leon joined, its publications were almost exclusively in the German language and only two members of its central committee spoke English.

De Leon was then a recent convert to Marxism. According to some accounts, he was born in Curaçao in 1852, and was educated in Holland and at the Columbia University Law School, where he had taught international law until he abandoned that career to devote his full energies to radical journalism and politics. In 1886 he was impelled into the storm of labor agitation surrounding the Eight-Hour Movement and the Haymarket incident. He passed rapidly through the Single Tax movement, the Bellamyite Nationalist Clubs, and the Knights of Labor. By 1890 he had discovered Marxism and joined the SLP. Within a year his keen intellect and tireless energy had propelled him into the leadership of the organization and the control of its publications.

The People, the party's first regular English-language publication, first appeared in 1891, on a weekly basis. The title *Weekly People* was adopted in 1899 after a factional fight for the control of the party and the journal. From 1900 to 1914 it was published daily as the *Daily People*, reverting after that to the weekly schedule and title it has maintained since.

De Leon rapidly achieved a personal dominance over the SLP that has been as complete as any individual has ever exercised over an American political organization. He made *The People* an instrument for the presentation and explication of his own revolutionary theory and program. His goal was to strip socialism of all moral and sentimental considerations and to present it as a pure "scientific principle." De Leon exhorted his followers to "load your revolutionary ship with the proper lading of science" and avoid any "dillyings and dallyings with anything that is not strictly scientific or with any man who does not stand on our uncompromisingly scientific platform." During his tenure over the journal, *The People* poured out a steady commentary on Marxist theory, punctuated and flavored by De Leon's incessant polemical attacks on rival political and labor organizations and their leadership.

In the process, the editorial pages of *The People* presented and interpreted the main body of Marxist economic and social theory and did so at an exceptionally high level. De Leon has been cited, reportedly by Lenin himself, as the only American thinker to have made independent contributions to Marxist theory. This extended explication of Marxist texts was criticized as poorly calculated to reach and hold a mass working-class readership. ("The common herd cannot understand such stuff," complained a Massachusetts factory worker. "The masses are not at present educated in such a manner as to understand Karl Marx.") De Leon responded to this criticism with the serene prediction that the workers would find their way to Marxism and the analytical principles of *The People* when the inevitable operation of the social dialectic had inculcated them with the proper class consciousness. Meanwhile, he stated, there could be "no greater calamity" for a revolutionary party than to develop a constituency that did not understand what it was supporting."

De Leon proposed to prepare for the development of a genuine mass revolutionary situation and consciousness by constructing an elite, vanguard party. Ultimate victory, he proclaimed, would "depend on the head of the column—upon that minority that is so intense in its convictions, so determined in its action, that it carries the masses with it, storms the breastwork and captures the fort." The role of the political arm of the revolutionary vanguard would be to capture the machinery of the state. Notwithstanding De Leon's always militant rhetoric, this was not to be achieved by a violent uprising, but through the established electoral process. "The ballot," he insisted, "is the weapon of civilization" and the movement of the working class "must place itself upon the highest plane that civilization has reached." Having seized control of the state, the party would immediately abolish it and then immolate itself as well. "The political movement of labor that, in the event of triumph would prolong its existence a second after triumph would be a usurpation."

Power would then devolve on the economic arm of the revolutionary movement, industrially organized unions which would operate the means of production in accordance with the "easy" formula of "the wealth needed, the wealth producible, and the work required." Both the political and the economic organizations were indispensable to success: "without political organization, the labor movement cannot triumph. Without economic organization, the day of its triumph would be the day of its defeat."

De Leon's rigid insistence on absolute acceptance of those basic doctrines, at a time when American radical movements were generally characterized by spirited individualism and pragmatic ideological flexibility, embroiled him and *The People* in endless combat with heresy within and without the SLP. Throughout the 1890s *The People* recorded a dreary catalog of defections from and purges of the party provoked by De Leon's dogmatism. He expelled the influential radical clergyman, Herbert Casson, for proposing a working alliance with the Populists. The popular and successful Massachusetts unionist, James Carey, was ejected after casting, as a town alderman, an ideologically impure vote on a local issue. De Leon's authoritarian rigidity alienated Victor Berger and Morris Hillquit, who took a sizable following out of the SLP and into Eugene Debs' Socialist party. De Leon approached the limits of melodramatic absurdity when he formally excommunicated his favorite son, Solon, for disputing his analysis of the labor theory of value.

At the same time, De Leon hurled a storm of bitter invective at rival radical and reformist organizations. The Populist party epitomized "middle class corruption." The leaders of the Knights of Labor (after rejecting De Leon's bid for control of the union) were "a band of brigands . . . rotten to the core." Samuel Gompers and other leaders of the American Federation of Labor were "labor fakirs, doing picket duty for capitalism." All non-Socialist labor organizers fell into two categories: "some are ignorant, others are corrupt." The Socialist party (which included a sizable group of De Leon's disgruntled former adherents) was "the wretched Debserie," composed of "the moral and intellectual riff-raff from Russia," united with native "freaks, crooks and schemers—the flotsam and jetsam of society—a shivering monument to political-economic imbecility.''

These rhetorical extravagances were always related to a firm and logically consistent set of political principles. Moreover, De Leon's guiding precepts posed valid and serious questions about the tactical difficulties of organizing a successful revolutionary movement in the United States. These questions have been perennially revived and debated, and never satisfactorily answered, throughout the later history of American radical movements.

De Leon insisted that a revolutionary organization had to eschew the constant temptations to form alliances with nonrevolutionary forces in order to achieve piecemeal reform victories. To succumb to the impelling sense of ''the need to do something immediately for the working class'' would inevitably lead to the corruption of the radical leadership or the co-optation of its program. The ''ultimate victory,'' he argued, ''should be the aim of the Social reformer . . . Nothing short of socialism.''

De Leon's unending diatribes against the American Federation of Labor contained a shrewd and prescient analysis of the future development of the American labor movement. He warned that ''pure and simple, here and now'' unionism would, at best, produce organizations to ''perform ambulance service on the industrial battlefield'' and, at worst, become ''caricatures of capitalism'' controlled by corrupted bureaucracies with a vested interest in thwarting ''every intelligent effort of the working class for emancipation.'' His prediction that ''the trade union leaders will let you bore from within only enough to throw you out through the hole bored by you'' was an apt and succinct summary of the fate of the Left in the American labor movement.

Similarly, De Leon maintained that radical political organizations that allowed themselves to be diverted to the support of ameliorative reform measures would be inevitably destroyed by them. Their reform measures and the popular support attracted by them would simply be absorbed by conservative parties which would use them to buttress rather than demolish the capitalist social structure. Pursuing those principles with inexorable logic, De Leon gradually stripped the party and editorial pages of *The People* of every vestige of concern for short-run social and economic issues. In 1900, *The People* announced that twenty-one political planks, ranging from wages and hours laws through women's suffrage, had been eliminated from the SLP platform. No longer, De Leon announced, would the party have its revolutionary energies "consumed by the tape worm of immediate demands." *The People* was now an unsullied testament to the Socialist millennium, pure and sterile, protected by an impregnable ideological shield from the unpredictable vagaries and mundane concerns of the masses whose future it proclaimed —and totally incapable of exerting any influence over them.

In 1905, De Leon participated in the formation of the Industrial Workers of the World. He was largely responsible for drafting the famous preamble to the IWW constitution which, in accordance with De Leon's dicta, promised to avoid political affiliations and pursue the abolition rather than the reform of the wage system. But the pragmatic, spontaneous, and imaginative activists who gave the IWW its character and significance had little in common with and little patience for De Leon's dogmatism. After his inevitable break with them came in 1908, he revived and headed his rival revolutionary union, the Socialist Trades and Labor Alliance (generally known as the "Detroit IWW") but it, like the SLP, was quickly reduced to an isolated and impotent sect.

In the last five years of his life, the reiteration and elaboration of his theories in *The People* became De Leon's only concern and the chief effort of his devoted and docile organization, dominated, according to its official historian, by the "terrible task" of maintaining *The People* on a daily basis. In 1913, challenged by a cohort who asked how the SLP—by then hopelessly devoid of any potential for practical influence or activity—could any longer justify its existence, De Leon responded that its purpose and justification were to be found on the "composing and printing floor . . . throbbing with the activity of issuing four SLP journalistic publications, one of them a daily."

When he died a year later, in 1914, De Leon left behind not a political organization, but a personal cult that he had tirelessly pruned, purged, and molded into a pure extension of his own will. For the more than fifty years since his death the remnant of the organization has labored undeviatingly on the course he charted for it. *The People* survives to chronicle that lonely and barren effort.

Chico, California, 1973

Radical Review

NEW YORK, 1917-1919

JOSEPH R. CONLIN

THE *Radical Review* had a brief history, issuing only seven numbers between 1917 and 1919. It was primarily a theoretical journal, "devoted to the critical investigation of scientific socialism." As the emphasis on *scientific* socialism implies, the *Review* was quite outside the mainstream of American socialism. It adhered to the orthodox Marxism of Daniel De Leon at a time when De Leon's Socialist Labor party was a tiny sect virtually ignored by the relatively prospering and promising Socialist party of America. The journal was published in New York City by an independent company unaffiliated with the SLP. But its editor, Karl Dannenberg, and its major contributors were active in SLP affairs and the *Review* published the writings of the late De Leon and the SLP's national secretary, Arnold Petersen.

The Socialist Labor party deserves closer attention than historians have given it. With the exception of some local electoral victories in Massachusetts at the turn of the century, the party never made much of an impact on American politics. But the SLP was the first Socialist party organized in the United States, and it survives to the present. Moreover, despite its small size, the SLP has remained a vital organization with a coherent ideology which, so far as its members are concerned, stands as scientific sociology and as a revolutionary blueprint. Within this context, the *Radical Review* assumes an importance it never had as current literature.

The unique character of the SLP was the work of Daniel De Leon who, in 1890, took what was little more than a *Turnverein* and remade it in his image. Dutch-Jewish by ancestry, De Leon was apparently born in the West Indies, educated at several European universities, and lectured in Latin American law and diplomacy during the 1880s at Columbia University. He turned his attention to Marxism after 1886, soon gained control of the SLP, and literally ruled the party until his death in 1914.

De Leon's influence on the SLP and, thus, on the *Radical Review*, took several forms. The fiercely intellectual "professor" molded the SLP into an organization passionately devoted to theory. Most of De Leon's Socialist contemporaries disliked both his ideas and his personality, but none could deny his brilliance as an ideologue. No less an authority in the field than V. I. Lenin was quoted as saying that De Leon was the only American to contribute substantially to Marxist thought. The SLP never managed to produce an intellect to succeed the master's but neither did the party stray from its concern with correct theory.

The *Radical Review* was rooted firmly in this tradition. If the American Socialist movement has had innumerable theoretical journals, none deserved the title more than the *Review*. Editor Karl Dannenberg set the style with a serialized essay on "Karl Marx: The Man and the Myth," which ran through most of its issues: Harry Waton, the second most prolific contributor, wrote a sequence on the "philosophy of Marx." Most of the other articles analyzed current events within the theoretical construct of Marxism-De Leonism.

Another legacy of Daniel De Leon was his supreme confidence in the scientific nature of his thought, a confidence reflected in his personal inflexibility and imperiousness. Critical socialists dubbed De Leon "the pope" for his insistence on ideological and organizational discipline. His successors, heirs of De Leon's intolerance but not his papal stature, looked more like martinets. One indication of the *Radical Review*'s organizational independence of the SLP, in fact, was the journal's unsuccessful attempt to transcend the party's orneriness. De Leon and the SLP never quoted heretics except to attack or ridicule them: the *Review* was rather tolerant. It published dissenting articles such as David Reisz's "Twofold Organization of the Working Class," and a rebuttal by J. Harrington, of the Socialist party of Canada, to the *Review*'s critique of his party. While editor Dannenberg noted that Reisz's argument deviated from the journal's point of view, he added that the article merited "careful perusal" and invited "a discussion of the propositions and deductions contained in the same."

This invitation to dialogue was alien to the dogmatic SLP and provides a hint of one of the journal's political purposes, the unification of the American Socialist movement. "The question of Socialist Unity presents a somewhat different aspect nowadays than it did before April, 1917," wrote Socialist Laborite Clarence Hotson. Common vulnerability to governmental suppression during World War I brought the parties "into a mutual attitude of greater sympathy. The force of events itself has tended to clear the ground and bridge the gulf that separated the two parties."

But the De Leonist tradition of ideological intransigence proved too strong for the *Review*. Dwight Macdonald has piquantly observed that American radicals' arrogance in their belief that they alone have the truth varies inversely with their strength. The weak *Radical Review*'s problem was that it was interested in fusion but not on a "give and take" basis. Having gestured cordially to the SPA, Hotson continued in the same essay: "While smaller in number, the SLP is proportionately superior to the S. P. in knowledge and clearness, and in straightforward adherence to principle." Any unification would, clearly and straightforwardly enough, involve the SPA's recognition of such SLP superiority.

When the SPA indicated that it was not interested in trading in its pragmatism for De Leonist leadership, the *Radical Review* reverted to assailing the SPA as of a piece with capital and plutocracy. By the time the final number was printed in early 1919, the conciliatory tone which had vaguely distinguished the *Review* from official SLP publications was gone. The journal's redundancy and the financial woes chronic to radical publications account for its unannounced demise.

The *Radical Review* is a valuable document for the study of American Socialist thought and the neglected history of the Socialist Labor party. It is not easy reading. The style of Socialist theoretical journals in general is not scintillating and the *Radical Review* was more turgid than most. But its contributors included some important Socialist analysts, and even the articles of less eminent radicals contain valuable insights. There are, finally, occasional gems such as a prognostication from Sen Katayama, an old hand in international Socialist circles. "The present war," Katayama wrote in October 1917,

. . . will be fought out in Europe largely as the result of the armed peace of European powers. The armed peace over the Pacific, especially between America and Japan, will be the next in the order of capitalist development. America's extraordinary expansion of armament, a factor that will soon come to be realized, will some day come to a clash with similar institutions of Japan. The next war will be still greater and deadlier than the present one, because it will be a racial war of two colors—brown and white. . . .

Chico, California, 1968

Industrial Unionist

NEW YORK, 1932-1950

MARTIN GLABERMAN AND GEORGE P. RAWICK

THE *Industrial Unionist* provides an interesting illustration of the impact of major events on an organization and ideology as self-sufficient and self-contained as the De Leonist Socialist Labor party. Daniel De Leon, who dominated American socialism in its early years, was a man of great intellectual powers and qualities of leadership. The Socialist Labor party, which he led, was originally the main American Socialist organization. After a major split, which led to the founding of the Socialist party under the leadership of Eugene V. Debs, the SLP rapidly became very doctrinaire and based entirely on the specific industrial unionism views of De Leon.

The *Industrial Unionist* was founded in 1932 by a group which called itself the Industrial Union party (or, at different times, League), which had split off from the Socialist Labor party. The split reflected the impact of the Great Depression and the inability of the SLP to adjust to new events. In particular, the substantial increase in strikes, and in industrial and social militancy generally, led to the belief that there should be a common ground on which this mass activity and a party of "genuine" socialism should meet. The dissatisfaction with the routine behavior of the SLP tended naturally to be couched in the familiar ideological terminology; that is, disagreements were presented in terms of greater loyalty to the ideas of Daniel De Leon and Marxism. The *Industrial Unionist* looked upon itself as the true organ of De Leonism in the United States.

The basic principles of the Industrial Union party remained essentially the same through all the years of its existence, with only slight verbal changes. Thus, it saw capitalism as a system characterized by an irreconcilable class conflict; the interests of capitalists and workers as diametrically opposed to each other; the capitalists as organized in various industrial and commercial associations; the workers as disorganized; the labor unions as basing themselves on the supposed brotherhood of labor and capital and therefore serving the capitalists, not the workers.

"Reforms only quicken its increasing degradation and prolong the prevailing system." The workers, the party stated, must organize politically and economically. On the political field the workers must "strive . . . to gain control of the political state by the civilized and legal means of the ballot, as guaranteed by the Constitution." On the economic field, workers must organize Socialist industrial unions which will be constructing under capitalism "the framework of the industrial government of the future, classless social order which must supplant the political state." The principles were essentially a combination of very violent denunciations of capitalism and reform and compromise with very moderate and peaceful proposals for achieving a complete revolutionary change. Basically, there was only one proposal on how to achieve power: vote the capitalists out and then turn all power over to the industrial unions.

A historical accident gave supporters of De Leon one connection with Marxist organizations abroad. Lenin had once praised De Leon as the only American who had made any original contribution to Marxism, and this led the De Leonists to include Lenin among the Marxists, who were otherwise limited to three: Marx, Engels, and De Leon.

The periodical contained its quota of doctrinal articles by De Leon and fundamental educational articles on economic and social questions, interpreted according to Marxist doctrine. Yet the concrete realities of the depression years were also noted in its pages. One of the factors that contributed to this was the actual participation of the Industrial Union party in industrial struggles in this period. In Jamestown, Pennsylvania, for example, the organization achieved a certain success in organizing furniture workers in the late 1930s and, for a time, was able to resist the competition of the CIO and the AFL. They rejected the whole conception of a union contract which imposed on the workers' organization the responsibility of joint participation with management in the day-to-day problems of running the plant. But, unlike the Industrial Workers of the

World (the Wobblies), the IUP attempted to build permanent shop organizations which, eventually, would become the industrial union government of the new Socialist society.

In the period of organization of the CIO the Industrial Union party could find a modest place for itself as part of the great number of different types of organizations being set up by workers all over the country. Ultimately, however, they could not maintain their industrial unions, and the shops in which they had influence became a part of the more traditional unions. Another aspect of this same movement was the support given by the *Industrial Unionist* to Harry Lundberg's Sailors' Union of the Pacific for its independent and class-conscious stand against both the old and the new labor federations. Here, too, their hopes ultimately were dashed when the need to defend the union against attacks by Harry Bridges' Longshoremen forced the Sailors' Union to become part of the AFL.

The consolidation of the years of unrest and organization within the CIO and also, to some extent, within the AFL, was reflected in the *Industrial Unionist* in the period immediately preceding World War II by the shift of the journal to a more abstract and traditional form of De Leonism. This carried with it less concern expressed or contact indicated with the reality of workers' struggles. The reversion was also expressed in a split. Abraham Ziegler, the national organizer, who was also the most prolific writer for *Industrial Unionist,* left with a tiny group and formed his own short-lived journal, *Modern Socialism.* By the beginning of the war, *Industrial Unionist* was reduced to mimeographed form for several issues before passing out of existence. It was revived temporarily in 1949-1950.

Industrial Unionist examined political events through essentially De Leonist eyes. Of some interest was its ambivalent attitude toward the Soviet Union. It supported what was called the industrial achievements of Stalin, the Five-Year Plans, and the building up of industry and agriculture. Beginning in 1936 (the year of the promulgation of the new Soviet constitution), the journal counterposed the political dictatorship to the Socialist industrial achievements. It rejected the Communist parties of the world as class collaborationists, and took the same attitude toward Soviet foreign policy. Ultimately, when Germany attacked Russia in 1941, the *Industrial Unionist* group defended the Soviet Union as basically a workers' society. Trotskyism (in the form of its American organi-zation) was attacked as both class collaborationist (willing to fight for reforms under capitalism) and dominated by foreign as opposed to American interests and concerns. The new unions of the CIO, as well as the old unions of the AFL, were consistently attacked as agents and supporters of capitalism.

Detroit and Rochester, Michigan, 1968

Labor Power

NEW YORK, 1939-1941

PAUL M. BUHLE

LABOR POWER, as the organ of a partially reconstructed De Leonism, gave expression to the pre-World War I radical politics of "Impossiblism," seeking to chart a new course with old maps as guides, at a time when the United States was plunged into the drastically altered world of the depression. *Labor Power* and its parent, the Industrial Union party (later the Socialist Union party), unlike the Socialist Labor party from which the IUP was a factional emanation, partially succeeded in perceiving the new realities. But in a time when Left hegemony was held decisively by the Communist party and the CIO and a second world war neared, the publishers found no room to grow or even maintain themselves as a political group, and by 1941 for all practical purposes dissolved.

The prophet of *Labor Power* was Daniel De Leon, who had died a quarter of a century before the periodical's birth. A Latin American-born, European-educated intellectual, De Leon had taught briefly at Columbia University in the 1880s before his conversion to socialism. Joining the largely German-American, isolated Socialist Labor party in 1891, he rapidly achieved domination of the organization through his editing of its organ, *The People*. De Leon's uncompromising hostility toward non-Socialist trade unions and any nonrevolutionary socialistic tendencies resulted in constant internal warfare within the SLP, culminating in the withdrawal of a sizable group, which helped to found the Socialist party. In that same year, 1899, a purged but politically adamant Socialist Labor party adopted a position similar to that of European "Impossibilists": it scorned any demands for reform under capitalism and called solely for the system's overthrow.

After 1900 De Leon's SLP was a personality-dominated sect. De Leon made his last bid for power on a national scale by popularizing the notion of industrial unionism through his influence in the Industrial Workers of the World, founded in 1905. Within his plan, shared by other syndicalistic Socialists, the workers would organize for the revolution industrially and politically, but would rule the postrevolutionary government directly through workers' councils. This plan eliminated the role of the State, regarded by reform-minded Socialists and later Leninist Communists alike to be a necessary tool in the transition period to communism. In 1908 the "anarchosyndicalists" in the IWW, opposing all political entanglements even before the revolution, expelled De Leon. Thereafter his union policy was followed only by a group of SLP unionists in the Detroit IWW, later called the Workers International Industrial Union, which practically disappeared as an organization after its unsuccessful role in the Paterson, New Jersey, strikes of 1911. In effect, the Socialist Labor party was reduced to political leafleting and election campaigning, utterly divorced from day-to-day struggles.

Yet De Leon, a failure in the arena of mass politics, remained a deeply revered leader within the ranks of the SLP and fraternal groups abroad. By virtue of his editorial role in the *New York Daily People* (which folded shortly before his death in 1914) and his public speeches, he remained even after his passing the basic provider of the ideas which bound together the SLP membership. While he lived, his ideas *were* those of the party, even when (as in 1905) they changed sharply to fit new conditions. Following his death, "Marxism-De Leonism" became a fixed doctrine to be avowedly followed even by groups which split from the SLP to work for a "true De Leonism."

In the last year of his life De Leon entrusted the SLP leadership to Arnold Petersen as the new national secretary, a position Petersen held until his retirement in early 1969. Over the years Petersen proved well suited for the task of maintaining political stasis in the SLP and preventing any alteration in its doctrine. The minor internal crises the SLP has faced, from the Russian Revolution to the emergence of the New Left, seem to have been overcome without any serious challenges to his leadership, and factional groups have departed in small and localistic processions. One such group emerged in 1932 as the Industrial Union League (later the Industrial Union party) with Sam Brandon as national secretary and Charles Neuschotz as editor of its official organ, the *Industrial Unionist*.

The IUP, though quite obviously limited in its resources, attempted to put a De Leonist program into action on a miniature scale. The United Furniture Workers of America (UFWA) a radical union independent of both the AFL and CIO, promulgated a constitution with a preamble almost identical to that of the original IWW preamble written largely by De Leon in 1905. Moreover, the UFWA endorsed the *Industrial Unionist* as its official organ and had one of its leading figures, Carl P. Anderson, on the IUP executive committee. But like the militant Sailors' Union of the Pacific, the furniture workers' union could not survive the pressure of the great labor bodies as a small, autonomous group. Thus all that seemed to remain for the IUP (a faction of which was rechristened the Socialist Union party in 1939, after a political fragmentation) was a repetition of the function of the Socialist Labor party: De Leonist propagandizing and analysis of world and national events.

After the worst of its factional fevers subsided, the new Socialist Union party evinced a determination to struggle within the existing unions for radical insurgencies and within the body politic for a revolutionary resistance to the coming war. This divergence from the practice of De Leonism was probably stimulated by Abraham Ziegler, editor of the Socialist Union party organ *Labor Power*, a lawyer who had been expelled from the SLP and joined the Industrial Union party in the mid-1930s. Yet the participation in mass struggles was only a half-step, for *Labor Power* constantly affirmed its bitterness for the "reform" parties, i.e., nearly all the other radical parties in the United States who called for substantive changes *within* capitalism before the revolution. And as the SUP believed that the day-to-day battles of the workers were generally useless and continued only because of ignorance, its participation must have had a cynical quality.

Certainly the pessimism, and implied cynicism, in *Labor Power* were not without objective cause in the real world. The problems of the Left by 1939 stood against any easy progress for a relatively small and doctrinaire radical group. Just as the early 1930s was marked by a great revolutionary hopefulness among Marxists, and a search by many for a revolutionary movement outside the Communist party, so the latter part of the decade was dominated by the rise of the CIO and the fight against fascism, which together drew attention from all Marxist groups except the Communist party. By 1939, the Communists were consolidating their rapidly growing membership, and the other groups stood together (only metaphorically, as internecine attacks proliferated) in a common shadow. The war seemed naturally to crowd out most other interests, and *Labor Power* gave many of its columns over to foreign .policy matters, the outcome of which it could not possibly influence. Thus its impotence to do more than analyze events was underscored. It repeatedly lashed out at the leadership of the Socialist, Socialist Workers and Communist parties, imploring the membership to come over to the SUP; needless to say, its appeals were not met with any noteworthy response.

For Ziegler himself, *Labor Power* was a way station to further advance beyond De Leonist orthodoxy through the short-lived *Modern Socialism,* which managed a few issues in 1941 before he was inducted into the Army. For the rest of the group, *Labor Power* had been the means of expressing dissent and a political posture, in the same fashion that other politically isolated groups express themselves. Realistically, there was little if any chance to reach a mass audience, but the group found at least an opportunity for self-expression, presenting its program on the printed page. Thus the SUP did make itself heard for those who would listen, but its message had been bypassed by the actual organization of the CIO industrially and the consolidation of industrial unions had finally met its historical rendezvous, leaving only scattered partisans to repeat his message again and again.

Madison, Wisconsin, 1969

Modern Socialism

NEW YORK, 1941-1942

GEORGE P. RAWICK

MODERN SOCIALISM appeared for four issues in late 1941 and early 1942. It was the personal organ of Abraham Ziegler, who from 1939 to early 1941, had been the national secretary of the small Socialist Union party and principal editorial contributor to its official organ, *Labor Power*. The Socialist Union party had split in 1939 from the Industrial Union party, which in turn had split from the De Leonite Socialist Labor party in 1932.

The Industrial Union party and its heirs and offspring were all attempts to break out of the rigid sectarianism of the De Leonite organization in the face of the ferment in the American labor movement that produced mass industrial unionism and the Congress of Industrial Organizations. The De Leonites had been advocating mass industrial unionism for so many years that when such a movement actually appeared, the official De Leonite party, the Socialist Labor party, could only react in a sectarian and hostile fashion. *Modern Socialism* is an indication of the impact of De Leonism on American socialism, and is a part of any history of that strand of socialism in the United States.

While Ziegler had become "convinced that there was no room for splinter groups in the movement and that they are a waste of time organizationally (moreover, the group was torn by internal dissension)," he felt the need to continue some form of Socialist discussion. Thus *Modern Socialism* evolved.

Almost all of the articles in the four issues of the journal were by Ziegler, although a few independent Marxists such as Paul Mattick and Fred Dyer did contribute articles with points of view not identical with that of the editor. There is a great lack of political and theoretical clarity in the journal, but for serious students of the history of socialism in the United States this periodical has significance.

Modern Socialism reflects certain problems that faced all branches of American socialism in the 1930s: the impact of Hitlerism, the degeneration of the Russian Revolution under Stalin, and the rise of the Congress of Industrial Organizations. While Ziegler was clearly no Marxist theoretician, he was able to react to the world about him. He looked for a democratic reformulation of Marxism and rejected the emphasis of the Socialist Labor party and its heirs upon the building of sectarian industrial unions controlled by the party, in favor of working with and in the mass unions.

Two questions were most important for Ziegler. Was a "Vanguard Party," based on a strictly monolithic conception of internal democracy, necessary in the struggle for socialism? And what should be a proper Socialist policy toward World War II?

The editor seems to have rejected the idea of the "Vanguard Party" in his search for a democratic Marxism. But he floundered, and eventually the magazine disappeared because he could discover no other basis for the existence of a Marxist organization.

The discussion the editor conducted on the war question, however, dominated the history of the periodical. In the first issue Ziegler argued that while the war is a struggle between the imperialist powers and thus reactionary, it is also, because of the threat of totalitarianism, a social struggle and, therefore, Socialists must find a way to support its progressive aspects. By the third number Ziegler had come to understand that there was no way to straddle the issue. He declared: "*Modern Socialism* bowing to hard political reality, has taken a firm stand in favor of full and complete military support, without equivocation or mental reservation, of the war against Nazism and its Japanese cat's-paw." The last issue of the journal contained the following note: "The undersigned having received notice . . . of his classification in Class 1A and his imminent induction into the armed forces of the United States, announces the suspension of *Modern Socialism* for the duration or such period as, when and if he returns once more to civil life . . . Abraham Ziegler."

Rochester, Michigan, 1968

The Militant
NEW YORK, 1928-1934

New Militant
NEW YORK, 1934-1936

Labor Action
SAN FRANCISCO, 1936-1937

Socialist Appeal
NEW YORK, 1937-1941

The Militant
NEW YORK, 1941—

JOSEPH HANSEN

SINCE its first issue of November 15, 1928, *The Militant* has expressed the political position of the Trotskyist movement in the United States. It was launched in opposition to the Stalinist faction that had been placed in command of the Communist party under a Kremlin ukase. From the beginning, *The Militant* stood to the left of the *Daily Worker*. It still remains there.

The primary aim of *The Militant* for the first five years was limited to bringing the views of the International Left Opposition, and particularly its leader, Leon Trotsky, to the attention of members of the Communist party in the hope of breaking the grip of the Stalinist faction and returning the party to observance of the revolutionary-Socialist program on which it had been founded. This meant defending the Soviet Union as a workers' state, but opposing Stalinist decay. In the United States it meant faithful adherence to the program of class struggle.

The first editorial board of *The Militant* consisted of James P. Cannon, Martin Abern, and Max Shachtman. Maurice Spector was added to this board a little later, his name appearing on the masthead of the December 15, 1928, issue. Arne Swabeck became the fifth member of the board on January 1, 1931. This board remained unaltered until *The Militant* changed its name to *New Militant* on December 15, 1934, as one of the results of the fusion of the original Trotskyist group, the Communist League of America, with the American Workers party led by A. J. Muste.

The five members of the original editorial board of *The Militant* were all well-known Communist leaders who had participated in founding the party. When they learned the truth about the differences in the Russian Communist party through documents that came into Cannon's possession at the sixth congress of the Communist International, they decided to break the censorship set up by Stalin. The editors decided to make the suppressed documents written by Trotsky and other leaders of the Left Opposition in the Soviet Union available to the entire international Communist movement. And they decided to do battle inside the Communist party for the program that the Left Opposition stood for—the program of Leninism to which they had been won upon the victory of the Russian Revolution in October 1917.

The members of the editorial board knew that the struggle would be difficult, although they did not appreciate how difficult it was to be in the face of the concerted attacks that descended on them from all sides, ranging from the liberals to the fascists. The attacks were not confined to ideology. The world movement suffered assassinations at the hands of Stalin's agents, long prison terms, and death in concentration camps and before the firing squads of the Nazis.

The editors of *The Militant* were not without influence when they came out in defense of the cause Trotsky stood for. In the American Communist party, James P. Cannon was a member of the Political Committee and the Central Executive Committee; Martin Abern and Arne Swabeck were members of the Central Executive Committee; Max Shachtman was an alternate. Maurice Spector was a member of the Executive Committee of the Communist International, chairman of the Canadian Communist party, and editor of *The Canadian Worker* and *The Canadian Labour Monthly*. All of them were public figures—Martin Abern and Max Shachtman as leaders of the Communist youth movement, James P. Cannon and Arne Swabeck as organizers and leaders in workers' struggles going back before World War I. Maurice Spector was an outstanding figure in the Canadian radical movement.

Their efforts met with a warm response from co-thinkers abroad. Trotsky, for instance, sent a message which was published in the June 1, 1929, issue. It may be worth quoting here, since the staff of *The Militant* shared his views on the points he made then, and the current staff, although completely renewed, has not changed in this respect:

The work to be achieved by the American Opposition has international-historic significance, for in the last historic analysis all the problems of our planet will be decided upon American soil. There is much in favor of the idea that from the standpoint of revolutionary order, Europe and the East stand ahead of the United States. But a course of events is possible in which this order might be broken in favor of the proletariat of the United States. Moreover, even if you assume that America, which now shakes the whole world will be shaken last of all, the danger remains that a revolutionary situation in the United States may catch the vanguard of the American proletariat unprepared, as was the case in Germany in 1923, in England in 1926, and in China in 1925 to 1927. We must not for a minute lose sight of the fact that the might of American capitalism rests more and more upon a foundation of world economy with its contradictions and crises, military and revolutionary. This means that a social crisis in the United States may arrive a good deal sooner than many think, and have a feverish development from the beginning. Hence the conclusion: It is necessary to prepare.

If those words of 1929 sound highly contemporary, the same can be said of much that appeared in *The Militant* in the early years. The concern of the editors was to advance the task of solving the truly great problems facing humanity in that era. Those central problems remain to be solved—in fact they have become exacerbated, now presenting the world with the alternative either of a planned economy on a global scale or a civilization reduced to radioactive ruins. Consequently, a surprising amount of material in *The Militant* remains timely and well worth considering. The obvious corrections and adjustments would, of course, have to be made since the course of the class struggle on an international scale proved to be more complex, tortuous, and drawn out than any of the original board expected.

The editors of *The Militant*—and a long succession of able revolutionary journalists participated in getting it out—sought to report these developments honestly and accurately and to influence their outcomes insofar as it was possible to influence them. The policy from the beginning was to maintain *The Militant,* not as a mere muckraking or sensationalistic journal, but as a *fighting* paper integrated with the supreme task of our times—to build a combat party of the working class in the tradition of Leninism. Thus the history of *The Militant* is an integral part of the history of the American Trotskyist movement.

When the Communist League of America fused with the American Workers party in 1934, the new organization was named the Workers party. The name of the paper changed accordingly, becoming the *New Militant.* James P. Cannon was designated editor under an agreement allocating leading posts in the new organization on an equitable basis between the two tendencies that had merged.

When promising leftward-moving currents appeared in the Socialist party shortly thereafter, the new organization sought another fusion. To accomplish this it was necessary for the entire Trotskyist tendency to join the Socialist party as a group. This operation was carried out openly and in agreement with the main leaders of the Socialist party, who at the time stood for, and advocated, an "all-inclusive" party, even going so far as to extend an invitation to all other currents to join. The Socialist party leadership, however, under pressure from the right wing, placed rather onerous conditions on the Trotskyists, the worst being an ultimatum to give up publication of their newspaper. This was acceded to, although with great reluctance. The last issue of the *New Militant* (June 6, 1936) announced the decision and, under the terms of the invitation that had been extended by the leadership of the Socialist party, appealed to all revolutionary-minded militants to join the "all-inclusive" setup.

The fusion between the left wing of the Socialist party and the American Trotskyists proved to be profitable for the Trotskyists. Very shortly it became possible to provide an avenue for expressing the revolutionary-Socialist views of the new combination. A weekly newspaper, *Labor Action*, was founded in San Francisco as the official organ of the Socialist party of California and James P. Cannon was invited to become its editor. The first issue appeared on November 28, 1936, during the general strike of the West Coast maritime unions.

Within the Socialist party, however, the very success of the Trotskyists made it increasingly difficult to speak out freely on some truly crucial issues of the time, particularly the Spanish Civil War, in which the policies of the Stalinists, the Social Democrats, and the Anarchists were paving the way for the disaster that eventually befell that very promising revolution. The right wing of the Socialist party became more and more fearful of the left wing's growing influence and strength, and initiated steps to contain and, if possible, shatter it. What the right wing intended was clearly signaled by efforts to muzzle the Trotskyists in particular. The Trotskyists therefore prepared for a factional struggle in which a split appeared inherent from the very beginning in view of the gravity of the differences.

Labor Action, which really represented a continuation of *The Militant,* became a casualty in this struggle, the last issue appearing on May 1, 1937.

In the Chicago area, the Trotskyists were joined in the fight by Albert Goldman, a prominent labor attorney, former member of the Communist party and then of the Trotskyist movement, who had gone into the Socialist party on his own several years earlier. He edited an officially recognized bulletin in the Socialist party, the *Socialist Appeal.* When the National Executive Committee voted the *Socialist Appeal* out of existence, this provocative action was countered in New York. The *Socialist Appeal* was adopted by the Socialist party of New York left-wing branches, as an official weekly organ and reissued in New York beginning August 14, 1937.

The struggle within the Socialist party came to a conclusion at an emergency convention of the left wing which opened in Chicago on December 31, 1937. The delegates founded the Socialist Workers party and named the *Socialist Appeal* as its official weekly organ.

This name remained on the masthead until the February 1, 1941, issue, when the name, *The Militant*, was resumed. The lead editorial in that issue explained why the change had been made:

By returning to this name, we symbolize before the workers of America and the revolutionary proletariat throughout the world that our party proclaims today that program of uncompromising international class struggle which we inscribed on our banner from the first moment of our existence.

The Socialist Workers Party has also been compelled by a reactionary federal law, the Voorhis Act, to discontinue its organizational affiliation with the World Party of Socialist Revolution, the Fourth International.

But by this banner, *The Militant*, we make known to the revolutionary vanguard everywhere that we remain loyal to our common goal.

It can be truthfully said that, in the years since then, *The Militant* has remained loyal to the program with which it began, although some of those who served on its editorial boards did fall by the wayside.

On December 13, 1944, another change was made. *The Militant* ceased to be the official organ of the Socialist Workers party. An editorial announced that it was to be published "henceforth solely upon the responsibility of The Militant Publishing Association, its owner and publisher." The editorial specified that all statements in that and future issues of *The Militant* represented the views of the officers and editors of the Militant Publishing Association.

This measure was taken because of the government's witch-hunt against those who opposed World War II as another imperialist carnage. The Socialist Workers party had already been singled out by the witch-hunters for special attention. The party leaders were tried in 1941 under the Smith "Gag" Act, being the first victims of that infamous law against freedom of thought and the press. Later, when the Supreme Court refused to hear their appeal, they had to serve prison sentences because of their views. *The Militant* came under heavy pressure because of its role in seeking to popularize the program of the Socialist Workers party and printing the speeches and articles of its leaders opposing the war aims of U.S. imperialism. Issues of *The Militant* were held up by the censors, and for a time it appeared that the Roosevelt administration would even seek to deprive *The Militant* of its second-class mailing rights.

The Militant, as indicated, began as a partisan political newspaper directed primarily to the cadres of the Communist party. Its audience was thus necessarily a limited one. This is reflected in the nature of the articles it featured, dealing with what many persons at the time thought were highly abstract and even hair-splitting questions: the difference between Trotsky's theory of permanent revolution and Stalin's concept of "socialism in one country," and how this difference had become involved in the revolutionary struggles of our time and what it signified for their success and for the defense of the USSR. These questions turned out to be very concrete. Looking back now, some of these articles, many of them bearing the signature of Leon Trotsky, remain among the most interesting and thought-provoking published over the years. Revolutionists of today will find much in them bearing on their own problems, even though much has changed in the intervening years.

In 1933, however, when events in Germany (in which the Communist party permitted Hitler to walk into power without a fight) made it clear that the Communist International and its sections were beyond hope of reform, the Trotskyists changed their orientation. Instead of addressing themselves mainly to the cadres of the Communist party, they turned directly to the broad layers of the American working class. This was reflected, of course, in *The Militant.* It sought a more popular appeal. Strike struggles, union problems, activities of the mass organizations —all these became of primary concern. *The Militant* began to establish a reputation for the honest and uncompromising way in which it covered the unemployed movement, labor's battles, and the struggle for black liberation. Its pages over the years thus constitute excellent source material for studies of these struggles, particularly as they were estimated by the Trotskyists from their international Marxist point of view. *The Militant* also contains an immense amount of first-hand information from participants in major battles of the working class over the years.

In making this turn, *The Militant* never lost sight of the revolutionary-Socialist goals to which it had been dedicated from the beginning. It continued to provide analyses, special reports, and a Trotskyist political orientation on all major developments in the world. It remained preeminently a paper with an international outlook.

Besides its record in World War II, the case of the Korean war offers a good example of the standard maintained by *The Militant*. It was the first newspaper in the United States, to my knowledge, to come out in complete opposition to Truman's course of involving America in the civil war in that land. There was no ambiguity about the unconditional support it offered to the Korean people. Its exposure of what it saw as the imperialist aims of the United States and what its military machine did to the Korean people in that war provides a model of revolutionary journalism.

The Militant followed the same basic policy in the Vietnam war, defending the right of the Vietnamese people to determine their own fate without interference from the United States or any other power. Thus *The Militant* was instrumental in popularizing the slogan, ''Bring the GI's home now.''

The Militant has always been particularly attentive to the struggles of peoples in the colonial world, and has a proud record in this respect. This record includes the reportage and defense of the Chinese revolution, the Algerian revolution, and above all the Cuban revolution with its special meaning for the working class in the United States as the opening of the Socialist revolution in the Western Hemisphere.

Cannon's editorship of *The Militant* ended many years ago. It might prove interesting to list those who succeeded him. Max Shachtman became editor on January 22, 1938, with two associate editors, Harold Roberts and Frank Graves. On August 13, 1938, George Clarke succeeded Frank Graves as associate editor and was in turn succeeded by Felix Morrow on January 14, 1939. On February 10, 1939, Emmanuel Garrett and I were added as staff members. The staff was later reduced, and on August 8, 1939, Felix Morrow and Emmanuel Garrett became associate editors. On December 1, 1939, the associate editors were dropped, and Felix Morrow and Max Shachtman were listed as editors. This arrangement lasted until April 13, 1940, when an editorial board was set up consisting of Felix Morrow, Max Shachtman, and Albert Goldman. This was very short-lived because of political differences coming to a head at the time, and on April 20, 1940, the editorial board was reduced to Felix Morrow and Albert Goldman. This combination lasted until July 5, 1941, when Felix Morrow became sole editor.

On January 31, 1942, Morrow was succeeded by George Breitman. On August 28, 1943, Farrell Dobbs was made editor and George Breitman managing editor. Farrell Dobbs became sole editor on October 16, 1943. His title was changed to managing editor on April 7, 1945, and then back to editor on December 21, 1946. George Breitman resumed editorship on January 3, 1949, remaining five years. He was succeeded by me on June 21, 1954. On December 27, 1954, Murry Weiss became editor and he was followed on July 30, 1956, by Daniel Roberts. Three years later, on July 13, 1959, I resumed editorship, with Daniel Roberts as associate editor, a title that was changed to managing editor on October 12, 1959.

On March 13, 1961, George Lavan became managing editor. After four years, on June 7, 1965, he was succeeded by Barry Sheppard. On November 20, 1967, Barry Sheppard succeeded me as editor. At present *The Militant* does not have a managing editor.

Although some of these changes reflected political differences, most of them simply signified transfer to other duties in the revolutionary Socialist movement. In the case of Daniel Roberts, leukemia brought a tragic end to the career of a most energetic and promising revolutionary journalist and Socialist fighter.

Staff members were not listed on the masthead during the war hysteria of the 1940s and the following period of McCarthyism because of the need to protect them from reprisals in the professional fields where some of them derived their living. This necessity, which may have been overemphasized, is rather unfortunate. Besides the failure to give credit where credit is due, the picture of the staff becomes somewhat distorted. One of the main secrets of the capacity of *The Militant* to maintain its high levels has been its staff work. In more than one instance it could be said with some justice that the staff had to endure an editor who faltered, proving its capacity to meet its deadlines and cover the crucial events despite the added handicap of the editor. The motto of *The Militant* has always been, "No temperamental star performers; but teamwork." Two outstanding staff members for many years were the labor specialist, Art Preis, and the cartoonist, Laura Gray, both of whom died at the height of their powers and productivity.

It should also be noted that at certain periods when the regular editor could not function at his desk (Farrell Dobbs, for instance, spent a year in Sandstone as a victim of the Smith Act while he was editor), the work was carried on by others who stepped in without demanding a credit line. Among these should be listed Frank Graves, John G. Wright, George Novack, William F. Warde, E. R. Frank, and Tom Kerry.

Finally, I should like to mention the business managers on whom a particularly heavy responsibility always fell because of limited funds and limited personnel. In the worst days, particularly the early 1930s, their achievements were often not far from miraculous. Up until the end of 1934, the post of business manager was not listed separately. During those years, Rose Karsner, Martin Abern, and Arne Swabeck carried out this assignment as well as other difficult tasks assumed by the small group of Trotskyists.

The first business manager to be listed was Cara Cook, whose name appears on the masthead of the *New Militant* from December 15, 1934, to February 2, 1935. She was followed by Hawthorne Winner, who served until May 18, 1935. The post then remained unfilled until the *New Militant* suspended publication.

Frank Stern was business manager of *Labor Action*.

In the *Socialist Appeal*, the first business manager was Bob Browne (January 22, 1938-April 23, 1938). He was followed by Sherman Stanley (April 30, 1938-August 4, 1939). In a reorganization of the staff (listed in the August 8, 1939 issue), Martin Abern was made general manager and Sherman Stanley assistant manager. This lasted until December 16, 1939. The following issue (December 23) notes that George Clarke was made general manager, Sherman Stanley being retained as assistant manager. Stanley was dropped March 9, 1940. These frequent shifts, as in the case of the editors at the time, reflected a deep-going factional struggle in the Socialist Workers party that broke out on the eve of World War II. Against a minority who wanted to drop unconditional defense of the Soviet Union as a degenerated workers state, the majority defended the position that constituted one of the main planks in the platform of the Trotskyist movement.

George Clarke remained general manager until August 10, 1940, when he was given a different assignment. The post was then filled by Ruth Jeffrey (August 17, 1940-April 5, 1941). She was followed by Lydia Beidel (April 12, 1941-January 3, 1942).

During the rest of the war no business manager was listed because of the witch-hunt atmosphere. Those who served during this period were Reba Aubrey, Jeff Thorne, and Justine Lang.

On April 18, 1949, the post was again listed, with my name appearing as business manager. I served in that capacity until June 14, 1954, when I became editor.

The next business manager was Dorothy Johnson (June 21, 1954-November 28, 1955), followed by Anne Chester (December 5, 1955-January 14, 1957), Frances James (January 21, 1957-February 10, 1958), Beatrice Allen (February 17, 1958-March 23, 1959), and finally Karolyn Kerry, who served almost nine years (March 30, 1959-December 25, 1967). The current business manager, Beverly Scott, began on January 1, 1968.

New York, 1968

Young Spartacus

NEW YORK, 1931-1935

PAUL M. BUHLE

YOUNG SPARTACUS, an organ of the Trotskyist youth movement, was an expression of a period in the troubled development of a Left Opposition to the Communist party and the Young Communist League in America. Ironically, the Left constituency in the United States, where radical political parties have been relatively the weakest in Western nations, provided the strongest base for Leon Trotsky's followers and was consequently an agitational center for Trotsky's world revolutionary strategy. But even in America the evolution of the opposition was marked by a response, rather than an aggressive attitude, toward the Communist party's twist and turns, and the fate of Trotskyism was sealed in that period by the Communists' sheer size and ideological hegemony among the Left's following. *Young Spartacus* struggled as one part of a larger movement and, after limited success, was formally dissolved together with the adult organization.

From the birth of an American Communist movement in 1919, internecine warfare was a political way of life for the Left. Along with the government's suppression of radical activities from 1919 to 1921, the bitter feuding between the Communists and Socialists, and among the Communists themselves, helped to reduce the size of the two principal Communist groups to minuscule proportions. Limited in membership generally to a foreign-speaking constituency, the Workers (Communist) party liquidated its "underground" apparatus, and unsuccessfully attempted both to inject itself into a farmer-labor third-party movement and to gain a base in the American Federation of Labor unions by the mid-1920s. At the close of the decade, the party was scarcely closer to a

337

mass breakthrough, and was further splintered by the expulsion of the Trotskyists in 1928 and the "Lovestoneites," or Right Communists, the following year.

The Trotskyists barely numbered a handful in the early years of their existence as a separate group, and they were limited, by practicality as well as intent, to agitation among the members of the Communist party. They battled as an expelled (but utterly loyal) faction, calling for redress of grievances, democratic internal party life, and, above all, a repudiation of the Moscow "Third Period" line, which designated Socialists "Social Fascists" and which called for the construction of revolutionary independent (or "dual") unions with little actual mass support.

Young Spartacus was the publication of the Trotskyists' National Youth Committee and later of the Spartacus Youth League, which, unlike the politically autonomous "New Left" movements some three decades later, were rather simply mechanisms for reaffirming and spreading among youths the program of the parent organization—thus parallel in role if not in opinions to the Communists' Young Communist League (YCL) and Socialists' Young People's Socialist League (YPSL). Within the general definition there were, however, some significant disagreements among the Trotskyist leadership concerning the proper position of the youth movement in the general structure. Max Shachtman, who led a substantial faction away from the Socialist Workers party (Trotskyist) in 1940, believed that his fellow leader, James P. Cannon, was hostile to any youth group by dint of the latter's training in the prewar Industrial Workers of the World, where age, like race, was largely disregarded. Shachtman appeared to be reflecting his own experience in the Young Communist League of the 1920s in calling for a greater emphasis on building youth strength (thus granting more political suffrance for "immaturity") and a more popular line toward non-Communist youth. Although the implications of this difference should not be exaggerated, it may well have reflected the tensions burdening nearly all radical movements from the 1920s onward, as the proponents of the orthodox, worker-oriented approach clashed with the proponents of a newer approach directed at youth (even nonworking-class youth) who seemed to be in more constant revolt than workers.

In *Young Spartacus*, the tension was rarely explicit, for the paper claimed to appeal only to working-class youths and those college students who were willing to leave their individualism behind for the sake of the class struggle. This orientation put the paper, and the organization it reflected, historically between the Intercollegiate Socialist Society of pre-World War I days, which operated for the Socialist party almost exclusively among upperclass and elite-bound youth, and a New Left that has worked with students rather indifferent to their class origins. For *Young Spartacus*—at least formally—all college students were designated by the "fundamental principles of Marxism" as bourgeois, petty-bourgeois, or would-be petty-bourgeois, leaving little of their revolutionary potential to the imagination.

The paper reflected the character of internal life in the Trotskyists' early period. Trotskyist youths distributed the paper and debated YPSL members and anarchists. Most of all, they attempted to "show up" the YCL leadership while educating YCL members through verbal confrontations at mass meetings. Before 1933, *Young Spartacus* often commented that Trotskyists had been forced to defend publicly the Communist position and the Soviet Union because the Communists, due to their leadership, were unable to do so adequately themselves. And this provided the theme for their journal.

By mid-1933, when Trotsky moved beyond the hopes of reforming the Communist party, the logical orientation of *Young Spartacus* had shifted. Increasing emphasis was laid upon attracting semipolitical youth, but the recruiting successes recorded in a vigorous and hopeful fashion were minor. Just prior to the fusion of the Trotskyist organization with the American Workers' party in late 1934, the National Youth Committee's membership was reckoned at about 200, and the adult group's at around 450. They constituted in every sense the "hard core," weathered and tempered by the class and factional struggles. Compared to their meager numbers six years before, the membership rise was encouraging; compared to the thousands of youths in the Communist and Socialist youth groups, the 18,000 members of the Socialist party and the 23,000 of the Communist party, the increase was less promising. The rechristened Spartacus Youth League did indeed draw life from the burgeoning movements of the 1930s, but not fast enough to grow qualitatively into a powerful, mass youth organization.

The fate of the SYL and *Young Spartacus* was all but decided by the "French Turn," the amalgamation of the French Trotskyist organization with the Socialist party of that nation. Throughout 1935 the American Trotskyist organization waged a fierce internal battle, moving inexorably, with Trotsky's blessing, toward a rapprochement with the American Socialists they had previously attacked as traitors to the working class. As a condition of membership in the Socialist party, all Trotskyist periodicals were dropped and all formal organizations disbanded. Undoubtedly the most important role of *Young Spartacus* and the Trotskyist youth groups was to prepare young radicals for the factional struggles that raged from the Trotskyists' entry in the spring of 1936 to their expulsion in the fall of 1937. Although the Trotskyists failed to gain the working-class membership they had hoped to obtain in joining the Socialist party, they converted YPSL activists in great numbers.

The youth thus won from YPSL to Trotskyism departed in bulk with Max Shachtman from the Socialist Workers party in 1940 because of a series of internal differences among Trotskyists that were brought to a head by the question of support of the Soviet Union in the impending world war. The 1940 split marks the end of a kind of continuum between the earliest days of American Trotskyism and its maturity. The allegiance to Shachtman of the two most prominent members of the *Young Spartacus* editorial board, James Carter and Martin Abern (who had been a leader of the YCL in the 1920s and was first chairman of the Trotskyist National Youth Committee), like the allegiance of YPSL leader Hal Draper, was a sign of the general relationship between the Shachtman group and young Trotskyists. The real political differences thus had a stylistic component, with Cannon representing the older, union-oriented movement and Shachtman the agitational, more experimental tendency.

Young Spartacus, while a child of both parents, thus resembled one more than the other. With the energies each provided, the paper might in another time have possessed unusual powers of appeal. But it was not a memorable agitational success: incessant intergroup disagreements reinforced its isolation, and the Trotskyists' move into the Socialist party shortened its life. Like other limited successes and real failures of the radical Left, it served at best to train its creators and a few readers, and at worst to reinforce the bitterness of lost opportunities.

Madison, Wisconsin, 1969

Class Struggle
NEW YORK, 1931-1937

ALAN BLOCK

ALMOST from the very beginning the Communist International was split over the issue of "socialism in one country" or "world revolution." After the death of Lenin and the ascension of Stalin to power, Trotsky came to be on the outside of the correct party position. Finally, in 1928, when Trotsky was forced to leave the Soviet Union, the American Communist leadership mirrored this division by splitting with the American Communist majority which solidly backed Stalin.

The Left Opposition in the United States was led by James P. Cannon and Max Shachtman. They formed a group called the Communist League of America (CLA). The CLA placed particular emphasis on the point that they still considered themselves a part of the Workers (Communist) party (WP), and hoped to correct the larger party by criticizing it from a factional point of view but still from within the party. Cannon stressed that unity was what he was concerned with, and that when he and Shachtman and the others rejoined the WP, it would be a much stronger party and much clearer in its ideology.

Some in the CLA, however, did not share the concern for ultimate loyalty to the party and thought rather that revolutionary interests might be better served by not only opposing the party on the level of theory but also on that of action. Thus in 1931, the Communist League of Struggle (CLS) and its official organ, *Class Struggle,* came into being out of the Cannon faction, with Albert Weisbord at its head.

Weisbord had gained national recognition in the Passaic textile strike of 1926, a strike that the Communists felt was important because it was led by them. Before Passaic he had graduated with honors from Harvard

Law School and passed through the Young People's Socialist League (YPSL) before he became a Communist. In 1929 he was expelled from the Workers party for reasons that were not quite clear. At this point, Weisbord retired from politics for a brief period, returned as a Trotskyist, and joined the Left Opposition. By 1931 he had moved outside the Left Opposition toward a policy and program of his own.

Basically the CLS defined its differences with the Cannonites over several basic issues, such as the united front, the Labor party, and mass work. The CLS was in favor of a united front based on individual issues, and consequently joined the Mooney Defense and other united front groups. The Labor party question was a substantive one. Trotsky believed that a large Labor party soon would take root in the United States and supplant the two-party framework. The *Class Struggle* took the position that since the growth of a Labor party was inevitable they should participate in leading and building the Labor party. In 1932, Trotsky pointed out that to build a permanent Labor party would be to create a formidable obstacle to the future proletarian revolution. The CLS then altered its position to include participating in but not leading a Labor party. The CLS was firmly in favor of doing mass work.

The first number of *Class Struggle* declared that it was not a sect "but a two fisted hard group of Communists." *Class Struggle* was extremely critical of the Cannonite group on this issue, despite the fact that the Cannonites did not claim to do mass work. Another issue especially irritating to Weisbord was that, in a very un-Leninist way, the CLA, and the WP also, had turned over their membership lists to the Post Office in order to obtain second-class mailing privileges. Throughout the existence of *Class Struggle*, the CLS refused this tactically unrevolutionary act and paid a higher postal rate rather than submit.

During the entire publication of *Class Struggle*, Weisbord was the main contributor. The magazine was mimeographed and appeared at irregular intervals. Reflecting the small membership of the CLS, the circulation of *Class Struggle* was not very large. A not too sympathetic observer estimated the membership of the CLS at thirteen, and even if we double that figure, it must still be considered a very small group.

But despite its limited circulation *Class Struggle* always kept its adversaries alert. At one point the CLS was even able to create a small faction within the more eager Communist League of America members who wanted to do mass work. The membership in the CLS seemed to remain stable with occasional converts from the other Communist groups. It is paradoxical, but not very surprising, that despite its relatively small membership the CLS occasionally found it necessary to resort to expulsions.

Class Struggle contained articles on the world political scene as well as on domestic labor struggles. During the seven years of the magazine's existence, Weisbord made several tours abroad and reported on the condition of the Left Opposition in various countries. While he was away Vera Buch, the assistant editor, ably carried on the journal.

In the spring of 1932, Weisbord visited with Trotsky for three weeks in Turkey. Just as in the larger WP, whenever the factional infighting became too hot, the opposing sides would go to Moscow for a decision; so Weisbord went to Prinkipo in an effort to win Trotsky over to his position. Although Trotsky failed to shift his support to the CLS from the CLA, as the legitimate Left Opposition group in the United States, it appears that Weisbord received a sympathetic hearing, because articles and letters by Trotsky began to appear with ever greater regularity in the pages of *Class Struggle*. It was in 1934, when Trotsky advised the International Left Opposition to join the major Social Democratic parties, that the CLS broke with Trotsky.

Throughout its life the CLS always supported the USSR, despite its criticism of the Stalinist leadership. The attacks on the other Left Opposition factions, although always consistent in their vehemence, decreased in frequency, and for a time in 1933 there was even talk of merger with the CLA. By the beginning of 1934, however, cooperation was again out of the question and the two groups entered into a period of renewed hostility.

In the spring of 1936, the CLS and *Class Struggle* moved to Chicago in order to be "in close touch with the workers of the basic industries." In Chicago much of the infighting seems to have disappeared as the CLS became involved in organizing a militant Negro center on the South Side of the city.

With the coming of the Spanish Civil War, *Class Struggle* became more concerned with the international situation and the possible spread of fascism. In its often polemical style, *Class Struggle* found that it could not support the Spanish Marxist POUM (Workers party of Marxist

Unification) "in the sense of joining or agreeing basically with its line,"
although the CLS was able, in reality, to support the POUM with funds.
The last issue of *Class Struggle* was devoted entirely to Weisbord's
observations from Spain, where he described fighting within the Loyalist
groups in Barcelona and noted startling evidence of French help to
Franco sympathizers.

New York, 1968

Revolutionary Age

NEW YORK, 1929-1932

DONALD CLARK HODGES

THERE is a touch of irony in the fact that the majority leadership of the Communist party of the USA, which had been expelled from the party at the instigation of the Comintern only a few months after rolling up a staggering victory at the party's convention early in 1929, should have chosen for the title of its newspaper that of an earlier paper put out by the left wing of the old Socialist party during and following America's involvement in World War I. The original *Revolutionary Age* had been uncompromising and unremitting in its struggle against opportunism and social reformism in the old Socialist party. In contrast, the new *Revolutionary Age* was to represent the views of the majority leadership, which had been driven from the Communist party for right-wing deviations and factionalism allegedly in support of just such an opportunist and social reformist line. The party's leaders had refused to recant and submit to the discipline of the Executive Committee of the Comintern, which demanded that it abdicate in favor of a Stalinist minority led by Foster, Bittelman, and Browder, who counted for support on a bare 10 to 20 percent of the party's membership.

In fact, the picture was far more complicated than either the expelled leadership or the expelling Executive Committee of the Communist International (ECCI) was prepared to admit. The precise ground for expulsion was not right-wing opportunism at all, but rather the failure of the majority leadership to recant and submit to the discipline of the Comintern. Why, then, did the majority leadership not submit? It was not, as *Revolutionary Age* would have us believe, because of revolutionary principle alone. Actually, in an effort to mollify Stalin's agents in

345

America, the majority leadership went so far as to introduce at its March convention an altogether opportunistic resolution calling for Bukharin's dismissal from the presidency of the International. But even this was not enough. In effect, Stalin would settle for nothing less than the abdication of the leadership, asking that Lovestone and Pepper be withdrawn from work in the United States and sent to Moscow. The autonomy of the American CP was at stake, but so were the jobs of its elected representatives. It seems that the latter counted on retaining their posts despite pressure from Stalin, the CPSU (Communist party of the Soviet Union), and the ECCI.

They were mistaken in this assumption. To be sure, they managed to win their first battle inasmuch as the convention, ignoring instructions from Moscow, gave Lovestone and his supporters ten of the fourteen seats on the party's Central Committee. After the convention, a delegation of ten members went to Moscow to present its case before a special ECCI commission. However, the commission continued firm in support of its preconvention February letter to the American Communists, condemning both the majority and minority leaderships for factionalism involving unsubstantial, exaggerated, and artificial differences, without any regard for building a mass party of American workers. Besides calling for the liquidation of factionalism, the foundation of a normal party life, and the drawing of workers into the leadership, this letter had reaffirmed the practical necessity of self-criticism and iron party discipline, based not only on the unconditional subordination of the minority to the majority, but also on the unconditional recognition of the decisions of the Comintern. Accordingly, the members of the majority leadership who held posts in the Comintern—Lovestone and his leading supporters, Gitlow and Wolfe—were removed from their positions. And in New York, the Central Committee dominated by Lovestone's own supporters not only endorsed this action of the ECCI, but followed it up by expelling Lovestone, Gitlow, and Wolfe from the American Communist party.

Betrayed by their own followers, the majority leaders suddenly found themselves in the unenviable position of a minority without a party. Only about two hundred of the party's 35,000 dues-paying members chose to remain loyal to their duly elected leaders. Thus it was quite inaccurate and altogether misleading for the editors of *Revolutionary Age* to characterize it as the organ of the Communist party of the USA (Majority Group). In fact, it was the organ of a sect that gambled on eventual readmission into the party and the International, a hope that was never fulfilled. A decade or so after the first issue of the newspaper appeared on November 1, 1929, its editors, Lovestone, Gitlow, and Wolfe, would abandon communism along with Marxism-Leninism. The Communist Opposition, unlike the Trotskyist Socialist Workers party, disappeared from radical politics altogether, thereby testifying to a latent right-wing opportunism that was quite likely present from the beginning. In other words, we have indirect evidence from the leadership's subsequent abandonment of Marxism-Leninism that the Comintern's charge of right-wing deviations in the late 1920s was far from unprincipled name-calling and for the most part was accurate.

What, then, is the historical significance of *Revolutionary Age*? Its pages enabled the condemned to present a brief in their own defense, thereby affording us the opportunity to weigh the evidence against, as well as for, their alleged right-wing deviations. The Communist Opposition USA rejected this charge with the very first issue of its nominally revolutionary newspaper. Under the pretext of fighting the Right, we are told, the minority leadership of the party under Foster had been revising and distorting the Leninist line of the Comintern in an unprincipled series of turns and twists, leading alternately in Right-opportunist and Left-sectarian directions. Stalin's tactical zigzags, which led to an ultra-Left course following the expulsion of Trotsky and his followers from the Comintern and from the various Communist parties, were also to culminate in an ultra-Right course following the seventh congress of the International in 1935: the abandonment of a "class against class" policy for that of a Popular Front in which the issue was no longer the struggle against capitalism but rather the defense of bourgeois democracy against fascist aggression. If we are to judge the character of the Communist Opposition by its leaders' subsequent behavior, we must do the same for the Stalinist leadership of the Comintern and the various national parties under the direct or indirect influence of the CPSU.

The question at issue is whether the majority leadership objectively functioned as the agents of social democratic tendencies within the Comintern and Communist party of the USA. Let us consider first the behavior of the Lovestone group at the sixth congress of the Communist

International, held during July-September 1928, at which a new Left course was officially embarked on with its formal approval. The sixth congress noted that the chief danger and deviation within the Communist parties was to the right of the tactical course outlined at the ninth ECCI plenum in February 1928, implying the virtual abandonment of united-front tactics with Social Democrats and other working-class parties in favor of an all-out class struggle against the influence of Socialists and Social Democracy within the labor movement. The main report had been drafted and delivered by Bukharin, then president of the International and the most influential spokesman for the more moderate and thinking elements within the CPSU and the Comintern. Thus there would seem to be little ground for accusing him of right-wing tendencies at the time, although his criticism of such tendencies was qualified by the recommendation that the struggle against them be waged, above all, by reasonable and persuasive methods.

The Lovestone group had originally believed that, once the Trotskyists were expelled, right-wing opportunist tendencies had become the main disruptive factor within the party and the International. Yet they apparently shared Bukharin's conciliatory approach. In the interest of party unity, he had argued, right-wingers had to be persuaded of their mistakes rather than arbitrarily silenced or summarily expelled. Not for nothing was *Revolutionary Age* subtitled "For Communist Unity in the Revolutionary Class Struggle." The focus on unity, however, was interpreted by the Stalinists as a form of conciliationism and disguised assistance to right-wing elements. In an address delivered at a session of the Central Committee of the CPSU in April 1929, on "The Right Deviation in the CPSU," Stalin was already accusing Bukharin of being the leader of a new right-wing opposition within the party. In brief, Bukharin's errors were traceable to his going soft on the struggle against social democratic traditions in the Communist parties—in other words, to stopping short of driving the Right deviationists out of the party.

The theoretical basis of Bukharin's conciliationism was conceived as hinging on the following theses: (1) that within the USSR the agricultural sector would evolve into socialism without a fierce class struggle against the *kulaks* or upper stratum of landed proprietors; (2) that a general abatement instead of intensification of the class struggle between workers and capitalist elements could be expected in the course of Socialist development; (3) that the upper stratum of peasants in the Soviet Union no longer consisted of rich proprietors or *kulaks* in the prerevolutionary sense, but actually of near-paupers indistinguishable for practical purposes from the middle and poor peasants; (4) that the Soviet state should put a brake on its role as regulator of the market and permit the free play of prices in the agricultural sector, which was tantamount to raising the price of grain; and (5) that the starting point of agricultural reconstruction is not a rapid rate of industrialization but rather the development of individual peasant farming. There is little doubt that Bukharin's domestic policy would have slowed down the rapid industrialization and the socialization of agriculture in the USSR. His international program adopted by the sixth congress, however, was at least in harmony with social and economic conditions in Western Europe and the United States, and far more capable of implementation than the ultra-Left course of the Stalinist Third Period.

To be sure, during the Popular Front course initiated by the seventh congress, the Stalinist majority at the helm of the CPSU and the International was to prove no less capable of out-Righting the Right than of adopting tactics further to the left even of the Trotskyists. In fact, this very talent for sharp turns, flexibility, and maneuvering substantiates the charge of the Lovestone group that the Stalinist bureaucracy represented an eclectic or sectarian-opportunist policy combining Left dogmatism with Right conciliationism, weighted according to the circumstances. In contrast, the position of the Communist Opposition was consistently cautious, just as the tactics of the Trotskyists were marked by unflagging militancy.

The presence of Right-opportunist tendencies within Stalinism, however, is insufficient to support the Communist Opposition's claim that its own position was faithful to the main tendency of Marxism-Leninism rather than a position basically to the right in the Communist political spectrum. Despite the ultra-Right line of the seventh congress, the rightist tendencies characteristic of Stalinism were never more than tactical short-run affairs, whereas the rightist posture of the Lovestone group and the followers of Bukharin in the Soviet Union had crystalized into a fixed and consistent policy. Precisely the strategical rather than the merely tactical character of the Communist Opposition made of it a permanent grouping or faction within the CP (USA) and the International. Since the Trotskyists also constituted a faction, the various parties were confronted with the prospect of a major discussion and debate at every congress of every party, including the Comintern, which was bound to interfere with practical work and the unity of action required of a revolutionary struggle against almost overwhelming odds. But the rationale for eliminating factionalism had its price, notably a reinforcement of the powers of the existing authority within the several parties and the Comintern, and hence the permanent accession to power of the Stalinist central apparatus.

The Stalinists themselves exaggerated the danger to party unity of the existence within the party of more or less permanent left and right wings, especially in view of their own capacity to swing in either direction depending on the ebb and flow of the revolutionary struggle. Moreover, they were flatly mistaken in attributing a petty-bourgeois class character to Trotskyism, as in conceiving of the Communist Opposition as a shield for bourgeois elements within the party. Already the Trotskyists had been branded as counterrevolutionaries, a charge subsequently leveled against Bukharin and the Right Opposition as well. Yet the charge was fantastic even in the objective sense of the Opposition's having played into the hands of the enemies of socialism.. It amounted to sheer fabrication by the entrenched Stalinist bureaucracy and ended by weakening rather than strengthening the various Communist parties and the International. Any mass political organization must be capable of tolerating divergent tendencies, including permanent Left and Right groupings, if not ultra-Left and ultra-Right ones. It was one thing forcefully to dissolve the anarchosyndicalist Workers' Opposition; it was quite unnecessary to apply the same methods against Trotsky and Zinoviev, who were objectively willing to abide by Communist discipline. It was one thing to have broken organizationally with the Social Democrats; it was another matter to force a split with the Communist Opposition where the differences were over tactics rather than fundamentals.

Unlike the Trotskyists, who interpreted these differences in terms of a basic or class struggle among the proletarian Left, bureaucratic Center, and petty-bourgeois Right elements within the International, the Communist Opposition conceived of the various factions as differing mainly on secondary questions of strategy and tactics. Differences on such questions, no matter how serious, were deemed compatible with membership in the Comintern, provided they did not strike at the fundamental principles of communism. Despite the Trotskyists' so-called ultra-Left mistakes on matters of strategy and tactics, the Communist Opposition was in favor of readmitting them into the Comintern provided only they would renounce Trotsky's thesis concerning a Soviet Thermidor —whether interpreted as a complete denial or a partial denial of the character of the Soviet Union as a proletarian state. On the premise that membership in the Comintern is conditional upon agreement with Communist fundamentals, however, the Opposition argued that Trotsky's continued affirmation of the bureaucratic degeneration of the Revolution in the Soviet Union placed Trotskyism at odds with one of the basic principles of the Communist International, while providing legitimate grounds for the expulsion of Trotskyists from the various Communist parties. Here again, in its unremitting struggle against Trotskyism, however, we have evidence confirming the Communist Opposition's basically rightist orientation within the international Communist movement.

In its newspaper *Revolutionary Age,* the Opposition had concentrated on the single most important source of the seemingly Trotskyist and ultra-Left course initiated by the Tenth Plenum of the ECCI. Specifically, the theses of the Tenth Plenum were rejected for arbitrarily revising the principles and program adopted at the sixth congress; for rejecting the basic Leninist thesis of the uneven development of capitalism and the practical necessity of different tactics under different conditions of capitalist development; for mistakenly reinterpreting the character of the Third Period (1929-1934) on the ground that the advances toward socialism in the USSR and the radicalization of the masses in Western Europe were undermining and bringing to an end the period of capitalist stabilization, whereas the increasing level of production in the West would suggest that a revolutionary upsurge was far from imminent; for sacrificing united-front tactics and collaboration with other working-class parties in order to wage a sectarian struggle against Social Democracy conceived as a form of social fascism; for abandoning the struggle against the actual Right danger of spineless flexibility and opportunist reversals of policy in response to momentary tactical setbacks; and for readmitting Trotskyists into the CPSU and the Comintern.

We have seen that *Revolutionary Age* is indispensable to understanding the full implications of the factional struggles between the left and right wings and the centrist majority in control of the Communist International. The theoretical foundations and strategical and tactical line adopted by the Communist Opposition are presented throughout its pages in a series of articles, documents, and resolutions. Among these the most significant and informative are perhaps Will Herberg's "The Tenth Plenum ECCI" (continued through the first five issues, November 1, 1929-January 1, 1930) and "The VI Congress and the World Situation" (January 15, 1930); Bertram D. Wolfe's "Is the VI Congress Being Revised?" (November 15, 1929); Jay Lovestone's "The Crisis in the Communist International" (December 1, 1929) and "The International Conference" (March 7, 1931); Ben Gitlow's "The United Front" (February 1, 1930); the Editors' "The Truth About the 'Corridor Congress' " (December 1-15, 1929); "The Economic Situation in the United States: From the Draft Thesis of the February Plenum" (March 15, 1930); "The Present Situation and Our Tasks: Draft Thesis for National Conference of CP-Majority Group" (June 15, 1930); "Trotskyism and the Communist Opposition" (resolution adopted by the National Conference of CP-Majority Group, September 1-October 1, 1930); "Platform of the International Communist Opposition" (April 25, 1931); and the "Resolution on the General Line and Inner-Party Course of the CPSU" (May 16, 1931).

The theses developed in these articles, documents, and resolutions need to be weighed, of course, against the quite different assessments by the Communist left wing and center concerning the international situation and the inner-party course of the CPSU. Accordingly, we must consult Trotsky's classic critique of the sixth congress, "The Draft Program of the Communist International: A Criticism of Fundamentals" (June 1928), along with the principal Stalinist arguments in support of the proceedings of the Tenth Plenum: the ECCI letter to the sixth convention of the CP (USA) of February 1929, Stalin's address on "The Right Deviation in the Communist Party of the Soviet Union," and the theses of the Tenth ECCI Plenum on the international situation and the tasks of the Communist International.

Tallahassee, Florida, 1968

Workers Age

NEW YORK, 1932-1940

DALE RIEPE

THE American Communist party resulted from a left-wing split in the Socialist party in 1919. In 1921 it appeared as the Workers party. By 1928 it expelled the Left (or Trotskyist) Opposition over the question of permanent revolution, and in the next year purged the Right (or Lovestoneite) Opposition because that group held that the United States was not ready for revolution. The Lovestoneites first published *Revolutionary Age* from 1929 to 1932; it was then renamed *Workers Age* and continued from 1932 to 1940, when it disappeared along with the Right Opposition, or Lovestoneism. Jay Lovestone was its first editor and Will Herberg its last. Other American writers for *Workers Age*, besides Lovestone and Herberg, were Benjamin Gitlow, Lazar Becker, Bertram D. Wolfe, Bill Haywood, Herbert Zam, and Charles S. Zimmerman. Contributors from abroad included August Thalhever, Rosa Luxemburg, Karl Radek, and M. N. Roy. The journal reprinted some of the works of Marx, Engels, and Lenin.

Students of the history of American radicalism will be fascinated by the changes of policy, doctrine, and tone from the first issues to the last. At first *Workers Age* carried optimistic, self-confident editorials and articles by members of the American Communist party (Right Opposition) and its sympathizers. It was in this period that the United States recognized the Soviet Union and that much social legislation benefiting the workers was passed. But as the Great Depression continued, a certain bitterness crept in because the Moscow trials had created disaffection, Soviet foreign policy seemed to have forsaken progressivism, the American national income was fourteen billion dollars less than it had been in

353

1929, and, although the production level of 1940 had attained the 1929 level, this was with an 8-percent increase in population. Moreover, Mussolini, Hitler, Franco, and Hirohito were nearing the height of their power, with Stalin presumably about to join their unsavory activity. But 1939 warfare among American intellectuals was the deadliest it had been since the Civil War.

Workers Age had moments of brilliant reportage and editorializing. Consider the following neat harpooning of technocracy by Herbert Zam: Technocracy is "a mechanical and reactionary utopia . . . operating on physical rather than on socio-historical laws." Under the headline, "Gandhi and the Class-Struggle," Gandhi is quoted as saying to Nobel Prize winner Romain Rolland: "My observations have led me to the conclusion that as far as England is concerned the unemployed have no reason to complain of capitalism." The editor swallowed his indignation enough to comment on "the crude obsolescence of the Mahatma's ideological furniture." An editorial written just before the 1932 election, when Franklin Roosevelt faced Herbert Hoover for the Presidency, stated:

> Democratic party strategy demands the nomination of a man with a big name . . . of a man with solid golden linings in his political vest. At the same time, this man must be able to sprout [*sic*] radical phrases, while resting on a rock-ribbed reactionary foundation. . . . Page Governor Roosevelt of New York.

In another place Westbrook Pegler is ticked off for his views of American Federation of Labor reforms. His solution, according to the editor, is "just what Hitler and Stalin might say—and do!" And there is more in this vein after the Hitler-Stalin nonaggression treaty of 1939. It was in the midst of such reporting that *Workers Age* was calling for labor unity! Among foreign writers none topped Rosa Luxemburg for her keen comments on alienation. In describing the problem of the *Lumpenproletariat* she said:

> With the stripping off of conventional barriers and props for morality and law, bourgeois society itself falls victim to direct and

limitless degeneration (*Verlumpung*) for its innermost law of life is the profoundest of immoralities, namely the exploitation of man by man.

Although in our day the radicalism of organized labor seems deader than a doornail compared to that of blacks and students, in the period of the Great Depression nearly the whole burden of social change rested on labor and a small group of radicals associated with its fortunes. Consequently, it was labor status, labor problems, and labor needs that were paramount in the weekly issues of *Workers Age*. It editorialized and columnized on the sharecroppers, treatment of blacks, minimum wages, worker protection in the mines and factories, unemployment benefits, and labor rivalry (such as between John L. Lewis of the miners and Sidney Hillman of the garment workers). George A. Watkins exposed "Slavery in the Ford Empire," and another article revealed that 20 percent of the children of workers in Wilkes-Barre were underweight. There were countless meetings advertised in the issues of *Workers Age*: meetings to set Tom Mooney free (Mooney was sentenced to death for allegedly bombing a preparedness-day parade in San Francisco in 1916); meetings protesting the Citizens Military Training Camps; meetings to protest attempts to exclude Soviet products; picketing of the British Consulate in New York to force the release of M. N. Roy, then a left-wing leader of Indian labor; conferences of the Young Communist League to protest war; antifascist meetings; and meetings to protest the Sino-Japanese War in China.

A touch of humor was occasionally, but not often, inserted into *Workers Age*. Reference was made to "Groucho-Marxism" and to the outlook of the Socialist party of Illinois with its "appeals for socialism by Abe Lincoln, John Stuart Mill, Victor Hugo and Hiawatha." A tragicomedy under the caption "Christ Is Risen" was reported when the unemployed workers marched in the Easter Parade on Fifth Avenue in 1934. Finally, during the first year of publication, a roving reporter gathered the following sermon extracts at various prominent New York churches on a Sunday morning. They show a certain accommodation to the times: "The search for money and power is not to be condemned." Apropos of the then recent bank closures: "If we had constant depositors in the savings bank of the spirit." "We do not make religion the business of our lives." And finally, a pithy example of the moral determinist view of history: "Vanity is the cause of war."

Besides the great theme of labor problems were secondary ones, including the antiwar and antimilitarism stance, and the theme that capitalism must be replaced by a more rational system—socialism based on Marxism (this focus pervades every issue of *Workers Age*). Finally, in the last two years of its publication, a fourth theme emerged: the anti-Soviet and anti-Communist (but not anti-Marxist) theme, which grew out of *Workers Age*'s response to the Soviet-Finnish War and the Stalin-Hitler nonaggression treaty. This major motif is exceedingly important for an understanding of the later weakening of the labor movement as it tried to effect social change and educate the workers.

The antimilitarism theme appeared in accounts of antiwar conferences and in complaints about American military intervention in El Salvador and in "Marine-ridden Haiti." Along with comments on the need to cut superarmaments, *Workers Age* ran ads by Norman Thomas and Bertram D. Wolfe to "Keep America Out of War." *Workers Age* published a table showing that the body count in the Sino-Japanese War was 8,400,000 Chinese casualties and 480,000 Japanese. It revealed the secret war expenditures of Great Britain, complained about how U.S. trade kept the Japanese supplied with crucial war material, and faulted Franklin Roosevelt for being "now on record as favoring a navy big enough to whip the world, even when the world is at peace."

Workers Age reported the Socialist reaction to America's problems during the epoch of her greatest economic and political disequilibrium. More than in the capitalist press, the full sweep of human emotions was vented, especially denunciation of the treatment of labor and the poor. Passion, hatred, pity, cynicism, and indignation were combined with much first-rate reporting. But *Workers Age*'s utopia floundered, as Werner Sombart once noted, "on the reefs of the roast beef and apple pie" that were to come with World War II.

Buffalo, New York, 1968

International Council Correspondence
CHICAGO, 1934-1937

Living Marxism
NEW YORK, 1938-1943

New Essays
NEW YORK, 1943

PAUL MATTICK

THE series of publications, which appeared during the years 1934 to 1943 under the title *International Council Correspondence*, later to be renamed *Living Marxism* and, finally, *New Essays*, expressed the political ideas of a group of American workers concerned with the proletarian class struggle, the conditions of economic depression and worldwide war. Calling themselves Council Communists, the group was equally far removed from the traditional Socialist party, the new Communist party, and the various "Opposition" parties that these movements brought forth. It rejected the ideologies and organizational concepts of the parties of the Second and Third Internationals, as well as those of the stillborn "Fourth International." Based on Marxist theory, the group adhered to the principle of working-class self-determination through the establishment of workers' councils for the capture of political power and the transformation of the capitalist into a Socialist system of production and distribution. It could be regarded, therefore, only as a propaganda or-

357

ganization advocating the self-rule of the working class. Because of the relative obscurity of this group and its ideas, it may be well to deal briefly with its antecedents.

Labor organizations tend to see in their steady growth and everyday activities the major ingredients of social change. It was, however, the unorganized mass of workers in the first of the twentieth-century revolutions that determined the character of the revolution and brought into being its own, new form of organization in the spontaneously arising workers' and soldiers' councils. The council, or soviet, system of the Russian Revolution of 1905 disappeared with the crushing of the Revolution, only to return in greater force in the February Revolution of 1917. These councils inspired the formation of similar spontaneous organizations in the German Revolution of 1918 and, to a somewhat lesser extent, in the social upheavals in England, France, Italy, and Hungary. With the council system, a form of organization arose that could lead and coordinate the self-activities of very broad masses for either limited ends or for revolutionary goals, and that could do so independently of, in opposition to, or in collaboration with existing labor organizations. Most of all, the rise of the council system proved that spontaneous activities need not dissipate in formless mass exertions, but could issue into organizational structures of a more than temporary nature.

In both Russia and Germany the actual content of the revolution was not equal to its revolutionary form. Although in Russia it was mainly general objective unreadiness for a Socialist transformation, in Germany it was the subjective unwillingness to institute socialism by revolutionary means that largely accounts for the failures of the council movement. The great mass of German workers mistook the political for a social revolution. The ideological and organizational strength of Social Democracy had left its mark; the socialization of production was seen as a governmental concern, not as the task of the workers themselves. The workers' councils, which had made the revolution, abdicated in favor of political democracy. In Russia, the slogan "All Power to the Soviets" had been advanced by the Bolsheviks for tactical and opportunistic reasons. Once in power, however, the Bolshevik government dismantled the soviet system to secure its own authoritarian rule. The Russian soviets proved unable to forestall the transformation of the soviet into a party dictatorship.

It is clear that workers' self-organization is no guarantee against policies and actions contrary to proletarian class interests. In that case, however, they are superseded by traditional or new forms of control, by the old or newly established authorities. Unless spontaneous movements, issuing into organizational forms of proletarian self-determination, usurp control over society and therewith over their own lives, they are bound to disappear again into the anonymity of mere potentiality. This is not true, of course, for the minority of conscious revolutionaries who expect and prepare for new social struggles, and to that end concern themselves not only with the critique of capitalist society but also with the criticism of the means required to put an end to it.

This accounts for the Left Opposition within the Communist movement, which arose as early as 1918 and directed itself against the opportunism of the Bolshevik party in its endeavor to secure the existence of the Bolshevik government. Although bad experiences with bourgeois parliamentarianism and with the class-collaborationist practices of trade unionism had turned Western Communists into antiparliamentarians and anti-trade unionists, and thus into supporters of the council movement, the Bolsheviks insisted on a reversal of policies and the return to parliamentarianism and trade unionism. The Communist parties were split and their left wings were excluded from the Communist International. Lenin's pamphlet, *Radicalism, an Infantile Disease of Communism* (1920), was written to destroy the influence of the Left in Western Europe.

With the prestige of success on their side, and with the material means available to government to influence or destroy rival social movements, the Bolsheviks succeeded in reducing Left communism to practical insignificance. But it was never completely extinguished and has continued to exist in small groups in a number of countries down to the present day. For a time, it even won a hearing in the United States, where the lack of revolutionary conditions condemned communism to exist in merely ideological form. The formation of groups of Council Communists was first made possible here during the Great Depression, which saw the spontaneous growth of organizations of the jobless and of councils of the unemployed.

With the demise of the unemployed movement, the group of Council Communists elected to continue to function as an educational organization. A split in the Proletarian party added to their membership and made possible the publication of *Council Correspondence*. At the founding of the group it adopted the temporary name United Workers party, soon to be changed to Council Communists. It was, perhaps, due to the character of the group and its intentions that it failed to attract intellectuals into its ranks. With the exception of articles translated from European sources, all the material published in *Council Correspondence* was written by employed or unemployed workers. Contributions were not signed because they expressed the opinions of the group even when written by individuals. There was, of course, no money available to pay for printing, and the magazine was produced by voluntary labor. Only with an increase in the number of readers, which coincided with a membership decline in the group, did it become both possible and necessary to print the journal. In view of the reduced membership, however, it was clear that *Council Correspondence* did not promote the growth of the organization but was practically no more than a vehicle for the elucidation of the ideas of council communism. For this reason the change of name to *Living Marxism* was decided upon. Eventually, however, the general decline of radicalism resulting from America's entry into World War II made the name *Living Marxism* seem rather pretentious, as well as a hindrance in the search for a wider circulation. It was changed to *New Essays,* but this did not yield the hoped-for results. After a few issues it became clear that a sufficient number of subscribers to make the magazine financially viable was not forthcoming.

Throughout the existence of *International Council Correspondence* no attempt was made to simplify its style or content to suit less-educated workers. The intention was to raise their level of understanding and to acquaint them with the complexities of social, economic, and political issues. The magazine was also written for politically advanced workers and for the Council Communists themselves so as to improve the collective knowledge of the group. It was a forum for discussion, unhampered by any specific dogmatic point of view, and open to new ideas that had some relevance to the council movement. The magazine eventually succeeded in attracting contributions from Socialist writers who were not associated with the group. And it had, of course, at its disposal the work of some academic people—for instance, Anton Pannekoek (writing under the pseudonym J. Harper), an advocate of the workers' councils since their very inception. Others, like Otto Rühle, had been active in the workers' councils in the German Revolution. It was Karl Korsch, however, who became *Living Marxism*'s most prominent academic contributor as well as theoretician of the council movement.

Because large-scale unemployment was the most important aspect of the depression years, it received special attention in *Council Correspondence*—particularly with regard to self-help organizations and direct actions that attempted to alleviate the miseries of the unemployed. Connected with this in a special sense, but also for general reasons, was a great concern with the inherent contradictions of the capitalist system and their unfolding in the course of its development. The nature of capitalist crisis was more intensely discussed, and on a higher theoretical level, than is generally the rule in labor publications, encompassing as it did the most recent interpretations of Marxist economic theory and its application to the prevailing conditions. The various articles devoted to this subject make their perusal highly rewarding even today, since they have lost neither their actuality nor their validity.

In political terms, the rising tide of fascism, and thus the certainty of a new world war, occupied most of the space in *Council Correspondence*—not only with regard to the European scene but also with respect to its interconnections with Asia and the United States. From its earliest beginnings, German "National-Socialism" was recognized as preparation for a war to redivide economic power on a worldwide scale favoring German capitalism. The reactions to fascist imperialism were considered as being equally determined by competitive capitalist interests. Fascism and war were seen as directed against the international working class, for both attempted to solve the crisis by capitalistic means in order to sustain the capitalist system as such.

The antifascist civil war in Spain, which was immediately a proving ground for World War II, found the Council Communists quite naturally—despite their Marxist orientation—on the side of the Anarchosyndicalists, even though circumstances compelled the latter to sacrifice their own principles to the protracted struggle against the common fascist enemy. The essays devoted to the civil war were of a critical nature and for that reason possessed a high degree of objectivity, which made the failure of antifascism—as a mere political movement—more explicit. Not only were the political-military struggles, foreign interventions, and frictions within the antifascist camp adequately dealt with, but even more attention was given to the short-lived collectivization of industry and agriculture in the anarchist-dominated centers of revolutionary Spain.

Insofar as the problem of the collective economy has been dealt with at all in nineteenth-century Socialist literature, it was in terms of the nationalization of productive resources and government control of production and distribution. Only with the Russian Revolution did this problem assume actual importance, even though the socioeconomic conditions in Russia allowed for no more than a state-controlled economy that retained all the essential economic categories of capital production. This system may best be described as state capitalism. In spite of its differences from the capitalism of old, it was, as far as the working class was concerned, merely another system of capitalist exploitation. The council movement did not recognize its planned economy as either a Socialist economy or a transition to such an economy, and opposed it not merely by denunciation but by developing its own concept of a Socialist society as a free association of producers in full command of all decisioning power connected with the production and distribution process.

The organization of socialism was, then, a recurrent theme in *Council Correspondence* and *Living Marxism,* for the questions it raised could be answered neither by the localized collectivization of economically backward Spain nor by the centralized government planning in equally economically backward Russia. Quite generally, however, Russia's state capitalism was either bewailed or celebrated as the realization of socialism—or, at any rate, as the road leading to it—and this illusion, though aiding Russian state interests, was detrimental to the international labor movement. It was the function of council communism, through its publications, to aid in the destruction of this illusion. There was no longer an urgent need to oppose Social Democracy. It had already, through its own practices, demonstrated its non-Socialist character and was now in the process of shedding its Socialist ideology as well. This, however, gave the no less counterrevolutionary activities of international bolshevism an unwarranted nimbus. Much space was, therefore, given to analyses of both the theory and practice of bolshevism, going back to its earliest critics, such as Rosa Luxemburg, and bringing this criticism forward by following the history of bolshevism down to World War II. This criticism was all-inclusive, philosophical, political, economical, and organizational, and expressed at an early date what became, only much later, a more widely accepted recognition of the true nature of bolshevism.

Criticism of the old labor movement, whether reformist or revolutionary in its tactics, did not exhaust the repertoire of *Council Correspondence*. Many of its articles and essays dealt with issues of a scholarly nature of more general interest, ranging from problems of psychology, sociology, and literature to such items as geopolitics, nationalism, and imperialism. Quite a number of these essays have been steadily reprinted by other publications and have served different authors as material for their own productions. Yet, for some years after World War II, the ideas propounded in the publications of council communism seemed to be totally lost. Since then, however, a new interest was undoubtedly fostered by the institutionalization of workers' councils, shop stewards, and workers' committees in almost all the West-European nations, by the rather emasculated workers' councils in the Yugoslav "market socialism," and, last but not least, by their emergence as revolutionary organizations in the recent social upheavals in "Communist" Poland and Hungary.

Cambridge, Massachusetts, 1969

Marxian Labor College Bulletin

SAN FRANCISCO AND CHICAGO,
1937-1939

The Marxist Review

CHICAGO, 1940

DALE RIEPE

THE MARXIST REVIEW was published in Chicago in 1940. Its predecessor, *Marxian Labor College Bulletin,* appeared between 1937 and 1939, first in San Francisco and then in Chicago. It served as the watchdog of the Marxist Workers party during the final years of the depression. Although many radical journals emphasized the more hopeful aspects of things to come, *MLCB* anxiously pointed out the pitfalls into which unwary workers were likely to fall. This it did in the journal as well as in the labor colleges at San Francisco, Chicago, and Flint. It provided constant analysis of the issues of the day, such as the weaknesses of capitalism in keeping its workers from starving, in depending upon militarism to prop up the decaying economy, in supporting reaction throughout the world. It was equally critical of the Communist party of America, the Third Communist International, the Socialist party of America, the Trotskyists, and the Anarchists. On the international scene it accused the Soviet bureaucracy and Stalin of dictatorial methods, it showed the reactionary nature of the Popular Fronts in Europe, and the bourgeois nature of the Loyalist government in Spain.

For most of its life, W. H. Camfield was editor of *MLCB* assisted by the following writers: Arthur E. Sanger, F. Miller, E. Harris, M. Prizant, Pauline Basich, L. Berman, James Kendall, Elin Barkman, Abou-

Khalil, and B. A. Patton. Among the American Socialist authors it approved, as seen by its book and pamphlet lists in each issue, were Anton Pannekoek, A. M. Simons, Ernest Unterman, and J. Howard Moore. It also advertised the usual classics of Marxism by Marx, Engels, and Lenin.

One of the most enlightening editorials, and an important contribution to the history of political radicalism in the United States, is entitled "Editorial on Splits." The piece is unsigned, but presumably was written by W. H. Camfield. Behind the Socialist party of America split of 1919 was a disagreement as to how much stress should be put on Marxist education. The first group to leave the SPA, and a forerunner of the Marxist Workers party, consisted of those who stressed the necessity of thorough grounding in Marxian theory and practice. The Socialist party of Michigan, another group who left the SPA, instituted a referendum to compel propagandists to explain religion from the standpoint of historical materialism. After the expulsion of this group came the removal of the Slavonian language federations, people emotionally influenced by the Russian Revolution. These gravitated toward the Third International, even though they were not keen students of Marxism.

Three new parties soon arose: (1) the Communist party of America (CPA), (2) the Communist Labor party (CLP), and (3) the Proletarian party (PP). The first two later united to form the Workers party, now the Communist party (USA).

There were more splits (the Trotskyists and Lovestoneites) but the CP finally remained quite stable, mostly by "suppression" of any questioning of the "line" dictated by the bureaucracy. Underneath the surface stability, however, there was, Camfield claimed, a great turnover in membership.

The Proletarian party was for a considerable time distinguishable from the other "Communist " parties by (1) its insistence on Marxian education, (2) its absence of immediate demands, (3) its explanation of religion by historical materialistic theory, and (4) by its uncritical support of the Communist International (CI), although it often maintained that the CPA was not "Communist."

On the international scene the PP sought alliance with the petite bourgeois and condoned abandoning the Communist party of China to Chiang Kai-shek. By 1931, some criticism of its international stand was made but was ignored by the leadership. At the next convention, in 1933, it took up the matter of the CI and also invited condemnation of (a) a separate Negro republic in the United States, (b) dual unionism, (c) the theory of social fascism, (d) the united front from below (the alliance of workers and farmers). By 1935, the PP had still not taken a critical stand on the USSR and vacillated regarding the views of the seventh world congress of the CI—the year that the CI stopped calling for class struggle and dictatorship of the proletariat and, instead, emphasized the saving of bourgeois "democracy" against the inroads of fascism. The PP concurred in this reformism because it feared to expel its opportunist wing and did not wish to offend the Soviet Union. The editorial concludes: "We refuse to be party to this" movement which is falling into the hands of reformists and people's fronts.

Concern about bacterial warfare appeared in a 1939 issue, but at that time not much had been done, according to Dr. P. A. Gorer, because there was not yet money in it. But, Gorer said, "The very fact that bacterial attack is a subject for public discussion is a sinister omen." Along the same line, P. M. S. Blackett is cited as pointing out that no science is immune to political activity and politics is tied to economics. The collapse of peace is the result of poverty, according to Blackett.

By the time *MLCB* moved to Chicago, and particularly when it changed its name to *The Marxist Review,* it became considerably more lively and varied in its coverage. Some relief to straight politicizing appeared in such editorials as "The Chicago Daily Snooze" where it claimed that Judge Gary, head of U. S. Steel Corporation, never saw a blast furnace until after his death. Articles such as "Simon Bolívar: Man of Straw" and Paul LaFargue's "The Right to be Lazy," although not intentionally funny, gave the impression that muckraking was still a viable and sometimes humorous technique in American journalism and political writing. The most macabre article to appear was entitled "Alley Rights," a comment on the permits issued in Gary, Indiana, to allow the unemployed to search through garbage for scraps of food. *MLCB* envisioned certain difficulties here, namely that: (1) some unemployed will unfairly get the scavenge in the Gold Coast districts, while their less fortunate brethren will be scavenging in the slums, (2) the college-educated will skim the cream of the garbage because of their superior educations, and (3) the Humane Society (SPCA) will demand that enough be left after the unemployed have taken their fill of the garbage to satisfy the needs of the stray cats and dogs.

In response to making a revolutionary saint of Simon Bolivar (1783-1830), the *MLCB* pointed out that certain facts must be considered. (1) Bolivar's first great act was to restore Spanish rule in 1812. (2) Next he turned over General Miranda, a colleague, to Spanish authority. (3) As general of an army of "revolutionaries" and dictator and "liberator" of Venezuela, his administration was so bad that the Spanish were encouraged to defeat him. Like General Douglas MacArthur after the defeat of the Philippines, Bolivar left his troops and fled, his only desire being to pose as dictator. To the relief of nearly everyone, he disappeared after the Colombia generals revolted against him and died at the age of forty-seven. Although Alcibiades openly fought on three sides of the same war, Bolivar did the same thing unintentionally.

MLCB gave considerable historical background to socialism and the history of labor struggles, along with making trenchant comments on the American political parties other than the Republican and Democrat (which were treated as not worthy of discussion). Instead, the Communist party of America, the Trotskyists, and the Socialist party come in for a fair share of vitriol. According to *MLCB*, the CPA called Franklin D. Roosevelt a fascist six years before, whereas by 1938 he had become their savior. Earl Browder, its leader, scarcely used the word "workers" or "Dictatorship of the Proletariat" in recent years as the USSR gyrated in world politics. His pact with Hitler and the war on Finland gained no friends for Stalin, but *MLCB* would not go so far as to say that the Soviet Union had turned capitalist. Its reasoning in "The USSR—Capitalism or Socialism?" was that in Russia there was no public debt, officials did not become rich (official salaries were low), there were no foreign concessions, and the two and one half million landlords and capitalists had not been replaced by a new wealthy ruling class. Furthermore, the new ideology of the people of Russia would not allow it and, finally, more money was paid out in wages than was earned by selling commodities. Despite all the cry about Russia being capitalist, the capitalist countries went into a fury over the war with Finland, having kept quiet as mice over the Japanese invasion of China, the Italian invasion of Ethiopia, Mussolini and Hitler being in Spain, and Germany in Austria. This is the best proof that the workers, not the capitalists, own the USSR!

The Marxist Workers party was adamant in maintaining that war is the product of capitalism and that the workers should not fight in any nationalist or commercial war. They reprinted parts of Louis Boudin's *Socialism and War* to stress this point. The CPA, they said, cannot be trusted in this since it does not represent the proletariat. The so-called Popular Fronts are also fakes. The German Social Democratic party and the Communist party in such "democratic" capitalist countries as France turned into a French nationalist movement in which an attempt was made to foster a Russian-French Alliance directed against the workers by means of petite-bourgeois policies. In Spain the Popular Front led to the suppression of the revolutionary workers. The Russian Communist party had strayed from "correct Marxist thinking" since Lenin died, according to *MLCB*. Trotsky improved nothing and Stalin had not spent time on theoretical or practical questions helpful to the revolutionary movement. The "Communist" International simply followed the lead of the ineffectual Russian CP. Let us remember, wrote the editor of *MLCB,* that the workers have only *one* enemy: "The capitalist class, whether it is embodied in fascism, democracy, or a communist party."

Buffalo, New York, 1969